THE DECLINE OF ENGLISH FEUDALISM
1215–1540

To
MY MOTHER

THE DECLINE OF ENGLISH FEUDALISM

1215–1540

by

J. M. W. BEAN

MANCHESTER UNIVERSITY PRESS
BARNES & NOBLE, INC., NEW YORK

©1968 J. M. W. Bean

Published by the University of Manchester at
THE UNIVERSITY PRESS
316–324 Oxford Road, Manchester, 13

GB SBN 7190 0294 X

U.S.A.
BARNES & NOBLE, INC.
105 Fifth Avenue, New York, N.Y. 10003

Printed in Great Britain by Butler & Tanner Ltd, Frome and London

CONTENTS

LIST OF TABLES

PREFACE

This book is an attempt to answer some of the legal problems encountered during researches into the economic position of the English nobility in the later middle ages. My original intention was to write a short monograph dealing with the development of the use. But I soon realized that this subject had to be set within a wider context. On the one hand, it was necessary to examine the consequences of feudal tenure from the *Magna Carta* onwards. On the other, the story had to be taken down to 1540. In consequence, I have strayed into fields in which I am conscious of my lack of specialist knowledge and have been forced to rely on the researches of others. I am especially conscious of what I owe to the guidance of a number of legal historians, not least when I have disagreed with them.

I have discussed a number of problems which must await a more detailed treatment than is possible within this book. One especially—the development of the equity jurisdiction of the court of Chancery in the late fifteenth and early sixteenth centuries—I must leave to legal historians. But I hope myself on future occasions to examine in detail the social and economic significance of the rise of uses.

I have benefited greatly from the advice and criticisms of Professor J. S. Roskell. Dr. Gordon Leff also read the typescript and made a number of helpful comments. My brother has assisted with the proofs and index.

J. M. W. Bean

ABBREVIATIONS

Bean	J. M. W. Bean, *The Estates of the Percy Family*, *1416–1537* (Oxford, 1958).
BIHR	*Bulletin of the Institute of Historical Research.*
BM	British Museum.
Bracton	Bracton, *De Legibus et Consuetudinibus Angliae*, ed. G. E. Woodbine (4 vols., New Haven, Conn., 1915–42).
Bracton's Note Book	*Bracton's Note Book*, ed. F. W. Maitland (3 vols., London, 1887).
Brook	Sir Robert Brook, *La Graunde Abridgement* (London, 1586).
Brook's New Cases	*Sir Robert Brook's New Cases*, ed. with translations by J. March (London, 1873).
CAD	*Catalogue of Ancient Deeds.*
Cam	H. M. Cam, *The Hundred and the Hundred Rolls* (London, 1930).
CCR	*Calendar of Close Rolls.*
CFR	*Calendar of Fine Rolls.*
CIPMA	*Calendar of Inquisitions Post Mortem and other analogous documents preserved in the Public Record Office* (in progress, 14 vols. published).
CIPMB	*Calendar of Inquisitions Post Mortem and other analogous documents . . . Henry VII* (3 vols.).
CLJ	*Cambridge Law Journal.*
CMI	*Calendar of Inquisitions Miscellaneous (Chancery) preserved in the Public Record Office* (in progress, 6 vols. published).
Coke, *First Institute*	Sir Edward Coke, *The First Part of the Institutes of the Laws of England; or, A Commentary upon Littleton* (3 vols., edition of 1794).
Coke, *Second Institute*	Sir Edward Coke, *The Second Part of the Institutes of the Laws of England, Containing the Esposition of Many Ancient and Other Statutes* (edition of 1797).
Coke, *Fourth Institute*	*The Fourth Part of the Institutes of the Laws of England, Concerning the Jurisdiction of Courts* (edition of 1797).
Constable	*Prerogativa Regis; Tertia Lectura Roberti Constable de Lyncolnis Inne anno 11 H. 7*, ed. S. E. Thorne (New Haven, Conn., 1949).

C.P. Chan.	Calendar of Proceedings in Chancery in the Reign of Queen Elizabeth (3 vols., Record Commission).
CPR	Calendar of Patent Rolls.
Digby	K. E. Digby, An Introduction to the History of the Law of Real Property (Oxford, 5th ed., 1897).
Dyer	Sir James Dyer, Reports of Cases in the Reigns of Henry VIII, Edward VI, Q. Mary and Q. Elizabeth, translated by J. Vaillant (3 vols., London, 1794).
Early Lincoln Wills	A. Gibbons, Early Lincoln Wills . . . 1280–1547 (Lincoln, 1888).
EHR	English Historical Review.
Fitzherbert	Anthony Fitzherbert, La Graunde Abridgement (London, 1577).
Glanvill	The treatise on the laws and customs of the realm of England commonly called Glanvill, ed. and translated by G. D. G. Hall, London and Edinburgh, 1965.
Hall	Edward Hall, Henry VIII, ed. C. Whibley (2 vols., London, 1904).
Holdsworth	W. S. Holdsworth, A History of English Law, vols. I (6th ed., London, 1938), III (5th ed., London, 1942) and IV (3rd ed., London, 1945).
Holmes	G. A. Holmes, The Estates of the Higher Nobility in XIVth century England (Cambridge, 1957).
LIQD	List of Inquisitions ad Quod Damnum, Part I (Public Record Office, Lists and Indexes, no. XVII; London, 1904).
Littleton	See Coke, First Institute.
L & P	Letters and Papers, Foreign and Domestic, of the Reign of Henry VIII, ed. J. S. Brewer, J. Gairdner and R. H. Brodie (22 vols. in 35, 1864–1932, London).
LQR	Law Quarterly Review.
Paston Letters	The Paston Letters, ed. J. Gairdner (new complete library ed., 1904, London, 6 vols.)
Plucknett, Common Law	T. F. T. Plucknett, A Concise History of the Common Law (5th ed., London, 1956).
Plucknett, Ed. I	T. F. T. Plucknett, Legislation of Edward I (Oxford, 1949).
Pollock & Maitland	F. Pollock and F. W. Maitland, The History of English Law before the time of Edward I (2nd ed., 2 vols., Cambridge, 1923).
PRO	Public Record Office. C. 1. Early Chancery Proceedings. C. 43. Common Law Pleadings.

C. 66. Patent Rolls.

C. 136–42. Chancery, Inquisitions *post mortem*, Richard II–Henry VIII.

C. 143. Chancery, Inquisitions *ad quod damnum*.

C. 145. Chancery, Inquisitions miscellaneous.

C.P. 40. Plea Rolls, Court of Common Pleas.

D.L. 29. Duchy of Lancaster, Ministers' Accounts.

E. 357. Enrolled Escheators' accounts, Lord Treasurer's Remembrancer.

K.B. 27. King's Bench, Coram Rege Rolls.

S.P. 1. State Papers, Domestic, Henry VIII.

Reg. Chich.   *The Register of Henry Chichele, Archbishop of Canterbury, 1414–1443*, ed. E. F. Jacob (4 vols., Oxford, 1938–47).

Rot. Parl.   *Rotuli Parliamentorum* (Record Comm.).

Rot. Parl. Hact. Ined.   *Rotuli Parliamentorum hactenus inediti, MCCLXXIX–MCCCLXXIII*, ed. H. G. Richardson and G. O. Sayles (for the Royal Historical Society, Camden Third Series, vol. LI, London, 1935).

Royal Wills   *A Collection of all the Wills of the Kings and Queens of England*, ed. J. Nichols (London, 1780).

S. C. Chan.   *Select Cases in Chancery, 1364–1471*, ed. W. P. Baildon (Selden Society, vol. X, London, 1896).

S. C. Council   *Select Cases before the King's Council, 1243–1482*, ed. I. S. Leadam and J. F. Baldwin (Selden Society, vol. XXXV, Cambridge, Mass., 1918).

S. C. Exch. Camb.   *Select Cases in the Exchequer Chamber before all the Justices of England*, ed. M. Hemmant (2 vols., Selden Society, vols. LI and LXIV, London, 1933 and 1948).

S. C. King's Bench   *Select Cases in the Court of King's Bench under Edward I*, ed. G. O. Sayles (3 vols., Selden Society, vols. LV, LVII and LVIII, London, 1936, 1938).

Select Charters   W. Stubbs, *Select Charters*, ed. H. W. C. Davis (9th ed., Oxford, 1913).

Sheehan   M. M. Sheehan, *The Will in Medieval England, from the conversion of the Anglo-Saxons to the end of the thirteenth century* (Pontifical Institute of Mediaeval Studies, Studies and Texts, VI: Toronto, 1963).

Somerville   R. Somerville, *History of the Duchy of Lancaster* (vol. I only published, London, 1953).

Test. Eb.   *Testaments Eboracensia*, vols. I–III (Publications of the Surtees Society, vols. IV, XXX and XLV, 1836, 1855 and 1865, London and Durham).

Test. Vet.	*Testamenta Vetusta*, ed. N. H. Nicolas (2 vols., London, 1826).
TRHS	*Transactions of the Royal Historical Society.*
WHC	*Calendar of Wills proved and enrolled in the Court of Husting, London, A.D. 1258–A.D. 1688*, ed. R. R. Sharpe (2 vols., London, 1889–90).
YBRS	*Year Books, 20–35 Ed. I and 11–20 Ed. III*, ed. A. J. Horwood and L. O. Pike (20 vols., Rolls Series).
YBVE	*Les Reports del Cases en Ley* (London, 1678–80) (the 'Vulgate' edition of the Year Books (except those of Richard II's reign), edited from previous printed editions by Sergeant Maynard).

Introduction: the Nature of English Feudalism

'FEUDALISM' is the invention of historians. It is easy to explain how they came to invent the word, since its root—*feudum*—was used in medieval times to designate the fee, a portion of land held in return for the performance of military service. But the middle ages knew no concept of 'feudalism'. For the phrase 'feudal system' we have to wait until the eighteenth century,[1] and for the word 'feudalism' itself until the nineteenth. The consequent absence of any technical meaning for this term, warranted by medieval usage, explains the variety of uses to which it has been put by historians. For some, for example, 'feudalism' has been a synonym for the secular way of life in the middle ages: for others, at best, a description of the social and political conditions in which a powerful nobility struggled to keep themselves independent of any central authority, at worst, another name for anarchy.

On this point English historians have been less prone than others to engage in confused and imprecise thinking. On the whole, they have tended to agree on the basic characteristics of feudalism. They have used the term to describe a system of land-holding in which land was held of the King whose predecessors had granted it to tenants-in-chief in return for military service. In order to perform this obligation these granted lands to mesne tenants who undertook in return to perform part of the military service required from their lords by the King. They in their turn, and their tenants also, granted out portions of the lands they had received in similar ways and for similar purposes. The resulting processes of subinfeudation could, and did, reach down from the greatest tenants-in-chief of all to men whose economic position was little different from that of the average peasant. However, no tenant lived for ever. The vassals created by this system often died leaving heirs who were too young to perform

[1] J. G. A. Pocock, *The Ancient Constitution and the Feudal Law* (Cambridge, 1957), p. 249.

the services which went with the estates they inherited. Moreover, if the heir was a female, the problem of her choice of husband might arise: there was the danger that she might choose someone on whom the lord could not rely for the performance of his services—perhaps, indeed, one of his enemies. Above all, there was the problem of what happened if a tenant died without any heirs. Because of these risks to the lord's position, feudal custom evolved a body of rules which carefully defined the rights exercised by the lord whenever his tenant died. These historians have labelled as the 'incidents' of feudalism.

In this view military service was the core of the relationship between the feudal lord and his tenant. To this the lord's rights on the death of his tenant were incidental—in the modern sense that they were not the essential part of the feudal relationship, and, in the sense of this word's original derivation, that they occurred on certain occasions only. The tenant's duty of military service was always there: the lord's right to the incidents of tenure could only accrue when his tenant died, and even then their precise nature depended on the age and sex of his heir.

This interpretation of the nature of English feudalism deserves to be treated with scepticism. The evidence on which it is based is largely derived from legal writers of the late twelfth and thirteenth centuries, the earliest of whom wrote a century or so after the Norman Conquest. It is, however, quite clear that many fees were not held by undisputed hereditary tenure in the immediate post-Conquest period.[1] It is difficult to decide how far this situation existed at every level of Anglo-Norman landholding. On the one hand, it is easy to understand why mesne lords were loath to engage in the permanent alienation of their demesnes and granted life-estates to their tenants. On the other, is it likely that

[1] Recently it has even been argued that the legal theory of hereditary tenure did not fully develop until c. 1200 (S. E. Thorne, 'English Feudalism and Estates in Land', CLJ (1959), pp. 193–209). But it is impossible to reconcile this view with the acceptance before this date of the lord's obligation to pay the debts of a deceased tenant out of the profits of his wardship of the heir's lands (Glanvill, p. 83). For another criticism see J. C. Holt, Magna Carta (Cambridge, 1965), p. 208. Nevertheless, the assize of mort d'ancestor indicates that the heir's right to inherit was far from certain early in Henry II's reign.

those who were tenants-in-chief accepted lands from the King without some sort of promise of security of inheritance for their heirs? All we can conclude from the evidence at our disposal is that the growth of hereditary tenure must have been a slow and haphazard process. Any attempts by the King to deny it to tenants-in-chief would be fraught with political danger.[1] And, if mesne lords resisted it on their fees, their tenants would have struggled to secure it. We must not, of course, import modern notions of hereditary tenure into this situation. In practice a son might be allowed to stay on the land that his father had held; and this might encourage the notion that the fee was hereditary. But permission to succeed was not in itself acceptance of a right to inherit.[2]

Why, then, did mesne lords allow hereditary tenure to develop? This question cannot be answered without explaining the motives which led them to create the earliest fees. No historian has yet satisfactorily accounted for the apparent readiness of lords to engage in the permanent alienation of their demesnes, thus depleting their future landed revenues. It is not enough to say that they wished to provide for the King's military needs, since, when the feudal host was summoned, their obligations could easily be fulfilled by sending household knights or hiring mercenaries. We can only solve this problem if we discard the notion that military needs alone explain the creation of feudal holdings. First, it is reasonable to infer that political motives played some part in this process. Both the King and his barons granted land as a reward for services. It is also possible that mesne lords gave lands in order to recruit future support against the King. Second, it is necessary to bear in mind the importance of mercenaries in the post-Conquest period. Mercenaries cost money; and many barons must have granted lands to those they had hired, either to pay off arrears of wages or to avoid paying out ready cash in future. Third,

---

[1] See e.g., R. H. C. Davis, 'What Happened in Stephen's Reign', *History*, *XLIX* (1964), 5–12.

[2] These remarks, of course, apply only to lay tenants-in-chief. We must take care to distinguish between their situation and that of the bishops and monasteries, whose estates existed before the Conquest.

there must have been a market in land among the barons and their followers. When lands were sold, it would have been necessary to make arrangements for the military services with which they were encumbered; and the conveyance would naturally have taken the form of subinfeudation.

The emergence of feudal tenures in the century following the Norman Conquest is thus the result of the complex interplay of a number of influences. On the one hand there was the land-hunger of the new aristocracy and their followers. On the other, there was the response of lords to this situation. One, or more, of several motives might explain why they granted lands. If a sale occurred, it is quite likely that hereditary tenure was established from the start. But in other cases this might not achieve acceptance for some generations. In all such transactions a dominant influence would be exerted by the need to provide for the King's military service, since any grant of land diminished the grantor's capacity to perform his duties. In consequence, the tenant received land together with the obligation of military service. But to assume that this constituted the sole motive for the transaction between him and his lord is an unwarranted assumption.

These considerations demand a readjustment in our present views of English feudalism. It is clearly wrong to assume that we can find the key to its origins in the later view that the core of the feudal relationship was the obligation to perform military service. When legal writers in the late twelfth and thirteenth centuries came to define feudal tenures, it was quite natural that they should take this view. They saw that the King had rights over the leading landowners of England, and they in their turn over those who held land of them. One right—that of military service—was always there, waiting for the royal summons. They lived in a world in which many held lands by payment of rent. But still more held it in return for the performance of labour services on the lord's demesne. They could not help thinking in terms of an analogy with rent and labour services and thus arrived at the conclusion that the feudal tenant held his land in return for the performance of military service. To the lord's other rights they assigned a secondary role, because they lacked the feature of continuance during the lifetime of the tenant.

But this interpretation of its tenures distorts the nature of English feudalism. Many fees were undoubtedly originally created for the lives of the tenants. In their case, when a tenant died, a lord must often have been willing to allow his heir to remain upon the land. And the continuance of this practice for a number of generations must certainly have been a powerful influence in the creation of notions of hereditary tenure. Even so, over a period of generations lords would have clung to the idea that the land was theirs. The definition of rights which belonged to them on the tenant's death was the inevitable result of this attitude. Similarly, when lords sold land in the late eleventh and early twelfth centuries, it was in their interests to do so by means of subinfeudation. By this means they were able to lighten the burden of military service for themselves and at the same time, by defining rights which were theirs on the tenant's death, they obtained sources of future profit.

In this analysis the so-called 'incidents' of tenure were at least as important as military service in the creation of feudal tenures. Despite the extreme paucity of evidence during the period of origins, there is some in support of this theory. As early as 1100, at a time when we know scarcely anything about the conditions imposed when fees were created, Henry I's coronation charter shows that William Rufus had treated his rights over his feudal tenants as sources of revenue. Moreover, it is clear that these rights were not enjoyed by the King alone: the reforms granted by Henry I were to apply to mesne tenants as well as tenants-in-chief. In short, there are strong grounds for believing that English feudalism was in its origins as much a fiscal as a military institution. The term 'incidents' itself was unknown to the middle ages, but was invented by lawyers in the early seventeenth century.

During the century which followed 1100 the fiscal elements in feudalism became even more important. Scutage was increasingly employed to commute the personal performance of military service. The feudal levy had never provided the King with all his military needs: and now it was no longer the main source of the

King's army. When the period of the present study opens, its decline had already passed the point where it could still be reversed. Tenants-in-chief in the thirteenth century sent only a fraction of their *servitium debitum* to the field, paying scutage on the rest of their fees. By the end of the century the King was turning to commissions of array and the contract system for supplies of men for his wars abroad. Nor did scutage provide a satisfactory source of revenue in this situation: the complexities of tenure left by two centuries of subinfeudations rendered its collection a hopeless task. When the King wanted money for his wars, he now turned to taxes on personal property and customs duties on England's exports.

Thus in the period covered by the present work English feudalism is, to all intents and purposes, a fiscal system. It is impossible for a historian who studies it in this period to avoid using the language inherited from his predecessors. Hence the terms 'feudalism', 'feudal' and 'incidents' frequently appear in the chapters that follow. But they are used solely to define legal relationships between mesne tenants and their lords, and between tenants-in-chief and the King. Within this context our theme is the development of the feudal lord's fiscal rights over his tenants and their importance in the development of English land-ownership.

CHAPTER ONE

The Consequences of Feudal Tenure

ENGLISH historians have given a great deal of attention to the obligations towards his lord that feudal tenure imposed upon the tenant. But in recent years most of them have been concerned with the grievances expressed over the Crown's exploitation of its rights in the twelfth and thirteenth centuries and the efforts at definition and control eventually made in *Magna Carta*. The development of feudal revenues after 1215 has never secured the same degree of attention. The basic explanation for this neglect may be found in the absence of political conflict over the incidents of tenure after the reign of John. There can be no doubt, however, that the readiness of historians to equate feudal tenure with the performance of military service made them all the more prone to underrate the continued importance of feudal incidents.

Before we can restore them to their proper place in the history of English landownership in the later middle ages, we must examine their nature in detail and discuss the factors which influenced their structure in the three centuries which followed *Magna Carta*. On the one hand, we must investigate the resources which were thus made available to feudal lords. On the other, since they formed part of the financial obligations which fell on almost all the country's landowners, it is essential to analyse the attitude of feudal tenants towards them.

(i) THE INCIDENTS OF FEUDALISM

The incidents of feudal tenure formed a body of legal rights enjoyed by the lord over the lands held of him, giving him on a number of occasions a share of the revenues of the lands of his tenant. The existence of the incidents thus imposed a number of limitations on the tenant's ownership of his holding. At the beginning of the thirteenth century the reasons for this situation—that, in theory, at any rate, the tenant's holding had originally been carved out of the lord's demesne—had been forgotten. It was now accepted that all lands held under feudal tenure passed by hereditary right. Nevertheless, although for the tenant the incidents of his right had become encumbrances that went with the land, for the lord they constituted a source of income.

The least complicated of these incidents to describe is that of 'escheat'. On the death of a tenant without heirs, or in the event of his forfeiting his lands through felony or treason,[1] the land went back to its lord, because it was his ancestor who had originally granted it to the tenant's ancestor. Feudal custom had long laid down that a lord had a right to assistance from his tenants whenever he was in difficulties. By the middle of the twelfth century this general obligation had been converted into the right to demand a sum of money from each of his tenants. In general the occasions when this was exercised were those when the lord was under financial strain—when he had to find money to pay his relief to his own lord, to ransom his body if he had been captured in war, to knight his son or to marry his daughter.

The nature of the other incidents was governed by the age of the tenant's heir. If he was a child, the lord possessed the rights of wardship—that is, the custody both of the heir's body and of his inheritance—and marriage—that is, the right to marry the heir to a person of his lord's choice. In the case of a male heir, wardship lasted until he was twenty-one years of age, in the case of a female until she was fourteen, if married or betrothed at the time of her ancestor's death, and, otherwise, until she was sixteen. The lord's rights of wardship within these terms were absolute:[2] if the deceased ancestor had leased a portion of his lands, the lord had the right to expel the lessees who could then claim nothing

[1] The mesne lord could only exercise his right after the land had been held by the Crown for a year and a day (Holdsworth, III. 69–70).

[2] *Fleta*, ed. H. G. Richardson and G. O. Sayles, II (Selden Soc., LXXII, 1953). 21.

until the heir came of age.[1] Both wardship and marriage provided the lord with an important source of revenue. The right of marriage could be sold—to the heir when he came of age, to his own family or that of his prospective wife, or a third party. And, until he came of age, the lord could either retain the inheritance in his own hands or sell the right of wardship as a marketable commodity. These rules appear to have been finally established in the course of the first three-quarters of the twelfth century. Henry I's coronation charter in 1100 had promised that the wardship of lands held of him belonged to the widow or next-of-kin of the deceased tenant and stated that the same rule was to be followed in the case of lands held of his tenants.[2] It would be unwise to assume that this rule was an accepted part of the legal system at this time, since its inclusion in the coronation charter implies that William Rufus had ignored any rights which widows or next-of-kin had claimed. In any case, it did not remain law, since in the Assize of Northampton of 1176 the lord's rights of wardship were clearly accepted as part of the legal system without mention of any others who had rights or claims.[3]

All lords, great and small, benefited from wardship, but the chief beneficiary was the Crown, not merely because it was the greatest lord in terms of the extent of its territorial power but also because of the special right known as 'prerogative wardship':[4] if a tenant-in-chief died leaving an heir under age, the Crown had the right not only to the wardship of those lands which were held in chief but also to that of all the lands held by the deceased tenant of

[1] For references to the operation of this rule, see *CPR, 1237–42*, p. 231; ibid., *1266–72*, p. 448; ibid., *1292–1301*, p. 88; ibid., *1307–13*, p. 205; ibid., *1317–21*, p. 111. See also *Year Books of Edward II. 2 &3 Edward II*, ed. F. W Maitland (Selden Soc., XIX, 1904), pp. 84–6. The rule seems to have been abandoned in the early fourteenth century. If it had been retained, it would have made it difficult for secular landowners to engage in the large-scale leasing of their demesnes to tenants. But it lasted another century in the case of annuities from landed revenues (see below, p. 147).

[2] *Select Charters*, p. 118 (c. 4).   [3] ibid., p. 180 (c. 4).

[4] See *Glanvill*, p. 84. A reading of this passage as a whole shows that the writer has 'prerogative wardship' clearly in mind. He takes particular care to distinguish between the rights of the King and those of other lords.

other lords. In the later middle ages the Crown managed to extend the frontiers of 'prerogative wardship'. Its earlier efforts to do so failed. In 1215 in clause 37 of *Magna Carta* it abandoned its claims when the lands held in chief were in socage, in burgage, in fee farm or in petty serjeanty.[1] And in the reissue of 1217—a baronial gain made possible by the death of John—it undertook not to exact 'prerogative wardship' unless lands were held of it in chief.[2] By these means mesne lords were able to prevent the Crown from trespassing upon their rights of wardship by virtue of its prerogative. But royal administrators succeeded in recovering to some extent the ground thus lost, since by the middle of the fifteenth century it had become accepted law that the Crown could claim 'prerogative wardship' in respect not only of tenants who held of it in chief but also those who held of it as of three honours—those of Peverel, Boulogne and Hagenet.[3]

If a tenant died leaving an heir who was of age, the lord had the right to demand a 'relief' from the heir—that is, a sum of money had to be paid before he took the new tenant's homage, thereby recognizing him as the heir to the inheritance. This payment is, perhaps, the clearest indication we have in feudal law of the fact that a tenant had originally held his fief for life. The relief was, however, already an accepted institution in 1100 when Henry I in his coronation charter promised that a tenant's heir need not buy back the land but simply pay a 'just and lawful relief'.[4] As in the case of heirs who were under age, the Crown possessed an additional right which belonged to no other lord—that of 'primer seisin'. In the case of every inheritance a period of time elapsed between the death of the ancestor and the tenant's performance of homage to his lord. A tenant who held only of a mesne lord, or lords, was allowed to occupy the land immediately after his ancestor's death and the lord's seisin was purely formal in character, being concurrent with the real seisin of the heir.[5] But in the case of tenants who held of him, the King had the right to occupy

---

[1] *Select Charters*, p. 297.

[2] ibid., p. 343 (*c*. 38). This was accepted as the law by Bracton (II. 253).

[3] Constable, p. 10.   [4] *Select Charters*, p. 118 (*c*. 2).

[5] Constable, Introd., p. xxi.

the land until homage was performed. There can be no doubt that the development of primer seisin is as old as that of feudal tenure itself, and, in particular, of the relief,[1] but we possess little information about its origins. In fact, it is likely that primer seisin was only properly defined as a separate right from the thirteenth century onwards when the Crown developed a permanent system for the administration of its rights as feudal lord. By the end of the fifteenth century the rules relating to it were fixed and certain. If the tenant held of the King *ut de honore*, the King enjoyed the profits of the land until the relief was paid. If the land was a tenancy in chief *ut de corona*, the King was entitled to a year's seisin, or a payment in lieu thereof. But profits of this kind were not confined to inheritances where the heirs were already of age. Associated with primer seisin were the profits which the King made from the livery of inheritances to heirs who had been in his wardship and had now come of age. The heir had to apply formally to enter into his inheritance—that is, 'sue for livery'— and, before he could do so, had to pay a sum equivalent to half a year's profits. A similar procedure was followed in the case of a tenant *ut de honore* and the same sum paid, although the legal term for the procedure was *ouster le main*. By the end of the fifteenth century the legal procedures which had to be followed when an heir in the King's wardship came of age had become so complicated as to face him, especially if he were a tenant-in-chief, with considerable risks, since any slip, however minute and technical, might result in the King's officials seizing the land once again, thus forcing the tenant to recommence the proceedings and in the meanwhile lose the profits of the land. An heir to an inheritance which was complicated because it lay in a large number of counties or was comprised of a number of originally different inheritances, might find it to his advantage to pay the Crown an additional sum for 'special livery' and thus avoid these hazards. Although it is difficult to be certain of the exact details, there can be little doubt that these procedures already existed in their main outlines by the end of the thirteenth century.[2]

[1] See Pollock & Maitland, I. 311–12; Holdsworth, III. 61.

[2] See the valuable discussion of these points in Constable, Introd., pp. xix–xxvii.

Records relating to the exploitation of the incidents of feudal tenure go back to the early twelfth century. The coronation charter of Henry I,[1] in promising that reliefs should be 'just and lawful' and that wardships should be held by the widows and next-of-kin of the deceased, shows that William Rufus had exploited both these incidents to the full. Moreover, Henry I's promise that these rules should also bind mesne lords indicates that they also were alive to the value of these sources of revenue. But the royal promises of 1100 were not kept. The Pipe Roll of 1130 shows that Henry I had by the end of his reign reverted to his brother's practices.[2] And there is abundant evidence that Henry II and his sons similarly exploited their feudal rights as one of the main sources of royal revenue. The absence of any rule or custom which regulated the amounts of reliefs demanded from tenants-in-chief enabled them to demand exorbitant sums. Moreover, especially under John, full advantage was taken of the political opportunities afforded by such reliefs. The sums demanded were often so high that they could not be paid immediately and the tenant-in-chief had to undertake to pay by instalments that were themselves so crippling that they provided, through the ever-present threat of distraint, a weapon which the King kept poised over his head. In this situation a tenant-in-chief who had recently succeeded to his inheritance could be kept cowed and impotent.

Such policies on the part of Henry II and his sons led to deep resentment among their tenants-in-chief. The incidents of feudal tenure bulked large in the efforts of the baronial leaders of 1215 to curtail the unbridled exercise of royal power. Inevitably, therefore, *Magna Carta* was a turning-point in the development of feudal incidents in England. The rules now laid down about the exploitation of these sources of revenue were motivated by the desire to prevent the Crown from continuing past policies. But the reforms of *Magna Carta* in these respects were to apply to mesne lords as well as the King, a decision which undoubtedly

[1] *Select Charters*, p. 118.

[2] See, e.g., F. M. Stenton, *The First Century of English Feudalism, 1066–1166* (Oxford, 2nd ed., 1961), pp. 219–20.

resulted from the baronial leaders' desire to carry their own tenants with them in the struggle against John.

The effect of clause 2 of *Magna Carta* was to make it impossible for the Crown in future to derive great profit, in either political or financial terms, from the right of relief. Those who succeeded to earldoms and baronies were now to pay £100. 'Glanvill' had regarded £5 as the sum due from a knight's fee to a mesne lord; and this figure was extended to all knights' fees held of the Crown. In consequence, the King's right to fix reliefs at will was at an end. Attempts were also made to limit the abuses which had occurred in the exploitation of wardship and marriage. A guardian was not to commit waste on the lands of a ward (clause 4); and these were to be given to him when he came of age in the condition in which they had been received (clause 5). No heir was to be disparaged through the lord's right of marriage—that is, married to a person of inferior social status. Two other clauses confined the lord's right to demand aids from his tenants to three occasions only— the ransom of the lord's body, the knighting of his eldest son, and the first marriage of his eldest daughter. Furthermore, such aids were to be 'reasonable'. The King (clause 12) was specifically forbidden to levy aids on any other occasions save by the 'common counsel' of the realm. And in another clause (15) he promised that he would not permit any of his subjects to take aids from their men on any occasions other than the three named.[1]

The reforms secured by *Magna Carta* did not provide an exhaustive treatment of all the abuses that might arise in the exploitation of feudal incidents. There is good reason to believe that some of those who took part in the drafting of *Magna Carta* wished to obtain a relief of 100 marks for barons;[2] but it was not until the *Confirmatio Cartarum* of 1297 that a baron's relief was reduced to this figure.[3] Other reforms affecting the exploitation of feudal incidents which followed *Magna Carta* were due not so

---

[1] *Select Charters*, pp. 293–5.

[2] J. C. Holt, *The Northerners: A Study in the Reign of John* (Oxford, 1961), pp. 114–15.

[3] S. Painter, *Studies in the History of the English Feudal Barony* (Baltimore, 1943), p. 63.

much to political pressure as to the discovery of abuses or legal difficulties by royal lawyers and administrators. The result was a group of statutes promulgated in the course of the thirteenth century which further defined the rights of lord and tenant in respect of feudal incidents. In 1215 *Magna Carta* had simply stated that aids were to be 'reasonable' and had not fixed their amount in monetary terms. Moreover, the two relevant clauses had been omitted from subsequent reissues. In 1275 the amount of future aids demanded by lords was fixed by statute in the case of those for knighting an eldest son and marrying an eldest daughter—at twenty shillings from a knight's fee and at the same figure from every twenty pounds' worth of socage land.[1] In theory these provisions did not apply to the Crown and were not extended to its aids until a statute of 1352.[2] In practice, however, the Crown after 1275 made no attempt to exploit its right to demand any sum it liked.[3] By this time taxation on movables had supplanted feudal aids as its main source of direct taxation.

Other statutes dealt with abuses in wardship and marriage. By c. 6 of the Statute of Merton of 1236, if an heir over fourteen married without the lord's licence, the lord could prolong his wardship of the heir's lands until he had received from the issues double the value of the marriage.[4] A lord who disparaged his ward by marrying her to a villein or burgess was to lose the wardship which was to be applied to the infant's use by her kinsmen. In 1275 the Statute of Westminster, I, c. 22 laid down that, if an heiress over fourteen refused a suitable match proposed by her lord, he retained his wardship until he had recovered the value of the marriage.[5] The same statute dealt with the tendency of a lord to keep an heiress unmarried beyond the age of fourteen in order to enjoy the profits of her lands and laid down that, if kept unmarried for two years after she was fourteen, she could have an action to recover her lands without paying anything for the marriage or wardship.[6] These reforms, however, left a curious situa-

[1] *Statutes*, I. 35 (Westminster 1, c. 36).
[2] ibid., I. 322 (25 Ed. III, st. 5, c. 11).
[3] On this point, see Plucknett, *Ed. I*, p. 78.   [4] *Statutes*, I. 3.
[5] ibid., I. 33. See also Plucknett, *Ed. I*, pp. 116–17.   [6] *Statutes*, I. 33 (c. 22).

tion in which, while a female ward was penalized for refusing a suitable marriage offered her or marrying without licence, a male ward could refuse a marriage offered him with impunity.[1] In 1285 the Statute of Westminster (II, c. 16) dealt with the conflict of claims over the marriage of the heir and the wardship of his body when he held of more than one lord and ordained that in such a case they were to go to the lord of the oldest feoffment.[2] This provision, however, was concerned only with such disputes between mesne lords: if some lands were held of the Crown as of an honour, then the King held the marriage and the wardship of the body.[3]

At the end of the thirteenth century, in consequence of *Magna Carta* and the reforms which followed, the structure of feudal incidents was virtually complete and remained intact until the abolition of feudal tenures in 1660. Yet the opportunities for financial profit available to lords in the later middle ages were distinctly different from those of the twelfth century. Reliefs exacted by the King, and by his tenants from their tenants, were now fixed in value. In consequence, not only were lords, including the King, unable to levy reliefs at rates higher than those fixed in 1215 and 1297, but with the fall in the value of money which occurred in the course of the thirteenth century a decline followed in the real value of the fixed monetary relief, a situation which the Crown in particular was helpless to avert or alter. A similar decline also occurred in the real value of aids. In the case of mesne lords, those which they were permitted to demand for the knighting of an eldest son and the marrying of an eldest daughter were now fixed in monetary terms, while the absence in theory of such a limitation in the case of an aid to ransom the lord's body would be more than outweighed by the disadvantages of such a situation. In the later middle ages, therefore, the feudal incidents of the greatest value were those which enabled a lord to tap directly the wealth of an inheritance—that is, those which enabled him to lay his hands on the lands of an heir through wardship. It is true that *Magna Carta* had forbidden lords to commit waste. But a

---

[1] Plucknett, *Ed. I*, p. 116.   [2] *Statutes*, I. 82.
[3] Constable, Introd., pp. xiv–xv.

general prohibition of this kind was not as binding as a reform which fixed the figures at which reliefs or aids could be levied. No doubt this consideration explains why the legislative reforms of the thirteenth century dealt with abuses or defects in wardship and marriage. But, although the lord's rights to marriage were regulated and competing claims over wardships henceforward submitted to a rule of law, wardship remained. From this particular incident of feudalism the Crown was the greatest beneficiary, partly becuase it was the lord of the country's greatest landowners, partly because 'prerogative wardship' enabled it to draw the revenues of all the lands of infant heirs who were its tenants-in-chief.

The growth in the comparative importance of wardship and marriage as sources of revenue in part explains why royal administrators in the thirteenth century gave increasing attention to the means by which the feudal incidents of the Crown were administered. The result of their activities was the appearance of a new official—the escheator—whose duty it was to enquire into and enforce the Crown's feudal rights.[1] In the twelfth century and into the reign of Henry III, these tasks formed part of the duties of itinerant justices who made the necessary enquiries, while the sheriff accounted at the Exchequer for any issues which arose therefrom. With the growth of royal administration under the Angevin kings there were substantial additions to the sheriff's duties and it was found desirable to remove some of these from him. Among these was the supervision of the King's rights as feudal lord. The employment of both the itinerant justices and the sheriffs for this purpose was cumbersome and inefficient. Indeed, it is likely that revenues had been lost in the periods which elapsed between the deaths of tenants and the enquiries of the justices. The main motive behind the appearance of the escheator was undoubtedly a more intensive and efficient exploitation of wardship and marriage and primer seisin. Although the Crown continued to draw revenues from reliefs, the fact that these were

[1] For what follows, see E. R. Stevenson, 'The Escheator', in *The English Government at Work, 1327–1336*, ed. J. F. Willard, W. A. Morris, etc., II (Cambridge, Mass., 1947), esp. pp. 113–21.

limited in value as a result of *Magna Carta* meant that they could no longer be used as political weapons. Both the fixed body of rules relating to, and the non-political character of, reliefs must have made it easier to erect a new administrative system to control the Crown's fiscal resources as feudal lord.

The final appearance of the office of escheator as it became known during the rest of the middle ages was the outcome of a long period of experiment. Early in the reign of Henry III the itinerant justices ceased to hold inquisitions concerning escheats and wardships. The office of escheator then appeared as a result of the reforms at the Exchequer which followed the 'ministerial' crisis of 1232: thirty-four pairs of escheators were appointed who were to answer for the issues of escheats and wardships in their respective counties at the Exchequer. From 1236 until 1275 these revenues were under the control of an escheator north of and south of the Trent respectively. But in the latter year the duties of the escheator were transferred to the sheriff. The motive behind this change seems to have been an attempt to classify royal revenues more carefully and thus increase the efficiency of revenue-collecting: the escheators had hitherto been responsible both for the King's feudal rights and for the administration of his demesnes and at the end of 1275 the latter were transferred to three stewards, each controlling a group of counties. But the office of escheator had not been abolished: the same person now held the offices of both escheator and sheriff and writs were directed to him in one or other of his capacities according to the nature of the business to be dealt with. This new scheme, however, broke down within a few years. By 1281 the office of escheator north of the Trent had been reconstituted and by 1283 that of the south also. The administrative importance of both these escheatorships and the extent to which their activities impinged upon the lives of the King's subjects can be gauged from the fact that they were among the offices of state to which, by the Ordinances of 1311, appointments were to be made in parliament.[1] They continued until 1322 when, as part of the reforms which followed Edward II's victories over his opponents and which historians have associated

[1] *Statutes,* I. 160.

with the Despensers, their place was taken by eight local escheatries, each controlling a group of counties. After the accession
of Edward III the two escheatries were restored until 1332, when
they gave place again to eight local ones, being restored once
more in 1335. In 1340 parliament insisted on a return to the
system of eight local escheatries, each escheator to hold office for
one year only and to be appointed by the chancellor, treasurer and
chief baron of the Exchequer. In 1341 the escheatries were re-
grouped to coincide with the shires and the respective sheriffs
were chosen as escheators. Within a few years the escheatries were
separated from the sheriffdoms and henceforward each shire had
its own escheator: there was no grouping of shires into regions,
but each escheator accounted for the issues of his shire's escheats at
the Exchequer. These arrangements continued for the rest of the
middle ages.[1]

Broadly speaking, the duties of the escheator were to take care
of the feudal rights and revenues of the Crown within his shire.
When a landowner died, it was his duty to hold an inquisition
concerning the extent and value of his lands and the tenures by
which they were held. If the King had any rights as lord, he
seized the lands into the King's hands and accounted for their
issues until ordered by the chancellor how to proceed with them.
He took the proof of age of heirs who wished to sue their lands
out of the King's hands. It was also his duty to assign dower to
widows and to partition lands among heiresses. The Chancery
developed a number of writs to control these and other functions.
Although an escheator could, on the death of a landowner, hold
an inquisition on his own authority, most inquisitions *post
mortem*[2] were held after he had received a writ of *diem clausit
extremum* from the Chancery: if further enquiries were necessary,
the writ appropriate to the case in question was available.[3]

---

[1] No studies of the development of the office after 1341 have been published.

[2] The practice of holding such inquisitions—the earliest extant belongs to
20 Henry III—may have begun before the procedure involved was formalized,
since the earliest surviving writ of *diem clausit extremum* in the form in which it
was later known belongs to 39 Henry III (*CIPMA*, I. vii).

[3] For full details of the writs which were available, see *CIPMB*, I. Introd.

The fact that the Crown in the late thirteenth and early four-teenth centuries developed the office of escheator meant that each shire now contained an official whose sole duty it was to safe-guard the royal rights to feudal incidents. There can be little doubt that the system by which such rights were administered in the twelfth and early thirteenth centuries was subject to many loopholes and delays and the Crown thereby lost revenues. Pro-vided an escheator was loyal and efficient, from the late thirteenth century onwards it became increasingly less likely that the Crown would be deprived of the rights and revenues which were its due. Indeed, it is clear from the frequent changes in the administration of escheats in the first fifteen years or so of Edward III's reign that the landowners of England were extremely conscious of the potential dangers in the office of escheator, which had now be-come an important force in local government. It has been sug-gested that the fluctuations in these years from one type of system to another were due to political causes, since the magnates ob-jected to the eight local escheatries because they had been intro-duced by the hated Despensers.[1] It is possible that this motive played some part in their abolition in 1327, but it is difficult to believe that it adequately explains all the changes which followed during the next fifteen years or so. It is much more likely that their attitudes to these were motivated by their interests as land-owners whose inheritances might be seized by the new royal officials. Control of the system of escheatries by two great officials north and south of the Trent respectively was not in their interests, partly because delays in holding inquisitions might easily result thereby, partly because it was less easy for them to keep a watchful eye on officials whose duties covered so large a region. The same objections, though to a lesser extent, applied to the eight local escheatries. But the office of escheator, however much it might be viewed with suspicion and even hostility, had come to stay. In the course of the changes of the early years of Edward III both Crown and magnates came to realize that the shire escheatry was a reasonable compromise between their interests.

[1] On this see S. T. Gibson, 'The Escheatries, 1327–1341', EHR, XXXVI (1921), 218–25.

On the one hand, a careful watch could be kept on a local shire official, probably a member of the local gentry, while delays in holding inquisitions or restoring inheritances could be avoided more easily than with a more distant official. On the other hand, the Crown retained in each shire an official whose duty it was to ensure that it lost none of its rights as feudal lord and overlord.

(ii) The Motives of Evasion

If we confined our study of feudal incidents to the rights of lords, we would provide a one-sided and, therefore, inaccurate assessment of their position in English landed society, since it would not include the tenantry over whom these rights were exercised. But, because of its provenance, the evidence at our disposal of necessity gives an incomplete picture. Because it consists largely of the administrative and financial records of the greatest feudal lord of all, the Crown, it inevitably gives prominence to the nature of the rights which feudal tenure gave the lord and the ways in which the King exploited them. We tend to know comparatively little about the attitude of tenants once the Crown's rights had been brought under control by *Magna Carta*. Our problem is complicated by the existence of 'prerogative wardship'. As a result of this custom the King's right of wardship dwarfed that of all other lords. For this reason most leading landowners tended to regard the King as the only one of their feudal lords of whom they need take any real account. At the same time, in the case of those who held lands of them and other mesne lords, and not the King, they naturally wished to enforce their own rights. In short, if we are searching for signs of a desire to remove altogether the bonds which bound a feudal tenant to his lord, we would expect to find them emerging in the lowest reaches of the feudal hierarchy. But these have left very few traces in our records.

Nevertheless, despite a paucity of evidence, from the early thirteenth century onwards it is possible to detect a change in the attitude of English landowners towards the incidents of feudal tenure. The *Magna Carta* of 1215 was descended from a number of 'charters of liberties', which, whatever their divergences in detail, were concerned largely with the limitation and control of the feudal powers of the Crown. The reissues of *Magna Carta* in the course of the thirteenth century, and the reduction of the baron's relief in 1297,[1] indicate that such considerations retained their importance in the minds of the King's leading subjects. But from this time onwards there are also clear signs of a desire on the part of some landowners to escape altogether the feudal incidents which were now under some considerable degree of control. How far a landowner might feel the need to do this would depend on the extent to which he was the feudal tenant of others. One who held of others by military service but of whom little was held by this tenure—for example, a knight who occupied a few small manors in demesne—would readily see the advantages of evading his lord's rights. On the other hand, a great landowner, however much he might find inconvenient, and possibly resent, the Crown's rights as feudal lord over himself, could console himself with the thought of the advantages and profits he himself enjoyed as feudal lord over others. But the value of these would depend on the extent to which his tenants succeeded in discovering means of evading his rights over them. If, therefore, the tenants of mesne lords began to find means of successful evasion, the more such practices grew, the more it would be in the interests of the leading tenants-in-chief to attempt to evade the rights which the Crown possessed over them, their widows, heirs and inheritances.

The beginnings of such developments can be discovered in the middle of the thirteenth century. C. 6 of the Statute of Marlborough[2] in 1267 dealt with fraudulent enfeoffments that had been made to deprive lords of their rights and expressly forbade two of the methods used for this purpose. In the first the tenant enfeoffed his eldest son and heir of the inheritance so that he was already seised of it when the father died. The second method of defrauding the lord was more complicated: the statute describes how the tenants

[1] See above, p. 13.
[2] *Statutes*, I. 20-1 (52 Hen. III, c. 6), discussed in Plucknett, *Ed. I*, pp. 79-81.

c

will lease for term of years ... wherein it is contained that they are
satisfied of the whole service due to them until a certain term; so that
such feoffees are bound at the said term to pay a certain sum to the value
of the same lands, or far above; so that after such term the lands shall
return to them, or to their heirs, because no man will be content to hold
them upon the price.

These details reveal the considerable ingenuity which was already
being used to evade feudal incidents. A landowner made a lease
of his lands for a term of years. But, since in the event of his death
leaving an heir under age, the lord could dispossess the lessee,[1] he
had a deed drawn up, or included a clause in his testament, stating
that he had already received the rents and other services which
were due during the whole of the lessees' term. In consequence,
the lord had to respect the estate in the land which the lessees
held. To ensure that the land was returned to his heirs, the original
lease stated that, at the end of the term, the lessees had to pay a
specified sum to the owner or his heir: the amount was fixed high
enough to ensure that the lessees did not find it to their advantage
to continue their estate. In declaring both these practices illegal the
statute did not permit lords to dispossess at will either heirs
enfeoffed under age or lessees under a fraudulent enfeoffment. It
stated that a lord must obtain a writ of ward and laid down the
procedure to be followed in execution of this writ. An inquisition
was to be held to enquire into the account of the enfeoffment
which the witnesses to the original deed could give and, in the
case of the fraudulent lease, into the amount of the sum payable
at the end of the lessees' term. In the light of such evidence it
should be decided in the royal court whether the enfeoffments
were made 'in good faith (*bona fide*),[2] or by collusion, to defraud
the chief lords of the fee of their wards'.

[1] See above, p. 8.

[2] Professor Plucknett comments, 'This reference to *bona fides* seems to be
wellnigh unique in English common law during the middle ages. ... The
single appearance of *bona fides* in the statute of Marlborough is therefore a
remarkable indication of the urgency of the problem which compelled our
law to make so adventurous a borrowing from an alien system' (Plucknett,
Ed. I, p. 80).

It is unfortunate that we do not know more about the origins of this particular section of the Statute of Marlborough. Unlike the statute's other provisions, it did not arise from any complaint made in the Provisions of Westminster of 1259. Until all the legal records have been thoroughly examined, it is not possible to be certain of the identity of the lords whose interests were being damaged by fraudulent enfeoffments. The word 'lords' as used in the statute itself could easily include the King himself, who was thus able in the future to benefit from its provisions.[1] But it appears likely, in default at present of more precise information, that this reform was framed in the interests of mesne lords, not the King. In the first place, the provisions of the Statute of Marlborough as a whole were intended to deal with grievances on the part of the landowning classes, some of which were expressed in the Provisions of Westminster of 1259. In the second place, the language of the statute gives the clear impression that it was mesne lords who had been wronged by fraudulent enfeoffments. In the third place, a search of the Patent and Close Rolls of Henry III's reign reveals only one tenant-in-chief—Peter de Goldington—who had enfeoffed an heir under age,[2] while no trace of fraudulent leases can be found there. Lastly, at least from 1256 onwards, the Crown's own interests were adequately protected, since by virtue of the edict of that year[3] it claimed the right to license all alienations by tenants-in-chief and to seize all lands held in chief alienated without licence.

The statute does not reveal whether landowners had been in the habit of disposing of the whole of their inheritances in fraudulent enfeoffments. Nor do the details it provides give a complete

[1] For some discussion of the interpretation of the statute in the late fourteenth and fifteenth centuries, see below, Chapter IV (i).

[2] His younger daughter (*CPR, 1247–58*, p. 177; *CCR, 1251–3*, p. 314). The latter reference implies that the King was able to claim her wardship and marriage because her father had not appointed a guardian for her.

[3] See section (ii) of Chapter II. It is, perhaps, worth noting that, when in 1289 the King restored an heir who was a minor to the lands with which he had been enfeoffed by his father, on condition that they be resumed if the father died while the heir was under age, no mention was made of the Statute of Marlborough (*CCR, 1288–90*, pp. 19–20).

picture of the relationship between them and those who helped them to carry out the frauds. When a landowner enfeoffed an heir who was under age, we must assume that he remained in occupation of the land. But, in the case of a fraudulent lease, this assumption would be unwise: it would be possible for the trans- action with the lessees to include a real financial bargain—for example, arrangements for the repayment of loans—and thus, in effect, be a virtual mortgage. By this means a landowner could simultaneously prevent his heir's wardship and marriage falling into the lord's hands and pay his debts. What does emerge clearly from the Statute of Marlborough is the fact that by means of the practices it forbids lords had been losing the wardship of the lands so granted away and, if these comprised the whole inheritance, the right of marriage also. It seems likely that it was found neces- sary to include in the statute a procedure for dealing with such cases in the future because lords, in a situation where the existing law gave them no redress, had been asserting their rights by force or superior position, aided by the collapse of law and order in the years 1258-65. It is important to note that the Statute of Marl- borough did not give a complete protection against the loss of all feudal incidents in such circumstances. Its provisions applied only to the loss of wardship and marriage as a result of fraudulent enfeoffments and it remained possible for an heir who was over age at the time of his ancestor's death to avoid the payment of relief by these means. Perhaps this omission in the statute's provisions reflects a contemporary awareness of the fact that reliefs were less potentially valuable than wardship and marriage and that it was the latter incidents which must be saved.

A tenant who engaged in one of these fraudulent enfeoffments, especially the method of a lease, both showed considerable in- genuity and ran some risks. His efforts would not have been worth while if it had not been in his interests to evade the feudal inci- dents which were his lord's right. The motives which lay behind such evasive practices were twofold. The first, a negative one, was the desire to avoid the inconveniences and embarrassments which might result for the tenant's heir and family from the lord's exercise of his rights. The second was more far-reaching and, if successful, might result in lasting damage to the relationship between lord and tenant—in simple terms, to deprive the lord of the profits which he derived from his rights in order that his tenant might profit from them in his stead.

The desire to avoid the personal inconveniences of wardship for the tenant's heir and family was a natural extension of the struggle against the lord's uncontrolled exercise of his rights which had been continuing since the reign of William Rufus. The provisions of *Magna Carta* and of the 'charters of liberties' that were its predecessors do not reveal how far those who framed them objected to the mere exercise of these rights by the Crown, as distinct from the injustices in their enforcement. Those who were tenants and possessed no, or few, tenants of their own may well at an early stage have resented their own liability to wardship. At any rate, in the fourteenth and fifteenth centuries there are clear indications that the fear remained that the Crown would exercise its feudal rights unfairly. Complaints of waste on the part of escheators were made in the *Articuli super Cartas*[1] of 1300 and in statutes of 1340[2] and 1362.[3] The records also contain a number of references to waste on the lands of heirs by the guardians to whom they were committed by the Crown—for instance, it occurred on the estates of John Mowbray, earl of Nottingham, in the reign of Richard II,[4] while in 1437 John Vere, earl of Oxford, claimed that the costs of repairs caused by damage during his minority would exceed 2000 marks and he had no remedy since his guardian had died before he came of age.[5] In the light of this and other[6] evidence there can be no doubt that the reforms of *Magna Carta* in respect of waste during wardship did not serve to control incompetent or avaricious guardians. Moreover, if the inheritances of important magnates could be damaged during wardship, the risks for lesser landowners must have been considerable.

Efforts were also made to control the Crown's right to grant wardships to persons of its choice. In a statute of 1340, on the

[1] *Statutes*, I. 140 (c. 18). [2] ibid., I. 285 (14 Ed. III, st. 1, c. 13).
[3] ibid., I. 374 (36 Ed. III, st.1, c. 13). [4] *CPR, 1381–5*, p. 182.
[5] ibid., *1436–41*, pp. 71–2.
[6] e.g. *CMI*, III. 56 (no. 157) and 125–6 (no. 353).

ground of waste committed by escheators, a return was made to the sort of reform extracted from Henry I in 1100, though apparently it was soon abandoned.[1] It was ordained that

if it be found that the heir is within age, and the next friends of the heir to whom the inheritance cannot descend, shall come and offer to take the said lands, yielding the value to the King, until the age of the heir ... by accord between the Chancellor and the Treasurer, they shall have a commission to keep the said lands by good and sufficient surety until the age of the said heir, and to answer the King of the value.[2]

In practice these provisions applied to wardships of lands held by knight's service of the Crown the rules which already belonged by law to those of socage lands. The desire to protect the interests of the heir is so strong that the statute goes one step further than Henry I's coronation charter and permits the wardship to be granted only to those kinsmen who cannot inherit. In 1376 in the Good Parliament the Speaker complained that royal wardships had been granted to persons unfit to hold them[3] and a petition was presented requesting that the statute of 1340 be observed.[4] In the parliament of January 1377 a petition was presented that the next friends of the heir should hold his lands at farm,[5] while in that of the following October there was another requesting the observance of the statute of 1340.[6]

In addition to the desire to control the administration of wardships, there is evidence that landowners resented the fact that, in the event of their premature decease, the choice of a marriage for their heirs was the right of their lord. Towards the close of the Hundred Years' War the Crown openly recognized the existence of this feeling. When preparing their expeditions against France, Edward IV[7] and Henry VII[8]—the latter on two occasions— promulgated statutes which granted a number of privileges to

---

[1] See above, p. 9.   [2] *Statutes*, I. 285 (14 Ed. III, st. 1, c. 13).
[3] *The Anonimalle Chronicle, 1333–1381*, ed. V. H. Galbraith (Manchester, 1927), p. 87.   [4] *Rot. Parl.*, II. 341 (no. 59).
[5] ibid, II. 368 (no. 24).   [6] ibid, III. 20 (no. 79).
[7] *Statutes*, II. 445–7 (14 Ed. IV, c. 1). This applied to royal tenants only.
[8] ibid, II. 528–30 (4 Hen. VII, c. 4) and 550–1 (7 Hen. VII, c. 2).

those landowners who went overseas in their service and among these was one whereby, in the event of their dying on active service, and leaving heirs under age, the wardship and marriage would be held without payment by the deceased's executors or feoffees. In 1512 Henry VIII granted this privilege by statute to anyone who in future served the King in his wars overseas.[1]

Similar concessions—generally of the marriage of the heir together with a part, or the whole, of the wardship of the lands— were granted by the Crown to a total of twelve individuals in the thirteenth, fourteenth and fifteenth centuries: to John FitzPhilip in 1235 if anything befell him overseas where he had gone as the King's envoy,[2] to Nicholas de Molis in 1252–3,[3] to Matthias Bezill in 1253,[4] to Peter of Savoy in 1253,[5] to Robert Aquilon in 1266,[6] to William of Valence, the King's brother, in 1270,[7] to William Inge in 1310,[8] to Humphrey Bohun, earl of Hereford and Essex, in 1319,[9] to William de la Pole in 1339,[10] to William Montague, earl of Salisbury, in 1340,[11] to Robert, lord Ferrers, in 1349,[12] and William de la Pole, marquess of Suffolk, in 1444.[13] It

---

[1] ibid., III. 26–7 (3 Hen. VIII, c. 4). This did not apply to those serving in permanent garrisons, on the Marches or overseas.

[2] CPR, 1232–47, p. 121 (wardship and marriage of his heir and wardship of lands held in chief granted to his wife).

[3] ibid., 1247–58, pp. 142 (his heirs to marry freely without impediment) and 184 (to dispose of the wardship of his heir and lands as he wished).

[4] ibid., 1247–58, p. 216 (to dispose of the wardship of his heirs and lands and their marriages at will).

[5] ibid., 1247–58, p. 220 (if he has a male heir of his wife, to assign or bequeath the wardship of the lands or of the heir to whomsoever he will).

[6] ibid., 1266–72, pp. 19–20 (to dispose of the wardship of the lands and the marriage of the heir by will and, if he fails to do so, the heirs may have their own wardship and marriage).

[7] ibid., 1266–72, p. 451 (his executors or assigns to have free disposal of the wardship of his lands and heirs and their marriages as directed in his testament).

[8] ibid., 1307–13, p. 267 (to grant the marriage of his heir to his executors or assigns).

[9] ibid., 1317–21, p. 391 (grant of custody of half the estates and the marriage of the heir).

[10] ibid., 1338–40, p. 386. The nearest kinsman to whom the inheritance could not descend in the event of the heir's death, was to have the custody of the body

is obvious that all these were very specially favoured on these occasions. Six of the grants were made in Henry III's reign. Of the rest, all except one were men to whom the King was under some special obligation—for example, two of those rewarded by Edward III included one of his leading generals and his leading financier in the early years of his French wars, while the grant made to the marquess of Suffolk in 1444 was clearly due to his influence at the court of Henry VI. Nevertheless, the paucity of such grants, especially after 1272, is itself an indication of the extent to which the privilege was regarded as exceptional by the Crown and treasured by the recipient.

In the light of this body of evidence, it is apparent that the country's leading landowners were anxious, if the Crown was prepared to co-operate, to remove their heirs from the inconveniences which were certain, and the risks which were possible, from wardship and marriage. There can be no doubt that similar considerations were in the minds of other, lesser landowners. However, it is difficult to believe that these motives in themselves would have resulted in widespread efforts to evade feudal incidents altogether. It is equally possible, and perhaps more likely, that the mere dislike of wardship and marriage would, if left to itself, have simply resulted in attempts at further reform of the system, as, for example, can be seen in the statute of 1340. But there were other features of feudal tenure which placed those who held thereby under financial strains which gradually led them to realize that, through finding means of evading the feudal incidents to which their heirs were liable, they could not only avoid the

---

and the lands, to answer in full for the issues thereof to the heir when he came of age. The heir was to marry whomsoever he wished.

[11] CPR, 1340–3, p. 57. The earl's executors, or whoever he should nominate in his lifetime, was to have the custody of the lands held in chief during the minority of the heir and answer for the profits as laid down by the earl in his testament. The heir was to marry with their assent and counsel.

[12] ibid., 1348–50, p. 301 (the custody of the lands and the marriage granted to him and his executors).

[13] ibid., 1441–6, p. 319 (the custody and marriage of the heir granted to his wife and executors).

irksome features of wardship and marriage but also themselves enjoy the revenues of which they had deprived their lords.

By the middle of the thirteenth century two rules of feudal land law must have proved irksome for many tenants on financial grounds. In the first place, a tenant could not bequeath by will any lands held under feudal tenure: all those so held by him at his death had to descend to his heir by the law of primogeniture. The evolution of this rule is a complicated story which is, as yet, not completely clear.[1] According to 'Glanvill'[2] a feudal tenant could only make a grant of his land on his death-bed if his heir consented and afterwards confirmed his ancestor's act. In fact, the right so exercised can hardly be described as a devise by will, since it was the heir's consent and confirmation which made the grant effective in law.[3] By the end of the thirteenth century the royal courts certainly condemned post-obit gifts of land. Their attitude can be justified in terms of the procedures they were following. In their view a conveyance of land could not be effective unless there was a real transfer of seisin from grantor to grantee: and it was impossible to see how a post-obit gift could be reconciled with this rule. It is, however, likely that their anxiety to adhere to their rule on this point was greatly strengthened by the desire to protect the interests of the King, who, as the greatest lord of all, had most to lose from the decline of services and incidents which would be bound to follow the acceptance of a freedom to devise. In the mid-thirteenth century there are slight signs[4] that some common

---

[1] See Pollock & Maitland, II. 326-9; Holdsworth, III. 73-6. The chief influence in creating this insistence on the rule of primogeniture must have been the need to protect the lord's services and incidents.

[2] *Glanvill*, p. 70, discussed in Pollock & Maitland, II. 328; Sheehan, pp. 270-4. In fact, a death-bed enfeoffment would often be ineffective because the grantor would not be able to transfer seisin properly, e.g. *Placitorum Abbreviatio* (Record Comm.), p. 272, col. 1 (Suffolk, Hil., 9 Ed. I).

[3] e.g. in 1232 the abbot and convent of Tewkesbury received the custody of a wood, which Gilbert de Clare, earl of Gloucester, was said to have bequeathed to them, to hold during the minority of his heir, on condition that they should surrender it to him, if, when he came of age, he did not wish his father's bequest to stand (*CPR, 1232–47*, pp. 6-7).

[4] See the discussion and references provided in Sheehan, pp. 279-80. It is

lawyers were trying to adjust their doctrines and permit devises. Bracton refers to a practice in which land was conveyed to a person 'to hold to him and to his heirs or to whomsoever he wishes to give or bequeath it'. In one passage he appears to think it possible to devise land by this means,[1] but in another[2] he rejects it, because of the difficulty of transferring a valid seisin. At any rate, the latter view must soon have prevailed. And in a case of 1293 the rule forbidding devises of land held under feudal tenure was treated as axiomatic.[3] By the end of the thirteenth century, therefore, nothing had been done to alleviate the discomforts imposed on feudal tenants by this rule. If they wished to salve their paternal consciences by leaving inheritances to younger children who would otherwise be excluded by the rule of primo-geniture, they could only do so while alive, thus depleting their own landed revenues. Moreover, they could only do so if such children were already over age. No such facilities existed if they were still under age at the time of their father's death. Nor could they make preparations whereby their landed revenues could be used after their deaths to pay debts or raise marriage portions for daughters. Under feudal law no such arrangements were pos-sible. If a tenant left an heir under age, his lord could upset the provisions he had made; and, if the heir was over age, his consent or confirmation would be necessary before they could stand.[4] There were also anomalies which must have made the rules of feudal land law even more irksome for many landowners. Lands

---

difficult to believe that the limited freedom of bequest to brothers or cousins given to Peter of Savoy in 1241 by Henry III when he was granted the honour of Richmond is evidence of any tendency among lawyers to permit bequests of lands held under feudal tenure. He was a close relative and favourite of the King and was thus in a specially favoured position.

[1] Bracton, IV. 283. He seems to think a writ of recovery by the legatee is possible.

[2] ibid., II. 149. [3] *YBRS, 21 & 22 Ed. I*, p. 70.

[4] For examples of heirs consenting to such arrangements, during their an-cestors' lifetimes, see *CCR, 1272–9*, pp. 332 and 346. A grant of 1279 to John Vescy whereby he was to demise lands worth £100 a year for ten years to pay his debts mentions the consent of his heir (*CPR, 1272–81*, p. 354).

which were held in gavelkind[1] or in free burgage in the major boroughs[2] could be left by will. A landowner, therefore, who was fortunate enough to hold lands in Kent or in London or in an important borough was in a more advantageous position than his fellows who did not. How far these advantages were exploited by those who possessed them it is impossible to say; but it is interesting to note that the records of the Hustings court of the city of London contain wills in which leading landowners, including earls, disposed of city properties.[3]

Allied with the desire to bequeath lands by will was the second disability which feudal land law imposed—the fact that a land-owner who died in debt was unable to employ for the payment of his creditors the revenues which accrued from his lands after his death. In fact, the available evidence indicates that the feudal tenant's position in this respect had deteriorated during the late twelfth and early thirteenth centuries. In the case of landowners who died leaving heirs under age, a measure of relief still existed in the latter half of the twelfth century: 'Glanvill' tells us that a lord who held an heir in his custody 'should discharge the debts of the deceased, so far as the estate and the length of the custody will admit'.[4] Just when this rule fell into abeyance it is difficult to say. If it was effective in the reign of John, it is odd that neither the Articles of the Barons nor *Magna Carta* mention it in 1215. Moreover, clause 10 of the latter—laying down that a debt owed to the Jews would not accrue interest during a minority[5]— implies that the lord's obligation to pay the tenant's debts during wardship had disappeared. However, the rule is mentioned by Bracton in somewhat vague and general terms, when he tells us that during wardship, as well as maintaining the heir as befits his station, the lord 'will acquit the hereditary debts in proportion to the quantity of the inheritance according to the time of the

---

[1] C. Sandys, *Consuetudines Kanciae: A History of Gavelkind* (London, 1851), pp. 281–6.

[2] Pollock & Maitland, II. 330; *WHC*, I. xxxv.

[3] ibid., pp. 218 (Henry Lacy, earl of Lincoln), 310 (Aymer Valence, earl of Pembroke) and 507–8 (Laurence Hastings, earl of Pembroke).

[4] *Glanvill*, p. 83.   [5] *Select Charters*, p. 294.

custody'.[1] It is noteworthy that Bracton specifically mentions 'hereditary' debts: it is possible that he thereby refers to those which the heir would be under an obligation to pay if he were of age, but we cannot exclude the possibility that he is thinking of permanent charge on the revenues from the estates. At any rate, it is difficult to see how the lord's obligation when Bracton wrote could have been other than a purely moral one which, however strong in the past, it would be hard either to enforce on him or for him to carry out in practice, especially since—as Bracton himself shows—the functions of the executor were expanding at this time. Certainly this rule was so far weakened by 1327 that a petition of the 'community of the realm' in the first parliament of Edward III complained that those who enjoyed the custody of wardships were being troubled with demands to pay debts owed to the Crown by the deceased.[2]

The rules relating to the debts of an ancestor who left an heir who was over age also altered in the course of the late twelfth and thirteenth centuries. According to 'Glanvill',[3] 'If the chattels of the deceased are not sufficient to pay his debts, then the heir is bound to make good the deficiency out of his own property.' The same doctrine is to be found in Bracton, but the language he uses at one point betrays the fact that the situation is beginning to change. Although two passages[4] are similar in their content to 'Glanvill', Bracton also tells us, in a context which appears to relate to chattels, not lands, that 'the heir of the deceased shall be bound to acquit the debts of his predecessor, as far as anything has come to him from the inheritance of the deceased, and no further, unless he wishes to do so of grace'.[5] Despite the wealth of argument and detail that he gives on many other points of law, Bracton is vague on this point and fails to define in precise terms the extent to which the heir was bound to pay his ancestor's debts. Indeed, the language he employs implies moral obligations which could not necessarily be enforced at law. In any case, other

---

[1] . . . *debita hereditaria adquietabunt pro quantitate hereditatis, et pro rata, secundum tempus custodie* (Bracton, II. 252).
[2] *Rot. Parl.*, II. 9b (28).   [3] *Glanvill*, p. 81.
[4] Bracton, II. 178 and 180.   [5] ibid, II. 180.

portions of his work show that any duties the heir might have had were beginning to be shared with his ancestor's executors: provided debts due to the testator had been acknowledged in his lifetime, the executors could sue for them in the ecclesiastical court and they could also be sued there if directed by the testament to pay the testator's debts.[1] Within the next fifty years or so, the powers of executors had further increased. The royal courts recognized their position for the first time: early in the reign of Edward I the Chancery had framed, and the King's court upheld, a writ of debt for executors and a writ of debt against them. In 1285 the Statute of Westminster, II, c. 23,[2] gave executors the right to employ the action of account. In 1330 they were given by statute an action of trespass against one who in the testator's lifetime carried off his goods.[3] In short, by the early years of the fourteenth century the heir's responsibility for the debts of his ancestor had been taken over by the latter's executors.[4]

This change in legal doctrines posed serious problems for the landowner who died in debt. While the lord or the heir remained under any sort of obligation to pay these debts out of the lands' issues, however rapidly that obligation was becoming a purely moral one, the possibility and, therefore, hope remained that at least some of the revenues of the inheritance would be used to pay off the deceased's creditors. However, by the beginning of the fourteenth century this hope had no basis in law. If the heir was under age, the lord took the profits of his lands for his own use: if he was over age, once the necessary formalities between him and his lord had been completed, he occupied the estates as completely his own and the only resources available to his ancestor's executors for the payment of debts and the performance of their other duties were the chattels and other financial assets of the deceased. In this changed legal situation it seems likely that many landowners, unless they had achieved an increase in personal wealth while in occupation of their inheritances, witnessed a real

[1] ibid., IV. 267, discussed in Pollock & Maitland, II. 345–6.
[2] *Statutes*, I. 83.   [3] ibid., I. 263 (4 Ed. III, c. 7).
[4] On the rise of the executor, see Pollock & Maitland, II. 336, 343–8; Holdsworth, III. 563–85.

diminution in the financial resources available for the payment of debts and performance of their testamentary bequests.

There are clear indications in the records of government of the financial pressures which must have resulted from this situation. The Patent Rolls of the reigns of Henry III, Edward I, Edward II and Edward III contain a large number of grants in which the Crown promised to an individual landowner that, in the event of his dying in debt to the Crown, such debts would be secured from the heirs of the deceased, and not his executors. For instance, twenty such grants are recorded in the reign of Henry III, twelve of them after 1247,[1] and sixteen in the reign of Edward I, nine of them between 1294 and 1301.[2] This concession, when effective, must have resulted in an appreciable increase in the financial resources available to the executors for the performance of their duties. The extent to which the privilege was a treasured one[3] may be gauged from the fact that it was always given to leading magnates or to those whose services had been of special value to the King. It is especially noticeable that over half such grants made by Edward I occurred in the period of his difficulties with his subjects between 1294 and 1301.

Nevertheless, many landowners, including those who received such privileges from the Crown, must have continued to resent the fact that, in the event of their decease, they were unable to dispose of the revenues of their lands. A search through the Patent Rolls between 1216 and 1485 reveals that a number of them were more fortunate than their fellows in this respect, in that they received from the Crown grants whereby, for a number of years

---

[1] *CPR, 1225-32,* pp. 472-3; ibid., *1232-47,* pp. 288, 315, 454, 461, 477, 501; ibid., *1247-58,* pp. 34, 35, 108, 203, 212, 307, 458, 483, 503, 631; ibid., *1258-66,* pp. 9, 247.

[2] ibid., *1272-81,* pp. 113, 169, 354, 448; ibid., *1281-92,* pp. 38-39; ibid., *1292-1301,* pp. 83, 155-6, 168, 180, 241, 351, 508, 589; ibid., *1301-7,* pp. 160, 463-4. William Beauchamp, earl of Warwick, received two grants and Henry Lacy, earl of Lincoln, three.

[3] In the case of such a grant made to Roger Mortimer in 1282, in the event of his dying of his present illness, it was stated that the privilege had never before been given (ibid., *1281-92,* pp. 38-9). But the list of previous grants disproves this assertion.

after their decease, some, or all, of the revenues of their estates could be employed by their executors in the payment of debts or performance of their testaments. In most cases the terms of the grant indicate that the executors were thereby to have the enjoyment of revenues which would otherwise have belonged to the Crown through the minority of an heir.[1] A number received such grants in the event of their deaths while on the King's service overseas—Edmund, earl of Lancaster, in 1276,[2] on the occasion of a journey to Navarre, John Hastings, going to Ireland in 1293,[3] Ralph Gorges,[4] Hugh Bardolf,[5] Henry Grey,[6] and Robert Fitz-Walter,[7] all going to Gascony in 1294, Roger la Warre,[8] going there in 1295, Edmund, earl of Cambridge, going on the King's service to Portugal in 1381,[9] Thomas, earl marshal and earl of Nottingham,[10] John, lord Beaumont,[11] and John Holland, earl of Huntingdon,[12] all setting out on the Irish expedition of 1394, and Edward, earl of Rutland, during his service in Aquitaine in 1401.[13] A number obtained such grants because they were going on Crusade—Roger la Zouche in 1220,[14] John of Brittany, earl of

---

[1] Unless otherwise stated in the relevant footnote, the grants comprised the whole of the estates of the deceased. In a few cases the revenues were to be received by persons nominated by the deceased or persons described as his attorneys, but it is not worth while to distinguish between these and executors.

[2] ibid., *1272–81*, p. 156. For three years.

[3] ibid., *1292–1301*, p. 31. Two of his manors for three years.

[4] ibid., *1292–1301*, p. 78. For three years.

[5] ibid., *1292–1301*, p. 87. Land to the value of 300 marks a year during the minority of his heir.

[6] ibid., *1292–1301*, p. 87. One manor for seven years.

[7] ibid., *1292–1301*, p. 88. He had previously been given a licence to demise his lands at farm for two years from Michaelmas 1294. In the event of his death within this term, leaving an heir under age, his executors were to receive the farms for the remainder thereof.

[8] ibid., *1292–1301*, pp. 152–3. Two of his manors during the minority of his heir.

[9] ibid., *1381–5*, p. 8. For one year.

[10] ibid., *1391–6*, p. 348. For two years.

[11] ibid., *1391–6*, p. 361. For two years.

[12] ibid., *1391–6*, p. 363. For two years.

[13] ibid., *1399–1401*, p. 531. For two years.

[14] ibid., *1216–25*, p. 246.

Richmond, in 1269,[1] Edmund, earl of Lancaster, in 1270,[1a] all to the Holy Land, Henry, duke of Lancaster, going to Prussia in 1351,[2] Thomas, lord Clifford,[3] and Thomas, duke of Gloucester,[4] both going to Prussia in 1391. A few are specifically described as being in return for past services to the Crown—to Robert Fitz-Walter in 1303, in consideration of his expenses in the King's service,[5] William Bohun, earl of Northampton, in 1347, in view of the debts he had incurred in the King's service,[6] the latter's son Humphrey, earl of Hereford, in view of his father's services and his own, in 1373,[7] and Edward, duke of York, in 1412, because of his financial preparations for service in France.[8] A number of grants, however, do not mention any special grounds at all—to Simon de Montfort, earl of Leicester, in 1236[9] and 1248,[10] Peter of Savoy on seven separate occasions between 1242 and 1261,[11] John of Brittany, earl of Richmond, in 1275,[12] John Warenne, earl of Surrey, in 1275,[13] Edmund, earl of Lancaster, in 1295,[14] Humphrey

[1] In January 1269 he received a grant whereby his executors were to draw the issues from all his lands until they had received 2000 marks to acquit his debts. In November of the same year they were granted them for two years after his death (*CPR, 1266–72*, pp. 314 and 395).

[1a] ibid., *1266–72*, p. 448. For seven years.

[2] ibid., *1350–4*, p. 191. For one year.

[3] ibid., *1388–92*, p. 363. Lands held in chief only, for one year.

[4] ibid., *1388–92*, pp. 477 and 482. For two years.

[5] ibid., *1301–7*, p. 154. Three manors for four years.

[6] ibid., *1345–8*, p. 539.   [7] ibid., *1370–4*, p. 233. For one year.

[8] ibid., *1408–13*, p. 401.   [9] ibid., *1232–47*, p. 155. For four years.

[10] ibid., *1247–58*, p. 26. For eight years.

[11] In 1242 the King promised that in the event of his death he would not lay hands on his lands or give seisin to his heirs until his debts were paid (ibid., *1232–47*, p. 279), a grant repeated in 1248 and 1249, with the addition of the performance of his testament in the latter year as a condition of the King's entry (ibid., *1247–58*, pp. 34 and 48). Grants in 1246, 1253 and 1256 provided for the repayment of loans received from Richard of Cornwall (ibid., *1232–47*, p. 479 and *1247–58*, pp. 181 and 469). In 1261 his executors were to hold the honour of Richmond for seven years for the execution of his testament (ibid., *1258–66*, p. 161).

[12] ibid., *1272–81*, p. 81. For two years.

[13] ibid., *1272–81*, p. 127. All his lands in Norfolk for ten years. Cf. ibid., *1–7*, p. 264.   [14] ibid., *1292–1301*, p. 156. For one year.

Bohun, earl of Hereford and Essex, in 1319,[1] John of Gaunt, duke of Lancaster, in 1369[2] and 1378,[3] Thomas Beauchamp, earl of Warwick, in 1383,[4] Edmund, duke of York (formerly earl of Cambridge), in 1386,[5] Thomas, duke of Gloucester, in 1393,[6] and Edward, duke of Aumale, in 1399.[7]

The number of individuals who at some time received a grant of this type between 1216 and 1485 was twenty-six, some being so rewarded on more than one occasion. The lowness of this figure, in view of the fact that it covers a period of over two hundred and fifty years, is an indication of the extent to which the Crown was loath to grant such concessions. Those who received grants of this kind without special services being specified as the reason were either members of the royal family or leading magnates who belonged to the court circle. Otherwise, it appears to have been exceptionally difficult to obtain a privilege of this type unless the King was in real need of the services of his subject. It is especially noteworthy that six of the grants belong to the years 1293–96 and of these five specify the services which the recipient was about to perform in Gascony, a fact which emphasizes the need which Edward I felt to overcome his subjects' hostility to serving there. Most of the grants, indeed, when the recipient was not connected by a close blood relationship with the monarch mention circumstances which were considered especially deserving—in a few cases a crusade, under Edward I service overseas, and in the late fourteenth century the King's wars in France. In most cases we are told that the purpose of the grant was to enable the recipient's executors, or other representatives, to pay his debts and otherwise perform his testamentary directions. It is interesting to note that, in the case of the grant made in 1295 to Roger la Warre, the raising of marriage portions for his daughters is given

[1] ibid., *1317–21*, p. 391. Half his lands until his heir came of age.

[2] ibid., *1367–70*, pp. 212–13. For one year.

[3] ibid., *1377–81*, p. 262. As in the preceding grant, the letters patent thereof being surrendered.

[4] ibid., *1381–5*, p. 270. For one year.

[5] ibid., *1385–9*, p. 134. For one year.

[6] ibid., *1391–6*, p. 222. For three years.

[7] ibid., *1396–9*, p. 517. Except the lordship of Gloucester. For one year.

D

as the nature of his need,[1] while that made to Humphrey Bohun, earl of Hereford and Essex, in 1319 was accompanied by another of the marriage of his son and heir in aid of the portions of his other children.[2]

For the historian who studies the financial situation and legal institutions of English landownership in this period the importance of these grants lies in their exceptional nature. Even if we add to their number those in which the Crown granted the wardship of the inheritance and the marriage of the heir to the father's executors, it remains true that very few of the country's landowners benefited from royal bounty of this type; and their number was virtually confined to the upper ranks of the nobility. At the beginning of the fourteenth century an English landowner who lay on his death-bed would almost certainly know that, when his end came, if his heir was under age, the resources of his inheritance would not be available for the payment of debts and the performance of testamentary bequests. If the heir was over age, although in theory it might be possible for him to assist the executors from the revenues of the inheritance, in practice it was unlikely that such help would be forthcoming. Moreover, unless he had been able to grant them portions of land during his lifetime, the only revenues which could be employed to provide for younger sons or purchase marriages for daughters would be those in the hands of the executors from the disposal of chattels from which they had also to pay debts.

For many landowners the legal rules which created this situation must have been the source of much bitterness. It is likely that their resentment was aggravated by the passing of the responsibility for the payments of debts to the executors, since this must have curtailed the sums available to them for other purposes and at the same time have made potential creditors additionally cautious about the chances of recovering their money.

Unfortunately, we do not possess the evidence to decide how far the devices condemned in clause 6 of the Statute of Marlborough were employed to avoid difficulties of these kinds. The practice of enfeoffing his heir under age undoubtedly would have

[1] *CPR, 1292–1301*, pp. 152–3.   [2] ibid., *1317–21*, p. 319.

provided the deceased's family with revenues which could have been used for the payment of debts and testamentary bequests, although complications might have arisen over ensuring that they were so used. A fraudulent lease could certainly have been manipulated for these purposes, since the lessees could have been the deceased's creditors or his executors. But in 1267 both these devices were henceforward denied to landowners. Their problems remained: lands held by feudal tenure could not be bequeathed by will, while their revenues could not be used by a deceased tenant's executors. In this situation landowners would seek for means whereby these rules of feudal tenure could be evaded. If successful, they were bound to deprive their lords of the incidents of feudal tenure.

CHAPTER TWO

The Struggle over Freedom of Alienation, 1215–1327

WHEN land held under feudal tenure was conveyed by the tenant to another, the transfer was effected in one of two ways. The grantee might take over the precise feudal position hithe to occupied by the grantor and thus replace him in the tenure of the fee, holding it from the lord as the grantor had done. The alternative method was subinfeudation: the grantor conveyed the land to the grantee to be held of himself by services defined in the charter of enfeoffment. The grantee thus became the grantor's tenant for the land and the grantor continued to hold it of his original lord, although not himself in actual occupation of the land. Of these two possible methods, subinfeudation was bound to be much the more popular. It was in the interests of any grantor to subinfeudate, since, while he was able to make his tenant responsible for the services he himself owed to his lord, he could also, when they occurred, enjoy the incidents of tenure he had so created. The efforts made by mesne lords in thirteenth-century England to restrict their tenants' freedom of alienation would not have been necessary if subinfeudation had not been the method of alienation in general use.

With the growing economic development of England in the twelfth and thirteenth centuries, the buying and selling of land held under feudal tenure was bound to increase. Since the majority of such transactions employed subinfeudation, on each occasion when a portion of land was so alienated one more sub-tenant was added to the line of tenants between it and the lord who in turn held it of the King. In such a situation the interests of feudal lords were damaged in two respects. In the first place, the services which were due from the tenant might be weakened. It is true that the tenant continued to be responsible in law for the services due from the land he held: it is equally true that it was in his interests, if and when he subinfeudated, to make careful provision in the charter of enfeoffment for the performance of the services due to the lord from that portion of his fee that was being alienated. But in practice the interests of lords could, and did, suffer. The tenant's own capacity to perform the services due to his lord was damaged, in that less land was now occupied directly by him. He might also meet difficulties in obtaining from his own tenant the services due from the land he had alienated. In the second place, the lord's profits from the incidents of feudal tenure were diminished. He retained his right to a relief and to the marriage of any infant heir. But, in the event of his tenant's death leaving an heir under age, he had the wardship of an inheritance which was reduced in size and value because of the alienation that had taken place.[1] In fact, the lord's losses through his tenant's alienation lay mainly within the sphere of wardship of the land during a minority. When the services were not performed, he was still in a position to seek the remedy of distraint and could thereby take into his hands the whole of the fee, including the land that had been alienated. No doubt the development of the action of replevin and the legislation of the thirteenth century relating thereto made this an increasingly less satisfactory remedy.[2] Nevertheless, the possible threat of its employment by lords must have minimized, if not entirely prevented, the loss of services through alienation. But a lord could only exercise his rights of wardship over the whole of the original fee after alienation had occurred if a minority of the alienee's heir coincided with that of the tenant, a situation which must have been somewhat infrequent. Undoubtedly, the consequences of this situation must have been felt more keenly by lords as the thirteenth century progressed and it became increasingly apparent that wardship of the land was the most valuable of the incidents of feudal lordship.[3]

[1] The Crown appears to have been aware of its own losses through the alienations of its tenants-in-chief as early as 1212, since in that year John ordered the sheriffs to make enquiries concerning all such alienations as had occurred (*Book of Fees*, I. 52).

[2] Plucknett, *Ed 1*, pp. 55–63.   [3] See above, pp. 15–16.

The extent to which a lord suffered through his tenant's alienation depended upon the identity of his tenant's grantee. If the land
had been alienated to the Church, the injuries to his interests were
much more serious than if the alienee had been a layman. Neither
he nor his heirs could ever benefit in the future from the incidents
of feudal tenure, since the Church was an undying corporation,
which never came of age, had an infant heir or committed felony.
Moreover, the fact that the grant had been made to the Church
made it more likely that loss of services would occur. In the
thirteenth century most grants to the Church would be made in
frankalmoign—that is, to be held in free alms, by services which
were intended to be purely spiritual in character. When making
a grant of this sort, the alienor was under an obligation to make
arrangements for the performance of the services which were due
from the land.[1] But his own capacity to perform them was
weakened since less land remained in his occupation, while, if the
Church undertook to perform them, a situation was created in
which it would be more difficult in practice for the lord to enforce
his rights.

During the first half of the thirteenth century the courts of law
gave no satisfactory redress to lords whose interests were injured
by the alienations of their tenants. Their grievances were known
to the government at the beginning of the minority of Henry III
and resulted in an attempt at reform. Clause 39 of the reissue of
Magna Carta which appeared in 1217 laid down that a tenant
should not alienate so large a portion of his fee that the remainder
was not sufficient to maintain the services due to the lord.[2] The
observance of this rule would have benefited the King as well as
other lords. But the fact that it made its appearance when the
King was a minor and the government under the dominance of
the magnates of the realm suggests that it was conceived primarily
in the interests of the King's leading subjects. In practice, however, it must have been difficult to use this piece of legislation to
impose effective restraints upon alienation. To have attempted to
do so would have meant litigation which would have revolved

[1] Pollock & Maitland, I. 245.
[2] *Select Charters*, p. 343. It was confirmed in the reissue of 1225 (ibid., p. 350).

around the extent to which the land that remained in the tenant's hands was enough for the performance of services, an issue which it would have been hard to settle in the lord's favour unless the injuries to his interests were both clearly apparent and substantial. Moreover, if a tenant alienated in a way that appeared to conform with this rule, there was no redress for the lord's loss of incidents. No doubt these considerations explain why this reform does not appear to have been interpreted by contemporaries as applying to all kinds of alienations, despite the apparent meaning of its language. The precise interpretation that was followed is a matter of some doubt. In one passage, which contains a clear reference to this reform, Bracton states that a person of religion could not acquire land of any fee unless the residue in the hands of the feoffor was sufficient for the performance of the services. Shortly after this, he makes remarks indicating that acquisitions of such land in frankalmoign were forbidden.[1] It does, therefore, seem certain that clause 39 of the *Magna Carta* reissue of 1217 was interpreted as applying, at most, to alienations to the Church. But we cannot be certain whether the reform of 1217 applied to all of these or only to those made in frankalmoign. It is possible that in writing the latter of these passages Bracton was making two assumptions: first, that it would only be possible to prove a breach of the rule of 1217 in the case of frankalmoign: and, second, that all alienations to the Church were made in frankalmoign. Nevertheless, the discrepancy between his two statements remains, though, of course, this might be explained on the ground of careless writing or faulty editing. At any rate, the view that the reform of 1217 definitely applied to alienations in frankalmoign is confirmed in a statement to this effect in a royal letter patent of 1238.[2] It is, indeed, unlikely that it was ever extended in the courts

---

[1] Bracton, III. 35 and 37. For further discussion of these passages, see below, p. 61.

[2] *CPR, 1232–47*, p. 234: 'it is manifestly contrary to the liberty which the king granted in common to the magnates in the realm of England that any one should grant his whole tenement in almoin'. The prior of Bricett had been so granted the whole of a tenement which was held of Robert de Tattershall who had disseised him. The prior then brought an assize of novel disseisin which

to any other kind of alienation, since it was only in the case of frankalmoign that it be possible to prove effectively that the lord's services would suffer.

The attitude of contemporary lawyers to the lord's rights and interests when alienation occurred is best examined in the light of the discussion of this problem which we find in Bracton.[1] According to him the lord could not claim in law that his rights had been damaged through the alienation of his tenant:

... as regards the power of the donee to make a gift over and to transfer to another the property granted to himself, some might say that he cannot do so, because by this means the lord loses his service; this, however, is not true—with all respect to the chief lords, be it said. And speaking generally, the truth is that the donee may grant the property and the land granted to him to whomsoever he pleases, unless there were some special provision against alienation at the time of the feoffment. For when anyone makes a gift of a tenement he gives away an ascertained tenement upon condition of receiving in exchange fixed customs and fixed services ... And he cannot rightfully claim anything more from the gift; let him therefore take what is his and go his way. For the gift is not made for the purpose of the donor's obtaining wardship and marriage of the heir, but for homage and service; nevertheless when the donor has the right to homage, and that kind of extrinsic service is due which belongs to the chief lord, then relief and the wardship of the land, and the marriage of the heir, shall become due when the occasion arises; and also incidents of tenure as for instance, the ex-

---

was, in these letters patent of 10 February 1238, respited until the coming of the justices at the first assize in those parts, or until the King's first coming there. The case which followed was noted by Bracton: the details given show both that the lord had been deprived of his services and that the rule of 1217 was regarded as being applicable. The prior quitclaimed all his rights in the tenement to Robert de Tattershall in return for the payment of 100s. (*Bracton's Note Book*, III. 263-4 (pl. 1248); see also his reference in Bracton, III. 37). In the latter he stated that the assize failed, but the account in his *Note Book* merely tells how the parties agreed to settle.

[1] Bracton, II. 140-3. The translation which follows is based on that of Digby, pp. 160-1, with amended punctuation to take Woodbine's text into account. The second paragraph of this passage is an *addicio* to the original text, but Woodbine states that it is Bracton's own (ibid., I. 381).

trinsic service due to our lord the king. The chief lord, however, shall never have all these incidents at once, but one of them only when the occasion happens, either relief or wardship and the marriage of the heir. And it may well happen that one of these incidents may constantly happen and another never at all. Hence if the lord have only a relief, let him be content therewith, although wardship and marriage of the heir are more valuable; and because when any one is bound to render one of two duties disjunctively, he discharges himself by paying or rendering one of them. Hence when any chief lord hinders his tenant from making a gift, he works him an injury and an open disseisin, in not suffering him to make use of his own property and his own seisin. The tenant however by such a gift works no wrong to his lord, although he does him harm; since the lord may have his relief from his own feof-fee and his heirs,[1] and although the tenant may do the lord harm, yet the act will not be wrongful for the reason aforesaid. . . .

If any tenant makes a gift, it may be questioned to whom he works a wrong; not to the lord, for the lord has all that belongs to him; and he had the tenement bound and burdened whatever may be the words of gift, and into whosesoever hands it may come. Nor does the feoffee injure the lord's rights, because it matters nothing to the chief lord who holds his fee, since the actual tenant is his tenant, although there be an intermediate lord. Further, if the lord allege that the tenant has wrong-fully entered upon his fee, I say it is not so, because the fee is not the property of the lord but the tenant, and the lord has nothing in the fee except the services due to him, and thus the fee is the property of the tenant, but subject to services to the lord; and if the lord prohibits the tenant from doing what he pleases with the tenement which he holds in his demesne, this will be an entrance by the lord upon the tenement of his tenant, and will work a disseisin, unless any other consequence follows from any condition or covenant contained in the gift itself, for any one can annex terms and conditions to his gift[2] and thus create a rule of law which must always be observed.

[1] Digby translates this clause: '. . . the lord may have his relief from the feoffee of the tenant'. But this construction of the original Latin *ipse dominus habere possit relevium de suo feoffato et ejus heredibus*, does not make sense, since it implies that Bracton was talking of alienation by substitution, thus making the whole of this discussion of the lord's losses through alienation quite pointless.

[2] By the middle years of the fifteenth century any condition restraining alienation in the deed of conveyance was regarded as null and void (Littleton, s. 360, quoted and discussed in Holdsworth, III. 85).

In this passage Bracton is clearly seeking to demolish arguments which had been advanced to the effect that the interests of a lord in law were damaged through alienations on the part of his tenants. Although at certain points his style is somewhat repetitive, it is hard to detect in his arguments and tone any traces of a lack of confidence in the position he occupies. Indeed, it seems likely that the tendency to repetition may be attributed to an anxiety to emphasize the salient features of the law relating to this problem.[1] A careful examination of this passage reveals that Bracton is advancing three arguments.

(1) Land was held of a lord in return for the performance of specified services.

(2) There was a basic difference in character between these services and the incidents of tenure. Whereas a tenant remained constantly under the obligation to perform the services to his lord, the latter obtained the incidents on certain occasions only. When these occurred, he did not enjoy all the incidents together at one and the same time but only received that incident which was appropriate to the status of the tenant's heir. He would secure either a relief or the wardship and marriage of the heir: it was impossible to obtain both.

(3) The land was the tenant's property to dispose of as he wished: the lord's rights in the fee did not extend beyond its services.

Bracton's discussion deserves careful attention because it reveals both the nature of the legal situation and the gulf which existed between it and the tenurial reality. His arguments show that in the middle years of the thirteenth century when he wrote there was no restriction on the tenant's right to alienate. At first sight it might be argued that there were two weaknesses in the doctrines he is expounding. First, his view that the lord will always have his services was unsatisfactory, if not disingenuous, in that it

---

[1] Cf. Pollock & Maitland, I. 332: 'The very earnestness of his argument shows that he has to combat a strong feeling'. There is nothing in Bracton's argument to suggest that his views would be disputed by his fellow lawyers. But it is likely that he felt it necessary to state the legal position emphatically in order to meet the complaints of mesne lords.

avoided the issue that services might be lost through alienation by tenants. Second, it would seem that legal doctrines, as they had evolved over the last century and a half, had come to give the performance of services an importance which did not exist in the minds of the lords who originally created the fees, since they must have created tenures partly, if not largely, in expectation of the profits of relief, wardship and marriage, and escheat. There is certainly no trace in Bracton's exposition of the fact that these incidents of tenure existed because, when fees were first created, the tenant had enjoyed no more than a life-interest.[1] But there can be no doubt that Bracton's arguments would have satisfied both himself and other contemporary lawyers. The first criticism he would have answered by pointing to the remedy of distraint and the second by citing the terms of any deed of enfeoffment. It is, perhaps, worth noting that, although Bracton in this passage was employing a concept which is virtually the same as that expressed in the modern term 'incidents', an examination of his Latin shows that he did not possess a generic noun which had this meaning but instead had to use a demonstrative pronoun in the neuter plural. The fact that no other means of expression was available to him is a further indication of the extent to which the legal doctrines of his day regarded the performance of services as the core of the legal relationship between a lord and his tenant.

Bracton was clearly aware of the nature of the grievances felt by mesne lords. Indeed, his statement that wardship and marriage were more valuable than the relief shows that he was thoroughly conscious of the economic realities of their position. He would not have denied that the rules of law bore no relation to, and gave no remedy in, an economic situation in which the financial interests of lords were damaged through their tenants' freedom to alienate. But his concern was to expound the law, not to reform it.

When we discuss the demands for reform which emerged in the course of the thirteenth century, we must remember that this same period witnessed a transformation in the economic structure of the incidents of feudal tenure. With the decline of the feudal

[1] S. E. Thorne, 'English Feudalism and Estates in Land', *CLJ* (1959), pp. 193–209.

host as a means of raising the kingdom's armed forces, the feudal tenant's forensic service—that is, the personal service owed to the King through his lord—ceased to be an essential need for the lord. The appearance of new forms of taxation, direct and indirect, meant that the Crown no longer found it necessary to issue a formal summons of the feudal host as a means of raising money through scutage. Indeed, this source of revenue had collapsed by the beginning of the fourteenth century.[1] At the same time reliefs and aids became fixed in monetary value.[2] As a result of these developments, wardship and marriage were now the most valuable of the incidents of tenure. And it is in the desire of lords to protect their revenues from these sources that we see the dominating motive behind those legal reforms of the thirteenth century which affected the tenant's right to alienate his land. The growing consciousness of the importance of wardship and marriage and the simultaneous decline in the comparative emphasis placed upon the lord's services may be illustrated from the language employed in the preambles of the relevant statutes. Clause 39 of the *Magna Carta* reissue of 1217 was intended to protect the lord's services. In 1279 the Statute of Mortmain complained that 'the services which are due of such fees and which at the beginning were provided for the defence of the realm, are wrongfully withdrawn, and the chief lords lose their escheats of the same'.[3] But in 1290 the Statute of *Quia Emptores* did not mention services but claimed that 'the same chief lords have many times lost their escheats, marriages and wardships of lands and tenements belonging to their fees which matter seems very hard and irksome for these lords and other great men'.[4]

The extent to which lords suffered in the ways described in these preambles depended upon their status and the size and tenurial structure of their estates. Any reform which dealt with alienations by tenants on a national scale would benefit the interests of both the Crown and other lords. But, unlike the latter,

[1] See H. M. Chew, 'Scutage in the Fourteenth Century', *EHR*, XXXVIII (1923), 19–41.

[2] See above, pp. 13–15.   [3] *Select Charters*, p. 451; Digby, p. 220.

[4] *Select Charters*, p. 473; Digby, p. 237.

the King was always lord and never tenant. In studying the reforms of the thirteenth century which affected the tenant's right to alienate it is essential to bear these points in mind. The attitude of the Crown towards its subjects' demands for reform was conditioned by the interaction of two influences. One was the political situation: the other was the nature of its own interests as feudal lord. If political circumstances were favourable, the Crown might well act in terms of its own needs only and ignore those of its subjects. When we study the attitude of mesne lords, we must ask how far they were united in their hostility towards their tenants' alienations. A great magnate would, of course, lose heavily. But, the lower a man's position in the feudal hierarchy, the less likely was he to feel strongly about the practice of subinfeudation. Indeed, those with few tenants would derive more benefit from their own freedom to alienate, which they exercised at the expense of those above them in the feudal hierarchy, than from the acquisition of any powers to restrain their own tenants from alienating.

(i) The Problem of the Church

Feudal lords received some protection against their tenants' alienations into the hands of the Church from the beginning of the reign of Henry III. The reissue of *Magna Carta* which appeared in 1217 contained two clauses which were framed in their interests. Clause 39 laid down that no man was to alienate so much of his land that the remainder was insufficient for the performance of his services.[1] Although the language of this clause appears to comprise all alienations, as we have seen,[2] proof of its effectiveness exists only in the case of those in frankalmoign. Since it was in alienations of this type that the lord's services were most likely to be damaged, it is possible that the framers of this clause in 1217 had alienations in frankalmoign in mind, a fact which may help to explain why the clause so soon came to be regarded as applying to them alone. At any rate, from then onwards there was, in

---

[1] *Select Charters*, p. 343.   [2] See above, pp. 43-4.

theory at least, some sort of control over the most damaging of the alienations that could be made to the Church.

Clause 43 of the same reissue stated that:

> It shall not be lawful for any one henceforward to give his land to any religious house in such a way that he resume it again to hold it of the house; nor shall it be lawful for any religious house to accept any one's land and to return it to him from whom they received it. If any one for the future shall give his land in this way to any religious house and be convicted thereof, the gift shall be quashed and the land forfeited to the lord of the fee.[1]

There were two distinct phases in this type of mortmain: the tenant conveyed his holding to the religious house, to be held of the lord; and the religious house then granted it to the tenant to be held of itself. By this means the tenant, while remaining in occupation of his land, gave the religious house feudal rights which promised a valuable casual income. It was clearly to their mutual advantage to make such a bargain. The lord, however, though he kept his services, lost all his future profits from the incidents of tenure. It is apparent that clause 43 dealt only with one of the ways in which the Church acquired land: it did not mention any of the other means employed by religious houses. Nor did it prevent alienations made to the mendicant orders or the episcopacy.

Thus the gains secured by mesne lords through the 1217 reissue of *Magna Carta* were far from substantial. If clause 43 was enforced, they had managed to stop one of the devices by which one section of the Church entered their fees and deprived them of their incidents. In the case of alienations in frankalmoign they were now in a position to insist that precautions be taken to ensure that their services remained intact. But this reform did nothing to protect their incidents. Moreover, it is difficult to avoid the suspicion that this reform must have been difficult to enforce in the courts unless a tenant had been careless in dealing with the performance of services when the grant in frankalmoign was made.

---

[1] *Select Charters*, p. 343.

For these reasons lords continued to nurse strong grievances about the encroachments of ecclesiastics upon their feudal rights. In 1258 the Petition of the Barons, c. 10 demanded that 'men of religion should not enter into the fee of earls and barons and others against their will (*sine voluntate eorum*), whereby they lose for ever wardships, marriages, reliefs and escheats'.[1] This complaint resulted in chapter 14 of the Provisions of Westminster of 1259 which stated that 'it is not lawful for men of religion to enter the fee of any one without the licence of the chief lord of whom it is immediately held'.[2] This reform clearly dealt satisfactorily with the lords' loss of incidents through acquisitions by the Church: henceforth they had the right to license such grants and the language employed in this law implies that they had the right to refuse their permission if their interests were injured. But it is by no means certain that this reform became a permanent part of the legal system. Twenty years later the preamble of the Statute of Mortmain rehearsed its terms after the words 'Where of late it was provided that . . .'[3] And the view that this law remained in existence is supported by the terms of a writ enrolled on the Close Roll in 1278, in which the sheriff of Leicestershire was ordered to summon the abbot of Croxton before the justices at Westminster to show cause why he entered upon a mesne lord's fee without licence.[4] Not only does the writ rehearse the terms of the reform of 1259 as if it were accepted law but it also states that it had formed part of the Statute of Marlborough. But, although this statute, promulgated in 1267 at the end of the period of baronial rebellion, had embodied most of the Provisions of Westminster, the extant text contains no mention of this particular reform. We cannot, of course, exclude the possibility that the text available to us is defective in this respect. On the other hand, it is conceivable that the influence of the Church over Henry III's government at this time prevented the inclusion in the statute of a reform which struck at its interests.[5] It is equally plausible to suggest that the Crown in 1278 found it convenient to claim that

---

[1] ibid., p. 375.   [2] ibid., p. 393.
[3] For the Latin text, see ibid., pp. 451–2; for a translation, Digby, pp. 220–1.
[4] *CCR*, 1272–9, pp. 500–1.   [5] Plucknett, *Common Law*, p. 541.

the reform of 1259 was part of the law of the land, since this was a time of conflict with the Church in England[1] in which any threat to its power to acquire land in the future might prove a useful political weapon.

At any rate, the reform of 1259 was resurrected in 1279 by Edward I in the Statute *de Viris Religiosis*, otherwise known as the Statute of Mortmain.[2] This took the form of a writ addressed by the King to the justices of the Common Pleas, requiring them to have its contents read before them and strictly observed. After rehearsing the terms of the reform of 1259 as part of the legal system and explaining the damage to lords' services and incidents which was caused when ecclesiastics entered upon their fees, it continued:

We therefore, intending to provide convenient remedy to the profit of our realm, by the advice of our prelates, earls, barons, and our other subjects who are of our council, have provided, laid down and ordained, that no religious person or other, whoever he may be, may buy or sell any lands or tenements, or under the colour of gift or lease, or by reason of any other title, whatever it may be, may receive lands or tenements, or by any other craft or device may presume to appropriate to himself under pain of forfeiture of the same, whereby such lands or tenements may in any way come into mortmain (*ad manum mortuam*).

It then gave explicit directions regarding the procedure to be followed if this prohibition was broken:

it shall be lawful for us and the other cihef lords of the fee immediate to enter into the land so alienated within a year from the time of the alienation and to hold it in fee as in inheritance. And if the chief lord immediate be negligent and does not enter into such fee within the year, then it shall be lawful to the next chief lord immediate of the same fee to enter into the same land within half a year next following, and to hold it as before is said; and so every lord immediate may enter into such land if the next lord be negligent in entering into the same fee.

---

[1] See e.g., F. M. Powicke, *The Thirteenth Century, 1216–1307* (Oxford, 1953), p. 476; D. L. Douie, *Archbishop Pecham* (Oxford, 1952), p. 119.

[2] It was promulgated on 15 November in the course of a parliament. For valuable comments on its contents and implications, see Plucknett, *Ed. I*, pp. 96–100.

And if all the chief lords of such fees . . . be negligent or slack in this matter for the space of one whole year, we, immediately after a period of a year from the time that such purchases, gifts or appropriations happened to be made, shall take such lands or tenements into our hand and shall enfeoff others therein by certain services to be done to us for the defence of our realm, saving to the chief lords of the same fees their wardships and escheats, and other things belonging to them, and the due and accustomed services for the same.

The statute thus forbade all acquisitions of land by the Church in the future. In the last resort the Crown itself would intervene to ensure the forfeiture of any land illegally alienated. This piece of legislation clearly went far beyond the Provisions of Westminster of 1259, which permitted acquisitions by the Church if licensed by the lord of the fee. But what occurred in 1279 was an absolute prohibition of all future gains by the Church.

There was, however, a considerable gulf between the language of the Statute of Mortmain, on the one hand, and, on the other, the policies that were both feasible and in the long run followed by the Crown. It is impossible to conceive that any government in the late thirteenth century could for any length of time have prevented the Church from acquiring land or its subjects from so conveying it. However much lords might complain, the Church had found it easy to expand its territorial resources: the reasons were to be found partly in the wealth which was available to it for making purchases but also in the deep desire of laymen of all classes to make ready for the after-life and arrange for prayers and masses for the souls of themselves and their ancestors. In such circumstances, it is difficult to believe that, when the statute of 1279 was promulgated, Edward I and his advisers seriously intended to adhere rigidly to its provisions. Relations between Crown and Church were strained at this time—indeed, the archbishop of Canterbury was forced to agree to royal demands at the very parliament at which the Statute of Mortmain was promulgated.[1] It is likely, therefore, that the threat of a future policy whereby the Church would be forbidden to acquire land was thought to be a useful weapon against the recalcitrant clergy.

[1] Powicke, op. cit., p. 476.

In fact, Edward I's government ceased to adhere to the strict terms of the statute within a few months of its promulgation and, instead, launched a policy whereby it permitted its subjects to make grants of land to the Church. It began to issue licences whereby such alienations were allowed, the first on 26 May 1280, 'notwithstanding the recent statute in mortmain'.[1] Table I reveals the types and totals of such licences issued between that date and the end of 1306.[2] Each of these licences was technically one of exemption from the statute of 1279. As far as we can tell,[3] the Crown did not grant a licence until an inquisition *ad quod damnum* had been held in the appropriate shire. Having by this means discovered the value of the lands to be alienated and the extent of any resulting losses of services and other rights, the officials of the Chancery were able to assess the amount of the fine paid for the issue of the licence.

Table I demonstrates the massive dimensions attained by exemptions from the Statute of Mortmain between its promulgation and the end of Edward I's reign. It would be wrong to assume that an enormous amount of land passed into the hands of the Church by these means. Many of the licences dealt with remarkably small portions of land, sometimes less than an acre. But every licence, however slight the Church's gains thereby, contradicted the legal principle established in 1279. The Crown was acting by virtue of its prerogative right to exempt individual subjects from the terms of any statute it promulgated. By so doing in the case of the Statute of Mortmain it was striking at the interests of mesne lords. It claimed and exercised the right to grant exemptions, even if the land concerned was not held directly of itself. Moreover, especially after 1300, it was ready to pardon unlicensed alienations in mortmain of lands held of mesne lords. Its actions thus overrode the Statute of Mortmain's careful statement of the rights of lords to the forfeiture of any lands alienated to the Church. In effect, therefore, the Crown was intervening between mesne lords and their tenants. And its licences of exemp-

---

[1] *CPR, 1272-81*, p. 372.
[2] Based on ibid., *1272-81, 1281-92, 1292-1301*, and *1301-7*, passim.
[3] For further details, see *LIQD*, pp. iii-iv.

tion cut right across the nexus of rights which were part and parcel of feudal tenure.

These activities of Edward I did not pass without protest on the part of mesne lords. In the parliament of January 1292 the King gave his consent to two petitions which imposed some limitations

TABLE I. *Alienations in Mortmain, 1280–1306*

When pardons for alienations already made were issued, they are included in the column total and also entered in brackets.

Year	Lands held of King in chief	Lands held of alienee's own fee	Lands of other tenures	Total
1280	—	—	12 (1)	12 (1)
1281	1	4	9	14
1282	—	4	6	10
1283	1	1	13	15
1284	—	4	20	24
1285	1	10	38	49
1286	2	2	35	39
1287	—	—	—	—
1288	—	—	—	—
1289	—	3	2	5
1290	1	—	54	55
1291	1	3	43	47
1292	1	9	60	70
1293	2	—	37	39
1294	2 (1)	—	14 (1)	16
1295	2	—	12	14
1296	1	—	6	7
1297	1 (1)	1	13	15
1298	4	—	5	9
1299	—	2	41	43
1300	4	1	38 (2)	43 (2)
1301	1	1	48 (4)	50 (4)
1302	2	—	26 (2)	28 (2)
1303	5	—	61 (7)	66 (7)
1304	3	—	57 (5)	60 (5)
1305	9	—	81 (13)	90 (13)
1306	4	2	67 (10)	73 (10)

upon his powers. In one he made two promises. First, writs of *ad quod damnum* would henceforth only be issued in response to a petition in full parliament. Second, religious houses would only be permitted to acquire land if they did not possess enough to live on.[1] It is obvious that the magnates wanted to keep a watchful eye on grants in mortmain and to ensure that these met a real need for endowments, not merely the greed of clergy who already had enough for their needs. The other petition[2] laid down the procedure to be followed by the Chancery before a licence was granted. Once the inquisition *ad quod damnum* had been returned, the clergy concerned had to produce evidence of the assent of the lord of the fee. Nor could further action be taken in the matter if the grantor did not retain lands of the fee in his own lands.

Both these petitions resulted from mesne lords' discontent over the Crown's encroachment on their rights. It is, however, unlikely that the January parliament of 1292 was the first occasion on which they gave vent to their grievances, since the Crown had been pursuing the policies complained of for over twelve years. In default of further information from the parliament rolls, some insight into the situation can be gleaned from the figures provided in Table I. After no licences had been issued in 1287 and 1288, and a mere five in 1289, the totals for 1290 and 1291 were 55 and 47, the highest so far achieved. It is possible that the virtual moratorium of three years was the result of pressure from mesne lords. But, in any event, the upsurge of licences in 1290 and 1291 must have inflamed their feelings. If so, it is likely that they gave vent to their resentment in one or more of the parliaments of these years. And, when the Crown eventually made concessions in January 1292, it was yielding to parliamentary pressures which had existed for months, if not years. At first sight, it is odd that the royal concessions did not immediately lead to a decline in the number of licences issued—the total in 1292 was the highest so far. But, if we assume that the Crown's policies had been under attack for some time, this is easily explained. It is likely that Edward I, in an endeavour to avoid substantial concessions, deliberately delayed the settlement of mortmain petitions received

[1] *Rot. Parl.*, I. 78 (no. 4).   [2] ibid., I. 83 (no. 13).

in 1290–1 and, perhaps, in preceding years. When agreement with mesne lords was reached in January 1292, the way was open to deal with many of these in the course of 1292.

If we examine the figures contained in Table I after 1292, we see that between then and 1299 far fewer mortmain licences were issued by the Crown. Yet, from 1299 onwards, the growth in their numbers was resumed, achieving a remarkably high level in 1305. It would be wrong to deduce from these facts the conclusion that the Crown performed its undertakings of 1292 for a few years only and then reverted to its previous policies. After 1292 the parliament rolls contain no mention of any further complaints by mesne lords. And it is difficult to believe that they would have remained silent over the continued encroachment on their rights, especially if alienations in mortmain on their fees occurred without their consent.[1] It is more likely that the comparative paucity of licences between 1293 and 1299 was due to caution in the use of the new procedures by all those involved— the Chancery officials, the clergy and would-be grantors. By 1299 their hesitations had disappeared.

All the available evidence thus indicates that the Crown's concessions of 1292 provided a final settlement of the problems of mortmain for mesne lords.[2] The requirement that their prior consent be obtained before the issue of a licence by the Crown gave them a measure of control over the growth of mortmain on their fees. A mesne lord could now insist that a tenant retain part of his fee. From the Church's standpoint there resulted a considerable amelioration of the complete prohibition of mortmain which had been issued in 1279. In short, the final settlement hardly differed from the reform promulgated in the Provisions of Westminster of 1259.

This achievement was the result of a campaign which mesne

---

[1] For references to the consent of the lord of the fee, see, e.g., *CPR, 1301–7*, pp. 241–2.

[2] For annual totals of mortmain licences during the reign of Edward III, see K. L. Woodlegh, *Studies in Church Life under Edward III* (Cambridge, 1934), p. 165. These suggest that mortmain had not grown beyond the dimensions achieved in the closing years of Edward I.

lords had been fighting for over seventy years. Their motives are clear enough. But those which led the Crown to assist them still await elucidation. In fact, the Crown had possessed adequate protection for its own interests for half a century before the Statute of Mortmain of 1279. On 1 February 1228 Henry III had issued writs to all the sheriffs of England the terms of which amounted to a legislative enactment.[1] In the first place, each sheriff was ordered to proclaim throughout his bailiwick that 'no one who holds of us in chief . . . in our demesnes, as he values his body and his tenement, may grant or sell or in any other way alienate anything of his tenement to any religious house or any ecclesiastical persons without our licence'. In the second place, the sheriff was to forbid 'any one holding of us in chief, whether a knight or a freeman, or any other, from transferring himself from the land which he holds of us to the land of any religious house or ecclesiastical persons in order to remain thereon, by which means we might suffer losses in services, tallages or any other things pertaining to us'. In the third place, he was to enquire by oath from the lawful men of his shire which tenants-in-chief had alienated land to men of the church and to make inquisition concerning the dates of the alienations and their value. A study of the details of these directions shows that the Crown did not distinguish with any special care between alienations by feudal tenants-in-chief and those made by the inhabitants of its demesnes, a fact which may be attributed to the failure of royal lawyers and administrators at this time to have developed the concept of the royal demesne as a separate legal and administrative entity.[2] The Crown wished not merely to prevent its tenants-in-chief from conveying their holdings into mortmain but also to stop ecclesiastical landowners from enticing royal tenants on to their own estates. Behind these orders to the sheriffs we see not only the desire to end the erosion of

[1] *CCR, 1227–31*, p. 88. None was sent to the sheriff of Cornwall.

[2] When in 1212 John ordered his sheriffs to enquire into all alienations that had been made by tenants-in-chief, some of them appear to have thought that they were supposed to enquire into alienations of the royal demesne. See the discussion in R. S. Hoyt, *The Royal Demesne in English Constitutional History, 1066–1272* (Ithaca, New York: 1950), pp. 151–3.

feudal services and incidents but also the urge to safeguard the revenues from the lands in the Crown's own occupation, especially the profits from tallages which would be depleted if the number of its tenants declined.

Nevertheless, the main interest of this royal ordinance of 1228 lies in its provisions regarding alienations made by tenants-in-chief to the Church. Hitherto this document has gone unnoticed by historians. But there can be no doubt that, from 1228 onwards, by virtue of the directions issued in it, the Crown forbade any grants of land held in chief to the Church which were made without its licence. Its terms imply, though do not clearly state, that lands so alienated would be forfeited.

A search of the chancery rolls of the reigns of Henry III and Edward I yields a substantial amount of evidence to indicate that this ordinance was enforced. No explicit reference to its existence has been traced; but there were a number of occasions on which the Crown intervened when the Church acquired lands held in chief. On 5 August 1234 a writ was sent to the sheriff of Sussex ordering him to proclaim throughout his bailiwick that 'no religious man, or other clerk or layman, was to receive anything, whether of gift or purchase, or in any other way whatsoever, of the land of Savaury de Bohun, until the lord King shall have ordained otherwise'.[1] On 3 December 1236 the King remitted to Alured Jordan of Bromsgrove his indignation against him for selling land which he held of the King to Bordesley Abbey without the King's assent: the abbey was not allowed to keep its purchase and, although the land was resorted to the tenant, the rent was raised from 25s. by 10s.[2] In 1238, after the monks of Coggeshall had bought land from a tenant-in-chief, the King insisted that they sell it to a secular person who was to hold it of him in chief by the due and accustomed services.[3] The same policy appears to have been pursued in the last decade of Henry III's reign, despite the difficulties caused by the political disturbances of this period. In 1262 the details of the royal mandate concerning a bequest in frankalmoign of a manor made by the deceased earl of Devon

[1] CCR, 1231–4, p. 491.   [2] CPR, 1232–47, p. 172.
[3] CCR, 1237–42, p. 34.

show that the manor had been seized by the escheator into the King's hands.[1] The firmness of the policy followed by the Crown is revealed by the details of another confirmation, made on 9 August 1267, of a lease of two manors for eight years to Lavendon Abbey: the abbey was forced to agree that, if it entered them in fee, they should be forfeited to the King.[2] Later the same month the King refused to ratify an alienation of a serjeanty held in chief, made to the Templars without his licence: the manor in question was seized and then restored to the grantor's son who made fine with the King.[3]

The same impression of royal policy emerges from an inspection of the chancery rolls of Edward I's reign. Soon after the new king's return to England from Crusade efforts were made to enquire into illegal alienations of lands held in chief. On 19 February 1274 he ordered the escheator south of the Trent not to permit men of the Church to enter the King's fees without licence and to take into the King's hands any fees so alienated: on the following 20 April a similar order was addressed to the escheator north of the Trent.[4] The early Fine Rolls of the reign contain a number of writs ordering the escheators to seize lands alienated to the Church.[5] The available evidence thus indicates that from 1228 onwards the interests of the Crown in respect of alienations in mortmain were well protected.

However, the motives of the Crown in issuing the ordinance of 1228 and the principles it followed in administering its policy of prohibition of alienations in mortmain deserve more attention. Two considerations suggest that the ordinance of 1228 was regarded as an implementation from the standpoint of the Crown of clause 39 of the *Magna Carta* reissue of 1217 which laid down that no alienations were permitted if the residue of the land in the hands of the tenant was insufficient to support the services which

---

[1] *CPR, 1266–72*, p. 735.   [2] ibid., p. 97.   [3] ibid., p. 101.

[4] *CFR, 1272–1307*, pp. 17 and 21. Article 14 of the inquest ordered by Edward I on 11 October 1274 read 'Concerning knights' fees, of whomsoever held, and lands or tenements given or sold to men of religion or to other persons to the king's prejudice, by whom and from what time' (Cam, p. 250).

[5] ibid., *1272–1307*, pp. 4, 22, 24, 25, 90.

were due.[1] In the first place, it may be significant in this connexion that Bracton made no reference to the ordinance of 1228. In one passage he stated that neither a tenant-in-chief nor a mesne tenant could alienate a portion of his holding to a person of religion unless the residue in the hands of the feoffar was sufficient for the performance of services: in another he treated grants of such land in frankalmoign as illegal.[2] His employment in the former of the phrase *propter constitutionem libertatis* shows clearly that he was thinking of clause 39 of the *Magna Carta* of 1217. In the second place, in a writ of 20 February 1256 the Crown, in explaining the reasons for its orders, mentioned *inter alia* that 'it had been provided and commonly laid down that no man of religion might enter the fee of any one without his assent and will'.[3] Examined in the light of Bracton's observations, this statement must be regarded as a reference to the reform of 1217. It implies that the latter permitted mesne lords to licence alienations of their fees to the Church and to refuse the necessary licence if the land that remained in the hands of the tenant was insufficient to maintain his services. It seems likely, therefore, that the Crown's lawyers and administrators believed that the edict of 1228 merely executed a policy which had been given the force of law in the 1217 reissue of *Magna Carta* and confirmed in that of 1225. A perusal of the chancery rolls shows that the Crown did not forbid alienations of lands held in chief to the Church altogether. In the course of Henry III's reign and those years of Edward I which preceded the Statute of Mortmain the Crown issued a number of confirmations of, and licences for, grants to the Church, some of

[1] *Select Charters*, p. 343.

[2] Bracton, III. 35 and 37. Professor S. E. Thorne (Constable, Introd., p. xxxviii and n. 151) cites these passages as evidence that 'a gift made by a tenant in chief to a religious corporation was invalid'. But this interpretation overlooks Bracton's remarks about mesne tenants. The first passage contains the words . . . *qui de domino rege tenuerit in capite, vel de alio* . . ., and the latter . . . *si quis tenuerit de domino rege in capite per servitium militare* . . . *vel de alio quam de domino rege* . . ., the subject of these clauses being the alienor. Even if he had not specifically referred to it in the first of these passages, Bracton's words would imply that he was thinking of clause 39 of the *Magna Carta* of 1217.

[3] *CCR, 1254–6*, p. 400.

them in fee.[1] While we cannot be certain that all of these related to holdings in chief,[2] it is likely that a substantial proportion did so.[2a]

The Crown's attitude towards such alienations after 1279 is not completely clear. The language of the Statute of Mortmain in itself certainly suggests that it was intended to apply to all lands in England. But it would be unwise to interpret royal policy in the light of this fact, since the Crown very soon jettisoned literal adherence to the statute as far as mesne holdings were concerned. Once, however, the Crown decided to pursue a policy of licensing mesne alienations in mortmain, did it adopt the same attitude towards such alienations of lands held in chief? The figures contained in Table I suggest that in the years 1280–97 few of these were permitted, especially if we compare their total with that of licences to alienate mesne holdings in mortmain. Moreover, there is some other evidence which indicates that some efforts during these years to amortize lands held in chief foundered through the Crown's refusal to permit them.[3] But, if we rely on the figures contained in Table I, we must conclude that the Crown's attitude

---

[1] CPR, 1247–58, pp. 139, 152, 557, 575, 583, 584; ibid., 1258–66, pp. 21, 261; ibid., 1266–72, pp. 97, 114, 201, 206, 236, 242, 335, 369, 411, 643; ibid., 1272–81, pp. 98, 153, 270, 336.

[2] Some may represent attempts by grantors or the religious houses concerned to strengthen the titles thus conveyed in view of the hostility of mesne lords to alienations of their fees. In one case the grantor's heirs were disputing the grant (ibid., 1266–72, p. 201).

[2a] For alienations of lands which were definitely held in chief, see ibid., 1272–81, pp. 153, 336.

[3] In August 1294 Edmund, the King's brother, sought to convey his manor of Shapwick in mortmain. But the inquisition found it was to the King's loss (PRO, Inq. a.q.d., C. 143/21/3), despite the fact that he held many other lands in chief. And he had to content himself with a licence to grant a rent of £30 from it (CPR, 1292–1301, p. 87). In the same year Isabel, lady Ros, petitioned for a licence to convey an advowson in mortmain. Although it was found by inquisition that it was not to the King's loss, she had to wait until 1301 for her licence (C. 143/21/17; CPR, 1292–1301, p. 570). In the case of two petitions to amortize from Edmund, earl of Cornwall, at about the same time, although the inquisitions failed to reveal loss, no licences can be traced (C. 143/22/2 and 22).

changed in 1298: in that year holdings in chief were involved in almost half the mortmain licences issued. And, in the years that followed, licences of this kind were issued in greater numbers than in 1280–93. It would, however, be unwise to assume that a deliberate alteration of royal policy occurred in 1298. The increase in the number of licences permitting the amortization of lands held in chief was by no means remarkable. For the same reason we cannot attribute this change to a bid for political support of the Church, even though the years in which it occurred were ones of crisis in England. In all probability what happened resulted from a combination of two influences. One was the gradual realization that there was no harm in the amortization of lands held in chief, provided the tenant-in-chief retained part of his holding: the fine charged for the necessary licence could provide some compensation for any losses of incidents. The concessions made by the Crown to mesne lords in 1292 must have made it especially aware of these considerations. The other influence was the Crown's change of attitude towards alienations in chief to laymen from 1294 onwards.[1] Once this occurred, it must have become increasingly difficult for royal administrators to preserve a separate policy towards mortmain.

The existence of the ordinance of 1228, and the Crown's enforcement of it, mean that we must reassess its behaviour during the events which culminated in the Statute of Mortmain of 1279. For half a century before the statute the Crown had been protecting its interests against the inroads of mortmain. Of all feudal lords it alone had the power to do so. The complaint made by mesne lords in chapter 10 of the Petition of the Barons[2] confirms that they were powerless to prevent the men of the Church from entering their fees and depriving them of their services and incidents. What, therefore, they in effect demanded in 1258 was that their interests be protected in the same way as those of the Crown.

The Crown, however, would derive no direct advantage from protecting mesne lords against mortmain. It is true that any

[1] See the discussion of Table II in section (ii) of the present chapter.
[2] *Select Charters*, p. 375.

reduction in the mesne lords' loss of services and incidents would indirectly benefit the Crown, since the value of its own future revenues from these sources, especially that of wardship, would deteriorate if mesne tenants' alienations in mortmain continued to go unchecked. But the most serious damage to the Crown's interests caused by alienations in mortmain occurred when these were made by the tenants-in-chief themselves and these it was in a position to control. The gains it might obtain by helping mesne lords to protect their interests would at best be marginal and might well in certain circumstances be outweighed by other considerations, perhaps calculations of political advantage.

In this analysis a desire for the support of the clergy in its relations with the baronage may well explain why the Crown did nothing before 1259 to aid mesne lords in their desire for the imposition of restrictions upon mortmain. It is equally likely that the absence of any definite proof that the reform of 1259 became accepted law may be due to the political influence of the Church on the government of Henry III which prevented its inclusion in the Statute of Marlborough of 1267. These points in turn suggest that Edward I's motives in 1279 in promulgating the Statute of Mortmain were political—the intention was to employ it as a threat which would bring the clergy to heel. It is difficult, in view of the protection already secured for the Crown's own interests, and its earlier failure to meet demands for reform, to believe that a desire to help mesne lords now played any part in the calculations of Edward I and his advisers. On the other hand, the magnates' need to have their own services and incidents protected must have secured their support for a statute which virtually outlawed alienations in mortmain. It is certainly impossible, in the light of the role of mortmain in the satisfaction of men's spiritual needs, to believe that the Crown seriously intended to abolish alienations to the Church for ever. Indeed, the first licence of exemption from the statute's provisions was granted only just six months after its promulgation.[1] From 1280 onwards the Crown not only infringed the statute by granting licences of exemption but also claimed and exercised the right to license

[1] *CPR, 1272–81*, p. 372.

alienations in mortmain on the fees of mesne lords, a claim which had no basis in feudal custom or in legislation. The protests of mesne lords in parliament in 1292 resulted in a compromise between the Crown's interests and theirs: the Crown continued to exercise the right to issue a licence permitting alienation in mortmain after the consent of the lord of the fee had been obtained and received a money payment in return for its grant of a licence. The Crown's actions suggest that it was deliberately playing off the Church against the lay magnates. And this impression is strengthened by its behaviour in response to the gravamina of the clergy in the November parliament of 1280. When they requested modifications in the Statute of Mortmain which would permit them to acquire lands which were of their own fees and which would allow poorly endowed religious communities and churches to acquire land, the King replied that such concessions could only be made by going against the counsel of the magnates of the realm and would be injurious to the welfare of the kingdom.[1]

In the light of these details there can be no doubt that the Crown in the course of Edward I's reign had exploited its leading subjects' resentment about the intrusion of churchmen upon their fees in its own interests. Although in 1292 the mesne lords secured some concessions which mitigated the extent of the Crown's unwillingness to protect their interests, they did so only after it had been encroaching on their rights for twelve years. And the Crown continued to exercise the right to license all alienations in mortmain which it had created for itself. As a result of the campaign against mortmain which they waged in the course of the thirteenth century, mesne lords had succeeded in bringing the worst ravages of such alienations under some degree of control: from 1292 onwards it was accepted in law that they could refuse the necessary licence if some land of their fee did not remain in the hands of the grantor. But the Crown, in addition to its own benefits from the ordinance of 1228 which the Statute of Mortmain superseded and its indirect gains from the protection now given to the interests of mesne lords, henceforward exercised the right to license all alienations in mortmain throughout the

---

[1] Douie, op. cit., p. 127.

kingdom. And the fines[1] it charged for granting licences can only be described as a new incident of feudal tenure. In its handling of the grievances of mesne lords over mortmain the Crown had followed policies which gave itself, and not its subjects, the chief benefits from the reforms that were achieved.

(ii) The Royal Ordinance of 1256

A study of the attitudes of feudal lords in the thirteenth century towards alienations by their tenants to other laymen raises much more complicated problems than any enquiry into mortmain. Two main reasons explain the difficulties of the subject. In the first place, it is far from easy to discover the attitudes of mesne lords. No doubt the nature of the consequences of such alienations explain the lack of evidence: whereas the incidents of tenure were destroyed by alienation in mortmain, they survived, although reduced in value, after alienations to other laymen. In consequence, mesne lords were less vociferous in their complaints than in the case of mortmain. In the second place, we are faced with a cleavage between the interests of the Crown and those of mesne lords, much greater than we meet in mortmain. The attitude of mesne lords towards their tenants' alienations was bound to be an ambivalent one. Although they lost through their tenants' freedom to alienate, they had no wish to forfeit that freedom of alienation which they themselves possessed in respect of their own fees. For this reason mesne lords never openly demanded control over all their tenants' alienations as they did in the case of mortmain in 1258. But the interests of the Crown, because it was always lord and never tenant, were completely different: it could only continue to lose its services and, much more important, see its valuable incidents diminish, if its tenants-in-chief remained free to alienate at will. In this situation the Crown obtained no help from clause 39 of the 1217 reissue of *Magna Carta*. As we have seen, this very soon came to be inter-

---

[1] In the early sixteenth century it appears to have been accepted legal doctrine that the fine charged was three years' value of the land alienated (*Brook's New Cases*, p. 47; Brook, *Alienations*, no. 29).

preted as applying only to grants in frankalmoign; and, in any case, even from this limited standpoint, it gave protection to services alone and made no mention of the incidents of tenure. Unlike mesne lords, the Crown found nothing in that situation to dissuade it from attempting to restrict the freedom of alienation enjoyed by its tenants.

It is not, therefore, surprising that the Crown intervened to protect its interests and bring alienations by its tenants-in-chief under control. On 15 July 1256 writs were addressed to all the sheriffs of England in the following terms:

. . . Because it is manifestly to our most grievous loss and unendurable damage to our crown and royal dignity that any one enters the baronies and fees which are held of us in chief in our kingdom and power at the will of those who hold those baronies and fees of us through which we lose wards and escheats and our barons and others who hold those baronies and fees of us are so weakened that they are unable to perform sufficiently the services due to us therefrom, whence our crown is seriously damaged; which matter we are unwilling to suffer any longer:

Of our counsel we have provided that no one henceforth may enter a barony or any fee which may be held of us by purchase or by any other means without our assent and special licence.

And on that account we strictly enjoin you in the oath by which you are bound to us and as you value your person and all your possessions that you do not permit any one henceforth to enter any barony or any other fee which may be held of us in chief in your bailiwick by purchase or by any other means without our assent and special licence.

And if any one may enter any barony or any other fee which is held of us in chief in your bailiwick against this our provision, then you are to seize the land which he has entered by that means into our hand and keep it safely in your custody until we shall have ordered otherwise. . . .[1]

The motives which impelled the Crown to promulgate this ordnance are clearly stated in its preamble in which special stress is laid on the loss of incidents which resulted from the uncontrolled alienations of tenants-in-chief. But the precise reasons

[1] CCR, 1254–6, p. 429, first printed and discussed in G. J. Turner, 'A newly Discovered Ordinance', LQR, XII (1896), 299–301.

which explain why it was issued at this date in Henry III's reign must remain obscure. It is possible to suggest that the Crown was in 1256 especially anxious about its financial position in view of its Sicilian ambitions and was, therefore, anxious to exploit its feudal incidents as efficiently as possible. But financial difficulties had existed at earlier stages in Henry III's reign and no similar edicts had then resulted. The legal origins of the ordinance are equally obscure. It cannot be explained as an attempt to protect the rights which the Crown had obtained under clause 39 of the 1217 reissue of *Magna Carta*. Although such an explanation may be possible in the case of the mortmain ordinance of 1228, it must in this instance be rejected on several grounds. Firstly, whereas the ordinance of 1228 was issued only eleven years after the reform of 1217, that of 1256 occurred after an interval of almost forty years. Secondly, the interpretation of the reform of 1217 had by then been narrowed to apply to frankalmoign only and was, therefore, most unlikely to be used to justify control over all alienations in chief. Thirdly, no attempt was made in the preamble of the ordinance of 1256 to justify its provisions in terms of previous legislation. Lastly, the grounds put forward by the Crown for this reform gave particular emphasis to the loss of wardships and escheats, whereas the reform of 1217 had been concerned solely with services. It might, of course, be argued that the existence of the ordinance of 1228 in respect of alienations in chief in mortmain encouraged the view that the difficulties caused by alienations to laymen might be tackled by a legislative enactment in the form of writs addressed to the sheriffs. But a direct connexion between the ordinance of 1256 and any other reform which is known to us could not have existed.

Nevertheless, a search of the chancery rolls of Henry III's reign shows that the Crown's action in 1256 was not without some administrative precedents. Throughout the period down to 1256 the Patent Rolls contain a large number of licences to lease lands. Some of these were licences to pledge lands which were granted to persons who were going on crusade or pilgrimage to the Holy Land.[1] But the vast majority do not fall within this category and

---

[1] *CPR, 1216–25*, pp. 287, 302, 320; ibid., *1232–47*, pp. 101, 231.

their existence must be explained by other means. It would probably be unwise to regard them as evidence that the Crown was licensing alienations for many years before 1256. Not only is it impossible to be certain that each refers to lands which were held in chief but alternative explanations for their existence can be suggested. One is that a licence might be secured by a lessor or a lessee—perhaps both—to secure evidence of the nature of his title: another is that the prior grant of a royal licence would prevent the Crown from exercising its right to eject the lessee if the lessor died leaving an heir who was under age.[1] But there are a few documents enrolled on the Patent Rolls which afford more certain precedents for the policy of 1256. In 1242 the King granted a licence for the recipient to dispose of, give, let to farm or bequeath all his lands.[2] In 1244 another person was licensed to receive lands late of the earl of Arundel from the earl's heirs.[3] In 1246 Fulk de Montgomery was granted a licence to give the whole or part of the land which the King gave him by charter to his grandson.[4] In 1254 the King ratified a final concord which related to a manor that was held in chief.[5] In each of these instances it might be argued that the licence was secured because the recipient wished to secure his title by means of a document enrolled in Chancery. But this explanation cannot hold in the case of a confirmation, made on 26 September 1255, of a lease of a manor made to Peter de Montfort by Roger Bertram: it was confirmed on condition that Roger should not demise the manor in fee to Peter or any other, or Peter receive it in fee, on pain of forfeiting it.[6] It is, however, impossible to decide how extensively the Crown exercised any right to control alienations in chief before 1256. In Henry III's reign no attempt seems to have been made to distinguish between licences on the one hand, and grants of confirmation or ratification on the other. But there is clearly evidence to suggest that the Crown was in practice exercising some such right for some years before July 1256, although the most cogent piece of evidence comes from September 1255. Judged

---

[1] See above, p. 8.   [2] *CPR, 1232–47*, p. 347.
[3] ibid., *1232–47*, p. 426.   [4] ibid., *1232–47*, p. 487.
[5] ibid., *1247–58*, p. 312.   [6] ibid., *1247–58*, p. 427.

from the standpoint of these details, the ordinance of 1256 was not a complete innovation: it seems to have enunciated a principle which had, to some extent, been followed by royal officials in their administrative activities for some years. Probably, therefore, we should regard the ordinance of 1256 as emanating from the growing consciousness of the royal prerogative, and the increasingly close definition of its rights,[1] which was so prominent a feature of royal government and its officials in the thirteenth century.[2]

We have to wait until after the accession of Edward I in 1272 before we can fully and reliably illustrate the effects of the edict of 1256. The Patent Rolls from 1256 onwards, especially after 1265,

[1] In a case in the court of King's Bench in 1279 the Crown claimed that it held an advowson through the forfeiture by felony of a tenant who had held it in chief. The earl of Gloucester, however, claimed that his father had been enfeoffed thereof by the felon's father. Despite the fact that this alienation had occurred after the promulgation of the edict of 1256, the King's attorney did not cite this in arguing that the tenant's alienation had occurred without royal licence but simply based the royal claim to the advowson on the ground that 'the lord king has a special prerogative attached to his crown, namely, that it is not lawful for anyone to alienate his fee without his special licence, nor was it usual or permissible for a fine of such alienation to be levied without his consent, and, if it has been levied without his consent, it cannot be prejudicial to him in anything, rather shall it be deservedly quashed as levied to the disinheritance of the lord king against the prerogative which the lord king and his ancestors have so far used' (S.C. King's Bench, I. 48).

[2] It would be unwise to regard the document known as *Prerogativa Regis* as a product of this attitude to royal power. It has been suggested that it was probably drawn up in the early years of Edward I's reign and before 1285, since it does not mention *De Donis* (Constable, Introd., xviii, n. 47). But there is no evidence that either it or an enactment on which it was based was ever promulgated as a statute. Its statement that 'No one who holds of the king in chief by military service can alienate the greater part of his lands so that the remainder may not suffice to perform service thence without the licence of the king' (ibid., p. 160) is certainly not an accurate statement of royal practice from 1256 onwards. In the light of this fact we must conclude that, if it was drawn up early in the reign of Edward I, its author was ignorant of official practice. But is by no means impossible that it was based on a document written before the promulgation of the ordinance of 1256. It is not necessary to assume that its definition of primer seisin was based on the Statute of Marlborough, c. 16, which did not create this practice. Cf. ibid., p. xxi.

contain a large number of licences and grants of confirmation or ratification. It is, however, difficult to be certain that all of these relate to holdings in chief. Moreover, after 1265 we are faced with the serious difficulty that we cannot be sure whether they are the result, not of the Crown's right to license alienations in chief, but of the confusion in landholding and its titles which resulted from the period of civil war. But the material contained in the Patent Rolls of Edward I can be much more reliably analysed. Table II summarizes the results of a statistical analysis of the granting of licences to alienate, and pardons for alienations without licence, in respect of holdings in chief, throughout the reign of Edward I and during his successor's until the end of 1310. It has not been taken beyond this date because the dislocation caused by the activities of the Ordainers might affect the value of any results.

The most remarkable feature of Table II is the transformation which appears to have occurred in the granting of licences by the Crown from 1294 onwards. In the years 1272–93 inclusive a total of 50 licences was issued—an average of roughly 2·3 a year. But in the years 1294–1310 inclusive the total was 543—an average of roughly 32 a year. In 1294 itself the total was 31, as compared with an average of 4 for the three preceding years and almost 19 for the three following years. In the case of pardons for alienations without licence, a change appears to have occurred from 1299 onwards. In the years 1272–98 inclusive the total of all such pardons entered on the Patent Rolls was a mere 3; but in the years 1299–1310 inclusive it was 126—an average of 10·5 a year—and in 1299 itself it was 8.

It would be wrong to assume that Table II includes the totals of all the licences and pardons granted in these years: it is possible that some were omitted from the Patent Rolls through the carelessness of Chancery clerks. It is, however, most unlikely that this occurred frequently in the case of licences, since alienees would be anxious to secure their titles to their acquisitions and would, therefore, ensure that the licence was properly enrolled. An omission to enter on the Patent Roll is much more likely in the case of pardons, since, when a pardon was granted, the writ directing the escheator to surrender the land to the alienee would

TABLE II. *Alienations in Chief, 1272–1310*

Year	LICENCES				PARDONS				Grand Total
	In fee	In tail (inc. free marriage)	For terms of years or life	Total	In fee	In tail (inc. free marriage)	For terms of years or life	Total	
1272	—	—	—	—	—	—	—	—	—
1273	—	—	—	—	—	—	—	—	—
1274	—	—	—	—	—	—	—	—	—
1275	2	—	—	2	—	—	—	—	2
1276	3	1	1	5	—	—	—	—	5
1277	—	—	1	1	—	—	—	—	1
1278	1	—	2	3	—	—	—	—	3
1279	2	—	1	3	—	—	—	—	3
1280	4	2	2	8	—	—	—	—	8
1281	1	—	—	1	—	—	—	—	1
1282	1	—	—	1	—	—	—	—	1
1283	2	—	—	2	—	—	—	—	2
1284	—	—	—	—	—	—	—	—	—
1285	2	—	1	3	—	—	—	—	3
1286	1	—	—	1	1	—	—	1	2
1287	—	—	—	—	—	—	—	—	—
1288	—	—	—	—	—	—	—	—	—
1289	—	—	—	—	—	—	—	—	—
1290	4	—	2	6	—	—	—	—	6
1291	1	—	—	1	—	—	—	—	1
1292	4	1	—	5	—	—	—	—	5
1293	3	—	3	6	—	—	1	1	7
1294	9	—	22	31	—	—	—	—	31
1295	13	2	7	22	—	—	—	—	22
1296	5	—	4	9	—	—	—	—	9
1297	12	3	10	25	—	—	—	—	25
1298	6	2	4	12	1	—	—	1	13
1299	6	1	4	11	2	1	5	8	19
1300	9	1	7	17	3	—	1	4	21
1301	9	2	3	14	3	—	—	3	17
1302	12	2	7	21	9	—	—	9	30
1303	16	5	3	24	12	1	2	15	39
1304	14	4	2	20	3	2	1	6	26
1305	25	1	3	29	16	—	3	19	48
1306	28	4	13	45	9	—	2	11	56
1307	6	5	3	14	11	1	2	14	28
1308	26	2	13	41	4	—	2	6	47
1309	23	3	10	36	11	—	2	13	49
1310	26	6	13	45	16	—	2	18	63

be entered on the Close or Fine Roll and, therefore, the enrolment of the pardon itself elsewhere might be considered superfluous. A search of the Close and Fine Rolls of 1272–98 has
brought to light 62 entries relating to the seizure of lands alienated
without licence. Even if we add this total to that of the pardons
enrolled in these years, we arrive at an annual average of 2·4 for
the years 1272–98, as compared with one of 10·5 for the years
1299–1310. In fact, of these 62 entries 42 belong to the years
1272–80, when the Crown was engaged in tracking down
evasions of its rights during the closing years of the previous
reign. It is likely, therefore, that many, if not most, of these entries
of 1272–80 relate to alienations without licence made before 1272.
In the light of these considerations, there can be no doubt that
Table II gives a reasonably accurate impression of trends in the
issuing of pardons and licences in the years 1272–1310.

How, then, must we explain the changes which Table II reveals? It is possible to argue that the paucity of licences before
1294, and of pardons before 1299, was due to inefficiency in the
exploitation of royal rights. If this were so, the sudden increases in
the numbers of licences and pardons would be due to an administrative revolution which ended a situation in which tenants-in-
chief had not bothered to sue out licences to alienate. There are,
however, a number of grounds on which this explanation must be
rejected. In the first place, it is odd that the insistence on a more
rigorous prosecution of royal rights did not affect licences and
pardons simultaneously. Indeed, we would expect such a new
administrative policy to bring many unlicensed alienations to light
immediately; and, although it might be some time before pardons
were granted, they would certainly have appeared some years
before 1299. In the second place, there is plenty of evidence to
indicate that royal rights over alienations in chief were stringently
enforced as soon as Edward I returned to England from Crusade
in 1274. Article 3 of commissions of enquiry launched throughout
the kingdom in October 1274 read: 'Also concerning the lord
king's fees and tenants; who hold them now from him in chief,
how many fees each of them holds; what fees used to be held in
chief of the king and now are held through a mesne lord, and by

what mesne, and from what time they have been alienated, how and by whom.'[1] Its words reveal the royal desire to control the subinfeudation of lands held in chief. Although few inquisitions *post mortem* and related documents have survived for this period, we possess some which show that the royal prerogative to license alienations in chief was taken seriously as far afield as Devon[2] and Northumberland.[3] Two cases emphasize the King's personal involvement in the enforcement of this aspect of his feudal rights. In 1280 Sir Nicholas Weston secured from the King in person the quashing of a fine of 100 marks for previous transgressions and a licence to alienate lands to the value of £10 a year.[4] When in 1290 Gilber Umfraville, earl of Angus, wished to settle a manor on his eldest son and the latter's wife, he petitioned the King in parliament.[5] In view of this there can be no doubt that the King was personally involved in, if not completely responsible for, the policies followed in such matters.

In the third place, anyone who acquired lands held in chief without licence ran serious risks. When an escheator discovered such an alienation, the land was seized. There is no evidence that it was treated as a forfeiture; but it was not restored to the alienee until he had made good the losses inflicted on the Crown by paying a fine and rendering homage to the King.[6] In fact, the land might remain in royal hands a considerable time during which its

[1] Cam, pp. 248–9.

[2] An inquisition held there in 1276 stated: 'These lands used to be held of the king in barony, but now are held in socage only and by a mesne . . ., to the king's decrease by the alienation. It is therefore in the discretion of the king and his council whether he will restore the lands . . . (to the alienee) . . ., for the jury do not consider any other injury to be done to the king or others than is abovesaid' (*CIPMA*, II. 124–5 (no. 201)).

[3] In 1290 an heir petitioned the King to quash a settlement made by his ancestor on the ground that the land was held in chief and had been alienated without licence: 'For those who hold in chief cannot alienate their lands without the king's leave . . ., for thus the king would lose wardships and marriages of those lands' (ibid., II. 471–2 (no. 776)).

[4] *CPR, 1272–81*, p. 391.   [5] *Rot. Parl.*, I. 54 (no. 101).

[6] On a number of occasions escheators were ordered to hold the lands, or replevy them to the dispossessed alienee, until the next parliament (*CFR, 1272–1307*, pp. 65, 270, 292, 310, 489).

revenues were lost. The most remarkable illustration of this is Gilbert Middleton's acquisition without licence from Ralph Gaugy in Northumberland. The escheator was ordered to seize the lands on 23 April 1274.[1] Although Middleton was a few months later allowed to hold them in tenancy,[2] it was not until 10 May 1279 that the escheator was ordered to restore them to him.[3] Moreover, an alienee who acquired without licence might endanger the interests of his heirs, since his title would be defective: in the event of his death before a pardon was obtained, they might meet difficulties in asserting their rights.

In the light of these arguments, we must conclude that, if some alienations without licence escaped the vigilance of escheators before 1294, they were too few to affect our interpretation of Table II's figures. In view of convincing evidence that the Crown was enforcing its rights, the paucity of licences before 1294, and of pardons before 1299, must be attributed to the Crown's unwillingness to permit alienations in chief. The sudden rise in the numbers of licences from 1294 onwards suggests that Edward I then decided to alter his attitude and adopt a more liberal policy towards requests for licences to alienate. In short, we must explain the statistics of Table II as a reflection of the Crown's attitude towards alienations in chief. The change which occurred in royal policy is strikingly illustrated in the treatment accorded to Gilbert Umfraville, earl of Angus. In the parliament of October 1290 he petitioned the King for a licence to enfeoff his eldest son and the latter's wife of the manor of Overton 'to hold of Gilbert the father himself in his lifetime and after his decease of the chief lords of the fee by the services due and accustomed'. His request was refused on the ground that the King had no wish to permit any intermediary between the lord and his tenant.[4] This incident, indeed, brings out very clearly the inflexibility of royal policy on this point: the intermediary would have been created for the earl's lifetime only and the rights of the King and the mesne lord would then have been restored. But in February 1306 Edward I granted the same earl a licence permitting him to assign to

---

[1] ibid., *1272–1307*, p. 21.   [2] ibid., *1272–1307*, pp. 32 and 55.
[3] ibid., *1272–1307*, p. 111.   [4] *Rot. Parl.*, I. 54 (no. 101).

Thomas his son land in chief worth £20 a year, to hold of the earl during his lifetime and after his death of the King,[1] the same type of grant as had been proposed in 1290. The contrast between the refusal of 1290 and the consent of 1306 brings home the nature of the King's *volte face*: he was now prepared to permit in chief what before he had refused to countenance in mesne. The figures contained in Table II indicate that his change of policy occurred in 1294. What his tenants-in-chief then obtained was a relaxation of royal control which gave them freedom of alienation provided they complied with two conditions. First, the alienee, if the land was conveyed in fee or in tail, was to take the same tenurial position as the alienor had held in chief. And, second, the royal permission to alienate was given in return for a fine.

This reconstruction of the situation leaves some problems unsolved. The nature of our evidence does not allow us to explain satisfactorily why several years elapsed before the Crown relaxed its attitude towards the granting of pardons. One possible explanation is that the Crown's change of heart emboldened some tenants-in-chief to proceed with their alienations without suing out the necessary licences. If so, there were probably a substantial number of pardons required by 1299. This was, perhaps, one element in the situation. But it does not account for the continued rise of the number of pardons after 1299. It is, however, likely that the apparent delay in relaxing the royal attitude towards pardons partly reflects the unwillingness of the royal officials entrusted with the administration of the new policy to surrender the whole of the powers they had previously exercised. They may well have taken the view that, since the Crown was now ready to grant licences, there was even less excuse than before for unlicensed alienations and, in consequence, have been uncooperative in the issuing of pardons. If so, we may here catch a glimpse of the professional pride and jealousy which sometimes led the King's officials to be more royalist than the King. Similarly, we cannot be absolutely certain that the Crown never refused licences after 1294. But the great increase in their numbers after that date makes refusals unlikely. Indeed, the insistence that

[1] *CPR, 1301–7*, p. 414.

the alienees hold in chief and the payment of a fine deprived the Crown of any interest in refusal. Above all, we do not know how the Crown's change in attitude was communicated to the tenants-in-chief. The most likely place and occasion was parliament. But the absence of complete parliamentary records makes this suggestion incapable of proof.

We are on somewhat firmer ground when we try to explain the motives which persuaded Edward I to alter his attitude towards alienations in chief. It cannot be a mere coincidence that from 1294 onwards he was involved in difficulties abroad which made him dependent on his subjects' goodwill. Demands for men and money for his wars led to increases in taxation, both direct and indirect, and to requests for personal service overseas. In this situation it is likely that he found it expedient to relax his previous attitude of hostility towards alienations in chief and permitted what, subject to certain limitations, amounted to freedom of alienation. This suggestion is supported by the evidence of a number of licences which refer to the services which the recipient was to perform in the King's wars. Twenty state that he is going to Gascony on the King's service—15 in 1294 itself, and 5 in 1295.[1] Ten, all in 1297, mention that he is going overseas on the King's service without specifying any destination.[2] Three—in 1296, 1300 and 1302—mention service in Scotland.[3] All these licences seem to be concerned with the dispositions that the recipients found it necessary to make when about to set out on the King's service: sometimes they wanted to raise money from their lands to fit themselves out or enlist a retinue,[4] sometimes they were anxious to take precautions against their failure to return.[5] These

[1] ibid., *1292–1301*, pp. 78, 80, 83–7, 96, 153, 157, 169–70.

[2] ibid., *1292–1301*, pp. 249, 252, 288, 292–3, 300, 302–5, 307.

[3] ibid., *1292–1301*, pp. 187, 502; ibid., *1301–7*, p. 40.

[4] Humphrey Bohun, earl of Hereford and Essex, granted lands for life to Bartholomew Enfield who was going with him, while Hugh Bardolf made similar grants to two others. John, son of William Greystoke, granted lands worth 10 marks a year for life to each of the two persons going in his place (ibid., *1292–1301*, pp. 84–5).

[5] Most of these licences relate to leases. It is possible that the details relating to royal service were inserted in order to emphasize the temporary nature of

details give us a real insight into the pressures which impelled the Crown to alter its previous hostility towards alienations in chief. When it came to demand its subjects' service overseas, it discovered that this policy was working against its own interests. No doubt this explains why out of 34 such licences, 21 were issued in 1294, the year of the change of policy. At the same time it is important to remember that licences of this type formed only one aspect of a wider problem. For some decades the Crown had succeeded in restricting alienations in chief to a mere trickle. The sudden increase in the numbers of licences from 1294 onwards is a striking indication of the strength of the feelings of the tenants-in-chief on this point, since they were not slow in taking advantage of the opportunities now given them. It is apparent that the much more liberal policy pursued by Edward I after 1294 was intended to remove a grievance about royal power at a time when he was in need of his subjects' help and goodwill. The Crown's difficulties, though not as severe as in the years 1294–7, continued during the remainder of Edward I's reign; and that of his son and successor was dominated by a series of crises between the King and his magnates. In this situation it was impossible to return to the previous policy of restricting alienations in chief. Indeed, Table II shows that there was a gradual increase in the numbers of both licences and pardons. In the years 1294–6 licences averaged 20·7 a year and in 1308–10 40·7 a year. In 1299–1301 pardons averaged 5 a year and in 1308–10 12·3 a year. Knowledge of the Crown's new attitude soon spread through the kingdom and alienations in chief became part of royal government and private landowning.

In this analysis the promulgation of the ordinance of 1256 was followed by real and effective efforts at enforcement. In the first twenty years or so of Edward I's reign the Crown successfully asserted its right to license all alienations of lands held in chief: and the available evidence demonstrates the serious difficulties which were placed in the way of any tenant-in-chief who wished to alienate. The odds were against securing the necessary royal

---

the arrangements being made and dius protect the lessor's title and that of his heirs.

licence; and, if he went ahead without it, his alienee acquired a defective title and the risk of seizure of the land. Tenants-in-chief must have welcomed the relaxation of the Crown's attitude from 1294 onwards. What then occurred was a much more liberal application of the ordinance of 1256, not a complete jettisoning of its principles. Royal licences were still required; and an alienation took place subject to the conditions on which a licence was issued. The usual practice, if the land was conveyed in fee or in tail, was for the alienee to hold in chief as the alienor had done; and a fine was paid. The ordinance of 1256, therefore, possesses a twofold importance. Its promulgation began a phase in the relations between the King and his subjects in late thirteenth-century England. And, by enlarging the functions of the royal prerogative, it eventually created in the fines paid for licences and pardons a new incident of feudal tenure.

(iii) The Statute of Quia Emptores

In July 1290 the feudal tenant's right to alienate was the subject of legislation in parliament. In the Statute of *Quia Emptores*,[1] so-called from its opening words,

our lord the King . . . at the instance of the great men of the realm granted, provided and ordained that from henceforth it should be lawful for every free man to sell at his own pleasure his lands or tenements or part of them so that the feoffee would hold the same lands or tenements of the chief lord of the same fee, by such services and customs as his feoffor had held before.

In this passage the statute laid down two rules for the future. Firstly, freedom to alienate was conferred on all free men. Secondly, subinfeudation was abolished. These changes went together: the language of the statute indicates that the abolition of subinfeudation made freedom of alienation possible. The rest of the statute was concerned with the application of these rules. It was laid down that, if part of a tenant's land was alienated, the services were to be apportioned between him and his alienee in proportion

---

[1] *Rot. Parl.*, I. 41a; Digby, pp. 236–8; *Select Charters*, pp. 473–4.

to the amounts of the fee held by them. The statute concluded with the statement that it was to apply only to alienations in fee simple. If, therefore, a tenant granted land for a term of years or in tail,[1] subinfeudation might still be employed. No doubt these exceptions to the rule laid down by the statute were permitted because such estates were not detached permanently from the tenant's fee, but returned in due course to him or his heirs, to be held as before.

Despite the apparent clarity of the statute's terms, the motives behind it have given rise to fundamental disagreements among historians. Maitland seemed to see in it signs of a cleavage of interest between Crown and magnates: 'The statute is a compromise; the great lords had to concede to their tenants a full liberty of alienation by way of substitution'. He further states that 'the one person who had all to gain and nothing to lose by the new law was the king'.[2] For Professor Plucknett, on the other hand, it is a reform of the land law in the interests of all lords, great or small, 'merely one of a long succession of conveyancing acts; with the modification of the *habendum et tenendum* clause of deeds as its immediate object'. He stresses the fact that the text of the statute states that it was 'promulgated' 'at the instance of the great men of the realm'. And he argues that, since it was already the case in law that a lord could not refuse a substituted tenant, '*Quia Emptores* on this point merely stated in statutory form a state of affairs which had existed informally for some years'.[3]

There are two serious weaknesses in Professor Plucknett's arguments. First, while it is true that that substitution was possible in law, there is no evidence that the practice was always, or even frequently, employed by tenants who alienated lands held by feudal tenure. Indeed, if any such tenant wished to alienate, it was clearly in his interest to employ subinfeudation, since by this means he secured for himself the incidents of feudal tenure. Second, unlike Maitland, Plucknett does not discuss in this connexion the Crown's right to license alienations by tenants-in-chief and the edict of 1256 is nowhere mentioned in his discussion

[1] *YBRS, 21 & 22 Ed. I*, pp. 640–1.   [2] Pollock & Maitland, I. 337.
[3] Plucknett, *Ed. I*, pp. 103–6.

of *Quia Emptores*. On the other hand, while both historians stress the statement that the statute was made 'at the instance of the great men of the realm', they differ over its interpretation.

The obvious starting-point for a discussion of *Quia Emptores* is the precise meaning of its provisions. Future alienations by mesne tenants clearly fell within its terms. But did they apply to alienations by tenants-in-chief? On this point the text of the statute gives us little help. The words, 'it shall be lawful for every free man to sell at his own pleasure his lands and tenements . . .' are vague and, in the light of a number of considerations, must be regarded as ambiguous. It may be argued, of course, that the phrase 'free man' (*liber homo*) might include the tenants-in-chief. But in reply to this it might equally well be suggested that, if it was intended to include them, more precise and specific language could have been employed. There are, in fact, three grounds for believing that the tenants-in-chief were not included in the statute's provisions.

In the first place, it can be convincingly argued that the Crown had no interest in so including the tenants-in-chief, since the edict of 1256 and the system whereby it licensed their alienations catered satisfactorily for its interests. It is, of course, true that indirectly the Crown benefited from the provisions of the statute, since the fact that subinfeudation now gave way to substitution meant that in future, when tenants-in-chief were under age, the Crown was able to enjoy the wardship of an inheritance in which the losses incurred through alienations by mesne tenants had been stopped. But this long-term advantage would by no means have compensated for the Crown's loss of its right to license alienations of lands held in chief. If the statute had been intended to apply to tenants-in-chief, there can be no doubt that it would have meant the end of a valuable function of the royal prerogative.

In the second place, there is the light which is thrown on this problem by an incident which occurred in the parliament which was held in October 1290, a few months after the promulgation of *Quia Emptores*. Gilbert Umfraville, earl of Angus, petitioned the King for a licence to enfeoff his eldest son and the latter's wife of the manor of Overton 'to hold of Gilbert the father himself in his lifetime and after his decease of the chief lords of the fee by the services due and accustomed',[1] a settlement which, since it involved some subinfeudation, was not permissible within the terms of *Quia Emptores*. It is quite apparent that the earl assumed that an alienation of a mesne holding by a tenant-in-chief did not necessarily fall within the terms of the statute, since otherwise no petition in these terms would have been presented. And this suggests that the Crown did not consider itself bound by *Quia Emptores*. The nature of the royal response—*Rex non vult aliquem medium, Et ideo non concessit*—confirms the view that alienations in chief did not come within the terms of *Quia Emptores*: although it adopted the principle which underlay the statute, the latter was not mentioned and the grounds of refusal were based simply on the King's wish to avoid any intermediary between the lord and the actual tenant of the land.

In the third place, the view that *Quia Emptores* did not apply to alienations in chief is supported by the conduct of the Crown in granting licences to alienate in the course of the fourteenth and fifteenth centuries. Despite the statute's provision that every free man should be free to alienate 'at his own pleasure', the licensing of alienations in chief continued. Indeed, out of a total of 593 licences issued in the years 1272–1310, 556 belonged to the years 1291–1310. Moreover, in issuing such licences the Crown followed principles which were different from those of *Quia Emptores* in one very important respect. While the latter's rule regarding substitution had been confined to grants made in fee so that estates for terms of years or in tail were exempted from its provisions, in the case of entailments of lands held in chief the Crown appears to have insisted, as a condition of its licence to alienate, that the tenant in tail hold of it directly, and not of the grantor.[2]

---

[1] *Rot. Parl.*, I. 54 (no. 101).

[2] On this point the evidence does not support the observations of Professor S. E. Thorne in Constable, Introd., pp. xiii–xiv, where he criticizes Constable's view that, when a tenant-in-chief alienated in tail or for life, the alienee held of the King in chief (ibid., pp. 135 and 144–5). In the case of grants in tail, an inspection of the licences and pardons entered on the Patent Rolls confirms that Constable has accurately reported royal practice. Indeed, had the Crown acted

In the light of this evidence, it is impossible to conclude that the Crown intended *Quia Emptores* to apply to tenants-in-chief. It is unfortunate that we possess no decision by a court of law on this point which belongs to the years immediately following the statute's promulgation. Indeed, no such ruling was made until over six hundred years later, in 1922, when the point was raised in the court of Chancery and was the basic issue involved in a judicial decision.[1] After reviewing the statements of different authorities, Mr. Justice Astbury came to the conclusion that *Quia Emptores* did not affect the position of the tenants-in-chief in respect of the alienation of their holdings. His judgement also contained the suggestion that the rule relating to substitution was, on the contrary, intended to apply to future alienations by them.[2]

---

otherwise, an impossible situation would have arisen, in view of the fact that most of the entailments effected in the fourteenth and fifteenth centuries were carried out by feoffees to whom the lands had been conveyed for this purpose. For a case of 1295, in which a father was given a licence to enfeoff his son and heir of lands held in chief provided the feoffee held in chief, see *CPR, 1292–1301*, p. 143. Constable's view, however, does not represent royal practice towards most grants for life in the fourteenth centuries but is obviously the result of the Crown's efforts in the reign of Henry VII to expand the number of tenants-in-chief. The case cited in connexion with his criticisms of Constable by Professor Thorne (ibid., p. xiv, n. 30) is hardly relevant, since it concerns lands held of the Duchy of Cornwall (*S.C. Exch. Chamb.*, I. 29–38).

[1] *In Re Holliday*. A petition was presented for leave to traverse an inquisition held in 1921 at Kendal, Westmorland, after the death of Thomas Holliday, who was illegitimate and unmarried and had died intestate. The question was whether his lands had escheated to lord Hothfield, the lord of the manor of Brough, or to the Crown. Since the lands were copyhold enfranchised in 1837 by the lord of the manor, lord Hothfield had seized them as his escheat on Holliday's death and had later sold them to the petitioner who had been ousted by the inquisition held in 1921. Whether or not his petition succeeded depended in the last resort on the issue whether, since the manor was held in chief, the lord had the right to enfranchise a copyhold without a royal licence. In the arguments that were propounded the *Prerogativa Regis* was regarded as an actual statute and the judge decided that it belonged to the early years of Edward I's reign, thus antedating *Quia Emptores*. The terms of the Statute of 1660 abolishing feudal tenures were also considered.

[2] The available reports differ slightly in the versions they give of the relevant portions of the judge's judgement. *The Times Law Reports*, vol. XXXVIII

But it is difficult to accept this latter view, since the Crown had no need for a statutory rule on this point. In practice it had for some time applied such a rule when issuing licences to alienate and no doubt, when this practice continued, it came to be assumed that tenants-in-chief must comply with the rule of *Quia Emptores* in respect of alienations in fee, even when they had failed to apply for the requisite licences before alienating. What in fact happened in the years that immediately followed *Quia Emptores* was that the rule laid down for mesne tenants by the statute coincided in respect of conveyances in fee simple with a practice on the Crown's part which antedated the statute.

The conclusion that the statute did not apply to tenants-in-chief does not necessarily mean that we can exclude from our calculations without further investigation the possibility that its promulgation had some influence on the way the Crown exercised its right to license all alienations in chief. Even if it retained and continued to exercise this right after 1290, it remains possible that it followed a less rigid policy. Perhaps, for instance, the principle that every free man should be at liberty to alienate 'at his own pleasure' was taken to mean that the Crown was under an obligation to issue a licence when requested to do so: damage to its interests would be avoided because, under the statute, sub-

---

(1921–2), p. 711: 'He thought that while the first half of cap. 1 [of *Quia Emptores*] enabling every free man to sell his lands did not affect tenants *in capite*, the second part providing that a feoffee should hold the lands of the chief lord was intended to bind them. . . . He considered that it seemed improbable that at a time when the power of the Crown was at its greatest the King would have suffered in the case of his own tenants the inconvenience from subinfeudation, which in the case of the great lords had been removed by *Quia Emptores*.' *The Law Reports, Chancery, 1922*, II. 709: 'The first of these provisions did not in my judgement affect the King or his tenants *in capite* in the sense of giving the latter any free right of alienation, but the second provision may, it is suggested, have been intended to bind them where they had made alienations of their lands under the above provisions of the prerogative ordinance [i.e. *Prerogativa Regis*], although they are not referred to in express terms.' He then went on to point out that 1 Ed. III, st. 2, c. 12, appeared to support this suggestion. The ordinance of 1256 is nowhere mentioned in the case, presumably because it did not possess the authority of a statute.

stitution, not subinfeudation, would be employed. An analysis of the numbers of licences in the years which followed the promulgation of *Quia Emptores* does not support this suggestion. It is true that, while a total of 37 licences was issued in the years 1272–90—an average of almost two a year—the total in the years 1291–1310 was 556—an average of almost 28 a year. But a study of the annual figures given in Table II reveals that this remarkable expansion in numbers did not occur immediately after the promulgation of *Quia Emptores* but began in 1294. The respective totals for the years 1291, 1292 and 1293 are one, five and six, figures which do not differ remarkably from those of some individual years before 1290.

Even if we thus exclude the tenants-in-chief from the operation of the rules of *Quia Emptores*, we remain faced with the fact that it did apply to their tenants, giving them freedom of alienation. Historians have hitherto assumed that this reform gave adequate protection to the interests of mesne lords, including those who were tenants-in-chief: as a result of the replacement of subinfeudation by substitution, the decline of their revenues from the incidents of tenure was stopped. But this view is based upon an incomplete understanding of the nature of the interests of mesne lords. *Quia Emptores* certainly removed their main grounds of complaint about their tenants' freedom to alienate; but two powerful grievances remained.

The first of these was the Crown's right to license all alienations of lands held in chief. As we saw in our discussion of Table II, such licences were rarely granted between the accession of Edward I and 1294. From that year onwards the remarkable increase in the number of licences issued is a powerful indication of the strength of the desire to alienate freely which must have been felt by tenants-in-chief. When *Quia Emptores* was promulgated, therefore, the Crown was still pursuing a policy which restrained its tenants-in-chief from alienating and, moreover, showed no sign of relaxing it. This situation must have inflicted much personal and financial discomfort on the tenants-in-chief. In times of financial difficulty they were unlikely to secure royal permission to sell or mortgage their holdings. Nor was there any real hope, when they wished to provide for younger sons or daughters, that the King would approve of the creation of entails or *maritagia* from lands held in chief. And, if a tenant-in-chief decided to go ahead without royal licence, what might then happen was a further ground for grievance. The lands might be seized by the escheator, kept in royal hands, and their issues taken by the Crown, until a pardon for the alienation had been secured. Although the alienees were sometimes permitted by the Crown to hold the lands in tenancy, a considerable delay might occur before a pardon was granted. Resentment against the Crown's claim to license any alienation in chief must have been especially strong among the leading magnates. On the one hand, they suffered from the Crown's rights like all other tenants-in-chief. On the other hand, they were powerless to prevent their own tenants alienating.

The second grievance which was not removed by *Quia Emptores* was one which would have been felt most strongly by the magnates of the realm. Because they were unable to compel their own tenants to secure licences to alienate lands held of their fees, they were unable to prevent alienations which were *deliberately* intended to rob them of their incidents—for instance, the conveyance of lands to a husband and wife jointly, so that in the event of the husband's death before his wife, leaving an heir under age, the lord would be deprived of the wardship. It is impossible to deduce from the available evidence the extent to which alienations of this type occurred before 1290. But two legal cases in the early 1290's make it apparent that they did, and that lords could be roused to anger by them.

Details of the first of these are to be found in proceedings enrolled on the roll of the parliament of January 1291.[1] Thomas of Wayland had abjured the realm for felony and had, in consequence, forfeited his lands—those held of the King to him and those held of other lords to them, after the King had held them for a year and a day. The proceedings concerned the manor of Sodbury which he had held of the earl of Gloucester. In 1278, by means of a final concord, he had conveyed it to a single feoffee who had then granted it to him and Margery his wife and Richard

---

[1] *Rot. Parl.*, I. 66–7.

their son: Thomas and Margery were to hold of the chief lords of the fee for their lives, with remainder to Richard and the heirs of his body, to hold of the right heirs of Thomas.[1] The effect of this settlement, if permitted to stand, would be to deprive the earl of Gloucester of his right of forfeiture. In fact, the proceedings enrolled on the parliament roll appear to have constituted some sort of test case, since a number of entries on the Close Roll show that Thomas of Wayland had effected similar settlements in the case of lands held of other mesne lords.[2] No doubt these were ready to let their claims be prosecuted by the most influential of them, since the earl of Gloucester was not only one of the most powerful magnates but also the King's son-in-law. The proceedings which ensued led to a search of the available records for precedents. No fault in law could be found in the settlement, especially since it was effected by means of a final concord. Moreover, a precedent was found in the thirty-second year of Henry III in which a wife's *maritagium* was exempted from the forfeiture occasioned by her husband's felony. The manor in question, therefore, was restored to Thomas of Wayland's wife, although she was at the same time enjoined to give no support or maintenance to her husband. The proceedings reveal the earl of Gloucester's complete inability to prevent the settlement being made or becoming effective despite the loss of his rights which it occasioned. The arguments rehearsed in his plea indicate that he understood clearly the issues involved about which he warned his fellow magnates present in parliament.

. . . Since it seemed to many that this could lead to the great prejudice of the lord King and the injury of his Crown and dignity. Because any one proposing or wishing to commit a felony could make a joint enfeoffment with his wife of his lands and tenements, as well of his

---

[1] In default of heirs of Richard's body, the manor was to remain to the heirs male of Thomas born of Margery, to be held of the right heirs of Thomas, with remainder in default of such issue to the right heirs of Thomas, to be held of the chief lords of the fee. Without this ultimate remainder, the validity of the settlement would have been much more doubtful. It affords striking illustration of the complicated nature of the tenures it was possible to create before *Quia Emptores*. See the comment in Holdsworth, III. 104.

[2] *CCR, 1288-96*, pp. 93, 95-6, 106-7.

inheritance as of purchase, with such intention that his lands and tenements after he had committed the felony and had abjured the realm
would remain to his wife . . . so that she would support her husband
himself from the profit of the same lands and tenements.

It is apparent that there was a real threat to the interests of lords
in any expansion of settlements of this type. The earl's warning
that the wife might be a 'person of straw' so that the husband
continued to enjoy the profits of the land was taken seriously by
the King and his council, who issued a clear warning to Thomas
of Wayland's wife on this point. But the settlement was effective
in law, the work, it should be noted, of one who was, before his
felony, Chief Justice of the Common Pleas. Neither it nor the
events that followed would have been possible if mesne lords had
possessed the power to control alienations by their tenants.

The second case, from the Year Book of 1293, is equally re-
vealing.[1] In a case of novel disseisin the counsel for the plaintiff
rehearsed the events which preceded the disseisin and were not
denied by the defendant.

. . . Geoffrey de Maubank heretofore held of Sir John Tergot by knight
service; which Geoffrey enfeoffed one John le Blound of the said tenements. Sir John Tergot was wrath with John le Blound because he
entered his fee without permission; so that John le Blound went to Sir
John Tergot and gave him a thousand marks to have his good will, and
Sir John Tergot executed to him a writing of grant and confirmation;
then John leBlound enfeoffed Geoffrey de Maubank and Maud his wife
of the said tenements to hold to them and their heirs; Maud survived
Geoffrey, by whose death all the right accrued to Maud because they
were joint feoffees. Maud granted the same tenements to Henry de
Guldeford for the term of Henry's life, and Henry was seised by virtue
of that grant until Sir John Tergot and others named, etc. he was
disseised.

Sir John Tergot seized the lands by force, apparently on the
ground that the lands belonged to him in wardship. But the assize
went against him on the grounds that his behaviour in seizing the
lands by force and ravaging its crops was not that of a guardian.
In this case also we witness the impotence of a lord in the face

[1] *YBRS, 21 & 22 Ed. I*, pp. 272–7.

of alienations which deprived him of his rights. Like Thomas of Wayland, the tenant had employed the device of a feoffee to execute a joint settlement. The lord's wrath at the alienation to the feoffee was such that the latter found it wise to pay him a very large sum to obtain a confirmation of the grant. Despite this payment, the lord appears to have insisted on the substitution of the feoffee for his original tenant, since we are told that he 'executed to him a writing of grant and confirmation'. Nevertheless, the feoffee then carried out a settlement on the original tenant and his wife without the lord's permission. The details in the Year Book discussion imply that, when the original tenant died, he left an heir under age, a situation in which the lord asserted his rights of wardship by force. The absence of any action at law by which he might claim his rights compelled him to resort to an arbitrary disseisin. Although the dates of the transactions recorded in this case are not known, it should be noted that the settlements effected by Thomas of Wayland occurred twelve years before *Quia Emptores*. It seems likely that in the intervening period, if not before 1278, other landowners had engaged in similar transactions. In view of the fact that both these cases had occurred so soon after the promulgation of *Quia Emptores*, it is difficult to believe that the ideas expressed by the earl of Gloucester and those which were acted on by Sir John Tergot at about the same time were absent from the minds of the magnates who were present in the parliament of Easter 1290. When they thought of the loss of incidents which might result from settlements effected by their tenants, they must have resented their own lack of any right to engage in similar transactions in respect of their holdings in chief.

This conclusion is supported by evidence which reveals that at least some of the leading magnates after 1290 did not observe the principle laid down for their tenants by *Quia Emptores* that every free man should be at liberty to sell his lands 'at his own pleasure' provided that the purchaser held them of the vendor's lord. The words of *Quia Emptores* do not necessarily confer upon the tenant a complete and absolute freedom of alienation: instead, they may be interpreted as merely giving him the right to alienate to a purchaser freely chosen by himself without hindrance from his lord. If this interpretation of the statute's words be accepted, it might then be argued that some sort of confirmation, if not licence, from the lord, and some sort of payment to him for this, were not expressly excluded by the statute's terms. The law, in short, would only be broken if the lord refused to accept his new tenant. It should also be noted that on this point the statute mentioned the tenant who alienated: the freedom it conferred was for him to sell, not for his alienee to enter. In view of this, it would be possible to argue that there was nothing in law to prevent lords from insisting that alienees obtain either letters of confirmation or licences to enter their fees. A large number of lords must have interpreted *Quia Emptores* along these lines, since twenty-five years after its promulgation it was necessary to supplement it by further legislation. In the Hilary parliament of 1315 it was agreed by 'the archbishops, bishops, abbots, priors, earls and barons and others of the realm . . . that henceforward they would neither demand nor take any fine from free men to enter lands and tenements which are of their fees, provided always that by such feoffments they were not deprived of their services nor their services lost'.[1] The promulgation of this reform is clear evidence that *Quia Emptores* required clarification in respect of its provision regarding freedom of alienation. It is important to note that the new reform made reference only to the practice whereby lords had charged fines for permitting entry into their fees and made no specific mention of fines for licences to enfeoff. It is, of course, possible that the reform was intended to include these as well but was badly drafted. But it is equally possible that, while no lords had levied fines for licences to alienate, a large number had charged them for licences to enter. Indeed, a careful reading of the words of *Quia Emptores* supports the latter suggestion. Because it mentioned the alienor, and not the alienee, the legal case for licences to enter was much stronger than that for licences to alienate.

To understand the influences which led to the reform of 1315 it is essential to remember that the great lords of the realm possessed a degree of power and influence which made it difficult

[1] *Rot. Parl.*, I. 298.

for their feudal tenants to depend completely on their legal rights in their dealings with them. In law, as we have seen from our discussion of Bracton's views, mesne lords had no right to interfere with their tenants' alienations. But, in practice, it is likely that they often intervened to protect their rights—to ensure, for example, that they were not deprived of wardship by the creation of joint settlements. If Sir John Tergot could employ force in defence of his interests, a great earl would be more likely to do so: indeed, the threat of his displeasure might suffice to bring his tenants to heel. Although lords had no right in law, at least in the view of Bracton, to interfere with their tenants' alienations, there can be no doubt that some did so by insisting on the alienees securing licences to enter their fees and paying for them. It is quite clear that the simple words of *Quia Emptores*—'it should be lawful for every free man to sell at his own pleasure'—mask a conflict of interest between mesne lords and their tenants. How far some of them demanded fines for licences to enter (or even to alienate) before 1290, it is impossible to say. But it should be noted that the complaint of the earl of Gloucester in Thomas of Wayland's case makes no mention of any such practice. If so powerful a mesne lord did not issue licences to enter at this time, it is unlikely that many, if any others, did so. On this ground, therefore, it might be suggested that the practice of issuing licences to enter began after the promulgation of *Quia Emptores*.

The reform of 1315 represented a surrender by mesne lords of the new powers some of them had created for themselves. We can only speculate about the motives which led them to take this step. The explanation may well lie in the political circumstances of the time: in a period of conflict with the King a reform of the grievances felt by lesser men was politically advantageous to the magnates. Indeed, from this standpoint it is interesting to see that the legislation of 1315 protected the lords' services but made no mention of their incidents, an omission which was definitely to the advantage of the tenants. At any rate, it is certain that the grievances of mesne tenants about the policies pursued by an appreciable number of lords led to an undertaking in the parliament of 1315 that fines for licences to enter would no longer be levied. The existence of this reform on the parliament roll is tangible proof of the view that the replacement of subinfeudation by substitution did not give mesne lords in 1290 all the legal changes they desired. Indeed, some of the most powerful of them did not keep the undertaking made in 1315.[1]

To explain the promulgation of *Quia Emptores* in the light of this discussion is a difficult and complicated task. On the one hand, we are faced with the fact that the tenants-in-chief did not obtain the freedom of alienation which was apparently conferred on their tenants and the Crown continued to operate the system whereby alienations in chief had to be licensed by it. On the other hand, there are powerful arguments which suggest that the great lords of the realm would not have been satisfied with the abolition of subinfeudation in itself. Moreover, these are supported by

[1] In a case of replevin in the court of Common Pleas in 1412, the defendant claimed that 'there is a certain custom from time immemorial that any man who shall have acquired lands or tenements held immediately of the Honour of Gloucester shall make fine, for the same lands so acquired, with the officers of the lord of the said Honour for the time being'. In the Year Book discussion Justice Hankford stated that 'In the county of Cheshire the Prince has a fine on every alienation, and also the Bishop in Durham, and I tell you that in these lordships if any tenant transfers, the land is seized until he pays the lord a fine.' Judgement was given to the plaintiff on certain technical points which did not affect the main point of law at issue. Indeed, Justice Hill emphasized that the decision of the court was not to be taken as laying down a rule that the tenants of the honour of Gloucester need not pay fines for lands acquired there (A. K. R. Kiralfy, *A Source Book of English Law* (London, 1957), pp. 74–82, with full details of the record and the Year Book discussion). These three lordships are the only ones in which such practices can be traced. In each case there are special circumstances which are not to be found elsewhere. In the case of the bishopric of Durham and the earldom of Chester the explanation undoubtedly lies in their lords' palatinate powers. And, in view of this, it is very likely that fines for entering lands held of them were demanded before *Quia Emptores*. Indeed, in the case of the earldom of Chester they may have resulted from an ordinance made by the country court in January 1260 (for this see Plucknett, *Ed. I*, pp. 105–6 and 108–9). The position regarding the honour of Gloucester is more uncertain. But it is quite possible that its officials did not consider that their lord was bound by the reform of 1315: at that time, after the death of the last Clare earl at Bannockburn, the future of the earldom was in dispute.

For an example of the practice in the earldom of Stafford, part of the honour of Gloucester, see *CIPMA*, XII. 38 (no. 43).

evidence that some of them at least refused to allow complete freedom of alienation on their fees, despite *Quia Emptores*'s avowal of the right of all free men to alienate 'at their own pleasure'.

It is impossible to approach the problems of interpretation which these conclusions raise in the simple clear-cut terms of 'the interests of the Crown' and 'the interests of the lords'. Some lords were not tenants-in-chief: many held only a small portion of their lands in this capacity. Such landowners would feel far less strongly than the major tenants-in-chief about the Crown's right to license alienations of lands held in chief. Indeed, they might well tend to range themselves on the side of those who were wholly mesne tenants and thus resented any attempt by mesne lords to license, or in any way interfere with, alienations made by themselves. The confused nature of the tenurial structure, therefore, makes it impossible to define the interests of feudal lords as a whole as a single entity. It is possible, however, to distinguish between the interests of great lords—the magnates of the realm—and the lesser landowners who would be their tenants. Some of the latter might be tenants-in-chief because a portion of their lands was held of the Crown; but many would hold little land of the Crown and many would hold all their lands of mesne lords. In social terms this group of lesser landowners would comprise the lesser gentry and the more important freeholders of the shire. The reform of the land law which would best suit their interests would be one in which all rights exercised by lords over their tenants' alienations, including those of the Crown over those in chief, were abolished. In default of the abolition of the special rights attached to the royal prerogative, they would have sought the reform achieved by *Quia Emptores*, as supplemented by the legislation of 1315. They themselves wanted to be free to alienate, while the abolition of subinfeudation would ensure that their own interests as lords did not suffer.

Now, in a system of land law constructed solely to meet their needs, the magnates would probably have desired the right to license alienations made by their tenants. But legislation in these terms in the late thirteenth century would have been impossible to achieve. From the legal standpoint, it would have found no basis in contemporary legal doctrines which, as we have seen, fully recognized the tenant's freedom to alienate. Those who would suffer as a result of the imposition of restraints on alienation were the knights and freeholders of the shire whose support in local affairs was valuable to the magnates. The thirteenth century had witnessed several developments which together revealed that these social groups were exercising an increasingly important influence in national politics—for example, the attention given by the baronial reformers to their grievances in the years 1258–65 and the summoning of the representatives of the commons to parliament. Any form of restraint which was imposed on mesne tenants' freedom to alienate by means of legislation on a national scale was unthinkable both in legal and in politico-social terms: it would have run counter to the whole character of the development of property law over the previous century and would have struck at the interests of classes whose members, however inferior individually to the magnates in terms of birth and wealth, were both numerous and collectively influential enough to make interference with their interests undesirable.

It is true that the abolition of subinfeudation was a valuable gain to the great lords, since alienation through substitution would safeguard their rights to, and profits from, feudal incidents. But it is difficult to believe that they were completely satisfied with a reform which did not go beyond this. Indeed, what best suited their interests would be one in which they secured the freedom to alienate which their own tenants enjoyed. In fact, however, in 1290 the Crown retained its claim to license alienations by tenants-in-chief and the right to levy fines when such alienations occurred.

In the light of this analysis the statement in the preamble of *Quia Emptores* that it was promulgated 'at the instance of the great men of the realm' may well touch on the events which preceded it, in that it indicates that the statute resulted from pressure brought to bear upon the Crown by the magnates. The King agreed to a reform which primarily benefited the interests of the tenants-in-chief and those lords below them in the feudal hierarchy. How far they pressed for an abolition of, or reform in, the Crown's control over alienations in chief we cannot say with certainty. But the existence of such pressure may well explain the ambiguity of the statute's language: 'from henceforth it should be lawful for every free man to sell at his own pleasure his lands or tenements . . .'. It is most unlikely that careful attention was not given to the drafting of a statute of such far-reaching importance. The fact, therefore, that there was a desire among the great tenants-in-chief for complete freedom of alienation for themselves probably accounts for the vague statement of a principle of freedom of alienation for all and, in particular, the use of the all-embracing term 'free man' (liber homo) in the text of the statute. Although under pressure from the magnates to grant freedom of alienation to tenants-in-chief, the King and his ministers may well have been unwilling to use more precise language which would have stated in clear terms what was a surrender of royal rights.

These suggestions are supported by the fact that the statute applied only to estates in fee simple and, in consequence, estates in tail and for terms of years were exempted from its provisions, so that these might continue to be held of the donor. In agreeing to their exemption the Crown was acting against its own interests and in favour of those of the landowning classes. Even if it retained its right to license alienations of this type by tenants-in-chief, the fact that subinfeudation was to continue when mesne tenants in the future alienated in tail or for terms of years was bound to reduce its potential revenues from wardship. It is true that the great tenants-in-chief would lose when their own tenants subinfeudated in alienations of this type. But their losses in this respect would probably be compensated for by their own freedom to subinfeudate when making grants in tail or for terms of years of lands which were held of mesne lords. Since most, if not all, magnates held portions of their inheritances of mesne lords, the exemption of estates in tail and for terms of years from the provisions of Quia Emptores was a substantial concession in their favour as well as that of their tenants.

How far these arguments imply the existence of an open conflict over alienations between Crown and magnates in the parliament of Easter 1290 is hard to say. There is certainly good reason
to believe that, in the face of the magnates' complaints about the
recent handling of *Quo Warranto* proceedings, the Crown found
it expedient to promulgate a statute which gave some redress to
franchise-holders.[1] But there is no positive evidence of a similar
clash over alienations. Signs of a conflict of interest between
Crown and magnates do not necessarily indicate the existence of
an open clash, let alone a parliamentary crisis. Moreover, it is quite
possible that *Quia Emptores* resulted from demands made, not in
this parliament, but in preceding ones—perhaps that of Hilary
1290. If so, when parliament assembled at Easter 1290, the
Crown might have had ready a measure which met some of the
magnates' grievances. At any rate, all the available evidence points
to the conclusion that *Quia Emptores* was a compromise between
the interests of Crown and magnates. Whether it was prepared in
advance of the meeting of this parliament or was hammered out
in the course of its meeting, the statute failed to meet the needs of
the magnates completely. Both they and the Crown gained from
the abolition of subinfeudation in the case of alienations in fee.
But the other issue between the Crown and the magnates—the
Crown's right to license alienations in chief—was left virtually
unsettled. It is likely that the statute's vagueness and ambiguity on
this point was intentional on the part of the royal lawyers who
were responsible for the work of drafting. On the one hand, the
Crown was unwilling to promulgate an enactment which contained the abolition or limitation of this aspect of its power. On
the other hand, pressure from the magnates made it desirable to
issue a statement of the principle that all free men should be free
to alienate in fee provided they proceeded by way of substitution.
We can only engage in speculation concerning the way in which
the statute was interpreted on this point by tenants-in-chief. It is
possible that the view was taken that, so far as alienations in chief

[1] Plucknett, *Ed. I*, pp. 45–8, whose arguments are supported and further
developed by D. W Sutherland, *Quo Warranto Proceedings in the Reign of
Edward I, 1278–1294* (Oxford, 1963), pp. 91–7.

were concerned, the statute was laying down a principle which would be followed by the Crown when it granted licences to alienate in the future: the Crown accepted that its tenants should be free to alienate in fee by way of substitution provided that the necessary licence or pardon was obtained. If this interpretation existed at the time of the statute's promulgation, it may help to explain the absence of any signs of open opposition.

If this view of the origins of the Statute of *Quia Emptores* is accepted, we are still faced with the problem of explaining why such a compromise lasted and, indeed, remained the most important single law relating to the land for the rest of the middle ages. Why did the magnates, despite the language employed by the statute, allow the Crown to continue to exercise its right to license alienations in chief? The answer may be found, partly in the political background of the next thirty years, partly in further developments in the land law. From 1290 onwards other issues engaged the energies of both the King and his subjects—the conquest of Scotland, troubles in Gascony, the crisis of 1297, the Ordinances of 1311, and then a struggle for power which ended in civil war. Within this period the events of crucial importance, from which stemmed all the later developments, occurred in the years 1294–7. The need to finance his wars impelled Edward I to impose taxation, both direct and indirect, affecting merchants as well as landowners, to an extent not experienced since the reign of John. Moreover, his methods raised issues of constitutional principle. Thus, within seven years of *Quia Emptores*, the political situation had been transformed. The relations between Edward I and his magnates were dominated by a contest over policies which affected, not the nobility alone, but the whole 'community of the realm'. In such a situation it would have been difficult for the magnates to press their grievances over alienations in chief. Dwarfed as these were by greater issues, they had no appeal to the lesser landowners and merchants whose support was essential in the struggle which produced the *Confirmatio Cartarum* of 1297.

How much the magnates regretted their inability to prosecute the interests of tenants-in-chief we cannot say. But by 1297 they must have become less anxious about such issues, since they were

now confronted with a more liberal royal policy towards alienations in chief. From 1294 onwards the Crown relaxed its previous
attitude of hostility and appears to have been ready to grant
licences to alienate if its interests were reasonably protected. It
must have been political pressures which forced the Crown to
adopt a more liberal policy: and, since these continued, the new
policy became a permanent feature of government. It is, therefore,
hardly surprising that, in a situation in which their grievances both
declined in political significance and were deliberately alleviated
by the Crown, the magnates were content to accept the continuance of the royal right to licence all alienations in chief. Nevertheless, there was always the possibility that some day the Crown's
rights would be exercised to their disadvantage. And this con-
tingency could be safely averted only by legislation in parliament.

    The dangers to the position of the tenants-in-chief which were
implicit in the rights of the Crown in respect of alienations were
brought into the open by events which occurred in 1319–20.
These arose from the ambitions of Edward II's favourite Hugh
Despenser the younger who, in order to round off the inheritance
he was engaged in building up in South Wales, sought to secure
the lordship of Gower, then in the hands of the last of the Braose
lords.[1] As a result of a settlement made some years previously
Gower came into the hands of Braose's son-in-law, John Mowbray. Since a royal licence for this alienation had not been
obtained, the lordship was seized into the hands of the Crown.
Despenser appears to have thwarted Mowbray's efforts to have
the alienation to him pardoned and to have claimed both that the
lordship had been forfeited to the Crown by the failure to obtain
a licence and that it was treason to deny the Crown's right to the
forfeiture.[2] It is probable that it was Edward II's intention to grant
Gower to Despenser, but the latter's ambitions were defeated by
a coalition of Marcher lords, frightened by the threatened increase in Despenser's power and, in the case of the Mortimers and
the Bohuns, angry at the apparent defeat of their own ambitions
to acquire Gower. The resulting war has a vitally important place

[1] For full details, see J. C. Davies, 'The Despenser War in Glamorgan',
TRHS, 3rd ser., IX (1915), 33–42.   [2] ibid., p. 38.

in the events which led to Edward II's victory over his opponents in 1322. But, from the standpoint of the land law, these events raised two issues.

First, did the King's right to licence alienations in chief extend to Marcher lordships? Mowbray and the other Marcher rebels claimed that by virtue of the custom of the March a royal licence had not been required for the alienation of Gower. The claim, however, was a doubtful one in law.[1] The Crown succeeded in ignoring it during the next two centuries without further protests, while there are grounds for believing that it had no basis in law or practice in the late thirteenth and early fourteenth centuries. It is difficult to believe that the Marcher lords did not invent it to justify their rebellion, anxious as they always were to enlarge their privileges. The second issue was more important: in the event of an alienation being made without a royal licence, was the land thereby forfeited to the Crown? If so, a serious threat existed to the well-being of every tenant-in-chief, great and small. Any conveyance of their holdings would be fraught with risks; even in the case of a settlement within the family, failure to respect the right of the Crown might result in the permanent loss of part of the inheritance. In claiming the forfeiture of Gower of Despenser's

[1] On this point Conway Davies seems somewhat confused. At one stage he suggests that the exception of Gower from an earlier settlement on Mowbray was due to 'unwillingness on the part of Brewosa to prejudice Marcher privileges' (ibid., p. 37). But elsewhere he states that 'Brewosa had excepted Gower from the settlement because he wished to offer that portion of his hereditary possessions for sale to several lords' (ibid., pp. 34–5).

In view of the policies he followed towards Marcher lords, it is difficult to believe that Edward I would have been willing to accept the claim that their privileges exempted them from the obligation to sue out licences to alienate. In 1317, after the death of John Knoville, the Crown did not accept the escheator's excuse that he had been unable to hold an inquisition in the case of certain of his lands because they lay in the Marches of Wales and insisted that he proceed with it. He met resistance from the steward of Thomas, earl of Norfolk; but it is not clear whether this was in defence of Marcher privileges or of the earl's claim that the lands were held of him (*CIPMA*, VI. 5 (no. 16)). On the other hand, in 1299 Humphrey Bohun, earl of Hereford, successfully contested the King's claim to primer seisin within the lordship of Brecon (ibid., III. 421 (no. 544)).

instigation, the Crown was seeking to treat alienations of lands held in chief without licence on the same basis as alienations in mortmain without licence. The terms of the ordinance of 1256 contained nothing to justify this claim. A study of the Patent Rolls of Edward I and II shows that, when alienations without licence had occurred before this, the Crown had always been content to grant a pardon in return for the payment of a fine.[1] The claims put forward in 1320 were thus, in terms of previous practice, an innovation.

However much they lacked foundation, they could not be allowed to stand. In 1327, in the first parliament of Edward III, a statute was promulgated which was, in effect, an enactment of a petition[2] presented by the 'community of the realm':

> Whereas divers people of the realm complain that they are aggrieved, because lands and tenements which are held of the King in chief and alienated without licence, have been seized heretofore into the King's hands and held as forfeited, the King shall not hold them as forfeited in such a case, but wills and grants from henceforth, that of such lands and tenements alienated, there shall be reasonable fine taken in the Chancery by due process.[3]

There can be no doubt that this statute must be interpreted as a surrender by the Crown of the claims which had been put for-

TABLE III. *Alienations in Chief, 1323–31*[4]

Year	Licences	Pardons
1323	35	35
1324	50	56
1325	58	59
1326	46	35
1327	52	41
1328	51	25
1329	48	48
1330	46	25
1331	51	22

[1] See Table II.
[2] *Rot. Parl.*, II. 9 (no. 27); *Rot. Parl. Hact. Ined.*, p. 124 (no. 29).
[3] *Statutes*, I. 256 (1 Ed. III, st. 2, c. 12).   [4] *CPR*, passim.

ward and acted upon in 1319-20. The table which follows shows clearly that the Crown had continued to grant pardons when alienations occurred without licence during the last years of Edward II's reign. It cannot, therefore, be argued that the statute reversed policies which had been in operation on some scale for some years previously. Nor can it be suggested that it made alienations in chief easier and, therefore, more frequent. An inspection of the figures in the table shows that there was no significant change in the numbers of licences issued after the promulgation of the statute, while in the years 1328-31 the number of pardons was roughly two-thirds that of 1323-6.

The importance of the statute of 1327 lies in the control it imposed on royal rights over alienations in chief, ensuring that they were shorn of the dangerous claims made in 1319-20. A landowner who alienated lands held in chief had to obtain either a licence from the Crown prior to his alienation or a pardon after the alienation had been made. In the event of an alienation being made without licence, the Crown had the right to seize the land and receive its issues until a pardon had been granted. According to the statute of 1327 the fines demanded in return for licences or pardons were to be 'reasonable'.[1] An examination of licences issued from 1327 onwards reveals that the Crown generally took care that the tenant-in-chief retained some land after the alienation. Sometimes, indeed, when he wished to alienate the whole of his holding, it insisted that he retain a small portion—an acre, or a fraction of one—in his hands.[2] Nevertheless, within these wide limits, from 1327 onwards tenants-in-chief enjoyed freedom of alienation.[3]

By 1327 all feudal tenants in England had achieved freedom of alienation. But what they had won was not an absolute right to

[1] By the beginning of the sixteenth century it was accepted that a fine for alienation was levied at the rate of one-third the annual value of the land, while the fine paid for a pardon for alienation without licence was a whole year's value (*Brook's New Cases*, p. 47; Brook, *Alienations*, no. 29). Although Constable in 1495 (pp. 152 and 156) regarded the former figure as customary, he stressed that both rates lay within the Chancellor's discretion.

[2] See the details summarized in Table V.

[3] Cf. the remarks of Sir John Fortescue, *The Governance of England* (ed. C.

H

alienate as they wished. Tenants-in-chief had to obtain licences and pay fines for them. And no category of tenant secured the right to create whatever tenure he wished when he alienated. If the alienation was made in fee, it had to proceed by way of sub-stitution, not subinfeudation. In the case of mesne tenants, this rule was created by the Statute of *Quia Emptores*, and in the case of tenants-in-chief it was enforced by the Crown through its right to license all alienations in chief. Nevertheless, despite these limitations, a very substantial freedom of alienation now existed: in particular, tenants-in-chief enjoyed rights which were doubtful in strict law a few years before 1327.

The developments which produced this situation may be des-cribed quite accurately as 'a struggle'. When the thirteenth century opened, mesne lords were deeply concerned about their losses through subinfeudation. When alienations of their fees were made to other laymen, there are clear indications of their disquiet. And in the case of mortmain they certainly engaged in a struggle to protect their interests. The Statute of *Quia Emp-tores* is a powerful indication of the anxiety that mesne lords felt about the decline of incidents through subinfeudation. At the same time the Crown engaged in a struggle to secure, and then to protect, the right to control alienations in chief. In these events there were no remarkable crises or open clashes between the King and his subjects. In part their absence may be attributed to the competition of more immediate issues, in part to the complexity of the problems involved. The magnates of the realm would have been glad of the opportunity to press the interests of their class, whether against the Crown or against their tenants. But the

---

Plummer, Oxford, 1885), p. 134, discussing the various means by which the Crown might build up its territorial power: 'And by purchase, if this be done, there shall no man so well increase his livelihood as the king. For there shall none of his tenants alien livelihood without his licence, wherein he may best prefer himself.' But, if the Crown had manipulated its prerogative in this way to compel would-be purchasers to sell to itself, it would have broken the statute of 1327. It is only charitable to ascribe Fortescue's apparent ignorance of the law on this point to his long absence from the judicial bench at the time he wrote.

'community of the realm' was becoming more and more a political reality. On the one hand, the political issues between the Crown and its subjects affected the interests of all landowners, great and small, and even those of merchants. On the other, it was impossible for the magnates to persuade those below them in the landowning hierarchy to support a challenge to royal authority in which they had no personal interest. Thus much of the struggle over freedom of alienation is muted, leaving little trace in contemporary sources. It existed, but it lay beneath the surface of events. Hence the magnates secured the Statute of *Quia Emptores*, but failed to achieve the complete destruction of royal control over alienations in chief.

Nevertheless, in the end the Crown lost and its subjects gained. It managed to create two entirely new incidents of feudal tenure from which it alone benefited—the fines paid for licences to alienate in mortmain and in chief. But these by no means compensated for its losses. It failed in its efforts to control all alienations in chief. And, within the broad limits of the licensing system it had created, it had to concede freedom of alienation to all tenants-in-chief.

CHAPTER THREE

The Origins and Development of Uses

THE restrictions imposed by feudal tenure upon a landowner's right to employ the revenues of his lands after his death, and the lord's rights of wardship and marriage, together led to the growth of a legal device which had far-reaching effects both upon English land law and the development of feudal landownership as a whole.[1] It was known as the 'use', a vernacular term derived from the Old French *oeps*, which was in turn derived from the Latin word *opus*. Under this device one person, or group of persons, held a parcel of land to the use (*ad opus*) of another who in the law French of the period came to be called the *cestui que use*.[2] Land was granted to A to the use of B: the grant could have been made either by B himself or by a third party who intended that the land should be held for the benefit of B. In essence the use was a legal fiction. In practical terms B would be the real owner, since he would actually occupy the land and draw its profits. What happened was that a distinction was drawn between the actual occupation of the land and the view which the common law took of its ownership. In strict law—to use again the example already given—when land was granted to A to the use of B, A was the owner of the land at common law, since the conveyance was made to him, and not to B.

[1] For what follows see especially Pollock & Maitland, II. 228–39; Holdsworth, IV. 409–43; Plucknett, *Common Law*, pp. 575–82; A. W. B. Simpson, *An Introduction to the History of the Land Law* (Oxford, 1961), pp. 163 seq.; J. L. Barton, 'The Medieval Use', *LQR*, LXXXI (1965), 562–77.

[2] This is a shortened form of the phrase *cestui a que use le feoffment fuit fait*. The frequent employment of the abbreviation led to the assumption that *use* was a verb and thus the plural *cestuis que usent* appeared. Both contemporary abbreviations are used in the discussion that follows, rather than the somewhat anachronistic modern term 'beneficiary'. The latter is only used to refer to those who benefited from the directions given by a *cestui que use* to his feoffees.

Both the purposes behind, and the details of, the growth of uses present complex problems which require detailed enquiry. But the main features of the device deserve preliminary comment. The relationship between the person, or persons, who held the land at common law and the person to whose use it was held was basically that which nowadays exists between a trustee and his beneficiary. Because of this a feoffee to uses was under an obligation to respect and carry out the requirements and wishes of his feoffor. The latter could, if he wished, request his feoffee to make dispositions of the land during his lifetime. But he could also require him to dispose of the lands he held according to his directions after his death. As a result, it was possible, by issuing directions to the feoffee which were to take effect after the death of the *cestui que use*, for the latter to devise his lands by will. Landowners were now, therefore, able to circumvent that rule of feudal tenure which forbade the divising of lands by will.

(i) The Period of Emergence

Although the legal institution of the use was a phenomenon which emerged in England in the course of the later middle ages, the origins of the device can be traced back to a much earlier time. In the early middle ages the term *ad opus* is used frequently in the general sense of 'to the profit, or advantage' of a person or institution, when money or chattels changed hands. For example, it can be found in this sense in early Frankish documents and also in the Carolingian laws for the Lombards and, among English sources, in Anglo-Saxon land books and in Domesday Book. The term can also be discovered in English chancery rolls of the thirteenth century in connexion with the payment of moneys to royal officials for the profit of the King or the taking of goods from subjects for the King's use by way of 'prise'. Very often these instances of the employment of the term *ad opus* occur because it was necessary to define the relationship between the giver of money or goods, on the one hand, and the recipient, on the other, since the person who was actually taking possession was, in fact, not the real recipient but his agent.[1]

Such evidence indicates that lawyers and administrators from Merovingian times onwards were attempting to deal in precise legal terms with situations in which those who held goods or money in their hands were not, in fact, their owners in law. Nevertheless, the institution of the use which finally emerged was concerned with land. *A priori* it does seem highly likely that, quite early in the middle ages, the same problem was met in the case of land as occurred in the case of money or chattels—that the person who held physical occupation did so for the benefit of another. As early as the Frankish settlement of Gaul the Salic law reveals the existence of a person to whom land was transferred in order that he might make a grant in accordance with the directions of his grantor. In early German law he is called the *Salman*. It is clear that in most cases the conveyance by the *Salman* was to be carried out after the grantor's death and the grantor reserved the use of the land to himself during his lifetime. Since it was possible that the *Salman* himself might die before the grantor, the latter generally granted his lands to more than one *Salman*.[2] In England instances in which one man held land to the use of another can be found from the early twelfth century onwards. In Domesday Book we see that Eudo the king's steward held lands of Ramsey Abbey; but in an Abbey cartulary we are told that he held the land 'to the use of his sister'. Early in the twelfth century on one manor of Burton Abbey a certain Godfrey held land 'to the use of his little brother, until he shall have reached the age when he can and ought to render service to the abbey'. In a charter of *c.* 1127 a man, having declared that he had given land to his wife in place of her marriage portion, stated that he had given seisin to her brother 'in her place that he might maintain her and defend her from every injury'. On many occasions in the twelfth century we see lords acting in capacities analogous to those of the later feoffee to uses.[3] For instance, a vendor surrenders land to the use

[1] Pollock & Maitland, II. 229–30 and 233–5 and references there given.
[2] O. W. Holmes, 'Early English Equity. 1. Uses', *LQR*, I (1885), 163–4.
[3] Henry III appears to have acted in a similar capacity in the case of aliena-

of the purchaser by a rod and by the same rod the lord delivers the land to the purchaser.[1] A careful study of two of these examples shows clearly that we are dealing with a conception of a 'use' which is markedly different from the ordinary sense of 'to the profit, or advantage, of'. The Burton Abbey tenant holds the land until his younger brother comes of age, while in the case of the charter of *c.* 1127 the wife's brother is intended to look after her interests. Moreover, when a tenant surrenders land to his lord in order that it be conveyed by him to another, he is trusting his lord to carry out his wishes. In short, the conception of a trust has already begun to emerge as early as the first half of the twelfth century.

To judge from cases in the royal courts in the early thirteenth century, it had developed greater clarity by then. In an assize of novel disseisin in 1221 a guardian (*custos*) is seized of land to the use (*ad opus*) of an infant.[2] In an assize of *mort d'ancestor* of 1222 the defendant alleged that the deceased had held a rent *in custodia*, having purchased it to the use (*ad opus*) of the defendant with the defendant's money. The jurors virtually accepted this defence and stated that the deceased held the land *in custodia*.[3] In 1224 a man who was going to the Holy Land gave his land to his brother to keep it to the use of his (the grantor's) sons. Hearing that his father was dead, the eldest son demanded the land from the feoffee who refused to surrender it. A suit between them in the seignorial court was compromised and the land divided equally between them.[4] In a case of 1225 a man appears to have received land from the grantor on the understanding that he was to convey it to his

---

tions by tenants-in-chief, e.g., *CCR, 1261–4*, pp. 54–5 and 211, where the term *ad opus* is used.

[1] For full details see Pollock & Maitland, II. 231 and 235.

[2] *Rolls of the Justices in Eyre . . . 1221, 1222*, ed. D. M. Stenton (Selden Soc., vol. LIX, London, 1940), p. 447 (no. 1013). In another case in the same year a father acts as guardian (*custos*) of his son's land during the latter's absence in Ireland, but the term 'use' is not employed (ibid., pp. 114–15 (no. 257)).

[3] Pollock & Maitland, II. 235.

[4] *Bracton's Note Book*, III. 42–3 (pl. 999). The feoffee received his half for life only.

daughter and the grantor's son, presumably a marriage portion.[1] In a case of 1233 a man desired to enfeoff his son who was a child aged seven years. He gave the land to him in the hundred court and took his homage. After going to the land and delivering seisin, he committed the land to a third party to keep to the use of the son (ad custodiendum ad opus ipsius Petri) and afterwards to yet a fourth person for the same purpose.[2] It is possible to supplement this material derived from judicial records with some from documents, both royal and private in origin, which are entered on the chancery rolls. In 1246 the King ordered that seisin of the manor of Kirk Leavington be given to four sons of William Percy because

> William Percy three years before his death gave the manor . . . to Ingram de Percy, and William and Alan and Jocelyn, brothers of the same Ingram, his sons, . . . and committed it to the abbot of Sawley to keep to the use of his same sons (custodiendum ad opus eorundem), so that the same William de Percy received nothing from the issues of the said manor during the said three years.[3]

In 1257 Roger Cantelow and his wife granted the wardship and marriage of their heirs, and certain portions of land until they came of age, to Sir Adam de Cestreton: although the details are obscure and the term opus is not employed, the grantee's position can only be satisfactorily explained in terms of some sort of trusteeship.[4] We also find the term opus used on a number of occasions to describe the relationship between an attorney and the person on behalf of whom he was receiving land from a grantor.[5] Perhaps, the strongest indication of the extent to which opus can imply trusteeship by the middle years of the thirteenth century is the fact that the term is used by the King himself in connexion with

---

[1] *Bracton's Note Book*, III. 529 (pl. 1683).

[2] ibid, II. 575–6 (pl. 754). In another case a man bought land to the use of his second wife and the heirs of their bodies (ibid, III. 648 (pl. 1851)). His heir at law failed to recover it in an assize of *mort d'ancestor*. The term 'use' is, however, used in this instance less precisely than in the other examples in the *Note Book*— possibly in the sense of 'for the advantage of'—and we cannot exclude the possibility that the language used may describe a settlement in tail.

[3] *CCR, 1242–7*, p. 405.   [4] *CPR, 1247–58*, pp. 592–3.

[5] ibid, p. 205; *CCR, 1254–6*, p. 19.

royal property: in 1241 Henry III committed certain castles to John Lestrange who then swore on the Gospels that, in the event of the King's death, he would deliver them to the Queen to the use of the King's son and heir.[1]

Not all the uses of lands which can be traced from the first half of the thirteenth century exhibit the features of a trust. But it must be remembered that a high proportion of the examples quoted come from *Bracton's Note Book* and, therefore, other instances may yet come to light from judicial records which are still in manuscript. Indeed, it is likely that many landowners in the early thirteenth century committed lands to others to the use of their infant heirs. In c. 6 of the Statute of Marlborough in 1267 it was found necessary to forbid the practice whereby landowners enfeoffed heirs who were under age.[2] Since this reform had to be promulgated, it is probable that the practice was a frequent one. A landowner who followed it would have been faced with the problem of arranging for the care of his heir's inheritance in the event of his own death before the heir came of age. It seems likely, therefore, that the expedient of a use employed in the case of 1233 was a frequent one.

Further examples of uses of land which involved some sort of trust can be discovered in the late thirteenth and early fourteenth centuries. An inquisition of 1281 tells us how William Ferrers, earl of Derby, in 1251 granted three manors to his younger son William, to be held of the earl and his heirs. The son then had full seisin for over four years during his father's lifetime. The issues of all the manors, however, were collected by his guardian (*custodem*) and kept in ward (*custodia*) until the fifth year of the son's seisin when they were given to him.[3] Another inquisition of 1274 tells how a younger son of an Essex landowner was seised of a manor which was secured from his father through his guardian.[4] An inquisition of 1292, held on the death of Robert Burnel, bishop of Bath and Wells, describes how Sir Otto Grandison, before leaving

---

[1] *CPR, 1232–47*, p. 244. For other examples see ibid., *1258–66*, p. 588; *CCR, 1261–4*, p. 338, and ibid., *1268–72*, p. 236.

[2] *Statutes*, I. 20–1.   [3] *CIPMA*, II. 237 (no. 413).

[4] ibid, II. 44 (no. 63).

on crusade, granted his manors of Sheen and Ham to the bishop who held them at the time of his death. But the jurors explain that they do not know whether Sir Otto granted them to the bishop 'as bailiff' or whether he released all his rights therein to him.[1] Both their confession of ignorance on this point and the term 'bailiff' indicate that they had the possibility of a trust in their minds, a fact which implies that the device was not unknown to them. An inquisition of 1299 describes how a father granted ten librates of land to his son and heir and the latter's wife; but, because the son was under age, he gave him a guardian.[2]

It should be noted that the term *opus* is not found in any of these inquisitions. Instead, the person whose position approximates to that of the later feoffee is described as a 'guardian' or 'bailiff', the former term being reminiscent of the language used in the case in the King's court in 1222, in Bracton's case of 1233 and in the settlement made by William Percy. But cases of uses of land which do employ the term *opus* can also be discovered in the latter half of the thirteenth century. In 1259 we find land being purchased by a third party to the King's use.[3] In 1268 in two separate transactions lands were quitclaimed to feoffees to the use of another.[4] An entry on the Close Roll in 1268 reads,[5]

Be it remembered that Hugh Neville, son of John Neville, before his departure from England to the Holy Land, put in his place Hawisia Neville, his mother and John Neville, his brother, to let to farm all the lands and tenements of Hugh from the feast of the Nativity of St. John the Baptist in the fiftieth year of our reign for five complete years to whomsoever they wished in so far as they saw it to be to the advantage (*ad opus*) of Hugh, and to receive to the same use the lands which the lord King granted to anyone by occasion of the enmity conceived against Hugh, if it happened that they be restored to him.

In 1289 Ralph Grendon entered into a bond with Robert Burnel, bishop of Bath and Wells, to enfeoff the bishop, or another whom

[1] *CIPMA*, III. 47 (no. 65).   [2] ibid., III. 366 (no. 473).
[3] *CPR, 1258–66*, p. 48.   [4] ibid., *1266–72*, pp. 210–11 and 218.
[5] *CCR, 1264–8*, p. 254.

his wife-to-be should name, of lands worth £30 a year for her use for life.[1]

In the light of this evidence there can be no doubt that in the closing years of the thirteenth century lawyers and landowners in England were well aware of the possibility of transactions in which lands were granted to one person to the use of another. Indeed, in 1275 the Statute of Westminster I, c. 48[2] created a use as a statutory remedy. When a lord made a wrongful enfeoffment of land belonging to an heir who was in his wardship, the infant was now given an assize of novel disseisin against him; and, if judgement went against the lord, he lost all the lands belonging to the infant which were in his wardship. Instead, these were committed to the infant's next friend, 'to hold to his use'.[3]

These details, however, do not mean that the use of the later middle ages had fully emerged by the end of the thirteenth century. The term 'use' was not employed on every one of these occasions. The person in the position later occupied by the feoffee to uses was often described as a 'guardian' or 'bailiff'. Nor did contemporaries have a clear conception of his legal status. According to Bracton,[4] a 'guardian' did not enjoy seisin. But, although he tells us that an heir had an action against him, he fails to explain precisely where seisin lay while a 'guardian' occupied the land, an omission which the courts did nothing to repair.[5]

Towards the close of the thirteenth century the procedures employed to make settlements of land within families bring us much

---

[1] ibid., *1288–96*, p. 118.

[2] *Statutes*, I. 38, discussed by Plucknett, *Ed. I*, pp. 81–2.

[3] The phrase *ad opus* is used. In a similar context the Statute of Merton, c. 6, had employed *ad commodum* (*Statutes*, I. 3).   [4] Bracton, II. 135–6.

[5] In 1310 an heir failed to secure redress against his 'guardian' by means of a writ of waste (*Year Books of Edward II. 3 Ed. II*, ed. F. W. Maitland (Selden Soc., vol. XX, 1905), pp. 185–6), since this applied to feudal wardship only. His counsel argued that a writ of account could not lie, because the defendant had not acted as a bailiff. (Cf. *LQR*, LXXXI (1965), 563). In 1278 the Crown was uncertain which of two writs was available to James Shirley who sought redress against his son who refused to settle on his father for life a manor conveyed to him on condition that he do so after paying his father's debts (*Rot. Parl.*, I.2).

nearer the use in its finished form. If a landowner wished to entail
land on himself and his issue, or settle lands jointly on himself and
his wife so as to give his wife a life-interest, he was faced with the
difficulty that in common law he could not grant lands to himself.[1]
The solution of this problem was to grant the lands to one or more
persons who then reconveyed them to the grantor according to
the terms of the proposed settlement. Two features of such
transactions require special attention. In the first place, however
temporary the ownership which was thus transferred to the feoffees who performed the settlement, while it lasted it was real in
law: they took seisin and themselves delivered it when the settlement was effected, facts which are emphasized by the details in
several contemporary references to settlements.[2] In the second
place, a trust was reposed in the feoffees that they would perform
the settlement strictly according to the wishes of the grantor. Not
only do the details of these transactions imply this fact but it is
further attested by the terms of one royal licence to carry out a
settlement by this means. On 13 June 1290 Roger Bigod, earl of
Norfolk, received a licence to enfeoff 'some person in whom he
had confidence' of land to the yearly value of £300, to the end
that the feoffee might enfeoff the earl and his wife jointly.[3] It was
clearly necessary that the earl be able to repose trust in his grantee.
How far other landowners were content simply to repose a trust
in their feoffees that they would carry out settlements strictly
according to their wishes, we cannot say with certainty. In the
case of lands held in chief, the royal licence to alienate which was
required would provide some guarantee, since it would record
the terms of the proposed alienations in detail and would have to
be adhered to strictly; but in the early fourteenth century there
were some settlements effected without licences which were later

[1] e.g. Holdsworth, IV. 474.
[2] An inquisition of 1290 tells how a feoffee continued seisin and employed
the profits for eight days before he settled the land (*CIPMA*, II. 480–1 (no. 787)).
Another of 1322 stated that a settlement, although made by final concord, was
null and void because the feoffees did not take any of the profits of the land and
the tenants did not attorn to them (ibid., VI. 178–9 (no. 310)).
[3] *CPR, 1281–92*, pp. 363–64.

pardoned by the Crown.[1] In any case, the safeguard of a royal licence to alienate would not be available in the case of lands which were not held in chief. Some landowners who wanted settlements effected may have secured forms of undertakings in advance from their proposed feoffees in separate deeds of covenant or indentures.[2] And others may have had a clause inserted in the conveyance permitting their re-entry in the event of the feoffees' failure to perform. On the other hand, it is equally likely that many would have regarded the existence of such documents as damaging to their feoffees' titles and, consequently, to the validity of any settlements they carried out. For this reason they may have preferred to declare the condition whereby a settlement was to be effected at the time of their enfeoffment of the feoffees by word of mouth alone, a procedure which was quite sufficient to make the transaction a conditional feoffment at common law.[3]

In theory, a tenant could use his feudal lord to make a conveyance to the use of another, who, when the land was finally conveyed to him, would hold it of the lord. But, in practice, a lord would naturally be unwilling, unless possibly he was given some financial inducement, to carry out a settlement on a husband and wife jointly, since, in the event of the former's death leaving an heir under age, he would lose the wardship of the land. Feudal tenants, therefore, turned elsewhere for their feoffees, a situation which mesne lords were powerless to prevent.[4] Just when they began using feoffees to settle land held of mesne lords is uncertain. Thomas of Wayland used feoffees in 1278 to settle a manor on himself, his wife and son.[5] However, until the last decade of the thirteenth century two factors existed which were bound to limit the use of feoffees for such purposes. The first is the fact that before the promulgation of the Statute of *Quia Emptores* difficulties could easily have arisen over the tenures by which the lands so settled were held. The position would be quite straightforward if both the enfeoffment of the feoffees and their settlement were by substitution: but while a landowner could himself ensure that the

---

[1] For the earliest traced see *CPR, 1307–13*, p. 191.
[2] e.g. *CAD*, I. 306 (B. 963), 471 (C. 857).   [3] See *Rot. Parl.*, III. 61.
[4] See above, pp. 44–7.   [5] *Rot. Parl.*, I. 66–7.

enfeoffment he made was of this type, difficulties could easily arise when he tried to ensure that his feoffees settled the land in like manner. If, on the other hand, subinfeudation was employed throughout the land, when settled, would be held of the feoffees. After 1290 the position in law became clear and straightforward, since all conveyances in fee had now to be made by way of substitution: henceforth landowners could effect settlements using feoffees without any worries over possible tenurial complications. It seems highly likely that fears of these would have reduced the number of settlements made in this way before *Quia Emptores*. The second factor which inhibited the employment of feoffees for this purpose was the fact that the Crown, by virtue of its prerogative to license all alienations by tenants-in-chief, appears to have followed policies which must have prevented the latter from making settlements of lands held in chief. Certainly the type of settlement often made—one on a husband and wife jointly in order to provide for her in the event of her surviving him—would in the event of the tenant-in-chief's death leaving an heir under age deprive the Crown of the wardship of the lands so settled. For the first two decades or so of Edward I's reign the Crown appears to have been loath to grant licences to alienate. But from 1294 onwards it seems to have relaxed its attitude in this respect and from 1299 onwards it appears to have been easier to obtain pardons for alienations made without licence.[1] It would be extremely unwise to assume that no settlements at all employing feoffees were made in respect of lands held in chief before these changes occurred, since a few tenants-in-chief may have thought any risks involved worth while. But the pronounced relaxation in the Crown's attitude to such alienations which occurred in the 1290's certainly removed any possible barriers that had previously existed.

The disappearance of both these influences in the last decade of the thirteenth century led to a proliferation of settlements effected by means of feoffees. For example, the number of such settlements licensed by the Crown in the years 1294–8 averaged 2·6 a year: in 1325–29 the annual average was 16·4. This pronounced

---

[1] See the discussion of Table II.

expansion must have helped to produce in the minds of lawyers and landowners both a greater familiarity with the practice of employing feoffees and clearer conceptions of the nature of their functions. The fact that the feoffees who carried out a settlement obtained, for however short a time, a real seisin[1] was bound in the long run to suggest other functions for them to perform. For instance, why should they not effect the settlement after the death of their grantor? Or, in the intervening period, handle the revenues of the land as he had directed? The development of functions of this kind could not occur on any substantial scale until it was recognized that such feoffees were morally bound to abide by the wishes of their feoffor. The conceptions of trusteeship which already existed in the late thirteenth century must already have helped to produce such a principle. But the decisive contribution to its development must have been the employment of feoffees in effecting settlements. They could not have been employed by so many landowners if it had not been generally accepted that they must perform their duties strictly according to the injunctions of their feoffors.[2] At the end of the thirteenth century, therefore, the emergence of uses in the form which was known by the end of the middle ages was already very near at hand.[3]

Nevertheless, such examples of uses as can be found in the chancery rolls and other published sources of the thirteenth century all relate—with the exception of the settlements made by William Percy and the earl of Derby—to landowners who did not belong to the magnate class. It was, in fact, the first half of the fourteenth century which witnessed the appearance of enfeoffments to uses on the great landed estates of the realm, a process which is revealed by the Patent Rolls of the period. A search of these shows that during this period the Crown began to license

[1] In the early fourteenth century this remained true even if seisin was transferred by a formal ceremony in court in a *fine sur done grant et render*. But this device was rarely employed, probably because the title it gave was inadequate against others than the parties to it and their heirs. (Holdsworth, III., 241–2).

[2] See *CPR*, *1292–1301*, p. 540 for a settlement performed by the heir of the original feoffee.

[3] The importance of the employment of feoffees to effect settlements is discussed briefly by Plucknett, *Common Law*, pp. 577–8.

the alienation of lands held in chief to groups of persons, without specifying any details of any settlements which these feoffees were to perform. It is necessary to peruse the lists of feoffees in such licences carefully in case they were groups of relatives, since, if so, it is possible that the enfeoffment in question was merely some sort of family settlement which conferred estates for their lives on those so enfeoffed, with remainder in fee to one of them. But, when there is no evidence of close family relationship between the feoffees, it is safe to infer that we are dealing with an enfeoffment to uses. In addition, the Patent Rolls contain a number of letters patent of confirmation and *inspeximus* in which the Crown confirmed enfeoffments to uses of lands which were not held in chief. On 24 November 1304 Henry Bulebek received a licence to grant a manor held in chief to Eleanor Ewell, Geoffrey Neyrnut and William Neyrnut, to hold to them and the heirs of Eleanor.[1] But we cannot be certain that this was a case where the *cestui que use* was enfeoffed jointly with the feoffees, since the two latter appear to be related. However, on 1 June 1317 John Paynel obtained a licence to grant two of his manors held in chief to two other persons who appear to be unrelated.[2] Early in the reign of Edward III examples of enfeoffments to uses become more frequent. On 1 May 1331 John, son of Gilbert Mickleham, received a licence to enfeoff John, son of Adam Apperderle, and John, son of John Mickleham.[3] In 1332 David Strabolgi, earl of Athol, demised four manors to different groups of persons, at rents of one penny in each case, for periods of years—five in the case of three and ten in the case of one—and subsequently at substantial rents which were probably higher than the net values of the manors, an expedient no doubt intended to ensure their recovery by himself or his heirs.[4] Although these arrangements clearly relate to some sort of mortgage, it is noteworthy that they were made through the agency of feoffees. On 12 September 1333 two unrelated persons obtained a pardon for acquiring lands from a tenant-in-chief.[5] On 8 November 1333 Thomas Everingham

[1] *CPR, 1301–7*, p. 291. Cf. ibid., *1313–17*, p. 337.
[2] ibid., *1313–17*, p. 658.   [3] ibid., *1330–4*, p. 107.
[4] ibid., *1330–4*, pp. 305–6 and 308.   [5] ibid., *1330–4*, p. 468.

was given a licence to grant to two persons and the heirs of one of them a third of the manor of Garthorpe at an annual rent of 20 marks payable to him for life.[1] In 1337 two apparently unrelated persons obtained a pardon for acquiring certain lands in fee.[2] On 5 June 1337 two separate licences were granted to a tenant-in-chief to enfeoff two clerks of separate portions of land.[3] On 12 November 1337 Henry, earl of Lancaster, received a licence to grant a manor to his daughter Isabella and Henry de la Dale, for the life of Isabella.[4] On 10 June 1338 and 7 April 1339 respectively two tenants-in-chief were given licences to grant lands to groups of feoffees for life.[5]

These details comprise all those licences to alienate down to 1340 which might appear to refer to conveyances to feoffees to uses, although it would be unwise to assume that all of them fall within this category. In several of them land is conveyed to feoffees and the heirs of one of them, so that the feoffees were seised to the use of one of themselves, a practice which was employed frequently down to the sixteenth century.[6] From 1340 to the end of the reign of Edward III in 1377 the number of licences to make enfeoffments to uses enrolled on the Patent Rolls increases to a marked extent: they totalled approximately seventy, of which approximately two-thirds were issued in the last decade of the reign.[7] An examination of their contents shows that it was in this period that enfeoffments to uses became popular among leading members of the nobility. Portions of their inheritances, sometimes quite substantial ones, were so settled by Robert Ufford, earl of Suffolk, in 1342,[8] Thomas Beauchamp, earl of Warwick, in 1345,[9] Henry, earl of Lancaster, in 1349,[10] Edward, lord Despenser, in 1359,[11] Roger Mortimer, earl of March, in

---

[1] ibid., *1330–4*, p. 477.   [2] ibid., *1334–8*, p. 431.
[3] ibid., *1334–8*, p. 464.   [4] ibid., *1334–8*, p. 553.
[5] ibid., *1338–40*, pp. 101 and 216.
[6] For some discussion of this practice see below, pp. 154–5.
[7] Approximate totals are necessary since a number of the entries each comprise more than one licence or pardon.   [8] *CPR, 1340–3*, p. 502.
[9] ibid., *1343–5*, pp. 517–18.   [10] ibid., *1348–50*, p. 374.
[11] ibid., *1358–61*, p. 244. For another enfeoffment to uses by him, see ibid., *1374–7*, p. 289.

I

1359,[1] Henry, duke of Lancaster, in 1361,[2] Richard, earl of Arundel, in 1366,[3] John of Gaunt, duke of Lancaster, in 1366,[4] John Hastings, earl of Pembroke, in 1369,[5] Humphrey Bohun, earl of Hereford, at some date prior to his death in 1373,[6] Edmund, earl of March, in 1374,[7] Walter, lord FitzWalter, in 1375,[8] and William Ufford, earl of Suffolk, in 1375 or earlier.[9]

Thus there is abundant evidence that uses of land were becoming popular among English landowners in the first half of the fourteenth century. But the nature of the settlements so created requires deeper examination. Uses, in the sense in which they were understood in the late fourteenth and fifteenth centuries, could comprise several different types of settlements. The feoffees might hold the land to the use of a particular individual for his life, or some other specified period. Or they might have been given it for the purpose of effecting a settlement, in fee or in tail, on a man, or on him and his wife jointly, perhaps after a period of time in which its issues were to be employed by them according to directions they had received. But the most frequent, and, in both legal and social terms, the most important type of use was one in which the feoffees held land for the purpose of carrying out the directions which the *cestui que use* drew up in his lifetime but which were to take effect after his death.

The beginnings of this practice can certainly be traced in the thirteenth century. As we have seen, there are a number of cases in which a landowner made arrangements, in the event of his death, for the guardianship of lands which were held to the use of his children. And it is difficult to believe that those who did this omitted to issue directions regarding the disposal of the revenues concerned until the infant beneficiaries came of age. Similarly, a contemporary Durham chronicler tells us that William, the last

---

[1] *CPR, 1358–61*, pp. 266–7.

[2] ibid., *1358–61*, pp. 575–6 and 580. For the settlements carried out by the feoffees after his death, see ibid., *1361–4*, pp. 114 and 118, and *1364–7*, p. 50.

[3] ibid., *1364–7*, p. 198.   [4] ibid., *1364–7*, pp. 333–4.

[5] ibid., *1374–7*, pp. 72 and 78.   [6] ibid., *1374–7*, pp. 33–4.

[7] ibid., *1370–4*, p. 264.

[8] ibid., *1374–7*, pp. 122 and 191. In the latter case the feoffees appear to have been mortgagees.   [9] ibid., *1374–7*, p. 203.

of the Vesci lords of Alnwick, who died in 1297, had conveyed his estates there to Antony Bek, bishop of Durham, 'trusting in him that he would keep it to the use (ad opus) of his little illegitimate son William and surrender it to him when of age'.[1] Although there are strong grounds for disbelieving this story,[2] there can be no doubt that a well-educated contemporary thought it both credible and feasible. Moreover, he employed the expression ad opus in explaining the nature of bishop Bek's responsibilities.

Search of the extant inquisitions post mortem down to the death of Edward III[3] has brought to light a large number of instances in which, on the death of a landowner, his estate in a portion of his inheritance had been conveyed to a group of persons whose position appears to indicate that they were seised to his use. In 1316 the inquisition on the death of William Prutz, whose daughter and heir was over age and married, states that some of his manors, held of a mesne lord, had been alienated by him to three persons for their lives, at an annual rent of £24 to himself for life.[4] In 1317, in the case of John Knoville, whose heirs were three daughters, all under age, we learn that long before his death he had enfeoffed two persons of one of his manors to hold to them and their heirs.[5] An inquisition held in 1319 on the death of John Paynel, whose heir was a married daughter over age, describes the alienation to feoffees of some lands held in chief (with the King's licence).[6] In 1322 we are told that Gilbert Pecche, some of whose lands were held in chief and whose heir was under age, had twenty years before demised a manor held of the earl of Pembroke to two persons, their heirs and assigns, who were to render £30 a year to him and his heirs, after the expiration of a term which still

---

[1] *Historiae Dunelmensis scriptores tres* (Surtees Soc., vol. IX), p. 91.

[2] On this see my article, 'The Percies' Acquisition of Alnwick', *Archaeologia Aeliana*, 4th ser., XXXII (1954); also Bean, p. 5, n. 4.

[3] A search of those of the reigns of Henry III and Edward I has yielded no trace of uses, apart from the inquisitions mentioned above.

[4] *CIPMA*, V. 368 (no. 572). The feoffees took the fealty of the tenants on 20 January 1316 but had received no other issues.

[5] ibid., VI. 5 (no. 16). A penny rent and the services of one tenant were excepted.

[6] ibid., VI. 111 (no. 184); *CPR, 1313–17*, p. 658.

had six years to run.[1] In 1322 John Harcla on his death-bed granted eighteen bovates of land in Westmorland to Andrew Harcla, who was to enfeoff John's son, under age at the time of the grant.[2] According to an inquisition of 1328 two feoffees had recently been seised jointly with Philip Brenlees of the manor of Talgarth in Wales, to hold to them and the heirs of Philip's body.[3]

During the reign of Edward III the number of landowners who died leaving some portion of their inheritances in the hands of persons who appear to be their feoffees underwent a considerable increase. A summary of the contents of the relevant inquisitions

TABLE IV. *The Growth of Uses, 1327–76*

Ten-year periods:	1327–1336	1337–1346	1347–1356	1357–1366	1367–1376	Totals
Deceased who had conveyed to feoffees to uses[4]	7	9	22	36	56	130
—as percentages of totals of deaths recorded[5]	—	—	3·3	5·8	13·0	—
Deceased *cestuis que usent* who left heirs under age[6]	7	6	17	26	34	90
—who held of the King in chief	2	4	12	21	43	82
—who remained seised of all lands held in chief	—	1	8	14	27	50

post mortem is provided in Table IV, which is based upon a list given in Appendix II. In assessing the significance of this material it is important to remember that the surviving inquisitions do not

[1] *CIPMA*, VI. 212 (no. 353).   [2] *CMI*, II. 265 (no. 1072).
[3] *CIPMA*, VII. 143 (no. 177).

[4] Robert del Isle is not included: in his case an inquisition was held in 1342 because he had entered religion.

[5] Thirteen of these occurred in 1349. There is, however, no evidence to suggest that the Black Death encouraged the practice of providing for families by means of uses.

[6] The totals of deaths recorded in inquisitions *post mortem* in these years will be published separately.

give a complete picture of contemporary uses. It is possible that, when heirs were over age and no lands were held of the Crown, escheators did not bother to record details of uses. It is equally possible that they were less than thorough in searching out uses of lands held of mesne lords. Moreover, many inquisitions have not survived. We may, therefore, be certain that the details summarized in Table IV and Appendix II minimize, rather than exaggerate, the extent of uses at this time. Indeed, a close inspection of Appendix II reveals that, in comparison with other years, there were striking increases in the numbers of uses recorded in the plague-years of 1348–9, 1361–2, 1369 and 1375. There can thus be no doubt that the uses revealed by death in any given year were only a fraction of those in existence.

A careful analysis of such details as we possess yields valuable conclusions. In the first place, it is apparent that throughout the reign of Edward III there occurred a gradual increase in the numbers of landowners who resorted to enfeoffments to uses. In the second place, we can see that there was a pronounced upsurge in their popularity in the last decade of the reign when, in terms of percentages of the total deaths, more than twice as many landowners had employed uses as in the previous decade. In the third place, it seems likely that in most of the uses recorded in inquisitions *post mortem* there was a connexion between the existence of the use and a minority: 70 per cent of the *cestuis que usent* who died left heirs under age. In the fourth place, our evidence suggests that during the reign of Edward III enfeoffments to uses developed on the fees of mesne lords to a greater extent than on those of the King. Almost 40 per cent of the *cestuis que usent* held no lands at all of the Crown. Of the rest, almost 60 per cent had conveyed to uses only lands held of mesne lords and remained seised of all the lands they held in chief. Those who had conveyed to uses lands held in chief formed only 25 per cent of the total.

The impression that uses were more extensive on the fees of mesne lords than on those of the King is strengthened when we examine a petition presented by the magnates in parliament in 1339. This requested that 'remedy be ordained in this parliament concerning persons who, when dying, make alienation of their lands, and have themselves carried outside their manors, by fraud to deprive the chief lords of the same'.[1] In interpreting the imprecise language of this complaint we must reject any suggestion that it refers to normal conveyances of land, since it is definitely stated that its concern is with the deliberate evasion of the incidents of tenure. It is clear that the tenants took care to conform with the rules of the common law regarding the transfer of seisin and thus ensured that they were not in occupation at the moment of death. Yet they delayed their removal from the land as long as possible, a circumstance which, together with the accusation of deliberate fraud, suggests that the land continued to belong to their heirs. These features of the situation presented in the mesne lords' complaint can only be explained in terms of the creation of uses. The absence of any mention of the term 'use' need occasion no surprise, since the mesne lords were concerned with their loss of incidents, not with the legal definition of the practices responsible for this. There can, therefore, be no doubt that as early as 1339 uses were being employed by the tenants of mesne lords to evade the incidents of tenure. Indeed, such practices were so extensive as to lead mesne lords to demand redress in parliament.

Two general conclusions emerge from this discussion of the evidence relating to uses during the reign of Edward III. In the first place, the practice of enfeoffing feoffees to uses appears to have begun among the lower orders of feudal society. When we first begin to obtain substantial evidence in the inquisitions *post mortem*, it is clear that uses were much more frequently employed on the fees of mesne lords than on those of the Crown. The extant inquisitions contain no trace of many feudal tenants; and the parliamentary petition of 1339 probably refers to those who were not important enough to attract the attention of royal escheators. A study of Table IV shows that during the next forty years their social superiors, including great earls and barons, began to follow their example on an increasing scale. In the second place, the available evidence suggests that there was a change in character of uses in the early years of the fourteenth century. Those which can be traced from the thirteenth century are all

---

[1] *Rot. Parl.*, II. 104a.

connected with a *specific* purpose—the profit of an individual or the performance of a settlement. But most of the references to uses that we find in the early fourteenth century provide no precise indication of the purpose. Instead, we merely learn that a number of persons held at a landowner's death lands which formerly belonged to his inheritance. In view of the paucity of such references, it may be risky to argue from their silence in the matter of purpose. But, especially when we bear in mind the contents of the parliamentary petition of 1339, it is difficult to avoid the impression that a basic change in character had occurred. Whereas in the thirteenth century uses had tended to be created for specific purposes, now they were increasingly employed for the purpose of making arrangements which were to take effect after the death of a *cestui que use*.

These conclusions raise the problem of the relationship between a *cestui que use* and the feoffees who held lands to his use at the time of his death. By what means did he ensure that the estates held by them were dealt with according to his wishes after his death? In the first half of the fourteenth century there is very little evidence to help us solve this problem. It is possible that in many cases landowners were content to leave verbal directions to their feoffees, a practice that can still be traced in the early fifteenth century.[1] It is likely that many, either at the time of the enfeoffment of the feoffees or shortly afterwards, entered into indentures of agreement with the feoffees in which their duties were precisely defined. A copy of such an indenture, made by a leading magnate, has survived.[2] In 1345 the feoffees who held a large portion of the estates[3] of Thomas Beauchamp, earl of Warwick, granted him an annual rent of £373, an expedient which was undoubtedly intended to secure the profits of the estates to the earl in his lifetime, despite the vesting of the legal title in the feoffees. On his part the earl granted that, if he died within twelve years of the making of the indenture, the rent should cease to be payable until a total of £2733 6s. 8d. had been levied therefrom

[1] *C.P. Chan.*, I. xliii.
[2] *CPR, 1343–5*, pp. 517–18.
[3] None of these was held in chief.

and divided between his daughters.[1] Thereafter it should be lawful for the earl's heirs to re-enter and hold the estates for ever. It is, however, almost certain that, at the time this indenture was drawn up, landowners had already begun the practice of issuing directions to their feoffees in their testaments.[2] The first who is known to have done this was Sir Hugh Cressy who, in a testament dated 1 May 1346, ordered his feoffees to convey his manors of Risegate and Braytoft to his wife after his death.[3] It is likely that, if their testaments also had survived, we should know of many others who engaged in the same practice about this time, if not earlier. But it is equally likely that other landowners, especially those of the magnate class, had doubts about the wisdom of issuing directions to feoffees in this way, since less than two years previously the earl of Warwick made provision for his daughters' dowries by means of an indenture with his feoffees.

Any such doubts appear to have disappeared in the course of the next generation. Before Edward III's reign had ended we learn of a number of important landowners who had incorporated directions to their feoffees in their testaments[4]—Sir Guy Beauchamp in 1359,[5] Thomas Beauchamp, earl of Warwick, in 1369,[6] John Hastings, earl of Pembroke in 1372,[7] Sir William Burton in 1373,[8] Sir Roger Digge in 1375[9] and Sir Nicholas Lovaine in 1375.[10] The extent to which this practice was now thoroughly

---

[1] £1200 to Elizabeth, 1000 marks each to Mathilda and Philippa and £200 to Katherine.

[2] The word 'testament' is here used in the strict sense of the term, i.e. a body of directions concerned with the disposal of the deceased's chattels after his death and with the arrangements for his burial.

[3] *Early Lincoln Wills*, p. 16. A royal licence to enfeoff the feoffees was granted on 24 May 1346 (*CPR*, *1345–8*, p. 120) and another on 25 March 1347 to settle on the widow for life, with a remainder in fee (ibid., *1345–8*, p. 263).

[4] We cannot, of course, exclude the possibility that they had also made the same, or other, directions, in separate deeds.   [5] *Test. Vet.*, I. 63–4.

[6] ibid., I. 79; Holmes, p. 49, n. 3, quoting Register of Archbishop Whittlesey, f. 110.   [7] *Royal Wills*, p. 93.

[8] *Early Lincoln Wills*, p. 38.   [9] *Test. Vet.*, I. 90.

[10] ibid., I. 99. References to uses cannot be traced in the testaments of Sir Robert Hastings (1346) and Henry, duke of Lancaster (1361). Cf. Holmes, p. 55, n. 6.

accepted may be judged from the fact that, whereas Thomas Beauchamp, earl of Warwick, in 1345 employed an indenture with his feoffees to raise dowries for his daughters after his death, twenty-four years later he bequeathed lands to a younger son by means of directions to his feoffees which were incorporated within his testament.

In view of the extent to which uses were employed by this time, it is not surprising that during the last quarter of the four-teenth century parliament in its legislative activities began to pay attention to them. In the first place, when those found guilty in the parliamentary trials of the period were sentenced to the forfeiture of their estates, it was found necessary to insert in the relevant statutes provisions which brought lands held to their use within the terms of the forfeiture. The first instance of this practice occurred in the case of the sentence imposed on Alice Perrers by the Good Parliament of 1376,[1] a precedent followed by the Appellants in 1388[2] and the Crown in 1397[3] and in all the acts of attainder of the fifteenth century.[4] In the second place, the need arose for legislation to prevent the creation of uses for deliber-ately fraudulent purposes. A statute of 1376 gave creditors the right of execution on the lands and chattels of debtors who 'do give their tenements and chattels to their friends, by collusion thereof to have the profits at their will', thus hoping to avoid repayment of their debts.[5] A statute of the following year dealt with the situation in which plaintiffs in actions relating to real property were deprived of their rights because the defendants 'do commonly make gifts and feoffments of their lands and tenements which be in debate . . . to lords and other great men of the realm, against whom the said pursuants, for great menace that is made to them, cannot nor dare not make their pursuits'. It laid down that in such circumstances these enfeoffments should be regarded as

---

[1] *Rot. Parl.*, III. 14a.   [2] *Statutes*, II. 50–1 (11 Ric. II, cc. 2–3).

[3] *Rot. Parl.*, III. 377b–8b and 380b–2.

[4] e.g. ibid., V. 226, 349–50, 479–80, 513.

[5] *Statutes*, I. 398 (50 Ed. III, c. 6). A statute of 1377 (ibid., II. 12: 2 Ric. II, st. 2, c. 3) laid down the procedure to be followed when debtors, who had employed such practices, fled into privileged franchises.

null and void.[1] Although the abuses the statute was combating involved 'maintenance' by powerful men, it is clear that, from the purely legal standpoint, they acted as feoffees to the use of those they protected, since the statute ended by emphasizing that it applied to alienations in which 'the feoffors take the profits'. A statute of 1391 forbade the practice whereby uses had been employed to evade the provisions of the Statute of Mortmain[2] and compelled those churchmen who had profited from the granting of lands to their use to obtain retrospective licences of amortization.

In the light of all these details there can be no doubt that it was the reign of Edward III which saw uses become part of the accepted structure of English landownership. When Edward III came to the throne in 1327, the practice of holding lands to the use of another had been known for at least a century. And there are distinct signs that its popularity was increasing during the late thirteenth and early fourteenth centuries. But during the fifty years of Edward III's reign, especially its latter half, the available evidence indicates a rapid upsurge in the popularity of uses. Indeed, the most striking illustration of the acceptance of the device as a legal institution is provided by the King himself: when he died in 1377, Edward III left lands in the hands of feoffees to be handled by them according to his wishes.[3] The King himself was emulating the example of the magnates of the realm, just as they in the previous generation or two had copied the practices of their tenants.

(ii) The Problem of Origins

The problem of the origins of uses in later medieval England is twofold. On the one hand, we have to explain how this particular

---

[1] *Statutes*, II. 3–4 (1 Ric. II, c. 9). Suits were to be commenced within a year of the disseisin or right of action. In 1403 the plaintiffs in cases of disseisin were allowed to bring actions during the lifetimes of the original disseisors, although the time-limit for other plaintiffs remained as before (ibid., II. 134: 4 Hen. IV, c. 7). These provisions were further clarified in 1433 (ibid., II. 279: 11 Hen. VI, c. 3).   [2] ibid., II. 79–80 (15 Ric. II, c. 5).   [3] *Rot. Parl.*, III, 60–1,

device for settling land arose out of the legal institutions which were known to contemporaries. On the other, we have to discuss the reasons for its growth and popularity from the point of view of the social and economic needs of the landowning classes. Neither part of the problem can be understood unless considered in the light of the character of uses and the chronology of their growth. In the form in which they finally emerged uses involved the existence of one or more persons who were the owners at common law of a certain portion of land but in fact held it to the use of another—that is, they would employ the revenues, or the land itself, as directed by him, during his lifetime or after his death. Now, while it is possible to find persons who held land to the use of another in the thirteenth century, it is not until the end of that century that we begin to find any evidence that the feoffees who so held the land were employing its revenues, or conveying it, according to the directions of a *cestui que use*. Indeed, we have to wait a decade or two before our evidence becomes full and convincing on this point.

A number of historians have put forward theories explaining the origins of uses. But none of them is satisfactory, since in each case our attention is drawn to a legal institution or doctrine which, although analogous to the use, is in basic respects distinctly different from it. One analogy in the sphere of Roman law is to be found in the idea of *usufructus*[1]—the right to the temporary enjoyment of a thing, as distinct from the ownership of it. But the relationship between the owner and the usufructary was not that of the later use: the property was not held to the use of the usufructary, whose position was nearer that of a tenant for life or someone else with a more limited estate. A more impressive Roman analogy is to be found in the *fidei-commissa*.[2] This was a practice whereby a testator instituted an heir and at the same time requested him to dispose of the whole, or part, of his property in a particular way. This device certainly bears two similarities to the later use. First, it was developed as a means of evading legal

[1] For fuller details, see e.g., W. A. Buckland, *A Text-Book of Roman Law from Augustus to Justinian* (2nd ed., reprinted: Cambridge, 1950), pp. 268–74.
[2] ibid., pp. 353–9.

restrictions on successions and legacies in the later Republic. And, second, there was in the beginning no means of compelling the heirs so instituted to perform their obligations. In due course this device was absorbed within the jurisdiction of the courts and later Roman law, therefore, can be said to have possessed a system of testamentary trusts. But, interesting and attractive though the similarities between the *fidei-commissa* and uses may seem, there is no means by which we can establish a direct connexion between this particular institution of later Roman law and that of later medieval England. Indeed, the resemblance between it and the office and functions of the English executor is even more striking and, in the light of this fact, it would seem highly likely that any connexion between English law and the *fidei-commissa* is to be found in the office of executor, since the canon law which was administered in the ecclesiastical courts was much influenced by the doctrines of Roman lawyers. In any case, the details of the development of uses in England make it very improbable that there was any direct connexion between them and Roman law. If this had existed, we would expect to find the first traces of uses among the great landowners of the kingdom. Yet, as we have seen,[1] the first traces are to be found among lesser men, many of them below the knightly class.

The American Justice Holmes drew attention some eighty years ago to the possibility that the feoffee to uses was descended from the *Salman* of early German law to whom land was transferred in order that it might be conveyed by him according to the grantor's directions.[2] But, even if an institution so similar to the later feoffee existed in Western Europe so soon after the fall of the Roman Empire, we are still left with the need to establish a direct connexion between the *Salman* and the feoffee to uses. It is difficult to believe that doctrines identical with those of the *Salman* were flourishing in thirteenth-century England, since the available evidence indicates that the practice whereby feoffees to uses conveyed land after the death of their grantor only properly emerged at the end of the century at the earliest.

[1] See the details given in Table IV and Appendix II.
[2] O. W. Holmes, 'Early English Equity: 1. Uses', *LQR*, I (1885), 163-4.

Equally unsatisfactory as complete explanations are the views of Maitland and Holdsworth. Maitland[1] drew our attention to the growth of the Franciscan order in thirteenth-century England and the impact of their ideas upon legal institutions. Their attempt to live without property compelled them to distinguish between ownership and beneficial occupation, an effort in which they must certainly have been helped by the doctrines of Roman law on the *usufructus*. But evidence which Maitland himself adduced revealed uses of a sort in England before the friars came in any strength. In 1279 the papal bull *Exiit qui seminat* declared that the *usus* of which the friars were beneficiaries were not property. However, not only can plentiful evidence of uses be found in England before this date but the conception of a trust is expressed in a royal statute four years previously. Aware as he was of the defects and limitations of his predecessors' theories, Holdsworth attempted to solve the problem of origins by declaring that,

Though we must look to the Salman or Treuhand for the origin of the idea that property could be entrusted by its owner to a person who was bound to deal with it according to the wishes of the owner, the shape which that idea took in English law is wholly the result of the manner in which the interest, both of the man who thus entrusted the property and of the third persons for whose benefit it was entrusted, was protected by the Chancery. The use of today is product of the equitable jurisdiction of the chancellor.[2]

This view, though perhaps not a surprising one to meet in a lawyer looking backwards at the growth of an institution, judged from the standpoint of the historian puts the cart before the horse. The Chancellor's jurisdiction in uses arose from the fact that they already existed and fraudulent feoffees were becoming a serious nuisance.[3] Indeed, it developed in the course of the fifteenth century, whereas uses had already started to emerge a century before.

A careful consideration of the available evidence reveals three separate strands in the development of uses in England in the thirteenth and early fourteenth centuries. The first is the existence of a practice whereby a person or persons held land to the use of

[1] e.g. in Pollock & Maitland, II. 231 and 237–8.
[2] Holdsworth, IV. 417–18.   [3] See section (iii) of the present chapter.

another, the presence of which is attested from late Anglo-Saxon times.[1] It is possible to argue that it was influenced, if not created, by the *Salman* doctrines of early German law. But it is more likely that it had deeper and older origins and may itself have produced the *Salman*. However much lawyers might equate ownership and seisin in the later middle ages, it must be remembered that a legal profession as a distinct social entity was the product of Anglo-Norman and, more especially, of Angevin England. Before professional lawyers introduced their coherent doctrines and rigid definitions, men had handled the problems of owning land in a much looser way. It would not be surprising if circumstances arose in which a man found it desirable to hand his land over temporarily to another—perhaps, for example, the need to make a lengthy journey away from home. Similarly, he might look after the land of a female relative or an infant who had not yet reached the age of discretion. Indeed, it is circumstances of this type which provide the contexts in which we find the term 'use' employed in the twelfth and thirteenth centuries. Viewed from this standpoint, the uses of *Bracton's Note Book* and the early assize rolls are survivals of an earlier age, before the imposition of feudal tenures had transformed a loose body of customs into a rigid land law.

The second strand in the development of uses is the growth of a conception of trusteeship. In early times the distinction between this and uses as a whole would have been hard to draw. Indeed, it may be argued convincingly that a situation in which the relationships between the parties could be comprised within the phrase 'to the use of' would always have implied the reposing of a trust by one side in the other. Nevertheless, it is apparent that a clear conception of a trust had emerged in England by the end of the thirteenth century, to be found in a number of different contexts —in c. 48 of the Statute of Westminster of 1275 as well as in documents enrolled on the chancery rolls. The very fact of the emergence of an independent conception of trusteeship is bound to have led contemporaries to examine more carefully the nature of the relationships involved in uses and the benefits they promised.

[1] Pollock & Maitland, II. 229–30 and 233–5 and references.

The third strand was the most important, because it involved the development of an institution on which uses could be modelled. The late thirteenth and early fourteenth centuries witnessed the emergence of the executor as the agent who was responsible for the administration of the affairs of a deceased person after his death. By the middle of the fourteenth century his duties embraced not only the performance of the deceased's testamentary requests and legacies but also the payment of his debts.[1] It is probably in this aspect of the development of uses that we are closest to the influence of the Germanic *Salman* and the law of Rome. The former was the model on which Germanic peoples based their first attempts to create executors, while the Roman *fideicommissa* influenced its development through the medium of the canon law.[2] It is likely that it was the conception of the executor as the personal representative of a deceased person that led to an increasingly powerful realization among contemporary landowners and their legal advisers that those who had hitherto held land to the use of another during his lifetime could continue to hold it after his death and employ it or its revenues as he had directed them before he died. In a sense, therefore, a feoffee to uses came to be viewed as an executor who handled on behalf of the deceased, not chattels, but lands. There was, both in practice and in law, a distinction between the functions of the executor and those of the feoffee to uses. The executor undertook a trust which began after the death of the deceased, and carried out his duties by virtue of the probate of the testament by the ecclesiastical authorities. The position of the feoffee was more complicated. Owing to the rules of feudal law on this point it was not possible for the land to pass to him by virtue of the death of the deceased. If, therefore, he was to handle the lands thereafter, he had to receive seisin in the lifetime of the deceased. The solution of this difficulty was found in the manipulation of the uses which some landowners already employed, a development which was

[1] ibid., I. 336 and 343-8; Holdsworth, III. 563-85.
[2] On this point, see the valuable remarks in Sheehan, pp. 148-9. Previous discussions of the origins of the executor have underrated the influence of Roman law.

facilitated by the practice sometimes followed of leaving lands in feoffees' hands for long periods when away from home—for instance, when on crusade. In this way the functions of an 'executor' who handled land were grafted on to the ancient practice whereby land might be held to the use of another. The nature of the sources available to us makes it impossible to give positive proof of this theory of the origins of uses, since, while we have some information on the structure of legal institutions and the ways in which they were used, at no time do we possess any explanation of current legal changes by a contemporary. Nevertheless, the arguments which have been presented do possess the merit that they explain the emergence of uses in the late thirteenth and early fourteenth centuries, in the form in which they were later known, in terms of a legal development—the rise of the executor—which was occurring at the same time.

Our theory of the origins of uses is strengthened by the existence of evidence which shows that the landowners of this period were suffering from the effects of legal changes which had recently occurred and were certain to impel them to seek such opportunities of improving their position as were offered by the legal practices of the time. In 1267 c. 6 of the Statute of Marlborough[1] virtually outlawed the two methods which had hitherto been employed to evade the incidents of feudal tenure. Those who wished to engage in such evasion had now to find other means. Their motives in doing so would not merely have been the avoidance of relief, wardship and marriage for their heirs but also to organize after their deaths the exploitation of the revenues that would otherwise have accrued to the feudal lord. At the same time as the search for new methods of evasion was proceeding, certain financial pressures upon landowners were increasing. The exclusion of the heir from the administration of the affairs of a deceased, and the growth of the total responsibility of the executors for these, meant that the revenues from the lands of the inheritance could no longer be employed for the payment of debts. Uses, as they had emerged by the middle of the fourteenth

[1] *Statutes*, I. 20–1.

century, provided a means whereby landowners could not only evade the incidents of feudal tenure but also devise their lands and the revenues therefrom as they wished. In this analysis, therefore, the financial and legal situation of English landowners in the late thirteenth and early fourteenth centuries impelled them to find some means of devising land by will, despite its prohibition under feudal law. Although the rapid development of the office of executor during this period was partly responsible for their difficulties, it also showed the way out of them: its functions suggested how they might manipulate the practice of holding land to the use of another in order to solve their problems. In consequence an ancient practice became a legal institution with functions which revolutionized existing land law.[1]

Not all landowners were able to avail themselves of these opportunities as soon as they appeared. There was no obstacle in law to prevent mesne tenants from alienating their lands to whomsoever they wished. Indeed, since nearly all the evidence about their activities comes from the records of the Crown, it is quite possible that many mesne tenants began to grant their lands to feoffees to their use at earlier dates and to a greater extent than our sources indicate. But until the statute of 1327[2] there were serious risks attached to such alienations on the part of tenants-in-chief. Not only had a royal licence to be obtained but there was no absolute guarantee that it would be granted. If the alienation occurred without one, the land would be seized by the Crown. And, although it was the practice to restore it to the alienee after a fine had been paid, tenants-in-chief before 1327 could not have felt so certain on this point as to venture on any scale upon methods of settling land which had both the intention and the effect of evading royal rights.[3] Although a few examples of what appear to be enfeoffments to uses on the part of tenants-in-chief

---

[1] It is interesting to note that in a number of London wills of the late thirteenth century executors are directed to hold real property in trust for purposes laid down by the testator (*WHC*, I. pp. 1, 11, 26–7). But it would be unwise to see a connexion between this practice and the development of uses, since the lands concerned were held in free burgage and hence devisable by will.

[2] 1 Ed. III, st. 2, c. 12.   [3] See above, Chapter II (ii), passim.

K

can be found before 1327,[1] it was only after this date that they could make such arrangements with complete security from royal intervention. A royal licence for this purpose could be obtained once the necessary procedure had been followed: but, even if it was not, the resulting transgression upon the rights of the Crown would be pardoned upon payment of a reasonable fine.

Accordingly there are strong grounds for suggesting that uses during the period of their origins grew both at an earlier date and to a greater extent among mesne tenants than among tenants-in-chief. In some measure, of course, the distinction between the two types of feudal tenant is a legalistic one, since in practice those who held in chief of the Crown would very often also hold land, sometimes in considerable quantity, of lords other than the King. A study of the figures provided in Table IV shows that during the period when uses were emerging, when such landowners wished to create uses, they tended to choose for this purpose lands held of mesne lords, not the King. In 1327–76, out of a total of 130 deceased *cestuis que usent*, 81 were tenants-in-chief. But, of these, only 33 had conveyed holdings in chief to uses. There can thus be no doubt that most tenants-in-chief deliberately chose lands held of mesne lords for their enfeoffments to uses. There are clear signs that towards the end of Edward III's reign they became more ready to choose holdings in chief for this purpose: of the total of 33 who did so in the years 1327–76, 7 died in the years 1357–66, and 17 in the years 1367–76. It is possible that the tendency to create uses from lands held of mesne lords, rather than those held of the King, was due to the hostility felt by tenants-in-chief towards 'prerogative wardship'.[2] But there are other considerations which provide a more plausible explanation of this phenomenon. First tenants-in-chief must have deliberately exercised caution in their evasion of royal rights: when uses were first being

[1] In the event of serious losses being caused through such alienations, it was not wholly inconceivable that, in order to protect its interests, the Crown would make claims similar to those made in 1320–1 (see above, pp. 98–101).

[2] On two occasions they unsuccessfully demanded its abolition—in 1258 in c. 3 of the Petition of the Barons (*Select Charters*, p. 374) and in parliament in 1327 (*Rot. Parl.*, II. 10b and 12a, no. 35).

employed, and the Crown's attitude towards them was as yet uncertain, its intervention against uses must have seemed more likely
if holdings in chief were so settled. Second, in the case of mesne
holdings no licence to alienate was required.

Nevertheless, whatever their motives, it is quite clear that
tenants-in-chief in their earliest efforts to create uses lagged behind
mesne tenants and that, in consequence, when uses first emerged
in the late thirteenth and fourteenth centuries, they did so within
the lower ranks of English landownership. The leading landowners did not begin to employ the device for two generations
or so, although, since it must have been employed for some time
by those who held land of them, they must have been aware both
of its existence and of its potential advantages.

The reasons why in their employment of uses the magnates
were content to follow the lead of those who were their inferiors
in terms of both landed wealth and feudal tenure must remain
obscure. It is difficult to believe that the explanation lies solely in
the uncertainty which surrounded alienation of lands held in chief
before 1327, since they could easily have alienated lands held of
other lords. What, indeed, is especially noteworthy about their
attitude towards uses is the fact that they did not themselves
employ them to any marked extent until after *c.* 1340. It is, perhaps, more likely that the size of their inheritances made them
less prone to suffer from the restrictions of feudal tenure—for
example, they could without serious discomfort provide younger
sons with settlements in tail or daughters with *maritagia*, parental
duties which might seriously deplete the resources of lesser men.
Moreover, some magnates benefited from concessions given by
the Crown whereby on their deaths it sought the repayment of its
debts from their heirs, instead of their executors. When, however,
their own tenants began to enfeoff to uses on an increasing scale, they
realized both the extent to which this development was going
to deplete their own feudal revenues and the advantages that
might accrue to themselves if they followed suit. These arguments
must have seemed even more powerful after they had failed in
parliament in 1339 to put an end to their tenants' practices.[1]

[1] ibid., II. 104a.

In assessing the magnates' motives we must beware of exaggerating the influence of any decline that actually occurred in their feudal revenues. When they began to employ the device themselves, the damage caused by their tenants' uses cannot yet have been serious. But they must have realized that a continuous decline in their feudal revenues was now inevitable. Since this could not be prevented, their best policy was now to recompense themselves by seeking the same benefits as their tenants. To this the law relating to alienations in chief from 1327 onwards placed no obstacle.

The precise nature of the advantages which landowners hoped to gain when they created uses deserves more detailed attention. The fact that, when a *cestui que use* died, it was his feoffees who were seised at common law meant that the lands held by them escaped the incidents of feudal tenure to which they would have been liable if he had died seised himself. But it would be wrong to conclude from this that the motives which led a landowner to make enfeoffments to uses were basically fraudulent ones. Some historians have asserted that one of the purposes of such conveyances was to prevent the widow of a *cestui que use* from obtaining her dower after his death.[1] In view of the rules developed by the common law on this point by the beginning of the fifteenth century it is difficult to see how this suggestion can fit the facts. A widow had an absolute right to one-third of the lands which were solely held by her husband during her marriage and to which any issue she had by him might succeed. Even if part had been alienated by him before his death, she nevertheless had the right at common law to obtain the original dower from the alienees, a right which could, if necessary, be prosecuted in the courts.[2] It is possible that enfeoffments to uses made it more difficult for widows to assert such rights. But there is evidence to show that several widows in the fourteenth and fifteenth centuries successfully sued for their dowers against their husbands' feoffees in the court of Common Pleas.[3] Indeed, such directions to

[1] The list of complaints against uses (*temp.* 1536) printed in Holdsworth, IV. 578 (no. 16) gives this as one of their consequences.

[2] ibid., III. 193–4, with full references.

[3] e.g. *CPR, 1348–50*, p. 535; ibid., *1422–9*, pp. 281–3.

feoffees as have survived in wills and elsewhere contain abundant evidence that widows thereby often obtained estates for life which were more considerable than those they would have obtained through dower alone.

Evidence has certainly survived to indicate that fraudulent motives played some part in the early development of uses. Some persons in the middle years of the fourteenth century employed enfeoffments to uses to evade the Statute of Mortmain[1] or to ensure that their lands stayed out of the clutches of creditors. But, although some of the growing popularity of uses at this time may have been due to such motives, it is certain that their influence must have waned thereafter, since such practices were forbidden by statute—in 1376 and later in the case of frauds perpetrated on creditors and in 1391 in the case of evasions of mortmain.[2]

One other possible fraudulent intention requires more detailed investigation—the desire to avoid the dangers of forfeiture in the event of treason or felony on the part of the *cestui que use*. There are some strong reasons for thinking that this motive may have played some part in the origins of uses. In 1310 a statute promulgated in the Irish parliament laid down that the strict provisions of the law of forfeiture were to apply 'if any man enfeoff another of his land, with intent to enter into rebellion, or to commit any other felony, and after the felony committed, to have again his said land'.[3] It is clear from the language that is employed that the type of enfeoffment envisaged in the statute is akin to, if not identical with, an enfeoffment to the use of the grantor.[4] There can, therefore, be little doubt that those who feared the dangers to themselves and their families of the loss of their inheritances through treason or felony were already at the opening of the fourteenth century attempting to avoid them by means of settle-

[1] For illustrations in the case of Oxford colleges, see *LQR, LXXXI* (1965), 565.

[2] For fuller details and references, see above, pp. 125–6.

[3] *The Statutes and Ordinances of the Parliaments of Ireland*, I (Dublin, 1907), pp. 270–1 (c. 6).

[4] The language of the text contains nothing which supports the statement of Holdsworth (IV. 443, n. 2) that 'this would seem to refer to feoffments made on a common law condition and not to uses'.

ments which are best regarded as enfeoffments to uses. It is true that our only evidence is of purely Irish provenance. But it is difficult to believe that English landowners were not in touch with events in Ireland, especially since some of them held lands there. Moreover, it would have been remarkable if legal institutions in this respect were more advanced in Ireland than in England. The absence of references to similar transactions in England can no doubt be explained on the ground that the political events of Edward II's reign absorbed the full attention of both Crown and parliament. When the King and his supporters triumphed in 1322, their complete military and administrative supremacy made an English equivalent of the Irish statute of 1310 superfluous.

In fourteenth-century England the law relating to forfeiture was complicated by the uncertainty of the position regarding entails. In 1348 a person hanged for felony forfeited entailed lands,[1] while the Statute of Treasons of 1352 contained no explicit exemption of entails from its provisions.[2] Moreover, entailed lands had not been immune from forfeiture during the troubles of Edward II's reign. In the light of these considerations it is difficult to avoid the conclusion that, during the first half of the fourteenth century when uses were emerging, some, if not many, landowners must have employed them in the hope that they would thereby escape the forfeiture through treason or felony of the lands thus settled. It is worth noting that the ancestors of seven of the magnates who enfeoffed to uses in Edward III's reign—the duke of Lancaster, earls of Arundel, Hereford, Northampton and March, and lords Mowbray and Despenser—had forfeited all their estates, including all those entailed, in the years 1322-30. In assessing the strength of the desire to escape the consequences of treason or felony amongst the motives behind the emergence of uses it is necessary to distinguish between the leading magnates, on the one hand, and the rest of the country's landowners on the other. The former would be very much concerned

---

[1] *CMI*, II. 518 (no. 2062).
[2] Cf. M. V. Clarke, *Fourteenth Century Studies* (Oxford, 1937), pp. 131-2, where it is stated that the exemption was 'tacitly confirmed'.

with the dangers of treason in respect of possible forfeiture but would not feel especially anxious over the consequences of felony, since we may generally assume that their position and the influence they could command could secure for them an effective immunity from the ordinary criminal procedures which might result in a sentence of forfeiture. We cannot exclude the possibility that memories of the forfeitures of Edward II's reign and the early years of his successor helped to persuade them during the next generation or two to employ enfeoffments to uses, especially since these events had destroyed, and the Statute of Treasons done nothing explicitly to restore, any doctrine that entailed lands were exempt from a sentence of forfeiture. At the same time, however, it is unlikely that such motives were present in equal strength in the case of every magnates' decision to create a use, since most of them had no ancestors who had recently suffered forfeiture. In any case, the effects of the fear of forfeiture on the early development of uses must have been short-lived. From 1388 onwards the precedent set in the condemnation of Alice Perrers in 1376 was followed and every act of forfeiture and attainder passed in parliament expressly included in its provisions the estates which were held to the use of the attainted person.[1] In 1410 a feoffee of Henry Percy, earl of Northumberland, failed to recover a manor with which he had been enfeoffed to the earl's use and which had been forfeited through his attainder.[2] The hope might, of course, remain that the creation of a use would help to conceal the lands concerned from royal administrators. But, if it existed, it was a forlorn one and must soon have been recognized as such: the available evidence indicates that after every attainder, especially those of the Wars of the Roses, careful and successful investigations were made by the Crown, which for this purpose

---

[1] On this point see C. D. Ross, 'Forfeitures for Treason in the Reign of Richard II', *EHR*, LXXI (1956), 569–70. The sentence of forfeiture pronounced on Alice Perrers in 1376 stated that the forfeiture of lands held to her use was not to apply to the others convicted or be taken as a precedent for the future (*Rot. Parl.*, III. 14a).

[2] *YBVE*, 11 Hen. IV, Hil., p. 52, pl. 30; PRO, K.B.27/592/*Rex*, rot. 12.

often employed the services of commissioners specially appointed
to search out all the lands held by the attainted person.[1] While,
therefore, we cannot exclude the possibility that some of the
earliest enfeoffments to uses among the magnates were the consequence of their fears of forfeiture for treason, from 1388 onwards it becomes increasingly difficult to discern the presence of
similar motives behind enfeoffments to uses.

Landowners who did not belong to the first rank were in a
different situation, since they were much more likely to be involved in the hazards of criminal procedures which might result
in a felon's forfeiture. In this event any lands held to their use
would not be forfeited, since at common law they would not
be seised and, in consequence, their heirs would not be disin-
herited. But our evidence does not permit us to generalize about
the extent to which this fact may be regarded as a motive for
erecting uses. In default of a fuller knowledge of the working of
the criminal courts in the later middle ages and the precise quantity and incidence of sentences of forfeiture for felony, it is hard
to believe that many substantial landowners would need to fear a
sentence of forfeiture in normal conditions. But, the lower his
position in the social scale, the more likely a person was to fear
this danger and, therefore, regard it as a compelling reason for
granting his lands to feoffees to his use.

In the light of this discussion it would seem unwise to see in any
of these 'fraudulent motives' powerful reasons for both the

[1] There is an interesting piece of evidence which draws attention to the
possibility that during the Wars of the Roses landowners may have attempted
to evade forfeiture in the event of the defeat of their side by enfeoffing feoffees
who belonged to the opposing side. According to T. D. Whitaker (*History of
Richmondshire* (London, 1823, II. 261–2)) such arrangements were made by
Sir Thomas Harrington between November 1458 and the campaign which
ended in the battle of Blore Heath. But this story must be treated with caution.
It is based, not on a perusal of the original deeds, but on a summary of them
drawn up some years later in a dispute over the lands concerned with the
Mounteagle family. Later in the same passage Whitaker gives details which
conflict with this story: he tells us that the feoffees' attorney received seisin on
6 February 1457—that is, eighteen months before November 1458. I have to
thank Professor J. S. Roskell for drawing my attention to this reference.

origins and the spread of uses. It would be equally unwise to ignore the influence of the fear of forfeiture altogether. But its significance is a matter of doubt and is, in any case, confined to the period before the death of Edward III in the case of the nobility. However, it is hardly necessary to draw up a list of reasons for the employment of uses by English landowners when we know that this device enabled them both to evade the incidents of feudal tenure and at the same time to deal as they wished with the lands held by their feoffees. The connexion between these two motives is a complex one. On the one hand, when a landowner died leaving an heir under age it was the financial opportunities created by the success of evasive practices which enabled him to employ the revenues of the lands concerned as he wished after his death: their removal from the lord's hands during wardship immediately and inevitably raised the problem of how they were to be administered until the heir came of age. On the other hand, when the heir was over age, although the lord was deprived of his relief, the heir was deprived of the lands, perhaps permanently if his ancestor had directed his feoffees to convey them to someone else in fee. In the origins of uses we are dealing with a development in which the desire to evade the incidents of feudal tenure merged into the desire to devise land, if necessary away from the heir. It is extremely difficult to decide which of these motives was the more powerful during the period when uses were emerging, since it is only in the middle years of the fourteenth century that we begin to find details of the directions given to feoffees in the wills of *cestuis que usent*. It is, however, clear that, if landowners simply wished to evade the incidents of tenure, they did not need in the late thirteenth and early fourteenth centuries to resort to uses. There were a number of settlements which were perfectly legal, although they deprived lords of their rights. A tenant could enfeoff his heir and a stranger, the fee simple being limited to the heirs of the heir. Or he might convey to a stranger for life, with remainder to the heir in fee. Or he might make a lease for life, or a gift in tail to his heir, with or without a remainder over in tail. In none of these instances, if he died leaving an heir within age, would the enfeoffment be regarded as collusive. None fell within the terms of c. 6 of the Statute of Marlborough.[1] It is true that, where a stranger was involved, there was a real danger of difficulties over the relationship between him and the heir; and, for this reason, if such settlements had become popular, it would have become necessary to regard the stranger's position as akin to that of a trustee. In fact, however, settlements of this type are conspicuous by their absence in the available records. There can be no doubt that landowners made no noticeable effort to employ them.[2] Had they done so, it would have been easy to legislate against their activities, just as the Statute of Marlborough had dealt with certain methods of evasion. But the need for legislation never arose: when Coke summarized the law on this subject,[3] these devices remained legal.

In view of this, it is impossible to avoid the conclusion that evasion in itself was not the motive of those who created the earliest uses. They sought to pay debts out of their landed revenues and finance their family responsibilities. In so doing they were bound to deprive the lord of his rights; but this was the consequence, rather than the cause, of their activities. The absence of evidence prevents us from discovering which motive—the payment of debts, or family responsibilities—was the more powerful. It is quite possible that some employed uses for the purpose of making settlements which were to take effect after their deaths.[4] But, during the period when uses were emerging, the risks involved would deter most from following this practice.

A study of the printed wills of the late fourteenth and fifteenth centuries shows that the main advantages of uses to a *cestui que use* were twofold. First, he was able to provide his executors with the revenues needed for the performance of their duties, including the payment of debts. Second, he was in a position to make grants of

---

[1] *YBVE*, 33 Hen. VI, Pasch., pp. 14–16, pl. 6.

[2] See *CIPMA, passim.*   [3] Coke, *Second Institute*, p. 111.

[4] A contemporary Durham chronicler told how William, the last Vesci lord of Alnwick, conveyed it to Antony Bek, bishop of Durham, in order that he enfeoff his illegitimate son. There are strong grounds for disbelieving this story (see my article, 'The Percies' Acquisition of Alnwick', *Archaeologia Aeliana*, 4th ser., XXXII (1954); also Bean, p. 5, n. 4). But the chronicler thought the transaction a feasible one.

land to his widow and daughters and younger sons, or raise mar-
riage-portions. The widow could be given a life-estate greater
than the dower to which she was entitled by feudal custom. His
feoffees could be directed to grant lands in fee or in tail to younger
children. We can illustrate these various intentions from the directions that have survived from the latter half of the fourteenth
century. In the first extant testament which mentions feoffees, Sir
Hugh Cressy in 1346 ordered his feoffees to convey two manors—
apparently the whole of his inheritance—to his wife for life after
his death.[1] In one of the earliest testaments mentioning feoffees,
John Hastings, earl of Pembroke, declared, 'I desire that all my
debts be paid by the hands of my executors and by the hands of
the feoffees of my manors. Also I devise that all the moneys
above-named . . . in this testament be raised and paid from the
issues coming from the manors and lordships which the feoffees
on my behalf hold of my gift'.[2] In 1380 William, lord Latimer,
directed his feoffees to make settlements in tail, mainly on John,
lord Neville, and then ordered that 'if our movables cannot suffice
to acquit our debts and reward our servants as is devised in our
testament and to perform our will of the said testament, . . . all
the lands of our purchase are to be sold to those who wish to give
most'.[3] In 1387 Richard, lord Poynings, made simultaneous provisions for his debts and his younger children, when he ordered
his feoffees to retain four manors and certain rents in their hands
for twenty years in order to enable his executors to pay his debts
and provide for the marriages of his younger children.[4] The most
well-known example of a direction to feoffees in which they were
ordered to settle lands on younger children is that of John of
Gaunt, duke of Lancaster, who in 1398 in a 'codicil' of his testament directed his feoffees to make various settlements on the
Beauforts, his children by Katherine Swynford.[5] But thirty years
earlier, in 1369, in one of the earliest testaments that contains

[1] *Early Lincoln Wills*, p. 16.

[2] *Royal Wills*, p. 93. This testament was proved on 16 August 1376. A
second one, proved on the following 16 November, contains no mention of
feoffees (ibid., pp. 95–7).

[3] *Test. Eb.*, I. 115–16.   [4] *Test. Vet.*, I. 122–3.   [5] *Test. Eb.*, I. 236–9.

directions to feoffees, Thomas Beauchamp, earl of Warwick, had directed his feoffees to settle on his younger son William in tail male lands worth 400 marks a year.[1]

A discussion of uses during the period of their emergence would not be complete if it omitted to draw attention to the fact that their growth in popularity within the ranks of the nobility and gentry coincided with the opening stages of the Hundred Years' War with France in the reign of Edward III. A landowner who followed the King to France would know that he might meet his death in battle there. It is, therefore, worth considering whether the fear of death in the French wars prompted English landowners to make enfeoffments to uses and at the same time issue directions to their feoffees regarding the disposal of their lands in the event of their deaths on active service. A search of the available records brings to light several who made dispositions of this sort. In 1347 William Hastings, being about to go abroad, granted a manor to feoffees on condition that, if he died abroad, they should pay his debts and found a perpetual chantry for his soul, but, if he returned, he was to re-enter the manor and hold it as before.[2] In 1360 Sir John Colville granted all his lands to feoffees for the same reason, on condition that, if he returned, he should have them back, but that, if he should die, they should enfeoff his son and heir thereof.[3] In 1372, having granted most of his lands to feoffees and being about to sail for France, John Hastings, earl of Pembroke, declared that, after they had paid his debts from the revenues thereof, they were to enfeoff William Beauchamp.[4] In 1373, when about to leave on John of Gaunt's French expedition of that year, Sir William Cauntelo granted his estates to feoffees on condition that they should re-enfeoff him if he returned but, if he died, enfeoff Thomas, son of Sir Robert Roos of

---

[1] *Test. Vet.*, I. 79.   [2] *CMI*, III. 28 (no. 78.)

[3] *CIPMA*, X. 550-1 (no. 655). He died within a few months, but his son was over age. At first, however, this was a matter of dispute and the enfeoffment was regarded with suspicion by the Crown (*CPR, 1358-61*, p. 554; ibid., *1361-4*, pp. 3 and 147; *CCR, 1360-4*, pp. 215 and 225).

[4] ibid., *1374-7*, pp. 286-8. This declaration was in due course rendered invalid, since he returned from France and a male heir was born to him (ibid.).

Ingmanthorpe. It is interesting to note that the proceedings en
rolled on the parliament roll which give us these details mention
at one point that Sir William had stated that he wished to enfeoff
feoffees because Sir Ralph Hastings, who was going on the same
expedition, had made similar dispositions.[1] Sir Roger Grey in
1369,[2] William Luffwick in 1372,[3] Sir John Norwich in 1373[4]
and, at some date before 1377, Robert Bourdevile[5] all enfeoffed
feoffees before going on the King's service overseas. A search of
the licences to alienate to feoffees in the course of Edward III's
reign brings to light two which relate to dispositions made by
tenants-in-chief who were about to set out on overseas expeditions. In 1349 Henry, earl of Lancaster, who was going to Gascony
on the King's service, received a licence to grant lands and rents
worth £1000 a year for twelve years to certain persons who were
to provide from the profits for certain charges according to an
ordinance which he was to make.[6] In 1366 John of Gaunt, duke
of Lancaster, was given a licence to grant a number of his manors
to a group of feoffees who were bound in his behalf for various
sums of money which he had borrowed for the equipment and
passage of himself and his men on an expedition to Gascony.[7]

No doubt these details do not provide a complete list of all
those English landowners who conveyed their estates to feoffees
to uses in circumstances which were associated with their service
in the King's French wars. Even so, it would be unwise to see in
their fears of death in battle abroad an important factor in the
growth of uses in the fourteenth century. The evidence of such
motives at work which has been collected from the records of the
period is not substantial enough to justify such a view, since it is
clear both that many created uses who did not fight in France and
that many were doing so before the French wars started. But it
would be equally unwise to ignore the influence of the French
wars in this respect altogether. The head of a family and the owner
of a landed inheritance who was about to set out on an expedition

---

[1] He did return and was re-enfeoffed (*Rot. Parl.*, III. 79a-80b).
[2] *CIPMA*, XIII. 84 (no. 109.)   [3] ibid., XIV. 183 (no. 170.)
[4] ibid., XIV. 43 (no. 46.)   [5] ibid., XV. 6-7 (no. 16.)
[6] *CPR, 1348-50*, p. 374.   [7] ibid., *1364-7*, pp. 333-4.

from which he might not return would naturally think of the financial situation which would face his family in the event of his death and of the arrangements he would then like to be made concerning the disposal of his inheritance. When the wars with France started in the fourth decade of the fourteenth century, uses already existed to provide the most convenient means of dealing with these problems. However, the existence of such needs on the part of those who fought in France was not confined to the first phases of the Hundred Years' Wars but continued throughout the period of hostility with France.[1] Indeed, in the late fifteenth and early sixteenth centuries the Crown found it desirable to assist its leading subjects' needs in this respect in order to further the recruitment of contingents for service abroad. When Edward IV was planning his expedition to France, a parliamentary statute was promulgated which permitted royal tenants who went on the King's service to convey their lands to feoffees without payment of fines. It also laid down that, in the event of their deaths on active service leaving heirs under age, their feoffees were to hold all the lands concerned during the heir's minority, even though the feoffments were collusive—that is, deprived the Crown completely of its rights of wardship.[2] On two occasions when he too was planning to invade France, Henry VII found it necessary to make similar arrangements.[3] In 1512 the government of Henry VIII promulgated a statute which made such arrangements permanent and laid down that they should always apply in future

[1] See, e.g., the arrangements made by Sir Thomas Strickland when about to set out for France in the reign of Henry V (J. Nicholson and R. Burn, *The History and Antiquities of the counties of Westmorland and Cumberland* (London, 1777), I. 94).   [2] *Statutes*, II. 446–7 (14 Ed. IV, c. 1).

[3] ibid., II. 529–30 and 550–1 (4 Hen. VII, c. 4 and 7 Hen. VII, c. 2). That of 1490 granted concessions which were virtually the same as those given in Edward IV's statute. That of 1492 granted the lands of the deceased to his feoffees for a term of four years only during the minority of the heir. It also laid down that the King was to retain the marriage of his tenant's heir. But, although this statute's concessions were less than its predecessors', it did confer a benefit which is absent from their provisions, in that, if the tenant died within three years of his return from the King's service, his feoffees were to enjoy the wardship for the rest of the four years following his return.

to those landowners who went on royal service on expeditions overseas.[1] Each of these statutes mentions that these benefits are conferred on those setting out on royal service in order that they might provide for the performance of their wills.

The Hundred Years' War had other equally important, if less tangible, effects on the development of uses. Those who fought in France incurred expenditure in equipping themselves and those followers who belonged to their households, needs which must have strengthened their desire to make satisfactory provision for the payment of their debts. But the development of the contract system of military service over a period of numerous campaigns meant that they had to create a nucleus of personnel on whose services they and, through them, the King, could rely in time of war. Hence fees and annuities were granted out of estate revenues and the need to secure the permanent services of the recipient made it desirable to grant them to him for his life. Such practices had two consequences which were highly relevant to the development of uses. First, the net revenues of estates were reduced so that the financial pressures created by the existence of any debts were aggravated. Second, it was desirable for a landowner who granted fees and annuities for life to ensure that such dispositions were not interfered with after his death—for instance, in the event of the minority of his heir, when the Crown had the right to dispossess the recipients during the term of the minority.[2] Such considerations must have encouraged many to enfeoff lands to uses. It is, of course, most probable that the majority of those

---

[1] ibid., III. 26–7 (3 Hen. VIII, c. 4). Those serving in permanent garrisons on the Marches or overseas were excepted from the statute's provisions. It is noteworthy that the language employed in the text of this statute and both those of Henry VII indicates that their provisions applied to all military tenants, and not tenants of the King alone. But it would be wrong to assume that this constituted a real and effective intrusion by the Crown upon the rights of mesne lords. Each of these statutes assumes that the deceased will have made his will, since each states that the wardship is to be employed in performing it. Before these statutes mesne lords were already losing their rights through the existence of uses. And the statute of 1490 (4 Hen. VII, c. 17) specifically recognized their loss of wardship if a will had been declared.

[2] See above, p. 8–9. See also, e.g., *CPR, 1408–13*, pp. 391 and 393.

who acted thus from such motives belonged to the ranks of the leading nobility, since they alone possessed the resources which made possible the creation of a permanent nucleus of personnel from whom contingents for war service might be drawn. In this connexion the will drawn up in 1386 by Hugh, earl of Stafford, is especially interesting, since he explains that one of his intentions is that 'all our servants to whom we have granted lands or annual rents may be made sure of having and enjoying them for term of life in the best and safest manner'.[1]

In all these respects the wars with France and their social and economic consequences helped to create a climate which was favourable to the growth of uses. But it is essential to avoid construing them as decisive factors in the origins of uses. The motives which led the landowners of England, great and small, to engage in enfeoffments to uses lay deep within the social and economic needs of a system of landed inheritance which was based on primogeniture. And developments in English law and society in the thirteenth and early fourteenth centuries added to the primary paternal impulse to provide for younger sons and daughters the need to make provision for the payment of debts from landed revenues after death. For this, however, the existing rules of law made no provision. In explaining the spread of uses among the landowning classes of England in the fourteenth and fifteenth centuries we must thus give first place to the problems which would face any landowner who was also the father of a family. If the effects of the Hundred Years' War deserve attention—the fear of death on active service, the expenses of preparing for expeditions and, among the magnates, the provision of fees and annuities—they served only to bring home to those who fought abroad the financial needs and family duties which had already led to the emergence of uses.

(iii) THE PERIOD OF DEFINITION

By the death of Edward III in 1377 uses, although they had become one of the devices normally employed in the settlement of

[1] Lambeth Palace, Reg. Courtenay, f. 220, quoted in Holmes, p. 53.

land, had not yet been fully absorbed within the legal system. From then until the passing of the Statute of Uses in 1536 there followed a period in which the nature of the relationship between the *cestui que use* and his feoffees was protected and defined in the courts of law.

During this period the practices which had emerged in the course of the fourteenth century developed further. Landowners continued to incorporate directions to their feoffees within their testaments. But, as these directions became increasingly detailed and complicated, they began to issue them in a separate document, specifically intended for this purpose. This came to be known as the 'last will' (*ultima voluntas*), a term previously used to denote testamentary directions not made in the proper form.[1] Generally, though not invariably, it was entered in the probate registers when the testament was proved. The testament and 'last will' were not necessarily drawn up together—indeed, an examination of any probate records shows that periods of months, even years, might separate them. No doubt the practice of entering both documents in the probate registers began because the former often contained references to the revenues which were thereby made available to the executors and thus fell within the jurisdiction of the ecclesiastical authorities concerned with the probate of testaments.

Strictly speaking, therefore, as a result of the emergence of feoffees to uses, we see the appearance of a new type of legal document. The first landowner who is known to have employed a 'last will' was William, lord Latimer, who drew one up six weeks before his death in 1381.[2] Thereafter this method of issuing

---

[1] On the term 'testament' in its strict sense, and the use of the expression 'last will' by ecclesiastical lawyers, see *Reg. Chich.*, II. xix; Holdsworth, III. 537.

[2] *Test. Eb.*, I. 115–16. The testament was dated 10 July 1380 and the 'last will' on 13 April 1381. Written in French, the latter begins, *Remembrance de nostre darrein volente.* It should, however, be noted that its last clause is testamentary in character, comprising a bequest of money.

Holdsworth (IV. 420) states that, 'A will of 1355, which contains such directions (i.e. to feoffees to uses), is drawn up in the form of a deed, and perhaps operated as an intermediate settlement of the property comprised in it,' citing *Test. Eb.*, I. 67–8, and implying that it reveals an intermediate stage in

L

directions to feoffees became increasingly popular. A study of any of the probate records of the late fourteenth and fifteenth centuries shows that contemporary landowners and their lawyers were careful to distinguish between the testament and the 'last will'. Whereas in his testament a man bequeaths his chattels, using the words *do et lego*, in his *ultima voluntas* he disposes of real property, directing his feoffees thereto by the words *volo quod* . . .[1] However, though this distinction in terms of law and terminology was generally observed, it remained in some measure a theoretical one and many testators did not adhere to it absolutely. It remains in practice possible for the testament, though mainly concerned with chattels, to contain directions to the feoffees, while some testators ignored any careful distinction between the two types of document. We can also find examples of a 'last will' which contained directions which were testamentary in character.[2] It would, however, be wrong to assume that every *cestui que use* gave directions to his feoffees in his 'last will' or, possibly, his testament. Some entered into indentures of agreement with their feoffees the terms of which embodied their directions concerning the disposal of their lands or revenues after their deaths:[3] others drew up deeds poll before witnesses in which they declared their wishes.[4] Even in the early sixteenth century the practice existed whereby the original deed of enfeoffment rehearsed the terms of

---

the growth of the practice whereby directions were given to feoffees which were to take effect after the death of their feoffor. But an examination of the manuscript register in which the deed is entered (Borthwick Institute, York: Registers of Wills, I. fol. 38) does not support either Holdsworth's view of it or its implications. Although the title *Ultima voluntas* . . ., as in the printed text, is entered in the margin of the entry in the register, it is placed between two testaments proved respectively on 8 September and 6 October 1391. The deed, however, belongs to the year 1355. Although the presence of a copy of the deed in the register supports the view that it was some sort of death-bed enfeoffment, it is impossible to understand the legal or administrative reasons for its entry in the register almost forty years later. It would clearly be unwise to infer any conclusions from the register clerk's use of the heading, *Ultima Voluntas*.

[1] *Reg. Chich.*, II. xix.   [2] ibid., II. xx.
[3] e.g. *CAD*, I. 329 (B. 1201).   [4] e.g. ibid., I. 412 (C. 273).

the use to which the feoffees were seised[1] or a schedule was annexed which set out the details of the use.[2] Nevertheless, a search of probate records, inquisitions *post mortem* and collections of deeds indicates clearly that the 'last will' was the method of issuing directions to feoffees which most landowners favoured.

It is not difficult to explain the reasons for this preference. One of the chief reasons for enfeoffments to uses was the desire to repay debts from the landed revenues of a *cestui que use* after his death; yet this was a function of the executors which would have to be defined in a testament. There must, therefore, originally have existed a strong feeling that it was desirable to issue directions to the feoffees in a document which could be associated with the testament proper. Hence there appeared in this sense the term 'last will', hitherto associated with testamentary directions which were drawn up some time after the original testament. After the death of a *cestui que use* it was in the interest of his executors to encourage the practice whereby this 'last will' was entered in the probate register together with a copy of the testament. Moreover, this procedure had an additional advantage from the standpoint of the heirs and beneficiaries of the deceased, in that a permanent and trustworthy record of the deceased's wishes in respect of his landed property was preserved. Indeed, by the end of the fifteenth century there were compelling reasons why a *cestui que use* should avoid declaring the terms of a use in the original deed of enfeoffment. By that time it had become an accepted legal doctrine that a use so declared could not be changed thereafter.[3] Of course, if it was declared in the deed of enfeoffment that the feoffees were to

---

[1] e.g. T. Madox, *Formulare Anglicanum* (London, 1702), pp. 413-14 (no. 747) and 414-15 (no. 749), in both of which the feoffees were seised in tail.

[2] e.g. *CAD*, I. 81-2 (A. 696), 458 (C. 738); ibid., II. 8 (A. 1864).

[3] *Brook's New Cases*, p. 41; *YBVE*, 5 Ed. IV, Mich., p. 8, pl. 20. If the last will was annexed to the deed of feoffment, the position remained uncertain until 1540 when it was decided that, if a man made a feoffment to perform his will and the will was annexed to the charter of feoffment, and livery of seisin was made thereon, he could alter or revoke the will, though it took effect on the livery (Holdsworth, IV. 420, n. 1). See *CAD*, III. 506 (D.853) for a proviso that the *cestui que use* can revoke the will annexed in a schedule to the deed of enfeoffment.

perform the grantor's will, then the grantor was left free to declare that will in due course. But if a specific direction such as would otherwise be made in 'last will' was declared, both the *cestui que use* and his feoffees would be committed to its performance. The great merit of a 'last will' was that it could be destroyed and a new one made, or that its terms could be altered or added to in a codicil.

A landowner who enfeoffed feoffees to his use would be compelled to pay careful attention to the nature of the legal estate he so created. It was essential that he employ the services of, not one feoffee, but several. Although single feoffees are encountered in the early part of our period, three considerations made this practice undesirable. First, while one feoffee was suitable, and in the late thirteenth and early fourteenth centuries often was employed, for the purpose of effecting a settlement, the possibility that he might predecease the *cestui que use* made his employment undesirable in the case of a use which was to last a long time and was to extend beyond the death of the latter. Second, the position of the *cestui que use* and his heirs, or beneficiaries, was more secure if there were several feoffees. If lands were conveyed to one person only, it would be easy for him to claim that they were his personal property and dispose of them as he wished. But, if there were several feoffees, even if they all agreed to divert the lands to their own purposes, it would be much more difficult for them to justify their actions. Third, in the event of the death of a *cestui que use* leaving his heir under age, it was conceivable that a single feoffee might himself die during the period of the wardship leaving his own heir under age. The lord would then be able to exercise his rights of wardship and the *cestui que use*'s intentions regarding the lands would be frustrated. Similarly, if a single feoffee left a widow, she would be able to sue for dower in the lands; and, if he left no heir, the land would escheat to the lord who, of course, would not be bound by the use.

Nevertheless, the decision to employ more than one feoffee did not solve all the problems of a *cestui que use*, since he had also to decide what type of legal estate to convey to them. In theory, three possibilities existed. The first was to grant the feoffees an estate in fee in return for a rent, the payment of which might be

deferred until such time as the grantor's directions had been performed. To ensure that the feoffees then restored the land to the
grantor's heirs, the value would be fixed at a figure above the
annual value. However, such an arrangement was forbidden by
c. 6 of the Statute of Marlborough of 1267. And, even if it had not
been illegal, its usefulness would have been limited to the payment
of debts and the financing of testamentary bequests. Lands so
settled could not be sold: and, though it might have been technically possible to employ such arrangements to settle lands on
younger children or relatives, the procedures involved would
have been both complicated and cumbrous, giving the beneficiaries titles fraught with hazards. The second possibility was an
estate for the lives of the feoffees or for a specified term of years.[1]
This would certainly have the great advantage that at the end
of the term the *cestui que use* or his heirs would be certain to
recover the lands. But such an estate would deny him complete
powers of devise: although he would be able to pay debts by this
means or make funds available to his executors, he would not be
able to direct his feoffees to sell any of these lands or convey
estates in fee to his children. In consequence, though we do en-
counter a few cases of estates for lives or terms of years given to
feoffees,[2] this type of enfeoffment to uses was not common.

In fact, a *cestui que use* who wished to wield a full and absolute
power of devising his lands was compelled to employ the third
possibility—an estate in fee, since only this method enabled him
to avoid the limitations, inconveniences and dangers which might
be met in either of the other two. In this respect the development
of uses was assisted by the courts of common law: by the middle of
the fourteenth century they had evolved clear conceptions of the
different kinds of estate which might be held in co-ownership.[3]
It was now accepted that a conveyance to several persons 'and
their heirs and assigns' created a joint tenancy in which they were
seised in survivorship (*per jus accrescendi*): as each person died, the

---

[1] For a grant to feoffees for a term of one hundred years, see *CPR, 1441–6*,
p. 28.

[2] e.g. *CPR, 1340–3*, pp. 273–4; ibid., *1385–9*, pp. 311–12; ibid., *1408–13*,
p. 271; ibid., *1476–85*, p. 307.   [3] Holdsworth, III. 126–8.

title reposed in the surviving feoffees and eventually in the last survivor, descending, when he died, to his heirs. The creation of a joint tenancy of this kind had two advantages which together explain why nearly all the uses which are encountered in the later middle ages were effected by its means. First, the estate at common law so created continued after the death of the *cestui que use*. If, therefore, his heir was under age, wardship was evaded: if over, no relief was paid. Second, it gave greater security to the *cestui que use* and his heirs, since if the feoffees wished to defraud them of the lands, it was necessary for them all to agree on this course. When the purpose of the use had been effected, it was necessary for the *cestui que use* or his heirs to secure a release and quitclaim from the surviving feoffee or his heirs.[1] But, provided this precaution was taken, conveyance to a number of feoffees in survivorship gave all the facilities required by those who wished to create uses.

Nevertheless, the solution of these problems did not remove all the difficulties threatening a *cestui que use*: there was always the danger that his feoffees might refuse to carry out his directions, or even misappropriate the landed property they held in trust. There were a few expedients which might be employed to minimize these risks. Careful attention would be given to the choice of feoffees. Often, they would include churchmen, presumably because it was hoped that their consciences would be less likely to err than those of laymen. Magnates frequently chose men who were their estate officials, councillors or retainers because of the bonds of loyalty and service that lay between them. It was desirable that at least some of the feoffees were also executors of the *cestui que use*, since in their latter capacity they would be supervised by the ecclesiastical authorities and thus some indirect, however unofficial, control over their activities as feoffees would exist. A frequent expedient was for the *cestui que use* to be seised

[1] e.g. *L & P*, VII 384 (no. 1009): George Rolle to Lady Lisle, '. . . I advise you to search out the next heir of Fox, late bishop of Winchester being the survivor of all the feoffees of all the recoveries, requiring him upon the sight of the indenture and the recoveries to make a new feoffment to your friends to the uses contained in the said indenture'.

jointly with the feoffees to his own use, though this meant a prior grant to another group of feoffees who then conveyed him and others.[1] Sometimes his wife[2] would be one of the feoffees.[3]

A *cestui que use* would naturally not remain content with the choice of reliable persons as his feoffees but would also seek legal safeguards. At the time when uses were first developing it is likely that many *cestui que usent* entered into indentures with their feoffees, specifying the terms of the use. The great disadvantage of putting the precise details of the feoffor's intentions in an indenture was that it was impossible to alter or add to them without making a further indenture. For this reason many must have entered into indentures with their feoffees in which the latter simply undertook to carry out the directions of their feoffor regarding the lands entrusted to them.[4] But it was no doubt quickly realized that the existence of such indentures would make

[1] *CPR, 1354–8*, p. 270; ibid., *1385–9*, pp. 64, 110–11, 339–40, 399, 436, 439; ibid., *1388–92*, pp. 99, 255, 514; ibid., *1392–6*, pp. 272, 322, 611, 638, 659; ibid., *1396–9*, pp. 94, 185, 268, 588; ibid., *1401–5*, pp. 48, 91; ibid., *1405–8*, pp. 17, 286; ibid., *1408–13*, p. 193; ibid., *1413–6*, pp. 395–6; ibid., *1416–22*, pp. 151, 180, 247, 400; ibid., *1422–9*, pp. 4, 9, 224, 269, 290, 292; ibid., *1429–36*, pp. 86, 118, 184, 333, 446; ibid., *1436–41*, pp. 152, 289; ibid., *1441–6*, pp. 57–8, 176, 279–80, 311, 312, 331; ibid., *1446–52*, pp. 6, 245, 277–8, 284, 405; ibid., *1452–61*, pp. 86, 215, 363, 368, 422; ibid., *1461–7*, pp. 265, 459; ibid., *1467–76*, p. 13; ibid., *1476–85*, pp. 16, 173, 202; ibid., *1485–94*, pp. 116, 119, 200, 251; ibid., *1494–1509*, pp. 22, 135, 585.

[2] ibid., *1385–9*, p. 380; ibid., *1396–9*, p. 185; ibid., *1405–8*, p. 57; ibid., *1408–13*, p. 273; ibid., *1413–16*, pp. 18, 126; ibid., *1416–22*, p. 126; ibid., *1422–9*, p. 425; ibid., *1436–41*, pp. 119, 130–1, 395; ibid., *1476–85*, pp. 131, 207, 347; ibid., *1485–94*, pp. 200, 251, 268; ibid., *1494–1509*, pp. 22, 185.

[3] Occasionally a husband and wife would be seised jointly with their son as well as the feoffees (ibid., *1422–9*, p. 538; ibid., *1485–94*, p. 303) or seised jointly in tail (ibid., *1429–36*, p. 576; ibid., *1467–76*, pp. 157, 177).

[4] e.g. an indenture dated 30 December 1393 in which a group of feoffees conveyed to another group lands which they held of the grant of John Roos and Richard Roos 'under such condition that they perform the will of the said John Roos thereof when they were required to do so in his lifetime but in such a way that it would not be to the prejudice of the said Richard Roos or his heirs; and that after the decease of the said John they perform thereof the will of the said Richard Roos and his heirs in the aforesaid form whenever they were so required. And, if they refuse to perform the wills of the said John and Richard

it difficult to claim that the feoffees were seised of the lands at common law during the lifetime of the *cestui que use*. And, when the Chancery developed a jurisdiction over uses, this means of controlling feoffees became superfluous. For these reasons examples of this practice are conspicuous by their absence from the collections of later medieval deeds that have come down to us.[1]

One other precaution could only be employed by a *cestui que use* who was also a tenant-in-chief—the insertion of specific details of the purpose of the enfeoffment in the Crown's licence to alienate. But this practice on the whole appears to have been adopted only by a few magnates in the late fourteenth and fifteenth centuries.[2] Undoubtedly the need for a fresh licence, if the feoffor wished to alter his directions, discouraged other magnates or smaller landowners from following their example.

Of all the precautions against possible fraud or disobedience on the part of his feoffees that were available to a *cestui que use* none was absolutely effective. However much feoffees were bound to him by ties of friendship or loyalty, there was no certain guarantee that they would not turn against him or his family if the opportunity of their own advancement arose. Nor did the fact that the *cestui que use* was seised jointly with them impose any effective

---

in the aforesaid form, then the said John and Richard and the heirs of Richard will be fully permitted to re-enter the said lands and tenements and hold them in their original state' (Latin deed in Box A in the muniment room of Levens Hall, near Kendal, Westmorland, consulted and quoted with the kind permission of Mr. and Mrs. Robin Bagot). John's powers to devise were clearly not complete, presumably being confined to the disposal of the land's revenues during his lifetime. The most interesting feature of this document is the clause providing for re-entry by the heir in the event of the feoffees' failure to carry out their obligations. For a similar provision, in favour of the beneficiary, see *Rot. Parl.*, III. 80.

[1] Another possible expedient was a clause in the deed of enfeoffment providing for the re-entry of the feoffor if his wishes were not carried out (e.g., *CPR, 1388–92*, p. 99). But this did not ensure the performance of a will.

[2] *CPR, 1385–9*, p. 17 (Edward Courtenay, earl of Devon); ibid., *1399–1401*, p. 332 (Ralph Neville, earl of Westmorland); ibid., *1405–8*, p. 123 (Sir Roger Trumpington); ibid., *1416–22*, p. 108 (Thomas Montague, earl of Salisbury); ibid., *1429–36*, pp. 122–3 (Richard Neville, earl of Salisbury).

restraint. In the last resort, therefore, the *cestui que use* or his heirs, or those who were beneficiaries under his will, might be forced to seek a remedy against dishonest or recalcitrant feoffees in the courts of law. But in such a situation the common law in the fourteenth and fifteenth centuries was not in a position to take cognizance of uses and act accordingly. In fact, its view of the ownership of landed property could in no way be reconciled with the respective estates held by the *cestui que use* and his feoffees. Some historians[1] have suggested that the situation in the mid-thirteenth century was somewhat different: the courts of common law might yet have extended their doctrines and jurisdiction to bring uses under their control. It is true that some evidence exists to support this view. Uses were certainly encountered in the common law courts in the thirteenth century and the judges took cognizance of them. But, when such evidence is carefully examined, it becomes clear that considerable difficulties were met in dealing with uses. In one case in a seignorial court the plaintiff pleaded that the defendant held to his use, but the case was compromised and the land divided between them.[2] In other cases,[3] although the term 'use' (*opus*) may have been employed, its meaning is loose and ambiguous—in one case it covers an agreement to convey a marriage-portion, in another security for a loan and in others some sort of guardianship. These cases certainly justify the view that the lawyers were endeavouring to employ an expression which would imply a distinction between real ownership and temporary occupation and that this attitude was one of the influences which helped towards the emergence of uses. But this evidence in itself is both too sparse and too ambiguous to support adequately the argument that the courts of common law might have developed a jurisdiction which comprised uses. Moreover, uses, as they had evolved by the end of the fourteenth century, were an institution completely different from any within the common law. In them we see a distinction between ownership in law and ownership in practice which is the basis of their existence. Any suggestion that the courts of common law could have taken

---

[1] e.g. Holdsworth, IV. 415–16.   [2] *Bracton's Note Book*, III. 42–3 (pl. 999).
[3] e.g. ibid., II. 575–6 (pl. 754); and III. 529 (pl. 1683) and 648 (pl. 1851).

cognizance of uses is essentially a contradiction in terms, since their absorption within the common law would have removed a large part of their *raisons d'être*. It was the fiction at common law that the feoffees were the owners of the land that enabled landowners to evade the incidents of feudal tenure and at the same time devise their lands by will. If the courts of common law had gone beyond this fiction, it is impossible to understand how they could then have connived at the evasion of feudal incidents, especially in view of the fact that they were bound by c. 6 of the Statute of Marlborough.[1] And the suppression of evasive practices through uses would certainly have reduced the capacity and the incentive to devise land by will.

Could the courts of common law, then, give any protection to interests created under uses? A *cestui que use*, his heirs or beneficiaries might well argue that their feoffees were enfeoffed on condition that they perform duties laid down for them by their feoffor. But the doctrines of the common law in the case of conditional gifts were clear and precise and could not be manipulated to include all kinds of uses. Their nature was brought out strikingly by proceedings in parliament in 1379.[2] Edward III had enfeoffed his executors of lands purchased by him; but after his death the council of his successor Richard II prevented the feoffees from obtaining the revenues of the estates. The feoffees then complained in the Gloucester parliament of 1378 and the judges and serjeants were consulted on the points of law involved. Then, in the parliament of 1379, the feoffees requested that their petition, the question addressed to the lawyers and their answer be enrolled on its roll. From these documents it appears that Edward III had enfeoffed the feoffees without any condition on 5 October 1376 and had given them livery 'without any condition in writing or by word of mouth'. The King then, 'a long time afterwards' declared by word of mouth his wishes, of which details were given in the record. The judges and serjeants were asked whether these directions could be regarded as a condition by the law of the land, and the enfeoffment of the feoffees as a conditional gift. They answered that,

---

[1] See below, Chapter IV (i).   [2] *Rot. Parl.*, III. 60–1.

if the gift abovesaid was a simple one, as has been said, without speech (*parlaunce*) before the gift, or upon the gift, or upon the livery, concerning any charge or action that the feoffees must perform; that by no request made of them after they were in possession, namely, by the charter of the King which is of record, the said preceding gift which was simple could not be made conditional.

Thus the courts of common law would only compel feoffees to observe the wishes of a *cestui que use* if it could be proved that the original grant to them came within the definition of a conditional gift at common law.[1] But the practice whereby *cestuis que usent* delivered their instructions some time after the enfeoffment—like Edward III—created an interest which the courts of common law did not recognize. It is possible that some *cestuis que usent* employed conditional gifts in the common law sense when uses

---

[1] A case in Michaelmas 1387 appears to come within this category, since in it an heir enters for breach of condition by her father's feoffee (*Year Books of Richard II: 11 Richard II, 1387–88*, ed. I. D. Thornley, with commentary by T. F. T. Plucknett (The Ames Foundation, London, 1937), pp. xlix–l and 118–19). Though the pleadings bring to light a feoffment to uses, the case was, in fact, one of trespass. A landowner enfeoffed three friends 'on condition' that after his death they should enfeoff his widow for life, with remainder in fee to her child by him, as yet unborn. After his death, however, they enfeoffed the widow for life, with remainder to another person altogether, and it was his son and heir who entered in due course. The original feoffor's daughter and heir then ejected him and enfeoffed someone else who in turn enfeoffed the plaintiff. The disagreements between the parties appear to have led to an action in which the heir of the original remainderman was sued for trespass as a result of his entry upon the land in an endeavour to assert his rights. The details of the conditional feoffment and the feoffees' breach of it were pleaded as the basis of the plaintiff's case. A jury was empanelled to decide on the facts alleged. But, while the record in the Plea Roll certainly describes an enfeoffment to uses, it is worth noting that the discussion in the Year Book makes no mention of any feoffees but refers to two conflicting accounts of a settlement—one on a husband and wife, with remainder in fee, and one conditional in character—neither side producing a deed in evidence (ibid., p. 115). In view of these facts, it may be unwise to regard this case as evidence that the courts of common law might enforce uses in certain circumstances, since the plaintiff's case appears to have been based on the argument that the original enfeoffment fell within the category of a conditional feoffment at common law. Cf. Prof. Plucknett's remarks, loc. cit., and in *Common Law*, pp. 576, n. 5, and 677, n. 2.

were first developing. However, such instances must have been rare, since there were two powerful objections to enfeoffments to uses of this type. First, if the *cestui que use* died leaving an heir under age, the existence of a common law condition would make it easier for a feudal lord to argue and prove collusion. Second, the assistance which the courts of common law could give in such cases was a limited one, since only the original feoffor or his heirs had any right of action and other beneficiaries would be helpless. With the growing popularity of 'last wills' which gave interests to others than the heirs at common law of the original feoffor, uses which could be construed as conditional gifts at common law must have become proportionately fewer.

It is possible that some *cestuis que usent* made some attempt to secure the protection of these common law doctrines, even though the uses concerned did not conform to common law requirements. It may be unwise to generalize on this point, since most charters of enfeoffment have not survived and we are heavily dependent on the details contained in the licences to alienate granted to tenants-in-chief.[1] But a survey of the latter leaves the impression that in the fourteenth century the general practice was to make simple enfeoffments, without any mention of their purpose. However, in the next century, and the early sixteenth, it became increasingly common for a feoffor to state that the purpose of an enfeoffment was that the feoffees should perform his will. We cannot exclude the possibility that this practice arose because of an assumption that it made the performance of the will a common law condition. But no attempt appears to have been made to advance this argument in the courts. In fact, it was not discussed before 1539–40: and the view then taken was that an enfeoffment to perform the grantor's will was merely a declaration of purpose and at common law the heir could not enter for non-performance.[2] It is very difficult to see how the common law could have taken any other view on this point. On the other hand, at a time when the legal position of the *cestui que use* was insecure, the fear of litigation at common law may have impelled some feoffees to perform the wills with which they had been entrusted.

[1] *CPR*, passim.   [2] *Brook's New Cases*, p. 41.

Some historians have speculated on the reasons why the common law did not take cognizance of uses by means of the doctrines of *assumpsit* which were developing at this time.[1] *Assumpsit* formed the foundations of the later law of contract: as the Latin term indicates, its doctrines were concerned with the right of a person to have an action at law when duties undertaken on his behalf by someone else had been performed in an incompetent or inefficient manner, thus injuring his interests. From the standpoint of the *cestui que use*, his heirs or beneficiaries, an action of this kind in the courts of common law would have had the advantage that it was not necessary for a plaintiff to prove the existence of a condition, imposed at the time the enfeoffment was made: a general understanding that the feoffees were under an obligation to carry out his wishes would have been enough. But an examination of the growth of *assumpsit* shows that it developed both too slowly and too incoherently to be of any service to those who sought a court which could exercise control over uses. It is not until *Somerton's Case* in 1433 that we see fully developed the notion that a breach of an undertaking constitutes a deceit. Even so, the common law judges were prepared to provide an action in cases of misfeasance only—when damage was caused through negligence in the performance of any duties. It was not until the first decade of the sixteenth century that they began to allow an action for non-feasance—that is, failure to carry out duties undertaken. Yet the need for a court that would control feoffees to uses had existed for well over a century before this. Moreover, even if they had been fully available throughout this period, the doctrines of *assumpsit* would have provided an unsatisfactory means of dealing with uses. In the first place, as in the case of conditional gifts at common law, only the *cestui que use* or his heirs could take such action. And in this situation an heir who was losing part of his inheritance through the use would hardly be anxious to act on behalf of the beneficiaries of the deceased's will. In the second place, the relief that *assumpsit* gave would have been inadequate. The plaintiff, if successful, obtained damages. But what was

[1] For what follows see Holdsworth, III. 429-34 and Plucknett, *Common Law*, pp. 638-42.

required in the case of defaulting feoffees to uses was specific performance of their duties. In some respects *assumpsit* dealt with situations very similar to those which occurred when feoffees to uses were dishonest or inefficient. But its remedies differed substantially and fundamentally from those required by a *cestui que use* or his beneficiaries.

It is thus abundantly clear that the courts of common law in the fourteenth and fifteenth centuries were dominated by doctrines and procedures which made it impossible for them to develop a jurisdiction over uses. The victims of dishonest or inefficient feoffees were left with the last resort of the medieval litigant—the King himself as the ultimate source of all justice in the realm. Petitions were addressed to the council or the Chancellor. And, as this practice grew, there emerged a jurisdiction, forming part of what later becomes known as 'equity', whereby the Chancellor enforced the performance of the terms of uses. It is difficult to define in precise institutional terms the nature of the institution which began to deal with the grievances of *cestuis que usent* or their beneficiaries. It is likely that many of the earliest of such complaints were addressed to the King and his council, or the latter only. The precise details of the developments which led to the Chancellor alone exercising such jurisdiction are by no means clear.[1] As late as 1423[2] no clear distinction was drawn in this respect between his functions and those of the council, since in that year, although a plaintiff addressed his petition to the Chancellor, the defendants were summoned before the council.[3] But

---

[1] See B. Wilkinson, *The Chancery under Edward III* (Manchester, 1929), pp. 47–53.

[2] *S.C. Chan.*, pp. 119–20 (no. 122) where this case is dated 1422–6. It may definitely, however, be assigned to 1423, since the endorsement is dated May 15th and lists the councillors present when it was decided to subpoena the defendant. There was, in fact, such a meeting of the council on 15 May 1423 (*Proceedings and Ordinances of the Privy Council of England*, ed. Nicolas, Rec. Comm., III. 91).

[3] At the same time it should be noted that on 17 January 1423 one of the feoffees of the deceased lady Neville was examined before the council regarding the terms of her directions to them, though the reasons for the examination are not stated in the record (ibid., III. 20).

within a few years the Chancellor had taken over virtual control of jurisdiction in uses.[1]

It is easy to decide why petitioners in these matters addressed their complaints to these authorities and why they in the end succeeded in obtaining the remedies they sought. Neither the council nor the Chancellor was bound by the rigid rules of the courts of common law. It was, therefore, possible for them to examine complaints about defaulting feoffees simply from the standpoint of the truth or falsity of the petitioners' allegations. Moreover, they had in the writ of *sub poena* a procedure by which defendants could be compelled, under a financial penalty for non-appearance, to appear in person and be examined concerning the charges made against them.[2]

It is difficult to reach definite conclusions regarding the date when this jurisdiction first arose. On 22 January 1350 the Chancellor and treasurer and others of the King's council examined in the Chancery one Gilbert Blount, who was then ordered to appear before the treasurer and barons of the Exchequer on the following 25 January to do whatever should be ordained by them. His testimony described how he had been one of a number of persons who had been enfeoffed by one of the King's tax collectors of all his lands and chattels and the marriage of his heir. By selling the chattels and marriage they were to pay off all the debts he owed to the King and, if these were not sufficient, they were to sell the lands as well.[3] It is possible that this litigation resulted from a suit by the heirs for the recovery of the lands, or what remained of them.[4] But it would be unwise to assume, on the basis of this possibility, that this is a case in which the Chancellor and council protected the interests of residuary beneficiaries, since it is equally, if not more, likely that their desire to

---

[1] In July 1429 he examined the defendants alone and found in their favour (*C.P. Chan.*, I. xxi–ii), while in August 1438 he even examined defendants at one of his manors (ibid., I. xliii).

[2] J. B. Ames, *Lectures on Legal History* (Cambridge, Mass., and London, 1913), pp. 236–8, correcting the views of O. W. Holmes in *LQR*, I. (1885).

[3] *S.C. Council*, pp. 33–4.

[4] As is suggested in ibid., p. 34, n. 17. See also Holdsworth, IV. 420, and Plucknett, *Common Law*, p. 578.

examine Gilbert Blount arose from a wish to recover the debts owed to the King.[1]

In October 1375 the feoffees of the earl of Pembroke, who had died the previous April, appeared before the council.[2] They produced a schedule of his will, which had been drawn up in May 1372. It contained two main directions. The first was that, in the event of his death without issue, they were to enfeoff the King of certain lordships in Wales. The second was that they were to convey the remainder of the estates they held—virtually the whole of the rest of the inheritance—to Sir William Beauchamp, on condition that he bear the earl's arms and persuade the King to give him the title of earl of Pembroke. If he failed to meet these requirements, they were to settle the lands on Sir William Clinton on the same conditions. However, a son was born to the earl a few months after the making of this will.

It is not clear why these directions led to proceedings before the council. One possible explanation is that the Crown was pressing its rights of wardship and wished to oust the feoffees from the inheritance during the minority of the heir. The feoffees were summoned before the council to enquire into the legal basis of their claims to continue to hold the estates. This suggestion certainly receives support from the conclusion of the proceedings in which the council declared that 'because the said earl dying overseas has an heir of his body, who is now within age . . ., it is determined that the king shall have the wardship of the said castles, lands . . . until the lawful age of the said heir'. It thus took the view that the birth of an heir rendered the earl's directions to his feoffees null and void. But another explanation for these proceedings is equally likely. According to this the feoffees appeared before the council because they sought guidance about their duties. What was the legal position in the event of the infant heir's death within his minority? Would they then be under an obligation to carry out the late earl's wishes? It is quite possible that they were driven to take this course by pressure from Sir William Beauchamp. At any rate, it was more than possible that

[1] See the details of proceedings for this purpose in Dyer, II. 160a.
[2] *CCR*, *1374–7*, pp. 286–8.

the infant heir would die before he came of age. The proceedings certainly contain details which support these suggestions. The feoffees 'professed that they ever were and are ready truly to do their powers to fulfil all the wills and conditions in that schedule contained and to do nought contrary to the earl's will'. And Sir William Beauchamp appeared in person, 'praying the king and council and the said feoffees to keep whole and unimpaired the estate and right of him . . . and of his heirs therein'.

Whichever explanation is correct, we must see in these proceedings some signs of the search for a jurisdiction over uses. Even if the council's concern was with royal rights of wardship, a beneficiary appeared before it to claim his rights. And, if the proceedings did arise out of the feoffees' difficulties over their duties, both they and the beneficiary sought redress from the council. But it is very clear that the council was not prepared to adjudicate over the feoffees' duties towards Sir William Beauchamp. It might be argued that the council's decision that the birth of an heir rendered the earl's directions null and void was itself an interpretation of the feoffees' duties, since it carried the implication that the feoffees were then under an obligation to re-enfeoff the earl. But, where its own interests, as distinct from Sir William Beauchamp's, were concerned, the Crown did not stick to this principle: in the case of the Welsh estates dealt with in the earl's will, the King ensured that, in the event of the heir's death without issue, they would remain to him and his heirs.[1] The impressions we derive from a study of these proceedings of 1375 are thus far from clear. The behaviour of the feoffees and Sir William Beauchamp, and the King's own actions over the Welsh estates, all point to the existence of the idea that feoffees were morally and legally bound to carry out their feoffor's wishes. Moreover, these proceedings contain signs of an attempt to make the council into a tribunal which would enforce this principle. But the council on this occasion did not utilize the opportunity it was offered. All it did was enforce royal rights of wardship. This decision certainly implied a view of the feoffees' duties. But it did so because this was a principle which justified the ousting of the feoffees during the heir's

[1] ibid., pp. 248–9; *CAD*, III. 117 (A. 4889).

M

minority. There is no positive evidence in the proceedings of 1375 to indicate that the council regarded itself as a tribunal possessed of a jurisdiction over uses.

A few years later the council of Richard II's minority interfered with the performance of Edward III's will. Its actions imply that there was as yet no general acceptance of the doctrine that the will of a *cestui que use* must be respected. Indeed, the proceedings in the parliament of 1379 show that the late King's feoffees assumed that the only hope of asserting their rights was the argument that their enfeoffment had been a conditional gift at common law.[1] The roll of the Hilary parliament of 1380 contains a number of documents relating to a suit brought in the Chancery against the heirs of Sir William Cauntelo by Thomas, son of Sir Robert Roos of Ingmanthorpe, who claimed the Cauntelo estates by virtue of a conditional feoffment made by the deceased. The feoffees were examined by the Chancellor and the lords of the council, who also made other enquiries, but the suit appears to have failed.[2] It would be wrong to regard this case as evidence that a jurisdiction in uses already existed. While the plaintiff was the beneficiary of a use, his suit was brought against the heirs at common law, not the feoffees. Moreover, it should be noted that one of the heirs, John Hastings, earl of Pembroke, was a minor in the King's custody. The plaintiff's decision to prosecute his rights in Chancery may be satisfactorily explained as an attempt to avail himself of the rights of justice which belonged to the royal prerogative. He may also have been influenced by the existence in Chancery of procedures by which inquisitions *post mortem* might be 'traversed'. If, indeed, he was to secure his rights against the earl of Pembroke, either this procedure, or one very similar to it,[3] would have to be followed.

In the first decade of the fifteenth century the position becomes somewhat clearer. In the parliament of 1402 the Commons complained that

since rent-charges and also feoffments of tenements in demesne are made to dishonest persons by way of confidence to perform the wishes

---

[1] *Rot. Parl.*, III. 60–1.   [2] ibid., III. 79–80. Cf. *CFR, 1383–91*, pp. 349–51.
[3] For a description of this procedure, see below, p. 209.

of the grantors and feoffors, which dishonest persons fraudulently grant the said rents to other persons in respect whereof the tenants attorn and such feoffors also charge the tenements in demesne without the assent of their grantors and feoffors, who have no remedy in such case unless one be ordained by this Parliament.[1]

Since the petition clearly states that *cestuis que usent* have no remedy when their feoffees engage in frauds against them, it would seem certain that neither the Chancellor nor the council was yet prepared to intervene in such cases.[2] In his answer to the petition the King stated, 'Let this petition be committed to the King's council for their consideration until the next parliament'. But there is no trace of this matter in the records of the next parliament.

In studying the origins of a jurisdiction in uses, it is essential to distinguish between the interests of a *cestui que use* himself and those of his residuary beneficiaries. If an enfeoffment had been made to the use of the feoffor or his heirs or that of a third party, while he was alive, he himself would be able to seek any redress that was available in the courts. The court would have the advantage of hearing his version of the circumstances behind the enfeoffment; and, if it accepted his story, it would be able to direct the feoffees accordingly. But, once the original feoffor was dead, a different situation exised. The suit would have to be brought by the beneficiaries. And the issues which faced the court might well be extremely complicated, since it would have to disentangle different versions of the deceased's wishes. Faced with this prospect, long after they had been ready to enforce the wishes of a living *cestui que use*, the Chancellor and council might well be loath to take cognizance of the complaints of residuary beneficiaries. In studying the origins of jurisdiction in uses we are, therefore, dealing with two types of suit which need not necessarily have received the same treatment from the Chancellor and council. And this initial difficulty is complicated by the nature of our

[1] *Rot. Parl.*, III. 511, as translated in Plucknett, *Common Law*, p. 578.
[2] This conclusion is supported by *CPR*, *1401–5*, pp. 453–4. Shortly before his death in 1400 John, earl of Huntingdon, conveyed elsewhere a manor with which he had been entrusted to make a settlement, despite his being enfeoffed jointly with others.

evidence. For the early years of the fifteenth century few Chancery proceedings have survived; and, while their numbers increase markedly from the third decade of the century onwards, few of either these or the preceding ones are dated. Moreover, in nearly every case only the petition of the complainant has survived and we have no record of any judgement.[1]

In 1409 we meet the first case commenced by a living *cestui que use* in which we know that the Chancellor proceeded to judgement.[2] The petitioner, Joan Waterfall, a widow, alleged that she had enfeoffed William Swetnam and others now dead of certain lands and tenements 'to this intent, that they should refeoff the said Joan at such time as they were required to do so'. The record tells us that Swetnam appeared before the Chancellor by virtue of a royal mandate and, when examined, claimed that he and his co-feoffees were enfeoffed on condition that they should refeoff Joan for term of her life, with remainder to John Newton, son and heir of Robert Newton, and the heirs of his body, with a like remainder to William, John's son, with, on failure of such issue, a direction to sell the property to pay the debts of Robert, John and William. Two further enquiries were made of him. He was asked whether any of these conditions had been fulfilled and answered that they had not. To the question whether John and William Newton were dead or not, he replied that they were alive. 'Whereupon, in the said Chancery, in the presence of the said Chancellor and the Justices and Serjeants at law of the said lord the King and others of his council in the Chancery then present, it was considered that the said Joan be restored to her possession of the aforesaid lands.'[3]

Professor Hargreaves, who brought this case to light, has stated that 'from beginning to end it was dealt with from the point of view of the common law condition and not of the equitable use' and that it is 'strong evidence that uses to take effect *inter vivos*

---

[1] These remarks are based on a search of the original proceedings in PRO, C. 1/6–10.

[2] A. D. Hargreaves, 'Equity and the Latin Side of Chancery', *LQR*, LXVIII (1952), 487–9.

[3] She also recovered a box of muniments which she claimed she had given Swetnam on the same condition as the land.

were not recognized or enforced by the Chancellor in 1409'.[1] But it is impossible to see how the details he gives support these views. What happened in the case must be understood in the light of the original complaint by Joan Waterfall, in which she had claimed that Swetnam had refused to refeoff her at her request. By ordering that she recover her lands the court was accepting the truth of her allegations against her feoffee. The facts elicited by questioning him—the non-fulfilment of the conditions he alleged and the fact that the Newtons were still alive—would have served in the eyes of the court to point to the falsity of his claims and the truth of the plaintiff's allegations. It is true that the judgement of the court simply directed that Joan be restored, and did not order her feoffee to refeoff her, a circumstance which may suggest that the distinction between a use and a conditional gift at common law was imperfectly understood. Nevertheless, this case reveals that the court of Chancery was already in 1409 prepared to protect the interests of a living *cestui que use*.

It is impossible to determine precisely how long it had been exercising such a jurisdiction. It clearly did not exist before the Common's petition of 1402. But it is important to notice that the King had then undertaken to consider the Commons' grievance. It is, therefore, quite possible that the case of 1409 is the one definite survivor of a number of cases brought by living *cestuis que usent* in the court of Chancery in the years which immediately followed the Commons' petition of 1402.[2] Indeed, although the

---

[1] ibid., LXVIII (1952), 488–9.

[2] See *S.C. Chan.*, pp. 43–4 (no. 40) for a petition complaining that feoffees had refused to enfeoff the petitioner according to the terms of an agreement relating to his marriage, although he had carried out the undertakings he himself had given. This can certainly be dated after January 1398, the date of the agreement. And it was presented to Edmund Stafford, bishop of Exeter, whose second period as Chancellor ended on 28 February 1403. Since the parliament of 1402 lasted from 30 September to 25 November, we cannot exclude the possibility that it was presented between the latter date and 28 February 1403.

A case heard before the council in August 1402 is not relevant to a discussion of the origins of jurisdiction over uses, since the feoffees were joined with their *cestui que use* as plaintiffs (J. F. Baldwin, *The King's Council in England during the Middle Ages* (Oxford, 1913), pp. 522–3).

Commons in the parliaments of 1404 and 1406 showed a re-markable capacity for independence and criticism of the Crown, they made no mention of any failure to deal with their previous complaint regarding uses. In the light of this fact, it is reasonable to suggest that the royal council, when it considered the complaint of 1402, decided that the matter was best settled by its own intervention on behalf of the aggrieved *cestuis que usent*.

The origins of a jurisdiction in uses exercised after the death of the original feoffor present an even more complicated problem. The earliest case in which it can definitely be seen that the Chancellor was compelling feoffees to carry out the directions of a deceased *cestui que use* belongs to 1439.[1] On 13 November in that year Elizabeth, late the wife of John Burgh, deceased, and her husband's feoffees appeared before the Chancellor. She sought an order directing them to enfeoff her for life of her husband's estates, with various remainders in tail, according to directions given them in 1434. But the feoffees seem to have produced in evidence a will made by John Burgh in France in 1438, which, though it also gave his widow a life-estate, directed that the estates be settled in a different way after her death.[2] The Chancellor decided in favour of the directions made in 1434.[3] And, although this is not explicitly stated in the judgement, it is fairly clear that he made his decision on the ground that these directions were given in the form of a tripartite indenture. This was binding on the feoffees at common law, unless a further such indenture

[1] See *CPR, 1441-6*, pp. 112-13 (an exemplification) for a summary of the record. For the date of the parties' appearance and further details, the original (C. 66/454/m.1) has been consulted.

[2] The widow's motives are not clear, since, whichever will was performed by the feoffees, she secured a life-estate in all the lands. There are three possible explanations for her petition to the Chancellor. She may have been acting in the interests of the other beneficiaries, who otherwise might find it difficult to secure action from the Chancellor until after her death. Disputes over which of the two wills should be performed may have resulted in delays over giving her the life-estate. And the feoffees may have been in genuine difficulties over which will to enforce and arranged with her to bring an action which would produce a decision in Chancery.

[3] The exemplification was made at the request of Brian Roucliffe, who received an estate in tail under the earlier will.

was made, and could not be amended merely by the issuing of different directions in a 'last will'.[1] This judgement, therefore, possesses much legal interest in itself: although the Chancellor was exercising a jurisdiction outside the bounds of the common law, he was nevertheless employing common law rules in making his decision.[2]

The details of this case show clearly that in 1439 the Chancellor was ready to intervene in favour of the beneficiaries of uses set up by a deceased. There are, however, strong grounds for believing that he had been prepared to take such action for some decades before this date. In the first place, a great expansion appears to have occurred in the numbers of complaints relating to uses that came before the Chancellor in the first forty years of the fifteenth century. They formed 30 per cent of the 80 extant Chancery proceedings before 1426, 70 per cent of the 57 between 1426 and 1432, and 67 per cent of the 247 between 1432 and 1443.[3] Although some of the apparent increase may be due to the survival of a greater number of cases from the two later periods, these figures do indicate a marked expansion. And it is hard to believe that this would have occurred if the Chancellor had not been ready to deal with complaints of all kinds relating to uses. In the second place, in a case heard before him in July 1429 the Chancellor definitely enquired into the complaints of beneficiaries who were not the original feoffors.[4] Although he decided in favour of the feoffees, it is quite clear that he was prepared to take cognizance of such a case. In the third place, there is some reason to believe that the interests of all kinds of beneficiaries were protected in the court of the manor of Bromsgrove as early as 1422.[5]

[1] This point helps to explain the growing preference for 'last wills' attached to, or associated with, testaments.

[2] On this point in general, see the remarks of Prof. Hargreaves in *LQR*, LXVIII (1952), 488–9.

[3] These figures are derived from a London M.A. thesis by Miss Elizabeth Avery, 'Proceedings in the Court of Chancery up to *c.* 1460' (1958).

[4] *C.P. Chan.*, I. xxi–ii.

[5] An abstract of the customs of the manor, dated 1598, assigns the following ordinance to this year: 'It is found upon the oath of twelve men: if any tenant had enfeoffed his land within the lordship, to the use of any other, or unto

Since it was ancient demesne, the tenants enjoyed an immunity from the ordinary courts of the realm in respect of their land pleas. But it is difficult to believe that the manorial court was able to give a measure of relief to aggrieved beneficiaries that was denied in the Chancery at Westminster. We can, therefore, be reasonably certain that complaints made after the death of a *cestui que use* were being dealt with by the early 1420's. But it is difficult to decide whether an earlier date can be assigned to this type of jurisdiction. A decision by the council to take action on the Commons' petition of 1402 need not necessarily have resulted in action along these lines, since the language of the petition seems to refer to the grievances of living *cestui que usent*, and not their beneficiaries. Moreover, it is likely that the emergence of the new jurisdiction was a slow process: the decision to give litigants over uses the court they wanted must have raised many problems, including the establishment of rules by which such litigation was to be handled. The beginnings of this newly created jurisdiction must have been rudimentary: and in this situation the Chancellor and council may well have been loath to treat the complaints of living *cestui que usent* and those of beneficiaries on the same footing. It may thus have been some years before the new jurisdiction was widened to embrace uses of all kinds.[1]

---

strangers upon any estate or condition agreed between the parties, the custom is: if the same be not observed and kept according to that intent and purpose agreed upon: that he or they or their heirs to whom [*sic*] such feoffment was made may enter and possess the same, though he or they be not heir or heirs to the first giver, but strangers and the will of the first donor be observed in manner etc.' (A. F. C. Baber *The Court Rolls of the Manor of Bromsgrove and King's Norton 1494–1504* (Worcs. Hist. Soc., 1963), p. 155). Cf., however, the relevant footnote where it is pointed out that the court rolls of this year contain no mention of any such ordinance.

[1] Three petitions by beneficiaries may have been presented between 25 November 1402 (when the parliament of that year ended) and 28 February 1403 (when Edmund Stafford, bishop of Exeter, to whom they were addressed ended his second period of office as Chancellor) (*S.C. Chan.* pp. 48–9 and 69–70, nos. 45, 71 and 72). On the other hand, there are two letters extant in which the Prince of Wales (later Henry V) intervened to secure the performance of wills (*Anglo-Norman Letters and Petitions*, ed. M. D. Legge (Oxford,

At the same time as these developments were in progress the precise nature of the tribunal which dealt with such cases came to be defined. In the earliest cases of which we possess details it is impossible to distinguish clearly between the functions of the Chancellor and those of the council. But by 1430 the Chancellor appears to have taken over all matters of jurisdiction in uses, a development which may be attributed to the combined effects of two influences. The first was the increasing involvement of the council in political issues, especially during the minority of Henry VI and the years of royal helplessness that followed. The second was the nature of the duties already performed by the Chancellor. His department was responsible for the issue of all judicial writs, a point of great importance to litigants over uses, since it was by means of the writ of *sub poena* that defaulting feoffees were brought to court. Moreover, he already exercised judicial functions on what later came to be known as the 'common law' side of Chancery where he adjudicated in suits brought for the annulment of royal letters patent and inquisitions *post mortem*. In this connexion it is interesting to note that, when he first began to deal with uses, he employed procedures which he had hitherto followed in his 'common law' functions.[1]

Unfortunately, our knowledge of the principles by which the Chancellor judged the cases that came before him is very imperfect. It is fair to state that he enquired into the facts and into the truth of the allegations made by either party. But whether, having acted thus, he ought to make a judgement against the feoffees might raise difficult problems of law. The Year Books do not mention Chancery cases in the first half of the fifteenth century. But in the reign of Edward IV a number of reported cases reveal that certain rules of law had begun to emerge within the court of Chancery, the effect of which was to define the nature of the protection which it gave to the *cestui que use* and his

---

1941), pp. 297–8, nos. 231–2). In view of the Prince's youth in 1402, it is likely that they were written after that date. The fact that he was approached may suggest that the Chancellor was not yet ready to intervene on behalf of beneficiaries.   [1] *LQR*, LXVIII (1952), 498–9.

beneficiaries.[1] Two doctrines of special importance had made their appearance by the end of Edward IV's reign. The first arose from the fact that, in the case of estates held by feoffees jointly with one another, their joint interests at law descended to the one who survived the rest and, on his death, to his heirs at common law. If, then, beneficiaries were aggrieved concerning the conduct of feoffees and had not for some reason taken action against them while they were alive, could they take out a writ after the death of the last surviving feoffee? And, if so, against his heirs, or against his executors? In 1468 the position was doubtful since a discussion on this point was inconclusive.[2] However, the Chancellor in the course of a discussion in 1482 stated that records existed in the Chancery of cases where *sub poenas* had been granted against the heirs of feoffees. To this Chief Justice Hussey replied that all the judges had agreed thirty years before that a *sub poena* would not lie against the heirs. But the Chancellor retorted that, if this was the law, 'then it is great folly to enfeoff others of my land'.[3] There can, therefore, be no doubt that by this date, if a feoffee was dead, the Chancellor would give the beneficiaries relief against his heir, even though the common lawyers disapproved of his readiness to do so.

The second rule arose out of the difficulties that the Chancellor must often have experienced in deciding whether or not a use existed in face of the allegations and counter-claims of the parties before him. Although we have no precise information on this point, it seems likely that the feoffees must have often defended themselves by claiming that the grantor's enfeoffment of them was a simple grant, made without any conditions or trust reposed in them. Equally, a person or persons might deny any knowledge of a use but might claim that they held the land by simple grant of the feoffees to whom it had originally been conveyed to the use of a grantor or his beneficiaries. In 1465 it was held that a person

---

[1] For a general discussion of the legal problems created by uses, see Holdsworth, IV. 421–43.

[2] *YBVE*, 8 Ed. IV, Trin., p. 6, pl. 1.

[3] ibid., 22 Ed. IV, Pasch., p. 6, pl. 18. See also the translations in Digby, p. 326, n. 5.

who acquired lands from feoffees for a valuable consideration—
that is, by giving money or anything of value in exchange—
with the knowledge that his grantor held it as a feoffee to uses was
necessarily bound by the same use.[1] This view implied that if the
purchase was made without such knowledge of the use, the purchaser was not so bound and the beneficiaries would have to sue
against the feoffees. It seems likely, however, that difficulties over
whether an enfeoffment was to uses or not must have continued
for fifty years or so, since it is only in 1522 that we meet a definite
doctrine on this point. It was then held that, if an enfeoffment
was made without valuable consideration or any intention openly
expressed, the land so conveyed was *ipso facto* to be regarded as
held to the use of the grantor and it was for the purchaser to
prove otherwise.[2]

The fact that these doctrines took so long to emerge proves
that the growth of the Chancellor's jurisdiction over uses was a
gradual one. The available evidence indicates that relief was given
to the *cestui que use* against the original feoffees from 1409, and
possibly 1402, onwards: it was extended to their beneficiaries
within the next decade or so. Nevertheless, the plaintiffs would
always have been compelled to prove that a use existed and,
throughout the first half of the fifteenth century, would be in
serious difficulties if one, at least, of the original feoffees had not
survived. Down to some date between 1468 and 1482 the heirs of
feoffees who still held the lands with which their ancestors had
been enfeoffed could engage in fraudulent practices with impunity. Throughout our period, if a feoffee sold the land to
another without disclosing that he held it to the use of a third
party, neither the latter nor his beneficiary could recover it. And,
although he might be able to sue the fraudulent feoffee in Chancery, it would be extremely difficult to secure any damages
awarded to him. In short, in the first half of the fifteenth century
the relief afforded by the Chancellor to the *cestui que use* or his
beneficiaries against inefficient or fraudulent feoffees must have
been a limited one: and, although it had been extended by the

[1] *YBVE*, 5 Ed. IV, Mich., p. 7, pl. 16, translated in Digby, p. 327, n. 1.
[2] *YBVE*, 14 Hen. VIII, Mich., p. 7, pl. 5.

close of the century, serious defects in his jurisdiction remained. At the beginning of the Tudor period the Chancellor had not succeeded in remedying all the deficiencies of the courts of common law in respect of uses.

Nevertheless, whatever the weaknesses of the Chancellor's jurisdiction over uses, by the end of the fifteenth century two distinctly different views of the law of landed property can be found in England. From the standpoint of the common law courts the feoffees, and not the *cestui que use*, were the owners of the land.[1] There is clear evidence that common lawyers found considerable difficulty in reconciling their rules with the nature of the estate which the *cestui que use* in practice possessed. For instance, in the case of some estates held by feoffees to the use of others, the lands were regarded at common law as being partitioned equally between the feoffees.[2] Common lawyers explained the actual presence of the *cestui que use* upon the land by taking the view that he was the tenant at will of the feoffees.[3] On the other hand, the Chancellor, in effect, treated the *cestui que use* as the real owner, not the feoffees. As early as 1464 contemporary lawyers were well aware of the basic differences in character between the two jurisdictions. In a case of trespass the court of Common Pleas[4] refused to take cognizance of a plea that the defendant was seised to the use of another, a justice remarking that,

This is a good ground of defence in Chancery, for the defendant there shall aver the intent and purpose upon such a feoffment, for in the Chancery a man shall have remedy according to conscience upon

---

[1] Hence we see the feoffees, not the *cestui que use*, obtaining an *inspeximus* of a charter of free warren in 1381 (*CPR, 1377–81*, p. 610), a licence to crenellate in 1410 (ibid., *1408–13*, p. 232) and a licence to enclose and impark in 1444 (ibid., *1441–6*, p. 261).

[2] Ibid., *1422–9*, pp. 282, 488–9; ibid., *1429–36*, pp. 488–9.

[3] Littleton, ss. 462–4 (Coke, *First Institute*, II. 271). He discusses the question whether a deed of release executed by the feoffees of all their rights in the lands to the feoffor was good or not. The common lawyers were in disagreement, both over the answer and over the grounds on which it could be argued that such a deed was good.

[4] *YBVE*, 4 Ed. IV, Pasch., p. 8, pl. 9, translated in Digby, pp. 339–40.

the intent of such a feoffment but here by the course of the common law in the Common Pleas or the King's Bench it is otherwise for the feoffee shall have the land; and the feoffor shall not justify contrary to his own feoffment that the said feoffment was made in confidence . . . for the common law of the land is different from the law of Chancery on this point.

The evolution of the jurisdiction of the Chancery over uses was the consequence of the growing demand among those who created uses for a legal system whereby control might be exercised over their feoffees. A study of the origins of uses shows that they owed their existence to the interaction of two motives among the landowners of England in the later middle ages—the desire to evade the incidents of feudal tenure and the search for a method by which lands so held could be devised by will, generally in order to pay debts or provide for younger children. An examination of the growth of the Chancellor's jurisdiction over uses serves to emphasize the strength of the social and economic forces which led to both the appearance and the dissemination of uses. Uses were an accepted part of the structure of landownership long before the close of the fourteenth century, at a time when, if feoffees were recalcitrant, inefficient or dishonest, no redress could be obtained in the courts of law. And they continued to increase in popularity throughout the fifteenth century despite serious gaps in the protection which the court of Chancery could provide. It is apparent that in the last resort the advantages derived from enfeoffments to uses more than outweighed any risks.

In 1484 a parliamentary statute reduced the hazards that might face a *cestui que use*. It was laid down that he might make any lawful estate or conveyance of any lands held by others to his use and that this would hold good for him or his heirs against his feoffees.[1] This statute possesses remarkable interest from the standpoint of the development of legal doctrines, in that, by openly recognizing that the *cestui que use* occupied the land, it equated legal and beneficial ownership. But in 1484 its promulgation must have been the result of strong practical considerations.

[1] 1 Ric. III, c. 1 (*Statutes*, II. 477–8).

It was entitled as 'An act against privy and unknown feoffments' and its preamble recited the inconveniences of secret enfeoffments to uses. However, such grounds for legislative action had existed for a considerable time and, in view of the more urgent issues which faced Richard III and his advisers in 1484, it is difficult to believe that they alone explain the promulgation of this statute. No doubt the need was felt to find some means of reducing the volume of litigation over uses which was now reaching the Chancellor. Indeed, this must have become so considerable as to interfere with the Chancellor's performance of his other duties. The rule now laid down provided a means of insurance against disobedience or fraud on the part of feoffees. If this occurred, the *cestui que use* or his heir had a means of redress, because they could dispose of the land as if it were held in fee at common law.[1] It is true that this form of self-help was not available to beneficiaries of the wills of deceased *cestui que usent* and these would still have to seek redress from the Chancellor. Nevertheless, the statute must have reduced the Chancellor's judicial commitments, since it was now less likely that he would be presented with the complaints of *cestuis que usent* or their heirs.[2]

The most remarkable illustration of the popularity achieved by uses at the close of the fifteenth century is to be found in a parliamentary statute[3] promulgated in 1504. This laid down that, if a bondman conveyed lands acquired by him to feoffees to his use,

[1] This was the interpretation of the statute implied in C. Saint German, *The Dialogue in English, between a Doctor of Divinitie and a Student in the Lawes of England*, c. 7 (edition of 1613, p. 70): '. . . as to the Common Law the whole interest is in the feoffee, and if the feoffee will break his conscience and take the profits, the feoffor hath no remedy by the Common Law, but is driven in that case to sue for his remedy by *Subpena* for the profits and to cause him to refeoff him again, and that was sometimes the most common case when the *Subpena* was sued, that is to say, before the Statute of R. 3'.

[2] These, however, could not have entirely disappeared, since the statute did not remove all of them. Saint German pointed out (ibid.) that 'for the profits received, the feoffor hath yet no remedy but by *Subpena* as he had before the Statute'. Moreover, when *cestuis que usent* and their heirs availed themselves of the statute, confusion over titles must often have involved them in litigation that could not be satisfactorily settled in the courts of common law.

[3] *Statutes*, II. 660 (19 Hen. VII, c. 15).

his lord was to have any right to enter on them that would have been his if the bondman had been seised. The need to legislate in this way shows that the practice of enfeoffing to uses had permeated the lowest ranks of the peasantry, and was damaging the interests of manorial lords. Bondmen *cestuis que usent* were, of course, much more liable to the risks of fraudulent feoffees than free men, since it was more difficult for them to sue in Chancery. Yet, despite this, uses grew among them to an extent that required parliamentary reform. Even humble peasants thought that the advantages of uses more than outweighed the risks.

CHAPTER FOUR

The Decline of Feudal Incidents

THE existence of a use inevitably meant the withdrawal of incidents of tenure and, therefore, profits, which belonged to the feudal lord. When the *cestui que use* died, in the eyes of the courts of common law, any lands held to his use belonged, not to him, but to his feoffees. And, when these proceeded to employ the revenues of the lands for the fulfilment of directions given them in the *cestui que use*'s will, they were, in effect, defrauding the lord. If the heir was over age, he lost his relief: if the heir was under age, he was deprived of his rights of wardship and marriage. A feudal lord who lost revenues in this way could console himself with the thought that he also had the opportunity to exploit the advantages of uses and could thus in his turn deprive his lord as his tenant had deprived him. But compensation of this sort was not available to the greatest feudal lord of all, the King, since he was always lord and never tenant.

One of the most remarkable features of the development of uses in later medieval England is the fact that, although the device was being employed by landowners on an extensive scale from the mid-fourteenth century onwards, we have to wait roughly a century and a half before the Crown attempts to employ legislative weapons against uses and their consequences. In 1483 there was a short-lived effort at legislative control within the confines of the Duchy of Lancaster. But it is only in 1490 that the Crown promulgates a statute which sought to alleviate, from the standpoint of both itself and all other feudal lords, the worst encroachments made by uses into their revenues from feudal incidents. This phenomenon of a century and a half of legislative silence on the part of the Crown and other lords about their financial losses as a result of uses requires explanation. On the one hand, a study of the legal sources, the Year Books in particular, reveals that both lawyers and royal administrators were well aware of the existence of this problem and from time to time gave it some careful attention. On the other, an examination of the legal administrative resources which were available to the Crown shows that its interests were to a considerable extent allowed to go by default and that, if the will to exploit the instruments of its prerogative had existed, a more effective struggle to prevent the erosion of its feudal rights might have been possible.

In studying these problems we must be careful to distinguish between the mesne lords, on the one hand, and the Crown, on the other. A mesne lord who wished to combat in a particular case the evasion of his rights would seek his remedy from the courts of common law. But the Crown had in its escheators, and the system of inquisitions *post mortem* organized under the officials of the Chancery, means of enquiring into the conveyances and settlements made by any landowner. Its prerogative gave it the right through its escheators to seize all the lands of deceased tenants-in-chief: and the resulting seisin was a valuable weapon against any who wished to claim their rights and sue the lands out of its hands.

(i) USES AND COLLUSION AT COMMON LAW

For mesne lords who were aggrieved because of the losses they incurred through the employment of uses by their tenants there were two possible means of securing redress. The first was to seek such remedies as were available in the courts of common law: the second was to request legislative reform from the King in parliament. In the fourteenth and fifteenth centuries efforts were made to use both methods; but no real success was achieved until 1490 when Henry VII promulgated the first attempt at reform on a national scale.

Such resources as were available to mesne lords in the courts of common law were the result of c. 6 of the Statute of Marlborough which had been promulgated in 1267.[1] Its importance in this

[1] There is a valuable discussion of the Statute and the relevant case-law in Coke, *Second Institute*, 109-12.

N

respect was twofold. First, it introduced the concept of a feoffment which was 'collusive', as distinct from one which was made
in good faith and was not, therefore, deliberately intended to
defraud the lord of his rights. Second, it laid down the procedure
which was to be followed by the courts when lords wished to
take legal action against those who had deprived them of their
rights. This portion of the statute was intended to outlaw two
methods of evading the incidents of tenure which tenants had
been employing. The first, later described by Coke as 'collusion
apparent', raised no problems of legal interpretation, since the fact
that a tenant had enfeoffed his son and heir while under age would
be sufficient to prove that his lord had been defrauded. But the
second—the employment of fraudulent leases—described by
Coke as 'collusion averrable', raised more complex problems,
since it was necessary both to restrain lords from asserting their
rights without due legal process and to define the procedure
which was to be employed to prove the existence of a fraud. The
statute forbade lords to disseise their tenants' alienees without
judgement. Instead,

> they shall have a writ for to have such a ward restored to them; and by
> the witnesses contained in the deed of feoffment, with other free and
> lawful men of the country, and by the value of the land, and by the
> quantity of the sum payable after the term, it shall be tried whether such
> feoffments were made in good faith or by collusion to defraud the chief
> lords of the fee of their wards.

A strict construction of the statute's language would seem to
suggest that the procedure thus laid down was to be employed
only in the case of fraudulent leases. On the other hand, in the
writ of ward[1] which was thus made available a judicial procedure
was created which might be used by lords who were deprived of
their rights of wardship as a result of their tenants' uses. Whether
or not writs of ward were used in such cases successfully would

[1] For the process followed after the issue of a writ, see c. 7 of the Statute of
Marlborough (*Statutes*, I. 21). For details of the writ, the form of which depended on whether the lord claimed the custody of the land and the body or
merely the land, see A. Fitzherbert, *New Natura Brevium* (London, 1677),
pp. 308–9. See also Holdsworth, III. 17.

depend on the attitude of the courts of common law. If they were prepared to allow the writ to be so employed, they would be enlarging the terms of the Statute of Marlborough to comprise methods of evasion which had emerged after its promulgation. The distinction which the statute had made between enfeoffments which were collusive and those which were made in good faith was one which might easily be applied to enfeoffments to uses, a circumstance which must have encouraged both pleaders and judges to look favourably on the application of the procedures laid down at Marlborough to uses.

An examination of the Year Books and sixteenth-century abridgements reveals that such an enlargement of the terms of the Statute of Marlborough by means of judicial interpretation did in fact occur in the late fourteenth and fifteenth centuries. We first see it in 1358.[1] In 1371 Sir Amaury St. Amand brought a writ of ward against the two surviving feoffees of his tenant Leonard Carew.[2] In 1373 the abbot of Kirkstall took similar action against the feoffees of Robert Mauleverer.[3] In each of these cases the plaintiff claimed that the feoffees had been enfeoffed by the deceased tenant of all the lands held of him, on condition that they were to enfeoff his heir when he came of age.[4] The details of

---

[1] Fitzherbert, *Garde*, no. 33. The record has not been traced.

[2] *YBVE*, 45 Ed. III, Trin., p. 22, pl. 25; Brook, *Garde*, no. 16. A somewhat fuller account of the discussion may be found in BM, Add. MS., 32, 087, f. 78 v. The record of the case is PRO, C.P. 40/444/rot. 579. The Year Book discussion relates to the action brought by Sir Amaury St. Amand. But a similar action seems to have been brought by Hugh Courtenay, earl of Devon, in respect of lands held of him by the deceased (ibid./rot. 580). Both Sir Amaury and the earl claimed the custody of the heir as well as his lands. Thus, if they had both succeeded, the issue of priority of enfeoffment would then have arisen to decide which of them was to have the custody of the heir.

[3] Fitzherbert, *Garde*, no. 102 (Trin., 47 Ed. III). But there is a fuller version than Fitzherbert's in BM, Add. MS., 32, 087, f. 81. The case cannot be traced in *YBVE* or earlier printed editions of the Year Books. For the record, see PRO, C.P. 40/451/rot. 308 v.

[4] In that of 1358 it was claimed that the enfeoffment had been made on condition of finding two chaplains during the heir's minority. When he came of age, the feoffees were to enfeoff him or pay him £20 a year, the land being worth 10 marks a year. Cf. Fitzherbert, *Collusion*, no. 29, which is not relevant

the plaintiff's claims in a case which occurred in 1384 are rather more complicated.[1] John Kirkby of Hayton in Kent claimed that John Mocking had enfeoffed feoffees of the manor of Newstead which was held of him and had later died, leaving a son and heir aged two years. The feoffees were enfeoffed within the ten days before his death, on condition that they perform the will which was to be declared within the next two or three days. When duly declared, this laid down that Mocking's son and heir, his younger son and his two daughters were to receive all the profits of the lands held by the feoffees in the county of Kent in common for twenty years after their father's death. At the end of this term the feoffees were to enfeoff the heir or, if he had not survived, the next heir of John Mocking. It is quite likely that both the procedure followed by Mocking and the form of his directions were influenced by the attitude of the courts as revealed in 1371 and 1373. He took care to make his will, not at the time of his enfeoffment of the feoffees, but some time later, thus strengthening the fiction that they were the owners at common law. And he avoided any open direction that they were to enfeoff the heir when he came of age. The retention of the lands by them for a term of twenty years had virtually the same effect, since the heir was aged two, and his younger brother one, at the time of their father's death. But Mocking's usurpation of his lord's rights was less blatant than the one which had recently been held collusive.

Both the attitudes of the judges of the Common Pleas, and the arguments addressed to them in these cases, possess several features of interest. In each case they took the view that the facts as alleged by the plaintiff constituted sufficient grounds in law for the issue of a writ of ward and, in accordance with the procedure laid down in the Statute of Marlborough, the summoning of a local inquest by the sheriff to determine the matter. If the jurors confirmed the plaintiff's allegations, he would recover his rights. The

---

to this discussion, because it concerns a settlement on a tenant, his wife and heir made *before* the tenant's entry into religion (PRO, C.P. 40/390/rot. 113).

[1] R. Bellewe, *Les Ans du Roy Richard le Second* (London, 1585), pp. 99–100. For fuller accounts of the discussion, see BM, Lansdowne MS. 557, f. 64 and Lincoln's Inn MS. 77, f. 217 v. The record is in PRO, C.P. 40/495/rot. 289.

details of these cases, therefore, show clearly that the judges of the Common Pleas in the late fourteenth century were quite prepared to take cognizance of uses if it could be proved that they had led to lords being deprived of their rights of wardship. They did so by means of the procedures provided by the Statute of Marlborough, even though this meant going beyond a literal reading of its terms. Nor do the discussions recorded in the Year Books on these occasions contain any remarks which suggest that any of their colleagues or those who pleaded in the court took a different view of legal doctrine on this point.

In a case[1] which occurred in 1425 the plaintiff—Sir Richard Waldegrave—claimed that his tenant John Goldingham, thinking that his wife Elizabeth was pregnant, conveyed his manor of Belstead to feoffees

with the intention that, if the said Elizabeth had issue male of that pregnancy or of another afterwards conceived of him John Goldingham, then the same [feoffees] were to enfeoff that issue of the said manor of Belstead in fee when he came of age and that during the minority of that issue they were to receive and raise the profits of the same manor to the use and profit of the same issue.

The details of the plaintiff's case have two features of interest. First, we see here an extension of the principle laid down in 1371 and 1373 that an enfeoffment made on condition that the feoffees were to enfeoff the heir when he came of age was collusive, since this doctrine was now taken to comprise such an enfeoffment made when the heir was as yet unborn or even conceived. Second, the plaintiff sued out his writ of ward against, not the feoffees who had been enfeoffed by his deceased tenant, but the widow. Although neither the Year Book discussion nor the record of the case make this point clear, it would appear that the feoffees had transferred the manor to the widow who presumably held the body of the heir in her custody. In this case, therefore, it can be shown that a writ of ward was issued against the beneficiary of a use who enjoyed the wardship of which the plaintiff lord had

[1] *YBVE*, Hil., 3 Hen. VI, p. 32, pl. 23. The record is in PRO, C.P. 40/656/rot. 379.

been deprived. The court was ready to enquire not merely into the original enfeoffment of the feoffees by the deceased tenant but also into an estate which was created by them in the course of the performance of the duties that had been entrusted to them.

As a result of these cases—and, perhaps, others that have not survived in the extant Year Books—by the middle of the fifteenth century common lawyers had learnt to apply the Statute of Marlborough's provisions to enfeoffments to uses. They had developed a distinction between uses which were collusive of the lord's rights of wardship and those which were made in good faith. The resulting doctrines were stated most clearly in the course of the judges' discussion over a case of replevin in 1455.[1] A female tenant had enfeoffed feoffees who then enfeoffed her for life, with remainder in tail to her son and heir. He had entered on his mother's death, though still under age, and had permitted the plaintiff to place his beasts on the land. These had then been removed by the officials of the lord acting in the exercise of his rights of wardship; and it was they who, as the defendants in the case, claimed that the tenant's enfeoffment of the feoffees had been collusive. This plea raised a number of complicated issues, the chief of which was the problem whether, even if the original enfeoffment of the feoffees was collusive, it could be argued that the collusion terminated when they enfeoffed the deceased with remainder in tail. If so, of course, the second enfeoffment would have been made in good faith and the defendant's pleas would fail.[2] In the course of the discussion Justice Danby declared that, 'if the tenant enfeoffs a stranger with intent that he enfeoff the heir at his full age, that is obviously collusion; but, if the feoffment be made to the intent that he marry his daughters, or pay his debts and then enfeoff the heir, that is no collusion'. This view found its way into the early Tudor abridgements[3] and was accepted as authority in the early seventeenth century.[4]

---

[1] *YBVE*, Pasch., 33 Hen. VI, pp. 14–16, pl. 6.

[2] They might also fail because the lord had not chosen to claim his rights by suing out a writ of ward.   [3] Brook, *Garde*, no. 5.

[4] Sir James Ley, *A Learned Treatise concerning Wards and Liveries* (London, 1642), p. 42; Coke, *Second Institute*, 111.

In the light of these details there can be no doubt that the judges of the court of Common Pleas were ready, in so far as they were able to protect lords' rights of wardship, to take the existence of uses into account. Wardship was clearly an exception to the general rule that the courts of common law took no cognizance of uses.[1] But, however interesting the doctrines of the common law may be in this respect from the standpoint of the development of legal principles, they appear to have had little practical effect and to have given scarcely any protection to the interests of feudal lords.

In the first place, it is apparent from an examination of the cases that have been discussed that, to fall within the scope of common law doctrines of collusion, the tenant's enfeoffment of the feoffees must come within the category of common law conditions— that is, the condition must be stated, whether in words or in writing, at the time that the enfeoffment was made.[2] In the cases of 1358, 1371, 1373 and 1425 the plaintiffs appear to have claimed that the full terms of the condition were so declared; and it is noteworthy that in the Year Book discussion of that of 1371 it was mentioned that the condition was stated when livery was made to the feoffees. In the case of 1384 the enfeoffment appears to have been made on condition that the feoffees should perform the will that would be declared to them in due course. Although a century and a half later this would not have been accepted as coming within the category of common law conditions,[3] at this date there is no reason to believe that the courts had as yet developed this view. This aspect of the legal position clearly gave considerable opportunities to those who were attempting to evade the lord's rights of wardship by means of uses. If they refrained from declaring any conditions, they would be able to claim that the feoffees had been enfeoffed in fee and that no connexion existed between themselves and the land concerned thereafter. It is clear from the details of the cases that have been discussed that in each of them the defendants were fully aware of this consideration,

---

[1] Cf. e.g. Holdsworth, IV. 416–17, which does not take doctrines of collusion into account.   [2] See above, p. 159.

[3] *Brook's New Cases*, p. 41. See above, p. 160.

basing their defence on the claim that the enfeoffment had been made without condition. As we have seen, from the earliest beginnings of uses onwards, it was the practice to convey lands to feoffees to uses without any formal stipulations regarding the nature of the use to which they were seised. It is possible that the desire to avoid the risks of common law collusion played some part in the decision to follow this practice.[1] But in any event the fact that uses so developed put most, if not all of them, out of the reach of such remedies as were available to feudal lords in the courts of common law. It may, of course, be argued that in the late fourteenth century there was no certainty that the common law doctrines of collusion would stick rigidly to an insistence that all uses of which they took cognizance must fall within the category of common law conditions. In each case the issue of fact would have to be decided by a jury empanelled by the sheriff in the shire concerned. And it might be suggested that jurors would not necessarily stick closely to the rigid rules of common law but might be ready to find enfeoffments collusive without clear evidence of conditions stated at the time of the enfeoffment—for instance, the existence of an implied condition might be inferred from their knowledge that the land remained in the family of the deceased tenant. But it is unlikely, in view of the attitude taken by the common law judges in 1379,[2] that they would have countenanced such an approach if called upon to decide upon it in law. In any event, their attitude was never put to the test, since there is no mention of any such issue arising in the Year Books.

Even if such limitations had not been imposed upon the jurisdiction of common law courts in respect of the evasion of feudal incidents through uses, they would have run into serious difficulties in applying the distinction between enfeoffments made in collusion and those made in good faith which Justice Danby propounded in 1455. This doctrine is best explained as the result of an attempt by the common law judges to rationalize their failure to prevent the evasion of wardship by means of uses. They managed to define as collusive those enfeoffments in which the

[1] See above, p. 160.   [2] See above, p. 159.

tenant openly avowed his intention to deprive the lord of his rights. And, since there was no such open avowal when a man made arrangements by means of uses for the payment of his debts and the needs of his wife and his younger children, they were content to regard these as made in good faith. Some two centuries later Sir Edward Coke supported their attitude, writing that 'every man by the law of God and nature ought to provide for his wife and children, and he is worse than an infidel that doth not provide for his family: and by the law of God and of nations debts ought to be paid'.[1]

Nevertheless, there were serious deficiencies in this doctrine which would soon have been apparent had there been intensive efforts to administer it in the courts.[2] For example, wills of the sort that common lawyers accepted as having been made in good faith generally laid down that, once the funds necessary for the performance of the deceased's directions had been raised, the heir was to be enfeoffed of the lands. But what was the legal position if the heir was at that time still under age? This point touches on a fundamental issue. However much it might be stressed that a tenant in these circumstances was merely acting as a father was morally bound to do, the fact remained that feudal law made no provision for the paternal duties of tenants. The spending of revenues after a tenant's death on the payment of his debts or on the needs of children who did not inherit was an intrusion upon the lord's rights or wardship.

There is only one case in the Year Books in which these issues were ventilated—in 1440.[3] The plaintiff alleged that his tenant had enfeoffed feoffees on condition that they enfeoff his heir when he

<hr>

[1] Coke, *Second Institute*, 111.

[2] See also *YBVE*, Mich., 10 Hen. IV, p. 4, pl. 11. Chief Justice Gascoigne and Justice Huls argued that an enfeoffment in order that the feoffees enfeoff the heir when he came of age was not collusive, since the ancestor might survive and they have to enfeoff during his lifetime. But this case was a *scire facias* in Chancery, not a writ of ward in the Common Pleas. And this argument does not appear again in the Year Books.

[3] *YBVE*, Mich., 19 Hen. VI, pp. 29–30, pl. 54. It has not been possible to search the relevant plea roll for the record, since it is in too bad a condition for production in the PRO search rooms.

came of age: in the meanwhile the tenant was to take the issues during his lifetime, and the feoffees during the ensuing minority. If the facts were as alleged by him, the feoffment was collusive. But the defendant feoffees counter-claimed that they were to repay a debt of 100 marks and thereafter raise £40 to marry the deceased's daughter. Judges and counsel then discussed whether, if the feoffees were telling the truth, the enfeoffment could then be regarded as collusive and, if so, on what grounds.

The arguments propounded in this discussion possess great interest, since they show that much confused thinking lay behind the doctrines of collusion that were already accepted. Justice Ayscough declared that 'the issue will be on the fraud, and in no way on the feoffment'. This view contains the elements of a much more radical approach to the problem of collusive enfeoffments than had hitherto appeared. In the first place, it asks the simple question—has the lord been defrauded? No jury need find this difficult to answer. In the second place, by so doing it provides a means by which the courts could look behind the formal language of the deed of enfeoffment: and it by-passes any attempt by the feoffees to counter-claim that their enfeoffment was unconditional at common law. According to Justice Fulthorpe, the issue of collusion could be settled by asking the question—did the deceased feoffor continue to draw the profits after the enfeoffment? This was another simple question which a jury could easily answer. But Justice Newton disagreed, arguing that, if Fulthorpe was right, an enfeoffment made in order to enfeoff, not the heir, but a stranger at full age would be collusive. On this occasion both Ayscough and Fulthorpe seem to have realized that the key to an understanding of the problems of collusion lay in the nature of the lord's rights. In feudal law the lord had a right to the wardship of all the lands which his tenant held of him at his death. Though they did not state this principle clearly as the premise from which they were arguing, both justices—Fulthorpe, perhaps, more incisively than Ayscough—touched on the most fundamental of the difficulties posed by accepted doctrines of collusion. A *cestui que use* generally made arrangements which were to take effect after his death. Even if his directions to his feoffees dealt with his responsibilities towards his wife and children, these could only be performed by depriving his lord of his feudal rights.

Why, then, in view of these considerations, did the courts of common law fail to follow policies which effectively prevented the evasion of wardship through uses? Justice Fulthorpe's question —did the deceased draw the profits after the enfeoffment?—was fully in accord with the common law doctrines of the mid-thirteenth century. Bracton always took care to emphasize that every enfeoffment, if it was to be a valid conveyance, must be followed both by the delivery of seisin to the feoffee and by his continuous exercise of that seisin thereafter. In both his treatise[1] and his *Note Book*[2] he cited cases of novel disseisin in which sons claimed they had been disseised of lands of which they had been enfeoffed by their fathers: but, although the requisite formalities of conveyance, including the delivery of seisin, had been complied with, their pleas failed because in each case the father continued to exercise seisin. In one case the assize failed despite the jurors' finding that the father had been seised after his grant merely in the capacity of a guardian. Thus in terms of Bractonian law the courts would be able to destroy the fiction of the use: since the *cestui que use* remained upon the land, he would *ipso facto* be regarded as being in seisin. In the middle years of the fourteenth century many *cestuis que usent* must have been worried lest the courts adopt this attitude: in a parliamentary petition of 1339 the magnates complained that tenants who had enfeoffed feoffees on their death-beds then had themselves carried off their lands to ensure that they could not be regarded as having died in seisin.[3] For lords who had been deprived of their wardships through uses the employment of the simple question—did the *cestui que use* continue to draw the profits and thus die seised? —had two advantages. First, it relieved them of the need to proceed by means of the Statute of Marlborough: not only would it in effect render any arrangements made by the deceased tenant null and void but it would also enable the lord to enter upon the land without suing out a writ of ward. Second, it provided a plea

---

[1] Bracton, II. 149–52.
[2] *Bracton's Note Book*, III. 637–8 (pl. 1838).   [3] *Rot. Parl.*, II. 104a.

that could be used in a court of law to overcome an enfeoffment
to feoffees, despite its compliance with all the formalities required
by law. If a lord, having ousted the feoffees without suing out a
writ of ward, had an action for novel disseisin brought by them
against him, he had a defence. If, however, he preferred to employ
the procedures laid down in the Statute of Marlborough, he could
argue that his tenant's enfeoffment was proven collusive because
the feoffees did not exercise real seisin. But, although a few lords
may have ousted feoffees without writs of ward,[1] there is no
evidence that this occurred to any appreciable extent. And, apart
from the case of 1440, the Year Books reveal no trace of any
interest in the nature of the feoffees' seisin. Why, then, did lords
fail to employ this means of attack upon uses?

The explanation must be sought in the interaction of two influences. One was the nature of the evolution of the courts of
common law in the fourteenth and fifteenth centuries.[2] One
result of this was that they moved away from the Bractonian
doctrine of seisin and instead approached the problems of the
ownership of land from the standpoint of the formal construction
of conveyancing documents. Indeed, in a case heard in 1429 a
judge stated that 'if one enfeoffed another with the proviso that
the feoffor should take the profits, the feoffee would nevertheless
have them as the proviso was entirely void'.[3] His attitude is the
complete opposite of that of Bracton, for whom the proviso
would have made the feoffment null and void. Fulthorpe's views
eleven years later suggest that not all judges would at this time
accept their colleague's proposition; but the fact that it was
propounded indicates how far the courts of common law had
moved away from Bractonian doctrines. In reality, common
lawyers found it impossible to ignore altogether the taking of the
profits by the *cestui que use*. But they reconciled this situation with

---

[1] Henry, lord Percy, did so after the death of his tenant Walter Heslarton in
1349 (*CIPMA*, IX. 431–2 (no. 639)).

[2] See, e.g., Plucknett, *Common Law*, pp. 158–9.

[3] *YBVE*, Trin., 7 Hen. VI, p. 22, pl. 21. He was stating not merely his own
view but also that of his old master Sir William Hankford, Chief Justice of the
King's Bench, 1413–24.

the conveyance of the land to, and the vesting of the legal ownership in, the feoffees by taking the view that the *cestui que use* was
the tenant at will of the feoffees. This doctrine was commonly
held by the middle of the fifteenth century;[1] and it is interesting
to note that it was employed by the defendant feoffees in the case
of 1384 which has been discussed to explain the fact that their
feoffor remained in occupation of the land.[2] It is thus quite clear
that the attitude of the courts of common law was such that, if
feudal lords entered upon the lands of a deceased *cestui que use*
when his heir was under age, there was a very real prospect that
the ousted feoffees would succeed in an assize of novel disseisin or
an action for trespass.

The other influence which must have helped to dissuade
lords from a radical attack upon uses by denying the validity of
the feoffees' seisin was a general understanding that such matters
were covered by the Statute of Marlborough and that it would
be illegal to proceed except by means of a writ of ward. The way
in which the common lawyers interpreted the statute lends support to this suggestion. But it is quite clear that, however much
the court of Common Pleas might be prepared to take cognizance of the loss of the lord's rights through uses, few lords resorted
to writs of ward. Indeed, the six cases that have been discussed—
those of 1358, 1371, 1373, 1384, 1425 and 1440—are the only ones
that can be discovered in the extant Year Books and abridgements
in which problems relating to the issue of writs of ward against
feoffees to uses were discussed. A study of the arguments put forward on these occasions reveals that common lawyers never faced
up to the implications of such doctrines as they managed to develop on this subject, a failure that may undoubtedly be attributed
to the paucity of the occasions when the relevant issues were
raised in the court of Common Pleas. The inadequacy of these
doctrines thus underlines the reluctance of nearly all lords, when
their rights of wardship were evaded by means of uses, to seek
redress at common law.

In explaining why they were so content to accept the loss of
their rights, we must distinguish between the interests of the

---

[1] See above, p. 176.　　　　　　　[2] PRO, C.P. 40/495/rot. 289.

great ecclesiastical landowners and those of laymen. The bishops and abbots held land by feudal tenure and had many feudal tenants. But, when they died, their lands remained with the Church. It was thus impossible for them to recompense themselves for the loss of feudal revenues caused by uses by themselves employing the device. Why, then, did they not wage a campaign against uses in the courts of common law? The answer must be sought in the risks of litigation. A plaintiff in the court of Common Pleas ran the hazards of procedures which were extremely technical in character.[1] Defeat, and thus amercement, might well result from, not a faulty case in law, but technical deficiencies in its presentation. Even if the court consented to the issue of a writ of ward, there was no guarantee that the sheriff would return it with the jury's finding at the proper time and frequent adjournments might follow.[2] Moreover, it would always be necessary to ensure that the jury acted honestly and was not affected by any undue influence exerted by the feoffees or next-of-kin of the deceased *cestui que use*. Such hazards would be present in varying degrees in most litigation at common law, but there were two further risks that might be encountered in suing out writs of ward against feoffees. It was possible that they might employ the counter-plea that the lands in question were not held of the plaintiff, a possibility made very real by the confused state of feudal tenures.[3] And, since all the feoffees were joined together as defendants, the death of one of them after the case had started might result in the termination of the proceedings against the survivors and the plaintiff would have to commence an entirely new action against them.[4] In view of the existence of these hazards it is not surprising that ecclesiastical lords preferred to accept the existence of uses and the loss of feudal revenues this entailed. It is quite likely that,

[1] For full details see M. Hastings, *The Court of Common Pleas in Fifteenth Century England* (Ithaca, New York: 1947), pp. 157–217, esp. 211–17.

[2] These occurred in the cases of 1373, 1384 and 1425 discussed above.

[3] In the case of 1373 the feoffees claimed the lands were held in socage, not by knight's service, while in that of 1425 it was claimed that the deceased had held of a lord other than the plaintiff.

[4] This occurred in the case of 1384.

during the period when uses were first emerging, the same considerations dissuaded some lay lords from taking action against them. But, even so, they must soon have realized that any such efforts were against their own interests in the long run and that their energies were better employed in seeking the advantages which uses offered to themselves.

A search of parliamentary records in the later middle ages reveals only two occasions when demands for reform were made in parliament that seem to refer to the consequences of uses. In parliament in 1339 the magnates requested that 'remedy be ordained in this Parliament concerning men who when dying make alienation of their lands and have themselves carried out of their manors, by fraud to deprive the chief lords of the ward of the same'.[1] There can be no doubt that here we see evidence of the response of some lords to the evasion of their rights during the period when mesne tenants were beginning to employ uses on a scale that made their consequences felt: the vagueness of the petition's language may be attributed to the fact that clear ideas about the nature of the device that was being employed were still in the process of development, a fact which probably explains the absence therefrom of the term 'use'. But the complaint appears to have secured no official action.[2]

The other demand for legislative reform in respect of uses is much less easy to explain. In parliament in 1404 the Commons petitioned that 'it be ordained and established by statute to be made in this your present Parliament that at the time that . . . collusion and fraud be duly proved in the manner that is ordained in the Statute of Marlborough, that thenceforth the said gifts and feoffments be voided, quashed and regarded as null for all time'. The King's reply declared that

To avoid the perils and inconveniences that could occur in this case, the King by the authority of the Parliament wills to assign certain Lords, together with the Justices, to examine the matter comprised in this

---

[1] *Rot. Parl.*, II. 104a.

[2] But another request made by the magnates at the same time—that wardships be granted to those next-of-kin who could not inherit—did lead to a statute (14 Ed. III, st. 1, c. 13).

Petition: And . . . the same Lords and Justices may by the abovesaid authority provide remedy in this case as will seem best to them according to their wise discretions.[1]

In view of the popularity of uses by this date it is impossible to avoid the conclusion that they were the 'gifts and feoffments' to which the petition refers. But it is noteworthy that the petition does not demand their abolition, or even a reform which would prevent the loss of the lord's rights of wardship which they caused. All it requests is amendment of c. 6 of the Statute of Marlborough so that, once a feoffment was found to be collusive, it would *ipso facto* be null and void, whereas in the statute's terms the seisin of the deceased's feoffees was merely postponed until the heir came of age. The motives which lay behind this demand are far from clear. Two possibilities present themselves. The first is that the petition was framed in the interests of lords who saw in the provisions of the Statute of Marlborough on this point a threat to their position, in that they may have feared that feoffees who were successfully ousted by means of a writ of ward might remain a nuisance, perhaps engaging in litigation against them— the action of trespass might present them with a possible opportunity.[2] The second possibility is that the petition was framed in the interests of heirs which would be damaged if the feoffees continued their seisin after the expiration of the minority. Presumably they would then have continued, or even commenced, the performance of the duties which the deceased had enjoined upon them and which had been interrupted by the lord's assertion of his rights. In such a situation it might be some time before the heir occupied his inheritance. This explanation would on the whole seem more likely than the former, in that it touches on an aspect of the Statute of Marlborough which it is difficult to justify on grounds of equity. But neither of the possible explanations seem satisfactory if viewed in the light of the attitude of the

[1] *Rot. Parl.*, III. 558–9 (no. 63).

[2] It is worth noting that in 1364 in a case of collusion where the Crown asserted its rights of wardship (*CIPMA*, XI. 397–8 (no. 522)), it found it necessary to forbid the justices to hold assizes which the ousted feoffees arraigned before them (*CCR. 1364–8*, pp. 72–3).

courts of common law towards uses and, in particular, the fact that very little effort had been made to employ the Statute of Marlborough against them. Indeed, the most curious feature of the petition is the implicit assumption it contains that the statute was frequently employed by lords who were deprived of their rights by their tenants' enfeoffments. A third possibility might be suggested—that those behind the petition thought, however mistakenly, that the reform it demanded was the best means of making the Statute of Marlborough an effective weapon against uses. But this would presuppose a degree of legal ignorance and practical incompetence which it might be difficult to reconcile with the adoption of the petition by the Commons. At any rate, no more is heard of the deliberations of Lords and Justices which the Crown promised and the petition must remain something of a mystery.

The advantages which uses conferred on those who employed them were such that the failure of the courts of common law to develop effective doctrines of collusion, and the almost complete absence of attempts at legislative reform, need occasion no surprise. The courts would only have grappled with the fundamentals of the problems of collusion which uses posed if real efforts had been made to make use of the facilities they offered. But the lords who were deprived of their incidents through their tenants' uses were themselves tenants of other lords and, as such, they had a vested interest in the impotence of the common law and the absence of parliamentary action.

(ii) THE ATTITUDE OF THE CROWN

When uses first emerged, the resources which the Crown possessed to deal with the threat they posed to its feudal revenues differed from those of mesne lords in two respects. In the first place, mesne lords were helpless to prevent their tenants for enfeoffing to uses, since the latter had the right to alienate their holdings at will. But the Crown had a means of protecting its feudal rights in the licences to alienate which tenants-in-chief had to obtain in order to alienate their holdings. In the second place,

o

when a landowner died, the local escheator enquired into the amount and values of his estates, the identity of the lords of whom they were held, and the person and age of his heir. The inquisitions *post mortem* which were then sent to the Chancery, when collected together from all the counties in which the deceased had held lands, enabled the Crown's officials to decide whether he was a tenant-in-chief. A system of writs and, in the last resort, commissions of enquiry, provided a means of checking, if necessary, the details thus assembled, especially if there were grounds for believing that the King's rights might have been evaded. In consequence, the Crown was in a position to observe the extent of the employment of uses by its tenants-in-chief and the degree of their encroachments on its feudal revenues.

The system of licences to alienate was of limited value in controlling the expansion of uses. It applied only to lands held in chief and did not comprise those held of most of the honours that had escheated to the Crown or of the Duchy of Lancaster. The tenants-in-chief, therefore, were able to alienate at will all lands held other than in chief and the Crown was powerless to prevent the loss of its rights under 'prerogative wardship'. Even when a proposed enfeoffment damaged its rights, the Crown in law had no right to forbid it absolutely: as a result of the Statute of 1327,[1] even if the land was alienated without licence, although the Crown had the right to seize it, it had to restore it to the the alienee when a reasonable fine had been paid. Nevertheless, when an alienation was damaging to its interests, the Crown, by virtue of its prerogative, appears to have exercised the right to insist that the alienating tenant retained a portion of his holding so that he remained its tenant. An examination of the Patent Rolls of the late fourteenth and fifteenth centuries has brought to light a number of cases where, when a tenant-in-chief sought to alienate the whole of his holding, the Crown issued a licence on condition that he retained in his hands an acre, or fraction of an acre. This practice was followed in the case both of settlements of land which were made on a husband and wife jointly and of conveyances to feoffees to uses. It ensured that, when the alienor died, he re-

[1] See above, pp. 100-1.

mained a tenant-in-chief so that the Crown secured the wardship
of the land retained together with any rights of 'prerogative
wardship' and the wardship and marriage of the body of his heir
if he were under age. The following table summarizes the annual
totals of such entries as have been traced.

TABLE V. *The Protection of Royal Rights in Licences
to Alienate*

Year	Settlements	Uses	Year	Settlements	Uses
1373	—	1	1459	—	1
1384	—	1	1461	—	1
1388	—	1	1462	—	1
1393	—	1	1464	1	1
1400	1	—	1465	1	1
1401	1	1	1469	—	1
1402	2	2	1472	—	1
1403	3	—	1473	—	1
1406	1	1	1476	1	—
1407	2	—	1477	2	2
1408	3	—	1478	1	—
1429	2	—	1479	2	—
1430	—	2	1481	1	—
1431	2	1	1483	1	—
1432	—	4	1485	1	—
1433	2	—	1486	—	1
1434	4	3	1489	—	1
1435	—	2	1490	2	—
1436	—	5	1491	—	2
1438	1	1	1492	1	2
1439	1	2	1493	1	1
1440	2	1	1494	1	1
1442	1	—	1498	1	1
1446	—	1	1506	—	3
1448	—	1			

These figures show that the Crown was well aware throughout
the years in which uses were developing of the need to ensure
that a tenant-in-chief who became a *cestui que use* remained, in

however slight a degree, its tenant.[1] Out of 53 cases relating to uses, 9 occurred in the Yorkist period and 12 in the reign of Henry VII. No doubt their existence can be attributed to the revived interest during these reigns in the Crown's feudal resources. But it is remarkable that 24 cases are to be found in the reign of Henry VI, 21 of them in the years 1430–40. Probably these figures reflect in some degree a growing tendency on the part of tenants-in-chief to alienate the whole of their holdings. But it is extraordinary that the figures for the years 1430–40 are so high in comparison with those for the later fifteenth century, when there is a great deal of other evidence to reveal the care taken by royal officials to protect the feudal resources of the Crown. It is, therefore, difficult to avoid the conclusion that royal officials in the years 1430–40 must have been especially zealous about safeguarding royal rights. And, in default of any other explanation, we can only attribute their zeal to the concern about royal finances which is a prominent feature of the treasurership of Ralph, lord Cromwell (1433–43). At any rate, there can be no doubt that some efforts were made during the late fourteenth and fifteenth centuries to employ the system of licences to alienate so as to exercise some control over enfeoffments to uses by tenants-in-chief.[2]

The protection of the Crown's interests after a *cestui que use* had died presents a more complicated problem. The escheator, when he held the inquisition *post mortem*, would have to record therein the fact that the deceased had before his death conveyed lands to feoffees to his use. From the standpoint, then, of the exercise of the Crown's rights as feudal lord, these feoffees, not the deceased, were possessed of the land. When an escheator thus recognized the position of the feoffees, he was accepting a legal fiction which had the effect of depriving the Crown of rights which it was his duty to protect. However, a study of the sur-

[1] Cf. the implication in Constable, Introd., p. xiii, that the practice began under Henry VII.

[2] The practice would, of course, only achieve the intended result if an escheator was careful to record the fact that the exception had been made when he recited the terms of the licence in the inquisition *post mortem*. In the case of the alienations made by Sir Geoffrey Boleyn in 1462 the inquisition failed to do this (PRO, C. 140/10/21; cf. *CPR. 1461–7*, p. 141).

viving inquisitions *post mortem* of the fourteenth and fifteenth centuries reveals a number of methods by means of which escheators successfully defended the interests of the Crown. In each of these it was possible to uncover the actual situation which lay behind the fiction of the use and show that, despite his conveyance to feoffees, the deceased had remained in occupation of the land.

In the first place, the escheator could refuse to accept at their face value the deeds which were presented to him and the jury by the family or feoffees of the deceased. A rigorous enquiry into the circumstances and procedures by which the land in question was conveyed to the feoffees might bring to light some means of impugning the validity of the conveyance to them. When land was granted by one person to another, the conveyance was not effective until all the grantor's tenants, including his free manorial tenants, had attorned to the grantee—that is, formally recognized him as their lord.[1] In law a tenant who had not so attorned remained the tenant of the grantor. An investigation along these lines might, and sometimes did,[2] reveal that the deceased had remained seised of the services of some of his tenants. This information was especially valuable when all the lands held of the Crown had been conveyed to feoffees, since it enabled it to exercise its rights of wardship and marriage.[3]

It is difficult to decide from the evidence at our disposal how rigorously escheators enquired into the extent to which deceased tenants of the Crown had followed all the procedures that were required for the conveyance of their lands to feoffees. Although a number of inquisitions have survived from the late fourteenth and fifteenth centuries in which references are made to the extent of attornment by tenants, these form a small minority in

[1] Littleton, ss. 551 and 553.

[2] *CIPMA*, XI. 398 (no. 522); ibid., XII. 22 (no. 19); ibid., XII. 103–5 (no. 128); ibid., XIII. 5 and 107–8 (nos. 6 and 134); ibid., XIV. 18 (no. 17); ibid., XIV. 242 (no. 227); ibid., XIV. 270 (no. 267).

[3] Similar results might be achieved by an enquiry into the interval between the date of the enfeoffment and the day of death. In one case it was discovered that the deceased's attorneys had delivered seisin after his death (ibid., XII 5–6 (no. 7)).

comparison with those which merely record the fact that the lands in question had been conveyed to feoffees who are thus regarded as being seised at common law. We have no means of telling how far it is possible to infer from such a statement in an inquisition that the escheator had carried out all the necessary checks on the legal validity of the conveyance concerned. It is highly likely *a priori* that escheators failed to make all the enquiries that were possible. When a tenant had thus conveyed only part of the lands he held of the Crown, the latter did not suffer unduly from its escheator's laxity, since it retained the wardship and other incidents due from what remained. But, when the whole of the holding was granted to feoffees, the escheator's inefficiency might deprive the Crown of an opportunity to protect its rights. However, any increased zeal and efficiency in these enquiries by escheators would be bound in the long run to defeat their ends: landowners who were conveying to feoffees would take special care to leave no legal loopholes for the Crown. And, indeed, it is possible that such precautions on the part of the King's tenants largely explain the absence of references to attornment in the vast majority of the inquisitions *post mortem*. Moreover, it is important to remember that, however rigorous the enquiries made by the escheators into the validity of the conveyances made to feoffees, they did not thereby recover for the Crown its rights over the whole of the lands that had been alienated. A number of inquisitions show quite clearly that the Crown secured its rights of wardship only over those lands where the tenants had failed to attorn: where attornments had been performed, it had no alternative but to accept the position of the feoffees.[1] We must, therefore conclude that this method of combating the effects of uses was of limited value to the Crown. Its very employment implied that the position of feoffees was secure when the grantor's tenants had attorned to them. If a *cestui que use* was careful, he had nothing to fear from it.

The second means of dealing with its tenants' uses that was available to the Crown was more radical in its approach. Eschea-

---

[1] e.g. *CIPMA*, VIII. 312–14 (no. 467). Cf. *CPR*, *1343–5*, p. 332; *CIPMA*, XIV. 17–18 (no. 17). Cf. *CPR*, *1374–7*, p. 216.

tors appear to have employed the concept of a collusive enfeoff-ment—that is, one deliberately intended to deprive the Crown of its rights—in a number of inquisitions held on the deaths of royal tenants. When attempting to reconstruct the principles on which they based such an approach, it is important to remember that we are dealing with the practices followed by a large number of individual officials over a century and a half. Indeed, there were a few occasions when the Crown asserted its rights, not because the relevant inquisition made mention of collusion or fraud but because the Chancery officials assumed their presence from the details supplied by the escheator in his return. But, broadly speak-ing, there were two main grounds on which escheators arrived at findings of collusion. The first was the finding that the deceased had granted his lands to feoffees on condition that they should enfeoff his heir when he or she came of age. Examples of this can be found throughout the period when uses were developing, the first occurring in 1372.[1] Two features of this type of collusion deserve comment. First, the Crown's officials appear to have adopted the same approach as the courts of common law which also came to regard an enfeoffment of this type as collusive. It is especially interesting to note that the first assertion of royal rights on this ground occurred in 1372,[2] fourteen years after this view appeared in the court of Common Pleas.[3] But it would be unwise to assume that the royal officials were borrowing for the Crown's benefit the new common law doctrine: although an inquisition of 1361 in making a finding of collusion makes a

---

[1] *CIPMA*, XIII. 159 (no. 188); ibid., XIV. 270 (no. 267) (where the feoffees were to answer to the heir for the profits received by them during the minority); ibid., XIV. 94 (no. 98). For examples in the fifteenth century, see *CPR, 1452–61*, p. 46; *CIPMB*, II. 301 (no. 490).

[2] ibid., XIII. 159 (no. 188). This case is especially interesting because the Crown claimed rights of wardship only in respect of those manors of which the feoffees were directed to enfeoff the heir when he came of age. The widow was allowed to occupy those manors of which they were to enfeoff her for life (*CPR, 1370–4*, pp. 280–1). It is noteworthy that there had been no finding of collusion. But the Crown acted as if one had been made (*CFR, 1368–77*, p. 207).

[3] See above, p. 183.

reference to the Statute of Marlborough, c. 6,[1] it is equally likely that they were acting by virtue of the rights which pertained to the royal prerogative. Second, in findings of this type, in their efforts to avoid the evasion of royal rights, escheators appear to have searched beyond the terms of the original enfeoffment to the feoffees and enquired into its purpose.

The second kind of finding of collusion which can be traced is one which seems to have been based on the ground that the deceased had conveyed all the lands held of the Crown to feoffees.[2] There are, indeed, a few occasions when the Crown exercised its rights in respect of such lands even though the inquisition made no mention of fraud or collusion.[3] Unfortunately, we have no means of deciding how escheators judged between enfeoffments of this kind which were collusive and those which were made in good faith.[4] It is possible that enquiry was made into whether or not the deceased had remained on the land after the enfeoffment, though the relevant inquisitions make no mention of this fact. But, of course, in order to secure the protection of royal rights at law, it was sufficient that an inquisition made a finding of collusion without stating the reasons therefor.[5]

It is worth noting that the distinction which has been made between the two concepts of collusion employed by the Crown may be more apparent than real, since it is based, in the case of the first type, on the language used in inquisitions and this does not make entirely clear the nature of the evidence on which the finding was based. The statement that an enfeoffment was made on condition that the feoffees should enfeoff the heir when he came of age certainly looked into the purpose of the enfeoffment;

[1] *CIPMA*, XI. 398 (no. 522).

[2] ibid., XI. 398 (no. 522); ibid., XIII. 199 (no. 215); *CMI*, III. 57 (no. 158).

[3] It is in this sense that the term 'collusion' was employed in a statute of 1475 which assisted the creation of uses by those landowners who joined Edward IV's expedition to France (14 Ed. IV, c. 1).

[4] For examples of such a finding, see *CIPMA*, VIII. 313–14 (no. 467); ibid., XI. 183 (no. 209).

[5] The onus would then be on the feoffees to traverse the inquisition in Chancery.

but the language which is employed affords no proof that this purpose was stated either in a condition at common law made at the time of the enfeoffment[1] or in a will declared some time later. It is possible that the escheator and the jury he empanelled simply inferred the fraudulent nature of the deceased's intentions from the fact that he had conveyed the whole of his lands to feoffees and had then remained in occupation. It might be suggested that, since a number of findings of collusion of the second type occur before 1372, the first type then appears in response to the development of common law doctrines on this point; but examples of the former continue to appear thereafter. It is impossible to avoid the conclusion that these difficulties in the interpretation of our evidence are due to divergences of practice within the ranks of the escheators.

A third method of combating the consequences of uses for the Crown was the most radical of all. In most cases the enfeoffment of the feoffees was a legal fiction since the *cestui que use* remained upon the land. If the inquisition *post mortem* stated that he had done so and continued to draw its profits, this would constitute evidence that he had remained in seisin at common law and had made the enfeoffment for the purpose of defrauding the Crown of its rights. This mode of investigation, which had some basis in the doctrines of the common law, at least in the time of Bracton,[2] provided a sure means of overcoming the fictitious conveyance to feoffees. Several methods might be employed to enquire into whether or not the deceased had remained in occupation of the land. The jury might simply be pressed to give a truthful answer on this point: alternatively, the records of the administration of the deceased's estates might be searched—for instance, the question might be asked, in whose name were the courts held?—or manorial accounts might be examined to discover to whom revenues were paid. In the case of any inheritance in which enfeoffments to uses had been employed the evidence to prove their fraudulent intentions must always have been there, awaiting investigation. Clearly this means of enquiry and action available to the Crown was the most dangerous of all potential threats to uses and the

---

[1] See above, pp. 158-9.   [2] See above, p. 191.

advantages that royal tenants derived from them. But in fact it was rarely used[1] and most enfeoffments to uses made by royal tenants were allowed to stand without escheators making any effort to upset them.

All these details provide abundant evidence that the Crown possessed considerable resources to engage in a campaign to prevent the erosion of its feudal revenues by uses. Any attempt to assess the effectiveness of its employment of these powers over the whole of the fourteenth and fifteenth centuries would present an insuperable task. Not only would a thorough search have to be made of all the surviving inquisitions *post mortem* and escheators' accounts but the information obtained from them would have to be compared with the grants of wardships and other information entered on the Patent, Close, Fine and Originalia Rolls. Nor, when we discovered that the Crown was granting to a third party the lands of a deceased *cestui que use*, could we be certain that these necessarily comprised lands held to his use which other evidence— the relevant escheators' accounts, for example—revealed to have been seized by the Crown. In such circumstances the grantee might find it difficult to assert his rights over lands which were held by the feoffees, not the deceased, at common law, and might find it desirable to recognize their position, perhaps through a financial compromise. In the last resort it is very often impossible to trace the fortunes of portions of inheritances which were held by feoffees when grants of wardships made by the Crown merely specify that these comprised all the lands held by the deceased tenant without giving full details of all the manors and tenements transferred from the hands of its escheators to the grantees. More-

---

[1] There are only five cases in the extant inquisitions *post mortem* before the death of Edward III (*CIPMA*, XI. 243 (no. 309); ibid., XII. 12 (no. 12); ibid., XII. 354 (no. 371); ibid., XIII. 17–18 (no. 20); ibid., XIV. 242 (no. 227)). The last is especially interesting because enquiries were made into the collection of rents and the identities of those to whom they were paid. Cf. ibid., XIV. 101 (no. 104) where it is specifically stated that the feoffees were seised and the deceased took no profits except by their will. The question—who took the profits?—in 1410 prevented a feoffee of the attained earl of Nothumberland from recovering a manor with which he had been enfeoffed by the earl (*YBVE*, 11 Hen. IV, p. 52, pl. 30; PRO, K.B. 27/592/*Rex*, rot. 12).

over, in many cases, especially in the fourteenth century, not all the inquisitions held on the death of a tenant-in-chief or all the escheators' accounts of the relevant year of death have survived. In short, the vast labour which has been described would never answer all the questions of detail which we would want to ask. Yet, if we bear certain considerations in mind, it is possible to achieve some sound general conclusions regarding the situation of the Crown in the face of the growth of uses.

If the Crown was to prevent completely the evasion of its rights through uses, it would have to insist that its escheators enquire into whether or not its tenants continued to draw the profits of those lands of which they had enfeoffed feoffees. Such a task would have entailed a complex administrative operation in which all the royal officials involved would have required constant supervision and been required to exercise it themselves in the performance of their duties. The structure of government in later medieval England was such that this task could only have been achieved as a result of a personal intervention on the part of the monarch and his determination that his aims in this respect be ruthlessly accomplished. Moreover, such policies would have to be achieved against the vested interests of all his landowning subjects. It is hardly necessary to emphasize the fact that between the death of Edward I and the accession of Henry VII the English Crown was never in a position which made such policies politically feasible. When the King was not a child, he was faced either by a rebellious nobility or by the need to secure the support of his subjects for foreign ambitions which would, in any case, have absorbed his interest and all his energies. Nor was it possible for the Crown to avoid its losses through uses by refusing licences for its tenants-in-chief to alienate to feoffees. If attempted, such a policy could not have avoided losses of 'prerogative wardship' through uses, since there would have been nothing to prevent alienations to feoffees of lands held of other lords. But, in any case, it would have constituted a breach of the statute of 1327, since there was nothing in law to prevent alienations of lands held in chief provided some land continued to be held of the Crown by the alienor.[1]

[1] This point is ignored in Holmes, p. 57.

For these reasons a radical attack upon uses was not practical politics. Nevertheless, it was possible for the Crown to pursue a policy which, while it allowed its subjects to continue to employ uses, avoided the complete loss of its rights thereby. As long as it was able to ensure that a tenant-in-chief died holding some lands of the Crown, it was able to enjoy its rights as lord in respect of these and, if the heir was under age, his wardship and marriage, together with the 'prerogative wardship' of any other lands of which the deceased had died seised. Such an approach to the problem of uses was quite feasible provided that the officials of the Chancery performed their duties with diligence and efficiency. Of course, if these qualities had been exhibited in the procedure which preceded the issuing of licences to alienate, the problem of the complete loss of royal rights would not arise. But, when a tenant-in-chief died, two different situations might arise in either of which it would be found that the whole of his holding had been conveyed to feoffees who were thus seised at common law. In one it would be found that he had obtained, as a result of laxity on the part of Chancery officials, a licence to convey the whole of his holding in chief to feoffees. At the end of the fifteenth century it appears to have been accepted legal opinion that in such a case the fact that a licence had been granted would debar a finding of collusion.[1] But the point was never tested in the courts and, in any case, there was another approach available to the Crown which would by-pass any adverse legal doctrine on this point. The issue of a licence would have been made on the virtual understanding that the alienor was to convey a real and effective seisin to his feoffees and, therefore, the fact that the alienor would have remained upon his holding would have sufficed to render null and void any legal consequences of the issue of a licence to alienate.

[1] In 1497 in Stonor's case Justice Danvers stated that 'the King cannot aver collusion contrary to his own licence for if the tenant aliens, the King shall seize the land for the fine and not because of the collusion; and if he aliens by licence, the King cannot say that the feoffment was made to defraud him of the wardship, where he himself is a party to the feoffment' (*S.C. Exch. Chamb.*, II. 172). The position was altered after 1490, since from then onwards the Crown's interpretation of the statute of that year ensured that it could not be deprived of wardship of the body (see below, Ch. V (i)).

The other possible situation was one in which it would be found that the deceased tenant-in-chief had alienated the whole of his holding to feoffees without suing out a licence. Under the terms of the statute of 1327 the Crown was under the obligation to pardon alienations made without licence. But in this particular case the fact that the deceased had so conveyed the whole of his holding would constitute evidence of collusion and the terms of the statute of 1327 need not apply.

If the Crown secured a finding of collusion in an inquisition *post mortem*, the need for vigilance on the part of its officials was not necessarily over, since there was a possible means of recovering their rights open to the feoffees at common law. They could, if they wished, 'traverse' the findings which had resulted in their removal from the lands—that is, appear before the Chancellor to deny the facts recorded in the inquisition. If the lands remained in the hands of the Crown, the feoffees brought a petition of right; and, if the Crown had in the meanwhile granted the wardship to a third party, it was necessary to proceed by suing out a writ of *scire facias* to secure the annulment of the royal grant.[1] Whichever procedure was followed, a special commission was issued in Chancery to enquire into the facts in the shire where the lands lay. When this was held, it was essential to ensure that its findings were thorough and accurate and paid due regard to all the legal issues involved in the prosecution of the King's feudal rights.[2]

[1] This belonged to what later came to be called the 'common law' side of Chancery, for which see Holdsworth, I. 452; Constable, Introd., p. xix. If the inquests found in favour of the claimants, then the Crown and they pleaded to issue in the Chancery. From there the issue joined was sent to the King's Bench for trial. When this ended, the record and judgement were returned to the Chancery where, if the claimants had been successful, the necessary action was taken—either a writ ordering the escheator to deliver the lands or an annulment of the letters patent in which they had been granted to a third party. The whole record was entered in the *Coram Rege* Roll, *Rex* side. This procedure was created by statutes of 1361 and 1362 (34 Ed. III, c. 14, and 36 Ed. III, st. 1, c. 13).

[2] For examples of feoffees who brought such actions successfully, see *CPR, 1399–1401*, pp. 172–3; ibid., *1401–5*, pp. 172 and 499–500; ibid., *1416–22*, p. 338; ibid., *1422–9*, p. 538; ibid., *1436–41*, pp. 258–9; ibid., *1441–6*, pp. 183–4.

In view of the considerable legal and administrative resources of the royal prerogative, how successful was the Crown in protecting its interests? The easiest and most profitable way to answer this question is to investigate the extent to which tenants-in-chief managed to deprive the Crown completely of its rights—that is, convey the whole of their holdings to feoffees to uses without the Crown taking any action to recover its rights. For this purpose three periods have been chosen: in each the extant inquisitions *post mortem* and the relevant Patent, Close and Fine Rolls have been searched to discover how far royal rights were exercised in respect of deceased tenants-in-chief who had conveyed all their holdings to uses. The first of these periods—that from the beginnings of the emergence of uses to the death of Edward III—has been chosen because it was then that the Crown first became conscious of the threat uses posed to its feudal revenues. The second period covers the 12th–16th regnal years of Henry VI—from September 1433 to September 1438: it enables us to examine the situation in the mid-fifteenth century, at a time when Chancery officials were especially zealous to protect royal rights in licences to alienate.[1] And in the third period—the reign of Edward IV—we view a situation in which uses had been an accepted part of the structure of English landownership for well over a century and the Crown had been afforded plenty of opportunities to develop a coherent policy towards them.

Down to the death of Edward III nine landowners who left heirs under age are recorded as having conveyed all their holdings in chief to uses. In the case of Edmund Benstead,[2] the Crown exercised its rights of wardship and marriage:[3] it is not clear whether it simply overrode the deceased's feoffees or acted thus because he held other lands in fee not recorded in the extant inquisition. Despite his grant to feoffees, the inquisition held on the death of John Leyham in 1369 found that he had remained in seisin and had always drawn the issues.[4] The inquisition held after the death of Sir Ralph Hempnall in 1370 found that he had conveyed all his lands to feoffees who remained seised and to whom all the tenants

---

[1] See Table V.
[2] *CPR, 1334–8*, p. 557.
[3] *CIPMA*, VII. 398 (no. 568).
[4] ibid., XII. 354 (no. 371).

had attorned.[1] He had, however, done so without licence, an omission which gave the Crown an opportunity to assert its rights. In return for the payment of 500 marks the feoffees were granted the wardship and marriage of the heir and were at the same time pardoned for acquiring without licence.[2] The details of the negotiations which led to this settlement are unknown. It is, however, quite clear that the Crown in no way accepted the evasion of its rights. The sum of 500 marks was a considerable sum to pay for the wardship and marriage of a country squire, a point which justifies the conclusion that the feoffees were confronted with a choice between this and the holding of fresh inquisitions which would dispossess them. When Roger Widdrington died in 1372, the first inquisition held concerning his holdings in chief simply found that he had conveyed them to a group of feoffees. But the Chancery then issued a writ enquiring whether the feoffment had been made fraudulently; and the resulting inquisition found that this was so, though without specifying the grounds for this finding.[3] On the death of John Man in 1372, the first inquisition stated that the alienation had been made without licence and the tenants had not attorned. The second found that the enfeoffment had been made to deprive the King and other lords of their rights on the ground that the feoffees were to enfeoff his daughter and heir when she came of age and were in the meanwhile to answer to her for the profits.[4] In five of the nine cases, therefore, the Crown asserted its rights without serious difficulty. But in the remaining four—Walter Clerebek (1338),[5] Richard Danvers (1361),[6] Sir Roger Gyney (1376)[7] and Sir John Kiriel (1377)[8]—there is no evidence, either in the extant inquisitions *post mortem* or elsewhere, that the Crown made any effort to protect its interests.

[1] ibid., XIII. 64–5 (no. 85). [2] *CPR, 1370–4*, p. 255.
[3] *CIPMA*, XIII. 198–200 (no. 215). [4] ibid., XIV. 270 (no. 267).
[5] ibid., VIII. 99 (no. 157). See also *CPR, 1334–8*, p. 385, and *CCR, 1337–9*, p. 355.
[6] *CIPMA*, XI. 200–1 (no. 244). Seisin had been given to the feoffees on condition that they should appropriate the lands to the prior and convent of Southwick. His heir was a great-nephew.
[7] ibid., XIV. 263 (no. 255). [8] ibid., XIV. 299 (no. 313).

It would be wrong to conclude, on the basis of these cases of successful evasion of royal rights, that the Chancery officials of Edward III made insufficient efforts to prevent such practices. These cases form a very small minority of all those tenants-in-chief who had conveyed lands to uses. And there is much other evidence to suggest that royal officials were both vigilant and diligent. When John Hastings, earl of Pembroke, died in 1375, care was taken to enquire carefully into the details of the directions he had given his feoffees: it was discovered that these were based on the assumption that he had died without issue. While this might have happened if he had died shortly after making them in 1372, they were rendered null and void by the birth of an heir before his actual death in 1375. On these grounds the Crown asserted its full rights of wardship.[1] Indeed, a study of the extant inquisitions *post mortem* brings to light many occasions when the Chancery felt dissatisfied with the escheators' findings and ordered fresh inquisitions. Some uses came to light on the deaths of tenants who held of minors in the King's custody; and in some of these careful enquiry was made into attornment to the feoffees on the part of the deceased's tenants.[2] The most remarkable instance of the Crown's prosecution of its rights in the case of lands held of a custody is that of Giles Nekton, who died in 1361, a tenant of the abbey of Bury St. Edmunds, then in royal hands through a vacancy. The inquisition found that his grant to feoffees was fraudulently intended to deprive the lord of his rights—apparently on the ground that the whole of his holding had been conveyed: at the same time it stated that many of his tenants had not attorned to the feoffees.[3]

Perhaps the best illustration of the stringency and efficiency with which royal rights were enforced is what happened on a number of occasions when tenants-in-chief had conveyed to feoffees only lands which they held of mesne lords. In six such cases the Crown ejected the feoffees to assert its rights of 'pre-

[1] *CCR, 1374–7*, pp. 286–8.

[2] *CIPMA*, XI. 398 (no. 522); ibid., XIII. 5 and 107–8 (nos. 6 and 134); ibid., XIV. 18 (no. 17); ibid., XIV. 242 (no. 227).

[3] ibid., XI. 398 (no. 522).

rogative wardship'. In four of these it was found that the deceased had died seised, since he had continued to draw the profits of the lands despite his enfeoffment of feoffees.[1] In two cases—Sir William Ingoldsthorpe who died in 1363,[2] and John son of Sir Walter Baskerville who died in 1374[3]—the Crown's seizure of the lands held of mesne lords was based on a finding that the deceased had directed his feoffees to enfeoff the heir when he came of age. It would, however, be wrong to assume that these details reflect a general determination on the part of the Crown to override uses which deprived it of 'prerogative wardship'. These are the only instances of such a practice that can be traced; and the surviving inquisitions *post mortem* contain many other such cases where there is no evidence that the Crown ever asserted its rights.[4]

During the five years 1433–8 there were three tenants-in-chief whose heirs and lands escaped royal wardship altogether.[5] In one case[6] the Crown seems to have accepted the loss of its rights quite readily: a pardon, which rehearsed the terms of the inquisition *post mortem* and thus described the enfeoffment of the feoffees by the deceased, was granted to them for entering without licence

[1] ibid., X. 140–1 (no. 161); ibid., XI. 242–4 (no. 309); ibid., XII. 10–13 (no. 12); ibid., XIII. 17–18 (no. 20).

[2] ibid., XIII. 158–9 (no. 188); CFR, *1368–77*, p. 207. The conveyance to feoffees must have escaped the attention of the Crown for nine years, since, though he died in 1363, the inquisition dealing with these lands was not held until 1372.

[3] *CIPMA*, XIV. 94 (no. 98). He conveyed the manor of Cressage, held of the earl of March, to feoffees, on condition that they should employ its profits to repay a debt of £100 and enfeoff the son or daughter born of his wife when he or she came of age. In the meantime the residue of the profits after the repayment of the debt was to be used for the benefit of his soul and that of his mother. These directions differ from those in the other cases of collusion in that the residue of the profits was to be used for religious purposes; but this did not prevent the finding of collusion.

[4] See Appendix II. A list would be too lengthy for a footnote.

[5] PRO, C. 139/64/19 (Roger Saperton); –/64/21 (Richard Baynard); and –/74/27 (Richard de la Mare). Roger Saperton's daughter and heir was thirteen years of age and already married. Nevertheless, if only technically, her lands should have been in wardship (cf. CPR, *1429–36*, p. 367).

[6] ibid., *1429–36*, p. 368.

P

and a mere five marks charged for it. But, in contrast with this example of apparent laxity, we have the case of Thomas Sinclair, who died in May 1435, leaving three daughters under age as his heirs. Of three inquisitions held by local escheators in 1436–7, two stated that he had died landless in the shires where they were held; but in the case of Oxfordshire he had enfeoffed feoffees of all his lands and thus did not die seised of any there.[1] On 1 December 1438, for a sum of 200 marks, the Crown granted the wardship of the lands and heirs and their marriages to Sir Thomas Stanley and Thomas Pigot.[2] This was followed by a number of inquisitions, held under commissions of enquiry, which found that the deceased had conveyed all his lands in seven counties to feoffees to his use, in collusion to defraud the King and other lords of their rights.[3] Finally, letters patent of 16 December 1445 ordered the restitution to the heirs of all the lands in the King's hands through the death of Thomas Sinclair.[4] These details are especially interesting because of the ways in which the Crown managed to avoid the loss of its rights. It is true that they were enforced with some difficulty. Indeed, it was three and a half years after Sinclair's death before it realized that its rights were being evaded. Moreover, according to its own statement in the grant of 1438, it then learnt of its losses, not through its escheators, but by a petition, presumably from those who were anxious to acquire the wardship. Even when the Crown had sold the wardship, the rights of

---

[1] PRO, Chan., inq. p.m., C. 139/73/4. These give the date of death as August 1435. But on this the later, more accurate inquisitions have been followed. Although the alienation to feoffees in Oxfordshire was made without licence, there is no trace of the feoffees suing out a pardon. It is, therefore, possible that these lands remained in the hands of the Crown.

[2] CPR, 1436–41, p. 241.

[3] PRO, Chan., inq. miscell., C. 145/308/1. There are two interesting points regarding the findings of collusion. First, the feoffees are stated to have continued their possession during the lifetime of Thomas Sinclair. In view of this, it would seem that collusion was deduced from the fact that the deceased had conveyed to feoffees the whole of his holdings in chief in each county. Second, the findings comprised the lands held of mesne lords which were subject to 'prerogative wardship'. In the case of one manor in Suffolk Thomas Sinclair was found to have died seised.

[4] CPR, 1441–6, p. 443.

the grantees were far from secure. The terms of the letters patent
of 1445 indicate that they had so far been unable to enforce their
rights of marriage. Nevertheless, the Crown was able to sell the
wardship for a sum of money. And it is clear that the legal position
of the heirs was a risky one, until in 1445 they and their husbands
secured the royal licence to enter into their lands. The details of the
letters patent granted for this purpose indicate that the royal
licence was not granted until they had made satisfaction for their
marriages to those to whom the Crown had granted them. Unlike those inheritances in chief which did escape royal rights of
wardship in the years 1433-8, the Sinclair estates were valuable,
spreading over eight countries. Its fortunes suggest that, in the
last resort, the Crown's rights to a valuable wardship would be
protected, if not by its escheators, then by the acquisitiveness of
would-be grantees.

During the reign of Edward IV there were at least twelve
tenants-in-chief whose heirs and lands escaped royal wardship as
a result of uses.[1] Three cases in particular emphasize the extent to
which the Crown appears to have been content to accept the
consequent damage to its interests. In the case of Sir John Seymour
the inquisitions held on his death found that he had died seised in
fee; but his feoffees succeeded in traversing these findings.[2] Indeed, it is quite apparent that, when the special local inquests
summoned to enquire into the facts found that the lands had been

---

[1] (1) Bertram Harbottle (PRO, C. 140/7/11. Cf. *The Northumberland
County History*, IX. 266-8);
(2) Gerard Sothill (-, C. 140/9/18. Cf. *CPR, 1461-7*, p. 218).
(3) Brian Darell (-/C. 140/11/14);
(4) Sir John Seymour (-/14/32);
(5) Robert Bodenham (-/20/34);
(6) Thomas Horsey (-/28/32);
(7) Robert Cuny (-/37/34);
(8) Sir John Benstead (-/38/57);
(9) Sir Roger Ree (-/52/33);
(10) Sir Geoffrey Gate (-/56/50);
(11) William Dodesham (-/77/78; Cf. *CPR, 1476-85*, pp. 234 and 253);
(12) John Orde (-/83/22).
[2] PRO, K. B. 27/817/*Rex*, rott. 8-9.

conveyed to feoffees by the deceased, they made no effort at all to look beyond the formal terms of the deeds of conveyance.[1] The two other cases provide even more striking illustrations of the complete failure to press royal rights. Both Sir Geoffrey Gate and John Orde had enfeoffed their feoffees without suing out royal licences. The Crown, however, was quite content to pardon the feoffees' transgressions in entering the lands without licence. Nor can it be suggested that the royal officials made any effort to secure compensation for the loss of wardship by charging high fines for the pardons: in the case of Sir Geoffrey Gate's lands the fine amounted to a mere 40s.,[2] and in John Orde's to half that amount.[3] In the early years of the reign it is conceivable that some tenants-in-chief managed to escape royal wardship as a result of the dislocation in central and local government caused by civil war; but this situation did not exist at the time of the Gate and Orde feoffees' pardons. When they were issued, in 1480 and 1482 respectively, Edward IV was firmly in control of his kingdom and was giving much attention to administrative and financial reform.

In the light of the details assembled from these three periods, it is possible to reach some rough general conclusions about the Crown's exploitation of its feudal rights in face of the growth of uses. It is clear that some tenants-in-chief who were under age escaped the clutches of the Crown. The annual averages for 1433–8 and the reign of Edward IV are much higher than those for Edward III's reign. But, since the latter was a period in which uses were only just beginning to emerge among tenants-in-chief, it would be unwise to place any emphasis on this comparison. Nor is it fair to suggest that the instances of successful evasion of royal rights point to laxity on the part of the King's Chancery clerks and escheators. The task of searching out the realities which lay behind uses was a difficult one. And, while the Chancery was able

---

[1] For evidence that Sir John Seymour had remained in occupation of his estates after his enfeoffment of the feoffees and also details of his will, see the earl of Cardigan, *The Wardens of Savernake Forest* (London, 1949), pp. 118–20.

[2] *CPR, 1476–85*, p. 195.

[3] ibid., *1476–85*, pp. 318–19. For evidence that the Orde family continued to hold these estates, see *The Northumberland County History*, IX. 45–6.

to order fresh inquisitions if dissatisfied with those returned, its clerks had a multitude of duties to perform. Indeed, for knowledge of the death of a tenant-in-chief who was not a major landowner, the Chancery was always in some measure dependent on relatives or on individuals who wished to secure the grant of the wardship for themselves. If the King's officials omitted to notice that royal rights were being evaded, the fault was not entirely theirs. The existence of tenants-in-chief who escaped royal wardship may thus be partly imputed to the absence of persons who were anxious to obtain the wardship and marriage of the heir. If these appeared, even some years after the tenant-in-chief's death—as happened in the case of Thomas Sinclair between 1435 and 1445—fresh inquisitions could be ordered and, with the enquiries diligently pursued, royal rights be recovered. In fact, remarkably few tenants-in-chief evaded royal rights altogether by means of uses: and those that succeeded in this did not belong to the upper ranks of the country's landowners.

Nevertheless, it is difficult to avoid the impression that some deterioration occurred in the efficiency with which royal rights were prosecuted in the late fourteenth and fifteenth centuries. In view of the difficulties of comparison with Edward III's reign, a period when uses were emerging, we cannot argue that there was an increase in the number of tenants-in-chief who escaped wardship. A decline in efficiency may, however, be traced in two other aspects of the Crown's feudal rights. In the first place, the Crown appears to have accepted the loss of 'prerogative wardship' as a result of uses. The few precedents for the assertion of its rights that we have discovered in the reign of Edward III were not generally followed. In itself this is not surprising: the prosecution of this aspect of the royal prerogative, when the deceased had been seised of lands in chief and the basic royal rights of wardship and marriage were unscathed, must have seemed superfluous to most escheators. Indeed, most of them in Edward III's reign were content to let the Crown lose its 'prerogative wardship' to uses. During the next few generations, however, this situation of administrative laxity becomes one of legal doubt. Did a tenant-in-chief possess the right in law to deprive the Crown of 'prerogative

wardship', even though he had alienated the lands he held
of mesne lords in a way that would have been collusive had
they been held in chief? In a case of *scire facias* in 1407 this was one
of a number of issues discussed by the judges: they appear to have
taken the view that there was nothing in law to prevent the
evasion of royal rights in this way.[1] Legal opinion remained
divided on this issue at the close of the fifteenth century.[2]

In the second place, there appears to have been no real effort to
prevent the loss of wardship and marriage through uses when
lands were held of the Crown *ut de honore* or of estates that were
temporarily in its hands. It is quite clear, for example, that in the
Yorkist period the Crown felt unable to stop such losses on the
estates of the Duchy of Lancaster without legislation in parlia-

[1] For the discussion, see *YBVE*, Mich., 9 Hen. IV, pl. 20, pp. 6–7, and for the
record, PRO, K.B. 27/585/*Rex*, rot. 45. The estates concerned had belonged
to Sir Ralph Hempnall, who had died in 1391, leaving a son and heir who was
then under age and remained an idiot until his death in 1403. The whole of his
inheritance, including lands held in chief, had been conveyed by Sir Ralph to
feoffees who themselves in turn granted them to others after his death. After
the heir's death the surviving feoffee attempted to traverse the findings of inquisitions held by the escheator. In the case of each portion of the estates there
were two of these: one found that Sir Ralph had died seised, the other that he
had continued to draw the profits after the enfeoffment and that this had been
made in order that the feoffees might enfeoff the heir when he came of age.
Despite the views expressed on the 'prerogative wardship' aspect of the matter
by the judges, including Gascoigne, Chief Justice of the King's Bench, the
petitioner failed. As far as we can tell, the writ of *scire facias* was quashed on one
or both of two grounds. Firstly, the local inquest ordered by the court had
failed to deal with the earlier finding regarding the purpose of the enfeoffment.
And, secondly, the petitioner claimed that the lands were conveyed to him on
a date when they were in the possession of the escheator. But in February 1409
the King admitted the rights of the petitioner and surrendered the lands to
him. However, this concession was made in return for a fine of 600 marks: the
size of this figure suggests that the Crown considered its claims in respect of
'prerogative wardship' stronger than the judges had allowed (*CPR, 1408–13*,
pp. 49–50).

The reference to this case by Statham (*Abridgement*, trans. M. C. Klingel-
smith (2 vols., Boston, Mass., 1915), I. 372 (10) bears no relation to the extant
Year Book discussion and wrongly gives the Crown its rights in respect of
'prerogative wardship'.

[2] Constable, p. 19, n. 46; Coke, *Second Institute*, III.

ment.[1] Of course, those landowners who deprived the Crown of this aspect of its rights by means of uses were in a strong legal position: in law they were free to alienate their holdings as they wished and the Crown's legal status was that of any mesne lord. In theory, it would have been possible to discover that the deceased *cestui que use* had continued to draw the profits after the enfeoffment: in practice, to compel royal escheators and bailiffs to make such enquiries would have been an immense administrative task.

It is abundantly clear from the evidence that has been discussed that the Crown in the late fourteenth and fifteenth centuries never pursued a coherent and conscious policy towards uses. Its tenants deprived it of its feudal rights by these means; and the officials of the Chancery must have become increasingly aware of the Crown's growing losses.[2] Despite this, there was no legislation against uses on a national scale and no sign of any tightening-up of the administrative powers that could be directed against them. However, if we cannot perceive a coherent royal policy against uses, we can probably discern an attitude towards them. It is fair to assume that the officials of the Chancery always proceeded on the assumption that every tenant-in-chief must die seised of some lands. And, if this were the case, in view of the existing legal position the Crown's interests were reasonably well protected: though its feudal revenues might be depleted, the hard core of its rights—the wardship and marriage of tenants-in-chief who were under age—remained. In practice, it is clear that insufficient efforts were made to ensure that this principle was always followed. But, in cases of failure, what occurred was not a weakening of the basis of the Crown's legal and administrative resources but a failure of the will to exploit them.

Why, in view of its awareness of its losses through uses, did

---

[1] *Rot. Parl.*, VI. 207b, discussed below, Chapter V (i).

[2] The extent to which lands held in wardship by the Crown were depleted by uses was brought out into the open in 1436. In the assessment of the income tax of that year the feoffees of Thomas, late lord Morley, were among the major landowners of the kingdom who were specially assessed (H. L. Gray, 'Incomes from Land in England in 1436', *EHR*, XLIX (1934), 617).

the Crown not resort to harsher measures? Part of the answer must be found in the existence of many other problems which absorbed the energies of the monarch and his officials and diverted their attention from uses. What made their virtual acceptance of the situation all the more easy was the fact that the number of tenants-in-chief who escaped royal wardship altogether never reached alarming proportions. Indeed, there were two factors which ensured that, without any effort on the part of the Crown, it was kept within reasonable bounds. One was the fact that courtiers, influential magnates and even royal officials were always eager to win wardships and marriages and would not hesitate to bring particular cases of evasion to the notice of the Crown. Moreover, in the hope of their own gain, when inquisitions were held, they would add their influence to the authority of the escheator to ensure that the deceased was found seised of at least some lands in chief. The other factor was the existence of doctrines of collusion which made the conveyance to uses of all the lands held in chief a hazardous undertaking. In this situation, therefore, the Crown secured its rights, in some measure at least, over the vast majority of its tenants-in-chief. Those who slipped through the net cast by the legal and administrative resources of its prerogative were neither so numerous nor so wealthy as to constitute reasons for public embarrassment or serious financial concern.

(iii) The Loss of Incidents

Any attempt to assess the extent to which the revenues of feudal lords declined as a result of the growth of uses must distinguish between the interests of the Crown and those of mesne lords. The latter, however powerful, had no means in law of preventing their tenants from making enfeoffments to uses. Unlike the Crown, they were unable to insist on the right to license alienations of the lands held of them. Above all, they were powerless to prevent their tenants from so alienating the whole of their fees: when the tenant died, his feoffees were in law the lord's tenants and he held nothing in fee of the lord. In consequence, if the heir was over age, the lord lost his relief: if he was under age, the lord's rights of wardship and marriage were worthless. In the case of incidents which belonged to mesne lords, therefore, enfeoffments to uses could result in the loss of the whole of the incidents due to the lord. Indeed, any tie between lord and man, however legalistic, had now completely disappeared: the fact that the feoffees were the lord's tenants in law, although the *cestui que use* occupied the land, meant that the relationship between the lord and his tenant, in so far as it was expressed in feudal terms, was purely a matter of legal form. Feudal tenure bore no relation to the actual occupation of the land and brought no benefit whatsoever to the lord: indeed, where before there had been one tenant in law, now there were several 'men of straw'.

The extent to which mesne lords were prepared to accept this situation is illustrated by the paucity of the Year Book cases in which some of them attempted to assert their rights—four in the latter half of the fourteenth, and two in the first half of the fifteenth, centuries.[1] In all these cases the lords were claiming the whole of their rights of wardship and marriage—that is, both the land and the body of the heir. In the late fourteenth and fifteenth centuries lords, in attempting to assert their rights, do not appear to have tried to distinguish between their rights to the land and those to the body of the heir and argue that, while the deceased tenant's enfeoffment had deprived them of the land, it could not deprive them of the wardship of the body and the marriage of the heir. Such a claim would be bound to prove more difficult to press in a court of law than one relating to lands only, since the deceased tenant may have held of more than one lord and thus disputes might arise over the question of priority of enfeoffment. But, in view of the fact that claims of this type would provide a means of clinging on to a portion of the incidents that were disappearing, it is, perhaps, surprising that traces of efforts along these lines have not been found in the Year Books during the period when common law doctrines regarding collusive uses were being developed.[2]

[1] See above, Ch. IV (i), passim.
[2] *Cf. YBVE*, 12 Hen. IV, Hil., p. 13, pl. 5, where a lord sought a writ of ward of the body against a widow and failed because he neither exercised nor claimed wardship of the land. There is, however, nothing in the discussion to show that

In fact, if we can rely upon the details contained in the Year Books, no lord attempted to raise in the courts until 1536 the point that, when a tenant conveyed all his lands to feoffees to uses, the lord lost his rights of marriage of the infant heir. The details of the case then pleaded and discussed[1] illustrate the extent to which in this situation there occurred in practical terms a complete disappearance of the lord's rights. In Trinity Term 1536 the abbot of Bury St. Edmunds brought a writ of ward against a widow, demanding the body of a ward whose custody he claimed. Before her husband's death a group of feoffees had been seised to the use of him and his wife for term of her life and, after her death, to the use of him and his heirs. After his death, therefore, they continued to be seised to the use of the widow. The case was argued again in Hilary Term 1537, but without any conclusion. Two judges of the Common Pleas—Shelley and Fitzherbert, the latter the author of the famous *Abridgement*—took the view that the heir was out of ward. Both they and others who engaged in the discussion argued that the abbot had a tenant and thus could not claim the wardship of the deceased's heir, though the identity of the tenant was a matter of disagreement—Justice Shelley took the view that it was the feoffees, and two serjeants the wife.[2]

A situation in which mesne lords could not secure the wardship of the bodies of infant heirs and their marriages had far-reaching implications for the structure of family law, since it raised the question of the guardianship of the infants during their minorities. If the lord was unable to exercise his rights of wardship, a custom would have to be developed which provided for the guardianship of the heir. There is evidence to indicate that a number of landowners were much aware of this problem when they drew up their wills and made arrangements accordingly. In 1383, in de-

the widow held her estate through a settlement effected *after* her husband's death.

[1] Dyer, I. 7b–13a (no. 11).

[2] In a similar situation the Crown, following on the promulgation of the statute of 1490 and its interpretation from the standpoint of the royal prerogative, claimed the wardship of the body and the marriage (see below, p. 251).

claring the uses to which his feoffees were enfeoffed, Sir William Fraunk stated that, if he had male issue, such issue was to be discreetly governed by his feoffees and enfeoffed of all his lands by them when he came of age; he further directed that the profits they obtained from the heir's marriage were to be applied for the benefit of his sisters, or, if they were dead, for that of the testator's soul and the payment of his debts.[1] In 1400 the feoffees to whom the deceased Sir Robert Shardelowe had conveyed all his lands granted a manor to his widow for her life on condition that she find John his son and heir sufficient food and clothing for schools and nurture until he reached the age of twenty-one and then pay him £20 a year.[2] In 1431 the will of Thomas Stonor laid down that Thomas his son and heir was to be under the governance and supervision of Thomas Chaucer, who was to have the issues of one of his manors for the infant's sustenance until the age of twenty-one and that his marriage was to be sold by four persons (who included his wife and Chaucer) and the profits thereof, together with the issue of certain manors, be spent on the marrying of his five daughters.[3] In his will made in 1441 Sir John Hody, Chief Justice of the King's Bench, directed that his feoffees were to pay the issues of most of his lands to his executors 'for the finding of John my son and heir until the said John shall have attained the age of sixteen years', when they were to convey a sufficient estate in law to him and his heirs. A later clause reads, 'I will that the same John be under the custody of my executors'.[4] In the same year Sir John Seyntleger, after directing his feoffees to make settlements on each of his sons, including his heir, when they came of age or married with their assent, willed 'that from the remainder of the said issues the said my sons and daughters be found, sustained and governed in an honest manner according to the

---

[1] *Sir Christopher Hatton's Book of Seals*, ed. L. C. Loyd and D. M. Stenton (Oxford, 1950), pp. 336–7, no. 486. The lord who thus lost the wardship and marriage of the heir was John of Gaunt, duke of Lancaster.

[2] *CPR, 1452–61*, pp. 206–7.

[3] *The Stonor Letters and Papers, 1290–1483*, ed. C. L. Kingsford (Camden Soc., Third Ser., XXIX, 1919), I. 48. See also ibid., Introd., p. xxii.

[4] *Reg. Chich.*, II. 605–6.

discretion of the said feoffees until they be married in the afore-said form or lands or tenements be assigned and delivered to them'.[1] The following year Edward Tyrrell, after directing that his feoffees were to use the revenues of one of his manors for the 'finding' of his son and heir, declared, 'Also I will that Anne my wife and mine executors have the avail (*avayle*) of the marriage of Edward my son if he be within age at the day of my death in performing my will.'[2]

Similar illustrative material may be found in the probate re-cords of the archdiocese of York in the latter half of the fifteenth century.[3] In 1462 Oliver Mirfield willed that 'mine executors have the rule of my son and of my livelihood during the nonage of my said son'.[4] The details contained in the will of Ralph Snaith, drawn up in 1472, show that he had granted all his lands to feoffees: he directed that his wife was to have 'the rule and guid-ing' thereof and was to put his two elder sons into the Abbey of St. Oswald at the age of ten, making the necessary financial arrangements with the abbot and allowing his heir to have lands worth 20 marks a year at the age of twenty-one.[5] In 1478 Thomas Fulthorpe issued rather more complicated directions to his feoffees, virtually creating a use upon a use, which make it clear that the wardship of the body and the marriage of his heir were out of the lord's hands. He directed the feoffees of all his lands in Yorkshire and Durham to enfeoff Ralph Bulmer thereof so that he might have the custody and governance of William his son and Agnes his daughter until they respectively came of age and employ the issues for their maintenance and marriages.[6] In 1481 William Neville of Thornton Bridge directed that his son (who appears to have been his heir) be married by the counsel of his executors and,

[1] *Reg. Chich.*, II. 614.   [2] ibid., II. 631 and 635.
[3] In the case of each of the examples cited the printed text published by the Surtees Society has been compared with the MS. original in the relevant Register at the Borthwick Institute, York.   [4] *Test. Eb.*, II. 257.
[5] ibid., III. 204. It is clear from the details in the will that the heir was in-volved in these directions.
[6] Borthwick Institute, York: Archiepiscopal Registers, V, ff. 124v–125; *Test. Eb.*, III. 241. In both this and the wills noted in the next two references the printed text is seriously defective.

together with his two sisters, be maintained from the issues of his lands until he came of age.[1] In 1483 Richard Pigot willed that his wife and his executors were to have 'the rule and governance' of his heir during his nonage.[2] In 1484 Marmaduke de la River of Brandsby directed that his son and heir was to be *ad tutelam*[3] of his feoffees during his minority.[4]

A search of the record evidence that is available has revealed that none of these testators held lands of the King in chief.[5] The existence of this body of directions relating to the guardianship of heirs during their minorities shows that these testators considered that the fact that all their lands had been conveyed to feoffees enabled them to bequeath the guardianship of their heirs and their marriages like any other chattel. They appear, indeed, to have ceased to think in terms of feudal wardship but rather of a form of guardianship very similar to what may exist today. It is especially interesting to note that two of them were lawyers of importance and would, therefore, have given special care to their testamentary directions—Sir John Hody died Chief Justice of the King's Bench, while Richard Pigot was a serjeant at law. Most of the examples that have been quoted have been found in the Register of Archbishop Chichele of Canterbury and in the Yorkshire wills that have been printed by the Surtees Society. It is possible that, when more later medieval wills have been printed, more examples of the practices that have been noted will be available.[6] But, in the light of the evidence that has been discussed, there can be no doubt that many testators who had conveyed all their lands to feoffees thought that they thereby secured the right

---

[1] Borthwick Inst., York: Arch. Reg., V, f. 224v; *Test. Eb.*, III. 263.

[2] Borthwick Inst., York: Arch. Reg., V, f. 232; *Test. Eb.*, III. 286.

[3] The term *tutela* originated in Roman law, where it denoted the guardianship of an infant heir. See the references given in J. S. Roskell, 'The Office and Dignity of Protector of England, with special reference to its Origins', *EHR*, LXVIII (1953), 206. [4] *Test. Eb.*, III. 293-4.

[5] Thomas Stonor, however, held of the King *ut de honore* of the honours of Wallingford and Pontefract. See *The Stonor Letters and Papers*, 1. xi seq. and references cited. Doughton (Gloucs.), however, was not held in chief.

[6] A thorough search of the Early Chancery Proceedings would probably yield more examples of similar practices. See, e.g., PRO, C. 1/6/152.

to bequeath both the guardianship and the marriages of their heirs in their wills. This phenomenon is a striking proof not merely of the completeness of the mesne lords' loss of feudal incidents through uses but also of the fact that this situation was leading to the emergence of new conceptions of family law.

The resources of the royal prerogative enabled the Crown to avoid the worst of the ravages that uses could inflict on feudal revenues. In the first place, the right to license all alienations of lands held in chief brought a revenue from fines when such lands were conveyed to feoffees to uses. Although individual fines might sometimes be very large,[1] the volume of the issues from licences for enfeoffments to uses was not remarkable. For instance, in the first ten years of the reign of Henry VI (1422–32) licences to convey to feoffees to uses produced an average of £190 a year, while the equivalent figure for licences to create other types of estate was £117.[2] The growth of uses, therefore, did provide some slight financial gains for the Crown. It is difficult to avoid the impression that revenues from this source could have been much higher: favourites or influential magnates were sometimes permitted to create uses of lands held in chief without paying fines,[3] while the fines charged for some licences seem

[1] In the whole period 1377–1485 only five of those entered on the Patent Rolls were over £100: CPR, 1399–1401, p. 365 (£100); ibid., 1422–9, pp. 59–60 and 108 (1000 marks and 500 marks); ibid., 1429–36, p. 346 (£100); ibid., 1436–41, p. 359 (200 marks).

[2] Several reasons explain the choice of these ten years for the purpose of working out these figures. It is desirable to choose a period in the fifteenth century, since the practice of enfeoffing to uses was then quite extensive. These ten years fall within a period when the Chancery seems to have attempted to protect royal interests by means of licences to alienate to, perhaps, a greater extent than in other periods (see above, Table V). Moreover, they immediately precede the year in which Ralph, lord Cromwell, presented his estimates of royal revenues to parliament (Rot. Parl., IV. 433).

[3] CPR, 1399–1401, pp. 332 and 358 (Ralph Neville, earl of Westmorland, and Henry Percy, earl of Northumberland); ibid., 1408–13, p. 406 (Edward, duke of York); ibid., 1429–36, pp. 508 and 600 (William de la Pole, earl of Suffolk, and Alice his wife); ibid., pp. 514–15 (Richard, duke of York); ibid., 1436–41, p. 35 (John, lord Beaumont); ibid., 1441–6, p. 174 (cardinal Beaufort); ibid., 1461–7, p. 270 (Richard Neville, earl of Warwick).

extremely slight in view of the size of the estates conveyed.[1] A precise assessment of the extent to which revenues from this source compensated for the Crown's loss of incidents through uses is impossible. But it seems likely that they went a fair way towards compensating for one type of incident that was so lost— the reliefs that would have accrued to the Crown had the estates concerned continued to be held in fee: while reliefs for earldoms and baronies were fixed at £100 and 100 marks respectively and that for a knight's fee at £5, in the years 1422–32 the fines paid from a total of 95 licences and pardons granted for enfeoffments to uses averaged £20.

In the second place, the Crown possessed some sort of control over the extent to which it lost revenues from wardships and marriage through uses. As we have seen,[2] as a result of the system of licences to alienate and the investigations of its escheators, the Crown in general was able to ensure that most tenants-in-chief died seised in fee of some lands in chief so that the wardship and marriage pertained to the Crown. Some tenants-in-chief did succeed in conveying to feoffees to uses the whole of the lands they held in chief. But an investigation of the available evidence shows that such cases were few and did not include any land-owners of exceptional wealth. The fact that they occurred at all was not in itself a result of the creation of uses but rather the consequence of inefficient prosecution of the King's rights on the part of escheators and Chancery officials who could easily have exploited the legal doctrines relating to collusion to recover the wardship and marriage of the heir and of the lands.[3]

Nevertheless, if the Crown in most cases of tenants-in-chief who left heirs under age managed to avoid the complete loss of its rights, there are a few interesting pieces of evidence which suggest that the practice of granting their lands to feoffees to uses

[1] See, e.g., especially ibid., *1416–22*, p. 108 (Thomas Montague, earl of Salisbury); ibid., *1446–52*, p. 145 (John, duke of Norfolk); ibid., *1452–61*, pp. 199–200 (Ralph, lord Cromwell). In the first of these licences the recipient was going overseas on the King's service and, apart from family responsibilities detailed in the licence, had to make financial preparations for his journey.
[2] See above, Ch. IV (ii), passim.   [3] See above, pp. 202–17.

was leading some tenants-in-chief to doubt, or to resent, the Crown's right to the marriage of the infant heir and the wardship of his body. In a will drawn up between 1430 and his death in 1435 John, earl of Arundel, directed that his son and heir was to have a manor 'for his finding in his tender age', that two of his feoffees were to have 'the governance thereof to the profit and avail of our said son till that he be sixteen year of age and then he for to have full possession of the said manor at his own liberty'.[1] In these directions the earl does not attempt to claim or to bequeath the wardship and marriage of his heir. But he does make provision for his maintenance during his minority, a duty which belonged to the Crown, and, moreover, directs that a manor be delivered to him at sixteen years of age, whereas in feudal law he came of age at twenty-one.

In four other cases we see more direct encroachments upon the royal prerogative. In his will, drawn up in 1455, Thomas, lord Hoo and Hastings, as well as bequeathing money for their marriages, laid down that his daughters by his second wife, who, together with a daughter by a first marriage, were his heirs, were to be 'ruled, governed and married' at the discretion of his wife and his brother.[2] The widow of Robert Poynings, who was killed at the second battle of St. Albans in 1461, described in a letter to her brother Sir John Paston how

... as of my said husband's livelihood ... besides mine jointure, my said husband, when he departed towards the field of Saint Albans, made and ordained his will, that I should have the rule of all his livelihood, and of Edward his son and mine, and to take the issues and profits of the said livelihood, to the finding of his and mine said son, to pay his debts, and to keep the right and title of the same livelihood.[3]

In 1471 Sir Thomas Cobham willed that his daughter and heir who was under age should after his death be in the 'governance'

---

[1] *Reg. Chich.*, II. 544. The testament is dated 8 April 1430, but the will that follows (in the form of a tripartite indenture) bears no date.

[2] *Test. Vet.*, I. 274; C. Dawson, *History of Hastings Castle* (2 vols., London, 1909), I. 276 and 278.

[3] *The Paston Letters*, IV. 309. The problem of its dating is discussed in R. M. Jeffs, 'The Poynings-Percy Dispute', *BIHR*, XXXIV (1961), 161, n. 2.

of his wife.[1] Perhaps the most interesting case of all is that of Henry Percy, earl of Northumberland, who died in 1489. In his will, drawn up in 1485, we find the clause, 'Also I will that mine executors have the governance of mine heir, be it son, daughter, or daughters, and to be guided as the most part of my executors be agreeable to, till that my said heir and heirs come to the age of 18 years.'[2]

In each of these four cases it can be seen that the deceased has bequeathed the guardianship of his heir as if it were one of his chattels. Both Thomas, lord Hoo,[3] and Robert Poynings[4] appear to have conveyed all their lands to feoffees to uses and, therefore, to have hoped, because they held nothing in chief in fee, to remove their heirs from royal wardship and marriage. But this explanation cannot apply to Sir Thomas Cobham[5] and the earl of Northumberland,[6] since both died seised in chief. It is difficult to explain why their wills should contain clauses of the type that have been described, since both must have been aware of the fact that they were laying claim to a right which was not theirs. Several possible explanations present themselves. The first—that the deceased had previously been granted the marriage of the heir by the Crown—cannot be accepted, since in neither case can any such grant be traced. The second—that the executors were being directed to purchase the marriage and wardship of the heir from the Crown—must also be rejected, since, if this were so, the

---

[1] *Test. Vet.*, I. 324.   [2] *Test. Eb.*, III. 306.

[3] See, e.g., *CPR, 1422–9*, p. 533.

[4] See, e.g., ibid., *1429–36*, p. 414; ibid., *1461–7*, pp. 544–5.

[5] Sir Thomas may well have been under a genuine impression that he was not seised of any lands in chief, since a letter under the royal signet addressed to the escheator of Kent after his death which has survived among the extant inquisitions relating to his estates describes how 'by labour and instance of the late lord Mountjoy . . . an office was found in the lordship of Boxley in our county of Kent lately belonging unto Sir Thomas Cobham knight as holding of us the same by knight service by reason whereof the ward and marriage of Anne his daughter and heir was presented unto us and by us granted unto the said lord, it is so that the said office as we be credibly informed was found by covin contrary to the truth' (PRO, C. 140/39/58/m. 4). But the Crown retained its rights (*CPR, 1467–76*, p. 535).   [6] Bean, pp. 128–9.

Q

language employed would be more clear and precise in its meaning. In the third place, it might be argued that the language employed by Sir Thomas and the earl of Northumberland does not necessarily exclude the exercise by the Crown of its rights of wardship and might be regarded, within the limits permitted by the royal prerogative, as a mixture of hope and exhortation on the part of the testator—that his wife and executors respectively should protect the interests of the heir and that the heir should be guided by their advice. But the language used does not support this interpretation and, in any case, even if it were acceptable, it would still imply an invasion of the rights of the Crown. The fourth possibility is that the heirs had been betrothed in marriage already. This may be true in the case of the earl of Northumberland's heir,[1] but not in the case of Sir Thomas's, since her marriage was granted by the King to the duchess of Buckingham.[2] In any case, the fact would still remain that the deceased had usurped royal rights of wardship, since in both wills directions are given regarding the 'governance' of the heir during a minority. Lastly, the earl of Northumberland may well have employed the term 'heir' to include all those children to whom he was bequeathing interests in land. But this explanation, if true, shows how much uses had eroded the feudal concept of the heir. In any case, it cannot hold in the case of Sir Thomas.

Two conclusions emerge from a study of the contents of these five wills of tenants-in-chief. First, the cases of Thomas, lord Hoo, and Robert Poynings both show that these tenants-in-chief considered that the fact that all their lands were in the hands of feoffees to uses gave them the opportunity, if not the right, to make dispositions about the guardianship of their heirs during their minorities. Second, the earl of Arundel, Sir Thomas, and the earl of Northumberland had made dispositions in their wills which must be construed as, in varying degrees, intrusions upon the Crown's rights of wardship. It may be unwise to read too much significance into these portions of the wills of only three testators. On the other hand, it must be borne in mind both that many wills of this period have not survived and that in the case of

[1] Bean, p. 125, n. 1.   [2] *CPR, 1467–76*, p. 535.

the two earls we are dealing with leading members of the nobility. It is hard, in the light of the evidence we have discussed, to avoid the conclusion that in the case of the earls and Sir Thomas the fact that most of their lands were held by feoffees to uses had weakened their respect for, if not acceptance of, the Crown's right to the wardship of the heir. Both the earls must have been aware of the fact that their own tenants by means of uses were depriving them of their rights of wardship and marriage: they may well have been attempting to emulate the practices from which they themselves had suffered. The illegality of their dispositions does not lessen their desire to make them. Indeed, the contents of the wills of these three testators, two of them earls and one—the earl of Northumberland—the second most wealthy magnate in the realm, constitute a remarkable demonstration of the extent to which enfeoffments to uses were eroding the whole structure of the feudal incidents of the Crown.

It is impossible to achieve definitive conclusions about the extent of the Crown's financial losses from the growth of uses in the later middle ages. A great deal of evidence exists in inquisitions *post mortem* and the grants enrolled on the rolls of the Chancery and Exchequer. To attempt, even for a period of a few years, to co-ordinate details drawn from all these sources would be an extremely arduous, if not insuperable, task. Moreover, it is impossible to believe that the results achieved would be worth while. It is unlikely that the valuations contained in inquisitions *post mortem* give a reliable indication of the real value of the estates concerned. Nor can we assume that all grants of wardship made by the Crown were sales: many were not but were grants to courtiers or favoured individuals. Moreover, in the case of those that were definitely sold we cannot be certain that the prices paid were not deliberately reduced by the King or his officials in the interests of the purchasers. In any case, the receipts from feudal incidents were casual revenues, fluctuating from year to year. In some years they would be considerably higher than in others, because an exceptionally wealthy tenant-in-chief, or perhaps several, had died. For instance, in the estimates of annual revenues laid before parliament by Ralph, lord Cromwell, in 1433 the lands of the duke of Norfolk which were in the King's hands were valued at £1333 (gross and net) and those of other wards at £1605 (£1598 net).[1]

Nevertheless, although the nature of the evidence prevents us from making accurate financial calculations, we can put forward some rough general conclusions about the extent of the Crown's losses. The decline of revenues caused by the growth of uses did not affect equally all the separate incidents of feudal tenure. The fines paid for licences to alienate and pardons for alienation must have compensated in some measure for the loss of reliefs. But these were the least valuable of the incidents of feudal tenure and there was no compensation for the losses of primer seisin or the most valuable incidents of all—wardship and marriage. It was these which suffered most in the decline which occurred. In their case we must be careful to distinguish between those which came to the King *ut de corona*—that is, because the lands were held in chief— and those *ut de honore*—that is, because the lands were held of honours which were in the King's hands. In the case of the latter, because of the absence of a system of licences to alienate, the Crown lost its rights completely if the whole fee had been enfeoffed to uses, like any mesne lord. After 1399 the greater part of the losses in respect of lands held *ut de honore* must have been felt by the Duchy of Lancaster.

In the case of tenants-in-chief losses in respect of wardship and marriage were certainly substantial. A few minors escaped from the Crown's hands altogether as a result of enfeoffments to uses. Because the Crown did not possess the right to license alienations by tenants-in-chief of lands they held of mesne lords, it was powerless to stop the removal of these from 'prerogative wardship'. The proportion of his lands that a tenant-in-chief granted to feoffees to uses varied from individual to individual: it might comprise the greater part of his inheritance. Two examples may serve to illustrate the sort of situation that might occur during the fifteenth century. In the case of Robert, lord Morley, whose minority lasted from December 1435 until towards the end of

[1] J. L. Kirby, 'The Issues of the Lancastrian Exchequer and Lord Cromwell's Estimates of 1433', *BIHR*, XXIV (1951), 132; *Rot. Parl.*, IV. 433.

1439, his father's feoffees were assessed for the income tax of 1436 for a net income of £100 a year.[1] In the case of the minority of Henry, fifth earl of Northumberland, which lasted from April 1489 to May 1498, his father's feoffees received net revenues of £1575 a year.[2] If we take the lengths of the respective minorities into account, in the case of lord Morley the Crown lost net revenues totalling at least £400 and in the case of the earl of Northumberland a total of approximately £14,200. The Crown, therefore, must have lost very substantial revenues which would otherwise have accrued through wardship when its tenants-in-chief conveyed parts of their inheritances to feoffees to uses.

On the other hand, it would be unwise to assume that profits from the right of marriage declined in precisely the same proportion as those from wardship of the heir's lands. The purchaser of an heir's marriage, whether directly from the King or from an intermediary who was a royal grantee, would offer a price which took into account the size of the heir's inheritance and in doing so would give careful consideration to the value of the lands that would be his when the ancestor's will had been performed. Moreover, this aspect of our problem must also be examined from the standpoint of the financial resources that were available to the prospective purchaser of a marriage from the King. The wills of the late fourteenth and fifteenth centuries contain many examples of directions in which testators directed that revenues in the hands of their feoffees should be spent on the purchase of marriages for young sons or daughters. In consequence, it is difficult to avoid the impression that there was, as a result of the growth of uses, an increase in the amount of the financial capital available for the purchase of marriages from the Crown. In the light of all these arguments, we must conclude that the Crown's losses in respect of its right of marriage were considerably less than those in respect of wardship of the lands.

A careful examination of the evidence thus leads to the conclusion that the Crown's feudal revenues suffered less from the growth of uses than those of mesne lords. But, unlike the latter,

[1] H. L. Gray, 'Incomes from Land in England in 1436', *EHR*, XLIX (1934), 617.   [2] Bean, p. 129.

the Crown was always lord and never tenant: mesne lords, and in particular the magnates of the realm, were able to recompense themselves for their own losses by employing uses themselves, a course of action that was not open to the Crown. It was for this reason that the Crown was, in financial terms, the chief sufferer from the growth of uses. But the extent of its sufferings, and their precise incidence within the structure of feudal incidents, deserves careful attention, since it can be shown that the erosion of its feudal revenues occurred mainly in the sphere of wardship of lands. Moreover, it would be wrong to assume that its losses in this respect constituted a matter for concern throughout the late fourteenth and fifteenth centuries or that the Crown always desired a reform of this situation during the whole of this period. The extent to which it really felt its loss of feudal revenues depended on the extent to which it attempted to exploit them efficiently. In fact, wardships and marriages were often granted without payment or at cheap rates to courtiers or other favoured individuals. A real consciousness of the inroads that uses were making into the profits of feudal incidents could occur only when the Crown saw the need for action because it was attempting to exploit those revenues to the full and finding its efforts impeded through the existence of uses. Such an attitude was not present in the late fourteenth century or in the Lancastrian period when the Crown was preoccupied with the ambitions of an overmighty nobility in England and with its own aggrandisement in France. A determination to build up the financial power of the monarchy and thus to exploit the potential profits of feudal incidents to the full does not appear until the Yorkist period and, indeed, for its most striking and effective manifestations we have to wait until the reigns of the first two Tudors.

CHAPTER FIVE

The Royal Prerogative, 1461–1529: the Beginnings of Recovery

THE late fifteenth and early sixteenth centuries witnessed a revolutionary change in the attitude of the Crown towards its feudal revenues. Its intensive efforts to exploit the fiscal aspects of feudalism to its maximum advantage led under Henry VII to important administrative innovations, from which there eventually emerged under Henry VIII a new institution—the Court of Wards—which took the administration of these revenues out of the hands of the Chancery and the Exchequer. In the period down to the summoning of the Reformation Parliament in 1529 there were four separate phases in the development of the Crown's policies towards its feudal incidents. The first occurred under Edward IV, mainly in the latter half of his reign. Although we lack for this period the detailed evidence that is extant for that of the first two Tudors, it is quite clear that he made real efforts to increase his feudal revenues.[1] Commissions of enquiry were appointed to investigate the evasion of royal rights. Within the Duchy of Lancaster in the last four or five years of the reign there was intense activity over feudal dues. And according to a contemporary chronicler, referring to the year 1476, the King exacted heavy fines from those who entered on their inheritances without suing out royal licences.[2]

The second phase comprised the reign of Henry VII.[3] The

[1] For full details and references, see J. R. Lander, 'Edward IV: the Modern Legend and a Revision', *History*, New Ser., XLI (1956), 48–9.

[2] The second continuator of the chronicle of Crowland Abbey (W. Fulman, *Rerum Anglicarum Scriptores*, I (Oxford, 1684), 559).

[3] What follows concerning the reigns of Henry VII and Henry VIII is based on H. E. Bell, *An Introduction to the History and Records of the Court of Wards and Liveries* (Cambridge, 1953), ch. I; and J. Hurstfield, 'The Revival of Feudalism in Early Tudor England', *History*, New Ser., XXXVII (1952), 131–45.

policies which were in operation in the reign of Edward IV continued as did the King's personal interest in them. But three
features of Henry VII's policies require special emphasis. In the
first place, there was a remarkably heightened interest in the
nature and scope of the royal prerogative. As a result, the legal
doctrines relating to the feudal rights of the Crown were
thoroughly examined and their legal implications and niceties
discussed to a much greater extent than ever before. Of course,
a reading of the Year Books shows that the King's rights had been
the subject of comments by lawyers in the courts on numerous
occasions in the past. But what now occurred was an attempt to
organize a coherent body of legal doctrine in this sphere around
the so-called Statute *Prerogativa Regis*. Indeed, it is worth noting
that whereas Littleton had used the term 'prerogative' only twice
in his *Tenures*, written in the previous generation, the statute was
the subject of at least eight readings at the Inns of Court in
Henry VII's reign,[1] a fact which emphasizes the importance it had
now acquired in a legal education. In the second place, especially
in the second half of the reign, the Crown not merely enjoyed
its revenues from the incidents of feudalism but also exploited
infringements of its rights as an additional means of securing
financial profit. Landowners were fined heavily for what were
often quite technical offences, a policy which was associated with
the careers in royal service of Empson and Dudley. Its un-
popularity was to cost them their lives in the reaction against
Henry VII's policies which followed the accession of his son. In
the third place, the administrative problems met by Henry VII
and his officials in the exploitation of feudal revenues exposed the
need for organizing them in a centralized system. The result was
the appearance in 1503 of an official called 'the surveyor of the
King's prerogative' who came to be known as the master of the
King's wards and was responsible for the management and sale of
wardships.

The third phase comprised the first ten years or so of Henry
VIII's reign. The new King gave up the unpopular aspects of his
father's policies towards feudal revenues. Indeed, their adminis-

---

[1] Constable, Introd., pp. xlviii–li.

tration became a much laxer affair and the control of wardships was allowed to fall again under the control of the Exchequer. The beginning of the fourth phase can be assigned approximately to the appointment of William Paulet as joint master of the King's wards in 1526, since although he shared his office with others he combined it with that of receiver-general. From at least 1528 onwards we are witnessing the activities of not merely an administrative office but also a court, since the two joint masters from that year onwards handled the judicial business relating to royal wards. For the full effects of these developments we must wait until after 1529, when the Crown's policies were further transformed by the consequences of its breach with Rome.[1]

It is against the background of these administrative and financial changes that we must view the Crown's policies towards uses in the late fifteenth and early sixteenth centuries. The degree of success achieved by attempts to increase the Crown's profits from feudal incidents would depend on the extent to which it managed to avoid the evasion of these incidents through uses. Throughout the Yorkist and early Tudor periods this consideration was always in the minds of royal administrators who realized that their efforts to expand feudal revenues would be fraught with failure unless they at the same time took measures to bring uses under some sort of control. For such a purpose the administrative resources which were available to the Crown—its escheators and the powers they exercised—alone were insufficient. Over the previous hundred years or so uses had come to be accepted as the most convenient and advantageous means whereby a landowner could settle his land: and, provided he did not deprive the King completely of his rights, even the most efficient and zealous of escheators would generally do nothing to interfere with the arrangements he had made.[2] By the middle years of the fifteenth century legal precedents and administrative practice had combined to produce an impasse which could only be removed by means of legislative reform.

[1] See below, Ch. VI, passim.   [2] See above, Ch. IV (ii).

(i) THE YORKIST KINGS

Edward IV was the first King to attempt to deal with the problem of uses by means of a measure of parliamentary reform. In 1483, in the last parliament of his reign, he endeavoured to curtail the Crown's losses through uses within the Duchy of Lancaster. The main provision of the bill introduced into parliament laid down that

> our said sovereign Lord and his heirs, and our Sovereign Lady the Queen, severally have the ward of the body and marriage of every person being within age, to whose use the interest of fee simple or fee tail, of any lands, tenements or hereditaments so holden, shall . . . belong, as heirs by the death of any of his ancestors: and also the ward of all the lands, tenements and hereditaments so holden by reason of the same Duchy, or of any parcel thereof . . . any such recoveries, fines, feoffments or estates of trust had or made notwithstanding.[1]

If the heir was over age, the King or Queen were to receive the relief which would normally have been due before the creation of the use. As it stood, this provision was a radical attempt at reform: it restored the duke of Lancaster's rights to wardship, marriage and relief to the position they had occupied before the development of uses. There can be no doubt that this section of the statute embodied the words of the measure that Edward IV placed before parliament. But the text of the statute that was actually promulgated proceeds to weaken this provision substantially:

> Provided alway that this present Act extend not to the letter, nor be prejudicial to the performing of any will of any person made and declared, of the lands, tenements and hereditaments aforesaid: saving to our said Sovereign Lord the King and to his heirs, and to our Sovereign Lady the Queen, severally, such reasonable portion of the same lands, tenements and hereditaments, as shall be sufficient for the finding of such heirs during their nonage, according to their estate, degree or condition, the same Wills notwithstanding. And that immediately after such Wills performed, the heirs then being within age, our said Sovereign Lord the King and his heirs, and our Sovereign Lady

---

[1] *Rot. Parl.*, VI. 207b.

the Queen, severally may seise the residue of all the said lands and tenements, and them to have in ward, during the nonage of the said heirs.

In other words, until the deceased's will had been performed, the duke could only secure those revenues necessary for the maintenance of the heir. But, once the feoffees had carried out the deceased's directions, they had to surrender the lands for the remainder of the minority. The fact that these drastic alterations of the intended legislation were entered in the form of a proviso that was added to it can only mean that the King's proposal was amended when it went through parliament. And, since the text of the act has come down to us in this form, there can be no doubt that the King was forced to agree to the amendment. In short, the only reform he could achieve was embodied in his subjects' alteration of his original intention.

Even this limited gain was short-lived. Within twelve months, in the parliament of 1484, Richard III repealed his brother's act completely, stating that he did so because of the injury it had inflicted upon his subjects.[1] No doubt he did so in the hope of securing the support of the tenants of the Duchy of Lancaster for his *coup d'état*.

Nevertheless, despite the fact that it remained in force for less than a year Edward IV's attempt at reform does not deserve the neglect it has received from the hands of historians.[2] It was the first of several efforts to deal with uses by means of legislative reform in parliament. It was clearly Edward IV's intention to prohibit the evasion of feudal incidents which was the *raison d'être* of uses. Even the resulting legislation, as amended by parliament, proceeded from the fact that the *cestui que use* was the real occupier of the land. It thus proclaimed a principle which looked forward to Henry VII's statute of 1490 and to the Statute of Uses of 1536. It is important to note that the date of Edward IV's act falls within the period of intense activity in the exploitation of feudal dues

---

[1] *Rot. Parl.*, VI. 261b–262b.

[2] It was, however, noticed by Sir Edward Coke (Coke, *Fourth Institute*, p. 196).

within the Duchy of Lancaster during the last four or five years of his reign.[1] Indeed, the experience thus obtained may have emphasized the need for legislative reform.

However, it remains true that Edward IV waited twenty years before he attempted reform. And, when he did so, his efforts were confined to the Duchy of Lancaster. In the event, he had to make do with a reform which gave him only part of what he wanted. It would have been difficult for the Duchy's administrators to administer the act actually passed in 1483.[2] It would have required the supervision of the performance of the tenants' wills; and this would have entailed the creation of special administrative machinery the expense of which would probably have cancelled out any financial gains. However much Edward IV wished to extirpate the financial consequences of uses and understood how this might be achieved, the fact remains that he engaged in no such efforts on a national scale. Indeed, it can be shown that in a number of cases he failed to employ the existing resources of the royal prerogative to prevent the evasion of his rights by tenants-in-chief,[3] so that the Crown lost the wardship of the heir's body and his marriage as well as the wardship of the lands. Moreover, in some of these cases the feoffees' acquisition of the whole of the lands held in chief was pardoned after an inquisition *post mortem* had been held and, indeed, as a result of it, although the officials of the Chancery were in a position to make further enquiries into any possible evasion of royal rights.

The explanation for the Yorkist kings' failure to achieve more in the struggle against the financial consequences of uses must lie in the political circumstances with which they were faced. Uses had become part of the structure of English landownership and all landowners, great and small, had powerful vested interests in the retention both of uses and the power to devise lands by their means which resulted in the Crown's loss of the incidents of feudal tenure. Always aware of the dangers of rebellion, the Yorkist kings dared not risk the discontent which any attempt at radical

---

[1] Somerville, I. 243–6.

[2] No traces of any effects of the statute can be found in the surviving Duchy feodary accounts (PRO, D.L. 29/11, 873–4). [3] See above, pp. 215–16.

reform would be bound to arouse. The extent to which they were compelled to accept the employment of uses by those who held lands of them by feudal tenure is brought out by the provisions of a statute passed in the parliamentary session of January–March 1475.[1] In the course of preparing for his invasion of France Edward IV found it necessary, in order to recruit the support of his nobility and gentry, to make concessions which, in the event of death on active service, enabled royal tenants to deprive the Crown of its rights of wardship by means of enfeoffments to uses. Those who went with the King to France were to have licences under the King's Great Seal without fee or fine[2] to make feoffments 'to such persons as they shall please . . . to the intent that they may thereof make their will for payment of their charges and other things.' If they died on the expedition, leaving heirs under age,

then all manner of persons having any manner of estate by way of feoffment or otherwise, to the use of the same person or persons so dying, in any honours, castles and other the premises with their appurtenances, to the use and performance of the will of the said person which doth so decease, shall have the same without any interruption of our Sovereign Lord the King, or any of his officers or ministers, by reason of any office thereof to be found, although the said feoffments, estate or alienation were made or had by collusion[3] or otherwise entitling our Sovereign Lord the King.

The statute then proceeded to lay down that in these circumstances 'his said feoffees and also his executors shall have and enjoy the ward and marriage, with the ward of the same manors, lands and tenements so holden, during the nonage of the same heir, to the use of the same person so dying, and with the same to perform his will', a privilege which was to be granted to them in the form

---

[1] *Statutes*, II. 445–7.

[2] Licences granted to the following are enrolled on the Patent Roll: George, duke of Clarence; John, duke of Norfolk; Henry, earl of Northumberland; William, lord Hastings; Sir Robert Chamberlain; Sir Thomas Burgh; Sir William Parr; John Harcourt; Sir Richard Corbet; Giles Daubeney (*CPR, 1467–77*, pp. 513, 515–18, 520–1, 523, 529–31, 533, 539, 541).

[3] For a discussion of this term, as used in this context, see above, p. 204.

of letters patent. In a purely formal sense it is true that these benefits were conferred by the exercise of the King's grace and that both the licences to alienate to feoffees and the grants of wardships and marriages were to pass under the Great Seal. The terms of the statute indicate quite clearly that the concessions it gave were confined to those who followed the King to France. But the fact remains that in order to recruit the leaders of his army the King was forced to waive the rights of his prerogative in the event of their deaths on active service and to permit the gains they thus secured to be administered through the agency of their feoffees to uses.

(ii) HENRY VII

In the reign of Henry VII the Crown began to develop policies which were intended to bring uses under more effective control than before and at the same time stop some of the loss of feudal incidents they caused. In the parliament of 1489–90 a statute[1] was passed which was the first attempt to legislate against uses on a national scale.[2] Since it was only to come into effect in the case of those landowners who died after Easter 1490, it is reasonable to assume that it was passed in the third session of this parliament, which lasted from 25 January to 27 February 1490.

The statute's preamble shows that it was intended to supplement c. 6 of the Statute of Marlborough of 1267:

Where by a statute made at Marlborough it was ordained that, when tenants made feoffments in fraud to make the lords of the fee to lose their wards, the lords should have writs to recover their wards against such feoffees . . .; since the making of which statute many imaginations have been had and yet been used, as well by feoffments fines and recoveries as otherwise, to put lords from their wards of lands holden of them by knight's service; Be it therefore ordained, established and

---

[1] *Statutes*, II. 540–1 (4 Hen. VII, c. 17).

[2] See *Paston Letters*, V. 309 (no. 924) for a reference to a parliamentary bill of 1478, to take effect in Easter 1480. But an inspection of the original (BM, Add. MS. 27,446, f. 7) shows that it is a copy of the statute passed in 1490, '1480' being an error in transcription.

enacted . . . that the said statute of Marlborough be observed and kept in all manner of things after the form and effect thereof.

It then proceeded to legislate against uses:

if any person or persons . . . shall be seised in demesne or in reversion of estate of inheritance being tenant immediate to the lord of any castles, manors, lands and tenements or other hereditaments holden by knight's service in his or their demesne as of fee, to the use of any other person or persons and his heirs only, he to whose use he or they be so seised dieth, his heirs being within age, no will by him declared, nor made in his life touching the premises or any of them, the lord of whom such castles, manors, lands, tenements and hereditaments been holden immediately, shall have a writ of right of ward as well for body as for the land, as the lord should have had, if the same ancestor had been in possession of that estate so being in use at time of his death, and no such estate to his use made.

And it went on to lay down that, if in such circumstances the heir was of full age, the lord was to have his relief. In short, if a *cestui que use* died without making a will of his lands, the lord secured the incidents of tenure which would have been due had his tenant died seised.

Did these provisions apply to all feudal tenants throughout the kingdom? To answer this question it is necessary to remember that the statute, in effect, made two main provisions. First, it stated that a lord could secure his rights if the *cestui que use* died without making a will. And, second, it gave him the means of doing so through a writ of ward. The statute clearly applied to all mesne lords. For them its provisions were interdependent: they could only avail themselves of its benefits through a writ of ward. But did the statute also apply to the tenants of the Crown? It certainly could not have made the remedy of a writ of ward available to the King. This was by definition an exercise of royal justice on behalf of his subjects: when his own rights of wardship were evaded, he had always secured his rights through the resources of his prerogative, and he continued to do so. But did the Crown, however, benefit from the other main provision of the statute? In his reading on the *Prerogativa Regis* the contemporary lawyer Robert Constable, writing five years after its promulgation, considered that the statute applied to all royal tenants: when a *cestui que use* of lands held of the King died intestate, the King secured his right of either wardship or relief.[1] This view is confirmed by the extant inquisitions *post mortem* of Henry VII's reign.[2] And, when in 1530–1 the government of Henry VIII made a bargain with the nobility over its feudal rights, the resulting agreement[3] assumed that the statute applied to all feudal tenants in the kingdom, both royal and mesne.

There can be no doubt, therefore, that the Crown benefited from the statute of 1490. But, was it intended to benefit when the statute was promulgated? It is unfortunate that the only evidence available consists of the text of the statute together with details of royal practice after its promulgation. At first sight, the omission of all mention of the King's rights might seem to suggest that the statute resulted from pressure from the King's subjects and that he then took advantage of this. However, it would be unwise to draw this conclusion. Although the original c. 6 of the Statute of Marlborough had been framed in the interests of mesne lords alone, the Crown in the exercise of its prerogative rights had followed the same principles as had the courts of common law in interpreting the statute.[4] Moreover, the frontiers of the royal prerogative at this time were ill-defined. When, for instance, lands were held of an honour which had escheated to the Crown, the King was, technically at least, in a position little distinguishable from a mesne lord's. It would have been impossible to argue that he could not benefit from the statute of 1490 in the case of these lands. If so, it is hard to see how the Crown could have been expected to treat its tenancies-in-chief on a completely different basis. We must conclude that the Crown was responsible for the statute of 1490 and always intended to benefit from it. Its only hope of securing its passage through parliament lay in extending the same benefits to mesne lords as it sought for itself. In view of the resources of its prerogative, any special mention of the King's rights, as distinct from those of other lords, would have been superfluous.

[1] Constable, pp. 20 and 53–4, esp. nn. 134–5.   [2] *CIPMB*, I–III passim.
[3] Holdsworth, IV. 574–7, discussed below, Ch. VI (i).
[4] See above, Ch. IV (ii).

It would have been assumed that the provision regarding the *cestui que use*'s intestacy was of general application, while that relating to the writ of ward applied to mesne lords only.

The conclusion that the Crown was responsible for the statute of 1490 is supported by two other considerations. In the first place, there had been an attempt to deal with the loss of feudal revenues through uses seven years before. And it is likely that some of Henry VII's advisers had been involved in both the formulation and enforcement of the Yorkist legislation.[1] The results within the Duchy of Lancaster were far from satisfactory: the attempt at reform caused discontent among the tenantry, and this led to its repeal in 1484. The royal officials involved must have resented their failure and at the same time gained a better understanding of the difficulties in the way of successful reform.

In the second place, there is some evidence which may explain why the statute appeared when it did. No doubt Henry VII's more urgent commitments explain why he did not legislate in this matter in the first two parliaments of his reign. But, while we cannot exclude the possibility that the proposed legislation was under discussion in the first two sessions of the parliament of 1489-1490, the statute was not promulgated until the third and last session. There are certain circumstances which may have persuaded the Crown to act during the third session. On 28 April 1489, when the first session was already over, Henry Percy, earl of Northumberland, died, leaving an heir who was eleven years of age. Of his net landed revenues roughly three-quarters were in the hands of feoffees to his use.[2] The Percy inheritance was the largest inheritance then outside the hands of the Crown.[3] When the details of the earl's enfeoffments became known to the Crown, the extent of the losses it was incurring through uses must have been

---

[1] The most important example is Sir Richard Empson who became Attorney-general of the Duchy of Lancaster in September 1485. He had held the same office in the years 1477-83 and was retained as apprentice-at-law in 1483-4. He must, therefore, have been associated with the drafting of Edward IV's statute. See Somerville, I. 392-3 and 406.   [2] Bean, p. 129.

[3] The duke of Buckingham, who was the wealthiest magnate in the kingdom, was a minor. His estates had been in the hands of the Crown since his father's forfeiture in the previous reign.

driven home. In an indenture of agreement with the late earl's executors, dated 14 December 1489, the Crown brought pressure to bear upon the feoffees to extort from them some of the revenues that were to be in their hands during the heir's minority.[1] The bulk of the indenture's provisions concerned the purchase of a marriage for the late earl's elder daughter[2] and the upbringing of his younger children at the royal court.[3] But in the last clause the King promised that the feoffees should continue seised of the estates with which they had been enfeoffed

without trouble, vexation or perturbance of our said sovereign lord, his sheriffs, escheators or any other his officers or commissioners . . . And our said sovereign lord the King granteth and promiseth in the word of a king to the said executors of the said late earl that they have and shall have, take and perceive and peaceably enjoy all the rents, farms, revenues, issues and profits of the same castles, honours . . . and other premises . . . for the performance of the testament and last will

---

[1] See Bean, p. 134, n. 5 for full references. The abstract printed in *Materials for the History of Henry VII* (Rolls Ser.), II. 554–5, does not include the Crown's undertaking to respect the position of the feoffees.

[2] They were to pay a total of 800 marks a year until the purchase-price of her marriage had been raised. There is some doubt about the size of this sum. The indentures which were sealed have not survived and the extant copies give the figure of £4000. In his will the earl had bequeathed 3000 marks for this purpose (*Test. Eb.*, III. 306). But, while it is likely that the Crown forced the feoffees to bid higher than this, it is difficult to believe that they would have paid double the sum bequeathed. If the earl himself altered his bequest in a codicil or new will that has not survived, it is doubtful if he would have doubled the original bequest. For these reasons the figure of 4000 marks seems a likely figure.

[3] The King was to receive a total of 100 marks a year for the 'finding' of each of the earl's two daughters and his three younger sons—a total of 500 marks a year. In the case of the daughters these payments were to continue until they attained the age of twenty-one or married, and, in the case of the sons, until they were eighteen. In addition, a sum of 250 marks was to be paid for the children's 'finding' from Whitsun to Christmas 1489.

It would be unwise to see in these portions of the agreement signs of any pressure on the part of the Crown to extort money from the executors and feoffees. The children's mother was dead and the executors may well have considered that the best way to secure a proper upbringing for them was to have them brought up at the royal court.

of the said late earl without interruption of impediment of our said sovereign lord or any other in or by the colour of his title.

In return for this undertaking the Crown was to receive from the revenues of the estates in the hands of the feoffees 200 marks a year during the minority of the heir. It would be wrong to read sinister motives on the part of the Crown into the earlier clauses of the indenture: the late earl's will had directed his feoffees to purchase a marriage for his elder daughter, while it was quite natural for the executors to arrange an upbringing at the royal court for the younger children. But it is impossible to explain the existence of the last clause except in terms of the feoffees' response to the King's threat to upset their title. Nor can such action on the part of the Crown be attributed to the fact that the late earl's enfeoffments had deprived it of the wardship of all his lands, since he had died seised of some of the lands he had held in chief. We can only conclude that the Crown was determined to reduce as much as possible the extent of its losses through uses on this occasion. And for this purpose it employed the resources of its prerogative—in particular, the threat that its escheators would hold inquisitions that upset the feoffees' titles—as a means of blackmail. It is worth noting that, although the earl had died in April 1489, the first of the extant inquisitions held after his death is dated 23 January 1490—that is, five weeks after the agreement.[1] In the light of these details, there can be no doubt that, at the time the Crown was engaged in the preparation of the statute of 1490, it was negotiating an agreement that was intended to mitigate its losses through uses in the case of the second wealthiest baronial inheritance in the kingdom. It is likely that its discussions with the late earl's executors began shortly after his death in April 1489; and they must have been proceeding during the second session of the parliament of 1489–90. The actual agreement is dated ten days after the second session had ended. It is very difficult to believe that there was not some connexion between these events and a statute concerning the same problem which emerged during the next session of the same parliament. The extent of the inroads

[1] *CIPMB*, I. 228–9 (no. 547).

made by uses into feudal revenues was, of course, already well known: it would clearly be unwise to assume that the earl of Northumberland's death, by driving these home to the Crown, was responsible for the statute. But it may well have played some part in the decision to legislate in 1490, rather than defer the matter to a later parliament. At any rate, it is clear that, at the very time legislation was in preparation, the Crown was blackmailing the most important group of feoffees in the kingdom into surrendering some of the revenues in their hands. In view of this, it is impossible to believe that the Crown did not intend itself to benefit from the reform it promulgated.

The statute of 1490 was by no means a radical solution of the problem of uses. In comparison with the Yorkist statute of 1483 it made only a limited effort to reduce royal losses through uses. It is true that it applied to the whole kingdom, whereas its predecessor was confined to the Duchy of Lancaster. But the relief it gave the King was available only in special circumstances: if these were absent, he derived no benefit from it. By laying down that a lord could secure his rights if the *cestui que use* made no will it made it clear that, if there was a will, he lost them completely.

Why, then, did the statute of 1490 not make a more effective attack upon uses? It is especially important to answer this question, since the details of the Crown's agreement with the Percy executors indicate its anxiety to secure more than it was given by the statute. However, in the political circumstances of 1490 it would certainly have been unwise, and probably dangerous, for Henry VII to do anything which seriously reduced his subjects' benefits from uses. Indeed, the details of the Crown's agreement with the Percy feoffees themselves illustrate the weakness of its position: although they gave way, they were strong enough to stop it from securing more than 200 marks a year. In this situation the reform the Crown managed to secure dealt only with the fringes of the problem of uses.

Nevertheless, it would be foolish to argue that, because the statute permitted feudal tenants to will their lands, it was a reform of no importance. As its preamble indicates, it was the first legislative enactment dealing with the evasion of feudal incidents throughout the kingdom for over two hundred years. In effect, it broadened the terms of c. 6 of the Statute of Marlborough of 1267 and brought within the category of collusive enfeoffments those uses where the *cestui que use* had not declared his will at the time of his death.

It is impossible to find direct precedents for this approach towards uses in the preceding two centuries. But an investigation of the Year Books and inquisitions *post mortem* does reveal ideas which help to explain why this new doctrine of collusion was evolved. On the one hand, it would seem to be the corollary of the common law doctrines which permitted a man to declare his will to his feoffees provided his directions contained no element of open collusion.[1] The statute of 1490 by implication admitted that a man had the right to devise lands by will and thus accepted the implications of common law doctrines. It added another category of collusive enfeoffment to those defined by the common law; but in doing so it proceeded within the framework of the latter. It might be argued that, where a *cestui que use* died leaving no will, the facts implied either that his feoffees were to be seised to the use of his heir—during his minority if he were under age —or that they were to enfeoff him of the land. And either of these possibilities was collusion when the heir was a minor, if proved at common law, before 1490. On the other hand, there are grounds for suggesting that the administrative practice introduced by the statute was not a complete novelty. In the late fourteenth and early fifteenth centuries escheators occasionally recorded the contents of the deceased's directions to his feoffees in inquisitions *post mortem*. And in the Yorkist period the tendency to do so became quite pronounced.[2] We cannot be certain that this practice arose from escheator's zeal to search out cases of collusion, since it is equally possible that it was the result of a desire on the part of the feoffees or the next-of-kin to secure a record of the deceased's wishes. But, at any rate, it is clear that in 1490 escheators were already familiar with the practice of entering wills in their inquisitions.

[1] See above, p. 186.   [2] See PRO, C. 140, passim.

There are two ways in which the statute conferrred positive benefits upon the Crown. In the first place, a study of the extant inquisitions *post mortem* of Henry VII's reign shows that escheators on the whole made real efforts to enforce it, enquiring into whether a will had been made and frequently summarizing its contents in inquisitions.[1] Although most landowners took care to make their wills, some did not and the Crown was able to enforce its rights of wardship and relief. In this way, therefore, the Crown derived some direct financial benefit from the statute.[2] In the second place, the fact that escheators now had to enquire into whether or not the deceased had made his will meant that they were now more likely than in the past to scrutinize wills carefully so as to detect evidence of collusion in their provisions. The majority of inquisitions *post mortem* now contained summaries in varying detail of the deceased's directions regarding the landed property they comprised. A careful study of the details in the inquisitions, and a comparison between these and such grants of wardship and marriage as can be traced on the Patent Rolls, shows that the expression 'will' used in the statute was understood to comprise not merely a set of specific directions regarding the employment of landed revenues after the death of a *cestui que use* but also any other precise description of the purpose of the

[1] Occasionally the jurors simply state that the last will was produced to them (e.g. *CIPMB*, I. 503 (no. 1150) and 513 (no. 1163); ibid., II. 377 (no. 597)) or make some other statement—for example, that it was annexed to the charter of enfeoffment (ibid., II. 208 (no. 323), 468 (no. 717))—that gives positive proof that it had been declared. Cf. ibid., II. 257 (no. 417), where the jurors state that they are uncertain whether the deceased had made his will. When such details, or a description of the will's provisions, are absent, we are sometimes told that the deceased died without making a will (e.g. ibid., I. 507 (no. 1154), 528-9 (no. 1191) and 558 (no. 1248); ibid., II. 493 (no. 766); III. 511 (no. 999)). There are a few instances where we are left to infer the absence of a will from the fact that only the feoffment of the feoffees is recorded, e.g. ibid., II. 95 (no. 137), 103 (no. 153), 167 (no. 248) and 546 (no. 852).

[2] The most valuable wardship obtained through intestacy was that of Sir William Stonor's heir. For the important legal case which followed, see below, pp. 252-3. The case of Edward Trussell who died without making a will (ibid., II and III. Index, *sub* Trussell) must be excluded, since he died a minor in the King's custody.

use, provided it applied to the period after the death of the *cestui que use*. For example, feoffees could be seised to the use jointly of a husband and wife and, in the terms of the statute, provided the wife survived, could continue seised after the death of the husband. But, if the feoffees held merely to the use of a man and his heirs, whether in fee or in tail, the *cestui que use* was then regarded as having died intestate.[1]

However, despite the existence of evidence which proves that the statute was effective, the benefits derived from it by lords must have been marginal. The nature of its provisions must have caused many landowners to take special care to declare their wills: indeed, by implication it defined the conditions under which uses could be employed by tenants without fear of the interference of lords after their deaths. But, although in these respects the statute applied to all feudal lords, there were three important points on which the interpretation of its terms by the Crown's administrators and lawyers enabled the King to derive more gains from it than mesne lords.

The first of these points concerns the wardship of the body and marriage of an heir when the *cestui que use* held of the Crown in chief and had granted all the lands so held to feoffees. The problem then arose of whether the Crown had the right of the wardship of the body and the marriage of the heir if his ancestor had conformed to the statute of 1490 and had declared his will. When tenants who held of mesne lords enfeoffed feoffees of the whole of their holdings, the lords had no redress, a fact which is apparent from a case argued in the court of Common Pleas in 1536–7.[2] But in the same situation the Crown was able to exploit its prerogative. Constable in his reading of 1495 on the *Prerogativa Regis* clearly assumed that, even if a tenant-in-chief had alienated all his lands to feoffees and had then declared his will, the Crown retained its right of wardship of the body and the marriage of the heir.[3]

---

[1] See, e.g., ibid., I. 558 (no. 1248) and II. 438 (no. 682). Cf. *CPR, 1494–1509*, p. 432; *CIPMB*, II. 546 (no. 852). Cf. *CPR, 1494–1509*, p. 540.

[2] Dyer, I. 7b–13a (no. 11).

[3] Constable, p. 21, where it is explained that the seizure of the lands is only postponed until the will has been performed.

The fact that he took this view is confirmed at a later stage in his discussion where he states the same doctrine in respect of lands held of the King as of an escheated honour.[1] Comparison of a number of inquisitions *post mortem* with grants enrolled of the Patent Rolls confirms that the Crown exercised its rights in this respect.[2]

The second advantage which the Crown derived from its prerogative lies within the sphere of 'prerogative wardship'. What happened when a tenant-in-chief had conveyed to feoffees lands held of others than the King and had died without having declared any will concerning these, as distinct from those held of the Crown? On this point lawyers appear to have failed to agree. The issue was basically the same as that which related to the King's right to his 'prerogative wardship' in the case of lands held of others which had been alienated in collusion. On this also legal authorities disagreed at the end of the fifteenth century: while, for example, Constable in his reading on the *Prerogativa Regis* supported the King's right to have his prerogative, Frowyk and Spelman in their readings denied it.[3] In the case of 'prerogative wardship' under the statute of 1490 Constable took the view that the King could claim it if the *cestui que use* had not declared his will concerning the lands he held of others than the King.[4] The issue was discussed at length in Stonor's case which began in Trinity term, 1497,[5] and was the subject of lengthy arguments in the Exchequer Chamber, where it had been adjourned, in the

---

[1] Constable, p. 36: 'Si le tenaunt que tient de roy come deschet & dauters per priorite fait feffement en fee a son use . . . Et coment declare est volunte, cel volunte est forsque sur le terre, pur que soit volunte ou null volunte declare, le cors serra en garde & de ce le roy avera son prerogatyf en cell case de priorite, & uncor il navera le terre tanque le volunte soit performe, & si ne soit performe duraunt le nonage le roy navera le terre.'

[2] e.g. (1) *CIPMB*, I. 545 (no. 1224) and 551 (no. 1235). Cf. *CPR, 1494–1509*, p. 105. (2) *CIPMB*, II. 486 (no. 750), 488 (no. 755), 490 (no. 759), and 491 (no. 761). Cf. *CPR, 1494–1509*, p. 373. (3) *CIPMB*, II. 428–32 (no. 679) and 552–3 (no. 863). Cf. *CPR, 1494–1509*, p. 373.

[3] Constable, p. 19 and n. 46.

[4] ibid., pp. 20–1, and n. 48.

[5] *YBVE*, Trin., 12 Hen. VII, pp. 19–22, pl. 1.

following Michaelmas term.[1] There, of six judges who took part in the recorded discussion, two argued against the Crown and four in its favour.[2] But it is important to realize that this point was ventilated on this occasion only because ejected feoffees sought to traverse an inquisition and secure the removal of the lands concerned from the hands of the Crown. In practice, it is highly likely that the escheators had for some years before this paid scant regard to legal niceties and simply assumed that in such cases they were in a position to enforce royal rights.

The third point under which the Crown was in a position to press its rights under the statute of 1490 is a rather academic one. What happened when the feoffees completed the performance of the will before the minority of the heir expired? Constable argued that seizure of the lands by the King was only postponed while the will was being performed and that, once it was performed, the lands were in wardship.[3] His view, which, it is worth noting, can also be found in Edward IV's statute of 1483, was obviously a reasonable interpretation of the implications of the statute of 1490. But the support given to it by other authorities is implicit in their remarks, rather than explicitly stated by them.[4] The reason for this is not hard to discover: however unexceptionable in law, Constable's view, if adopted officially, would pose serious administrative difficulties. Careful enquiries would have to be made into the ways the feoffees spent their revenues and a thorough comparison made between the values of the lands enfeoffed and the specific financial directions made in a will. Moreover, considerable complications might ensue when some directions of the deceased took longer to perform than others. Indeed, the prosecution of the Crown's rights in this respect would have given rise to many counter-claims and evasions on the part of the feoffees, while it would also have necessitated the development of administrative machinery the expenses of which

---

[1] *S.C. Exch. Chamb.*, II. 161–75, which, however, does not include a later discussion in *YBVE*, Mich., 13 Hen. VII, pp. 11–12, pl. 12.

[2] In 1516 the judges were unanimous in the Crown's favour (Dyer, II. 174a; R. Keilwey, *Reports d'Ascuns Cases* (London, 1688), pp. 86 and 176).

[3] Constable, p. 21.   [4] See the views cited ibid., p. 21, n. 49.

might well have cancelled out any gains. In fact, no evidence has been traced to indicate that the Crown enquired into the performance of any will during the minority of the heir.[1]

It must be emphasized that the Crown secured these gains, not as a direct result of the statute of 1490, but by means of the interpretation of its terms in the light of the rights of the royal prerogative. In practice, only one of these points of interpretation could have conferred tangible benefits. The application of 'prerogative wardship' when the will had not been declared could not have resulted in a remarkable increase in revenues, since there were few landowners who did not take care to make wills in respect of enfeoffed lands not held in chief. The right to wardship of the lands after the will had been performed was in practice extremely difficult to enforce and, in fact, appears only to have existed in theory. The Crown's chief gain must have been the fact that it retained the wardship of the body and the marriage of the heir, even though all the lands of the tenant-in-chief had been conveyed to feoffees and the will been declared.[2] On the other hand, the statute did nothing to safeguard the royal right of primer seisin against uses.[3]

In any event, the statute of 1490, while the first attempt to legislate against uses on a national scale, was also the first legislative recognition on a national scale of the state of affairs in which, by employing enfeoffments to their use, tenants-in-chief were manipulating for their own purposes after their deaths revenues

---

[1] There are a few inquisitions *post mortem* of Henry VII's reign which mention that the deceased's will has not yet been performed or that his debts have not yet been paid (*CIPMB*, I. 373 (no. 847), 447 (no. 1041), 500 (no. 1146), 535 (no. 1202) and 561 (no. 1251); ibid., II. 17 (no. 11), 201 (no. 308) and 356 (no. 562). But it would be unwise to assume that these result from the enforcement of Constable's doctrine. It is more likely that the deceased's executors or feoffees secured the insertion of these details in the inquisition in order to have an authenticated record of them.

[2] There is some evidence to suggest that, even without the statute of 1490, such enfeoffments by a tenant-in-chief might be considered collusive (see above, p. 204). But doubt could exist on this point if such enfeoffments had been made with royal licence (see above, p. 208).

[3] Constable, p. 54, n. 135.

which belonged to the Crown. Such practices could continue provided landowners complied with the conditions prescribed in the statute. It is clear that the reforms obtained in the statute were the most that the Crown was able to achieve against uses. No doubt the passage of the measure through parliament was due to the fact that, while it gave mesne lords their rights in the event of their tenants dying intestate, it left unimpaired the advantages they themselves derived from uses provided they took care to declare their wills. The extent to which the Crown in the reign of Henry VII was forced to continue to accept the loss of feudal incidents caused by uses is underlined by the terms of a statute passed in the last parliament of the reign in 1504:[1]

> . . . if any bondman purchase any lands or tenements in fee simple, fee tail, or for term of life or term of years, and causeth estate to be made to divers persons to his use, or taketh estate to himself and to divers others jointly with him and to his use and behoof, . . . it shall be lawful to the lord of any such bondman to enter during the same use into the said lands and tenements and every parcel thereof so purchased by his bondman, in like manner and form as he might have done if the said bondman had only been seised of the said lands and tenements in fee or otherwise.

No doubt the Crown, as the lord of the largest number of bond-men in the kingdom, gained most from this statute. But only in the case of unfree manorial tenants did it succeed in securing legislation which in effect enabled it to oust their feoffees. In the case of those who held by feudal tenure it had no alternative but to accept the existence of uses and their consequences.

In fact, if the Crown was to prevent the loss of its feudal revenues through uses, either of two policies would have to be followed. One would have meant the complete abolition of uses; but this would also have removed from landowners all the advantages they derived from them. The other would have entailed a reform whereby, although uses were permitted, the incidents of feudal tenure were safeguarded. But this would have damaged the interests of the landowning classes and, indeed, have removed one

[1] *Statutes*, II. 660 (19 Hen. VII, c. 15).

of the main, if not the chief, advantages of uses. It is certain that, even at the end of his reign, Henry VII was not powerful enough to force through parliament a reform of this magnitude. Throughout his reign, therefore, the policy of the Crown towards its feudal incidents was dominated by its tacit acceptance of uses. If it was to secure a substantial increase in its feudal revenues, it had no alternative but to turn to indirect means—fines for technical offences against its feudal rights and methods which verged on, or approximated to, blackmail. In this sense the inroads which uses had made into its feudal revenues, virtually accepted as they were in the statute of 1490, forced the Crown to resort to the unscrupulous rapacity which is associated with the names of Empson and Dudley.

CHAPTER SIX

The Royal Prerogative, 1529–1540: from Victory to Compromise

HENRY VIII's conflict with the Papacy, beginning in 1529 and leading to his breach with Rome, presented the English monarchy with two simultaneous dangers—the possible resistance of the English clergy and their lay sympathizers to the King's will and the threat that the Emperor Charles V would engage in military intervention on the Pope's behalf. In such a situation it was imperative that the King avoid adding to his subjects' discontent by increasing taxation. Yet his foreign ambitions over the past two decades had left his coffers low and his present situation forced him to seek means of raising additional revenues. The solution to his financial problems was partly found in the exploitation of the most potentially valuable of the Crown's extra-parliamentary revenues—the incidents of feudal tenure.

From 1529 onwards the Crown endeavoured to increase its feudal revenues in two ways. On the one hand, it carried to their logical conclusion the administrative tendencies of the past half-century and in 1540 set up the Courts of Wards. From then onwards there existed a formal court of record, set up by parliamentary statute,[1] which handled all the business relating to wardships and took over all the functions in this respect which had hitherto belonged to the Chancery and the Exchequer. Moreover, in the following year[2] all liveries of lands were put under its control. In consequence, there now existed a department of state which administered the whole of the feudal revenues of the Crown. No doubt a powerful incentive towards this administrative reorganization was the fact that, when the lands of the monasteries dissolved in 1536–9 were granted to laymen, they

[1] 32 Hen. VIII, c. 46 (*Statutes*, III. 802–7).
[2] 33 Hen. VIII, c. 22 (*Statutes*, III. 860–3).

were to be held of the Crown in chief, a form of tenure which promised to boost revenues from feudal incidents in future years.

On the other hand, the Crown prosecuted policies which were intended to stop the losses of feudal revenues which were suffered through uses. After efforts which lasted for five years or so, it succeeded in securing the passing through parliament of the Act of Uses in 1536 which made it impossible for any landowner employing uses to evade the incidents of feudal tenure. But this complete success was short-lived. In 1540 the Crown had to accept the Statute of Wills which left landowners with the power to devise by will two-thirds of all the lands they held by feudal tenure. Nevertheless, even this reform gave Henry VIII a measure of control over the loss of feudal incidents through uses which had been denied to his predecessors for almost two centuries.

(i) THE PERIOD OF NEGOTIATION

Henry VIII and his advisers must always have realized the difficulties which lay in the path of any attempt to deal with the problem of uses, since these constituted a vested interest which had become part and parcel of the structure of English landownership. They appear to have decided that the best hope of success lay in producing a scheme which would confer some advantages on all landowners in general, and on the nobility in particular, thus ensuring that the reforms they envisaged secured the consent of parliament. The scheme[1] which was drawn up has survived in the

[1] For the view that the draft bill was not official, see the comments of Dr. E. W. Ives in *EHR*, LXXXII (1967), 677–80 (which appeared while this book was in the press). But the unrealistic nature of some of its provisions hardly justifies this attitude to what was, after all, only a draft. It is certainly likely that the government planned the registration of uses. In any case, the draft is in the form of a government bill and Dr. Ives himself cites evidence indicating an official provenance (ibid., p. 679, n. 2). Its date gives no support to the theory that it did not form part of the Crown's plans against uses, since no year is mentioned in the text. In the case of the agreement with the nobility the deletion ordered in Mich. 1531 (ibid., p. 679, n. 2) must refer to cl. 18, not cl. 19, since the latter's removal would have threatened the success of any legislative plans.

form of two documents—a draft parliamentary bill and an agreement between the Crown and the nobility which was to form the basis of another bill. Both were brought to light when the *Letters and Papers . . . of Henry VIII* were published and have been discussed by Professors Holdsworth and Plucknett.

The draft bill contained three main provisions.[1] First, all entails were to be abolished and none permitted in future, 'so that all manner of possessions be in state of fee simple from this day forward forever'. Second, no uses of any land were to be valid 'unless the same use be recorded in the King's court of common pleas'. Third, entails were still to be permitted 'to the noble men of this realm being within the degree of a baron'. No one was to be able to buy a nobleman's land without a royal licence. These provisions contained benefits which, it was hoped, would persuade the landowners who sat in parliament to accept the King's plans regarding uses. The interests of non-noble landowners were not neglected. Uses were to be permitted to continue and the stipulation that they were to be recorded at Westminster was one which might be welcomed by any *cestui que use* who was anxious about the possibility of fraud on the part of his feoffees. The abolition of entails would be unlikely to cause discontent provided uses were still permitted. In fact, the proposed reform recognized the fact that entails had been broken quite easily for many years by means of common recoveries. If a landowner wished now to control the devolution of his inheritance, he was more likely to do so by means of uses and carefully compiled directions to his feoffees—indeed, feoffees were often seised to the use of a beneficiary in tail. The text of the draft bill does not indicate whether its authors envisaged the continuance of settlements of this type, but, if uses were to continue, it is difficult to see how they could have been avoided. But, apart from these considerations, the draft bill recognized the fact that entails no longer fulfilled a useful purpose, since there was no obstacle at law to their being broken with impunity: their abolition would simply save those who wished to break

[1] Printed in Holdsworth, IV. 572–4.

them the expense and inconvenience of effecting common recoveries.

For the nobility alone the draft bill promised rather more. In the reservation of entails to them alone there was the prospect that they and their descendants would hold inheritances which devolved by laws of succession not available to lesser men. In short, if the bill became law, they would constitute a privileged social caste. Some historians have seen in this aspect of the proposed reforms signs of a deliberate policy on the part of the Crown to bolster up the social status and economic power of a declining nobility and thus reconstitute the crumbling social hierarchy of English society under the headship of the monarchy.[1] But, in the light of the actual context in which its policies were formulated, it is unwise to read such an imaginative concept of 'social engineering' into the Crown's schemes. It is difficult to reconcile this theory with the identities of many of the nobles who appear to have consented to the Crown's plans. Of a total of thirty,[2] nine were *parvenus*: in six cases[3] their families had only reached the peerage after the accession of Henry VIII in 1509, while three[4] began the Reformation Parliament as members of the Commons and only attained the Lords at the beginning of December 1529. It would seem more likely that the promise that entails would be confined to their class was intended as a sop to the pride of the nobility, an especially attractive one to the most recent recruits to their ranks. Nor can it be argued that the bill envisaged a permanent social hierarchy: the noble entails so proposed were not necessarily to be perpetual, since the Crown was to have the right to license the sale of any lands so entailed. It is, of course,

[1] e.g. T. F. T. Plucknett, 'Some Proposed Legislation of Henry VIII', *TRHS*, 4th ser., XIX (1936), 121-4.

[2] Professor Plucknett is wrong (ibid., p. 122, n. 3) in stating that the Speaker, Sir Thomas Audley, was one of those who gave their consent. This signature must have been that of John Tuchet, lord Audley.

[3] Thomas, lord Darcy of Temple Hurst; Edmund, lord Bray; Thomas Boleyn, earl of Wiltshire; Henry Pole, lord Montague; Thomas Stanley, lord Mounteagle; and Charles Brandon, duke of Suffolk.

[4] Andrew, lord Windsor of Stanwell; Thomas, lord Wentworth; and John, lord Hussey.

possible that the Crown and its advisers wished by means of such licences to control the devolution of all noble inheritances in the future and that the proposal to restrict entails to the nobility in reality masks such a plan.[1] But, in default of further evidence, it may be wiser to regard this aspect of the Crown's schemes as resulting from its anxiety to provide the nobility with some tangible benefits which would persuade them to agree to its plans regarding uses.

The agreement[2] with the nobility was a lengthy document containing twenty-three clauses, to which are attached in the only extant copy the names of the King himself, Sir Thomas More, the Chancellor, and thirty peers.[3] A study of its provisions shows that its authors were attempting to go beyond the statute of 1490 and to restore to the Crown part of its losses of feudal incidents when a *cestui que use* died leaving a will. Clauses 1 and 2 reiterated the King's right of 'prerogative wardship' when his tenant-in-chief died seised in fee or, having enfeoffed feoffees to his use, died intestate. Clauses 3, 4 and 5 comprise the most important provisions concerning the King's rights of wardship. Clause 3 declared that, if a tenant-in-chief had conveyed all his lands, both those held in chief and those held of mesne lords, to feoffees and then died leaving an heir under age, the King was to have a third of all these lands in wardship, 'notwithstanding any will, jointure or other use to the contrary hereafter to be limited or assigned'. In short, a tenant-in-chief was to be permitted to devise by will no more than two-thirds of all his lands. Clauses 4 and 5 extended this rule to tenants-in-chief who had conveyed part of their lands to feoffees. If the residue held in fee amounted to more than one-third of all the lands, then the King was to have the whole of it in wardship: if it was less than one-third, he was to have 'the third

---

[1] Cf. the terms of the indenture of 16 July 1532 between the Crown and the earl of Northumberland whereby the latter promised to allow the greater part of his estates to descend to 'one person of the name of Percy and of the blood of the said Percy' (Bean, pp. 151–2).

[2] Printed in Holdsworth, IV. 574–7.

[3] These names presumably represent the signatures of those who signed the original agreement.

part of the whole lands at his pleasure' (cl. 4). Clause 5 dealt with the case of a tenant-in-chief who had conveyed to feoffees only those lands held of mesne lords and whose holdings in chief amounted to less than one-third of all his lands. When this occurred, the King was to have in wardship all the lands held in chief together with as much of the enfeoffed lands as would bring the amount in wardship up to one-third of the whole. In clause 7 the King was given in wardship one-third of lands held of him 'by reason of any escheat, honour or otherwise', despite any uses created by the deceased tenant.

A number of clauses set out the King's rights when heirs who were of age sought livery of their inheritances. Clause 8 laid down that an heir who had been in the King's wardship was to pay for his livery a sum equal to one-third the annual value of the lands the King had held in wardship. Clause 12 stated that an heir who was of age at the time of his ancestor's death was to pay a half of one year's revenues of the lands 'to him descended from his ancestor in possession or in use' before he obtained the livery of his inheritance.

A comparison of these clauses and of others which carefully safeguarded the rights which the Crown thus obtained with the actual prerogatives enjoyed by it, especially as a result of the statute of 1490, shows that the agreement with the nobility promised very substantial gains. In the first place, whereas since 1490 it had been possible for a *cestui que use* to convey all his lands to uses so that the King obtained only the wardship of the body and had—in theory, at least—to wait for the lands until the will was performed,[1] it was now proposed to give the King the wardship of one-third of all such lands, even if these comprised lands not held in chief, despite the fact that the deceased had declared his will in respect of them. In the second place, whereas the statute of 1490 made no mention at all of the King's profits from liveries, these were specifically mentioned in the agreement which, in the case of an heir who was of age, stated that he must give one half of a year's revenues from all the lands descended to him, whether in fee or in use, so that the Crown's rights in this respect could not

---

[1] See above, pp. 251–2 and 253.

be evaded by the creation of uses. From the Crown's standpoint these were substantial gains which promised greatly increased feudal revenues in the future. But a further consideration of the agreement's clauses in the light of the statute of 1490 brings to light a curious gap in its provisions, in that it made no mention of the relief. The statute of 1490 had given the lord his relief when a *cestui que use* died intestate, leaving an heir over age: if there was a will, the lord appears to have lost his right to it. It is, perhaps, unwise to read any significance into the absence of any mention of the relief in the agreement with the nobility: we are dealing with a document which was to form the basis of future legislation and it is quite possible that an error of omission had occurred which would, in due course, have been rectified. But two other possible reasons for the omission are worth noting. The first is that royal administrators had now come to realize that reliefs, since they had been fixed in value since the thirteenth century, were an unrealistic and inefficient means of tapping the wealth of landed inheritances, whereas the rule that a fixed proportion of annual revenues be paid for livery gave the Crown financial rights which would not deteriorate through any fall in the value of money. The second possibility is that the Crown did nothing to protect its rights to reliefs in order to propitiate potential opposition to the proposed statute. The fact that reliefs as a source of revenue were decreasing in real value would have made this concession easier to make.

The Crown hoped to secure support for its proposals regarding feudal incidents by means of concessions which would benefit all the kingdom's landowners. Most of these are contained in the draft bill dealing with the future of entails. But the agreement with the nobility itself contains in clause 19 an important benefit from which all feudal lords below the King might hope to gain:

Also the King's highness is pleased that it shall be enacted that every of the said noble men, and all other his subjects and their heirs and successors of whom any lands or tenements be or shall be holden by knight's service, shall have full benefit and profit of the wardship of the third part of the whole of the same lands or tenements holden of the King's subjects as the case shall require, as by the said Articles is devised for the King's highness, his heirs and successors of lands and tenements of him holden and not in chief.[1]

The Crown, therefore, could claim that it was legislating in terms of the interests, not of itself alone, but all feudal lords in the kingdom.

No doubt the King and those who advised upon and drafted these documents hoped that those landowners who sat in parliament, whether in the Lords or the Commons, would take a balanced view of the Crown's proposals as a whole, weighing up their losses through the limitations imposed upon their power to devise against the other benefits conferred upon them. Non-noble landowners would make gains—freedom from the inconveniences of entails and the wardship of one-third of any fees held of them when the tenant died leaving his heir under age and having declared his will thereof. The hope of gain from the latter benefit would, of course, disappear if the tenant held other lands of the King in chief, thus exposing the whole of his inheritance to 'prerogative wardship'. Noble landowners would make the same gains but would also secure a legal privilege denied to those outside their ranks. Moreover, their own profits as feudal lords would be greater than those of commoners. It is, therefore, clear that the scheme whereby the Crown hoped to repair the damage which uses had inflicted upon its feudal revenues conferred some benefits on all other landowners, though the nobility gained more than the rest. The presence of the names of as many as thirty peers[2] on the extant copy of the agreement with the nobility suggests that the Crown must have felt confident about the prospects of its proposals when presented to parliament.

---

[1] Those who signed the agreement also undertook in cl. 18 that, if they died before it became law, it should nevertheless take full effect between the King and their heirs.

[2] It is important to note that the signatories did not comprise the whole of the nobility. The most important absentee was Henry Percy, earl of Northumberland (for whom see Bean, pp. 144–57). Another was Thomas Fiennes, lord Dacre (for whom see below).

In the absence of records of the day-to-day proceedings of the Commons in the Reformation Parliament, and of the Lords' Journals for its early sessions, we are faced with a difficult task when we try to reconstruct the details of the Crown's efforts to push its schemes through parliament. According to Holdsworth,[1] these events took place in two stages: first, the draft bill and the agreement with the nobility were drawn up in 1529, his words implying that efforts were then made to put them through; second, further efforts were made in 1532. This chronology of the events cannot, however, be accepted. Holdsworth was following the editor of the *Letters and Papers* who assigned both the documents concerned to 1529. But there are convincing reasons why this dating must be rejected. It is, of course, highly likely that both the draft bill and the agreement with the nobility belong to the same date, since only the matters dealt with in the latter adequately explain the proposals of the former. But the draft bill contains nothing which helps us to determine its date; and, therefore, we have to assume that it belongs to the same date as the agreement. The only way to determine this is to examine the names of those nobles who appear to have given their consent to the Crown's proposals. Three of them had sat as members of the Commons at the opening of the Reformation Parliament in August 1529 and were only admitted to the Lords on the following 1–2 December. In view of the fact that the first session of this parliament was concluded on 17 December 1529, it is difficult to believe that the agreement was drawn up before the end of that year and almost impossible to believe that efforts were made to push its provisions through parliament in 1529. But, since another peer who gave his consent—Thomas Grey, marquess of Dorset —died on 10 October 1530, it is clear that his consent at any rate must have been given before that date. The list of peers which appears on the extant copy of the agreement, however, comprises one which gives considerable difficulty from the standpoint of dating the document. Edward Stanley, earl of Derby, was still a minor at the time of the marquess of Dorset's death and did not receive his special licence of entry upon his inheritance without

[1] Holdsworth, IV. 450–3.

proof of age and livery until 29 January 1531. It is difficult to believe that the Crown would wish to receive his signature of agreement before this date, since, although given, its validity might later be contested by him or his heirs in view of the fact that he was technically a minor before entering upon his inheritance. It is true that he had attained the age of twenty-one in May 1530. But the agreement was intended to bind the heirs of those who consented to it so that the Crown's financial gains thereby would accrue even if its provisions did not become a parliamentary statute. It is fair to assume that the Crown would take care to ensure that this provision applied to the earl of Derby.

The difficulties with which we are faced when we seek to reconcile the cases of the marquess of Dorset and the earl of Derby need no longer trouble us if we cease to assume that all those peers whose consent was given gave it at one and the same time. It is quite likely that the process of negotiation with the nobility lasted some months and that some individual peers gave their consent at earlier dates than others. But the presence of the earl of Derby's name on the list suggests that these negotiations must have been very recent on 29 January 1531. On the other hand, they must already have been in progress at the time of the marquess of Dorset's death on 10 October 1530.

This discussion of the problems of dating the documents with which we are concerned does throw some light upon the chronology of the Crown's efforts to have them made into parliamentary statutes. It is clearly impossible to believe that any such efforts were made during the first session of the Reformation Parliament which, after the initial prorogation, lasted from 4 November to 17 December 1529. The second session lasted from 16 January to 31 March 1531.[1] But the date of the grant of a special licence of

---

[1] It is possible the agreement was completed in this session, legislation being intended for the next, since its rubric states that it was drawn up in a session of this parliament and was to be enacted 'in the next full Court thereof'. But we cannot be certain of this, since our copy is in a late sixteenth-century hand. The inclusion of the marquess of Dorset among the signatories was probably the copyist's error.

entry upon his inheritance to the earl of Derby makes it unlikely, though, perhaps, not impossible, that legislation against uses was introduced in this session. However, on this point we are fortunately able to use the evidence of the chronicle written by Edward Hall, himself a member of this parliament.[1] According to him, when the Supplication against the Ordinaries was presented to him on 18 March 1532, the King complained of the treatment which the Commons had given the proposals he had placed before them:[2] '. . . For I have sent you a bill concerning wards and primer seisin, in the which things I am greatly wronged: wherefore I have offered you reason, as I think, yea, and so thinketh all the Lords, for they have set their hands to the book.' The last clause leaves little doubt that the bill in question was based on the agreement which had been made with the nobility. It is noteworthy that the King's remarks contained no mention of any efforts in this respect made in a previous session. We must, therefore, conclude the first efforts to secure legislation against the consequences of uses occurred in the third session of the Reformation Parliament which lasted from 15 January to 28 March 1532.

Yet some doubts must remain about the exact nature of the proposals which the Crown then placed before parliament. After quoting the King's words, to the Commons, Hall went on to explain the events which had caused the King's anger.

The cause why the King spake these words was this: Daily men made feoffments of their lands with such remainders, that not only the King but all other lords lost their wards, marriages and reliefs, and the King lost also his primer seisin, and the profit of the livery, which was to him very prejudicial and a great loss: wherefore he, like an indifferent prince, not willing to take all, nor to lose all caused a bill to be drawn up by his learned counsel, in the which was devised that every man might make his will of the half of his land, so that he left the other half to the heir by descent. When this bill came first among the Commons, lord! how the ignorant persons were grieved, and how shamefully they

---

[1] His chronicle does not appear to have been used by Holdsworth.
[2] Hall, p. 203.

spake of the bill and of the King's learned counsel: but the wise men which saw and understood the mischief to come, would gladly have had the bill assented to or at least to have put the King in a surety of the third or fourth part, which offer I was credibly informed the King would have taken.[1]

On the other hand, a letter written to his master by the Imperial ambassador Chapuys contains details which it is not easy to reconcile with Hall's statements. On 14 February 1532 he wrote that '. . . the King has been trying to obtain in Parliament the third part of the feudal property of deceased persons, but he has not yet succeeded'.[2] This description of the bill suggests that it was based on the agreement made with the nobility some twelve months or so previously. However, we would expect Hall, a lawyer sitting in the Commons which discussed the bill, to have a more reliable knowledge of its provisions than Chapuys.[3]

Their two different accounts are not irreconcilable. A year or so had elapsed since the agreement between the King and the nobility had been made. It seems quite likely that in the intervening period the Crown decided to raise its demands and alter the proportion to be held in wardship from one-third to a half. If so, Hall's statement that the latter was the amount proposed in the bill would be correct. This would have meant, of course, a fresh agreement with the nobility. Hall's version of the King's words, if accurate, suggests that this is what happened, since the King stated that 'all the lords . . . have set their hands to the book', whereas a perusal of the list of names entered on the extant copy of the agreement with the nobility shows that it did not

[1] Hall, pp. 203–4.
[2] L & P, V. 380 (no. 805). It seems likely that a letter of 30 January 1532 refers to the same bill, although the version given of its proposals is a somewhat garbled one: '. . . it was discussed in Parliament that the King should have all the goods of lords who die, even when they leave a son of full age' (ibid., V. 362 (no. 762).
[3] For some discussion (though in another connexion) of the reliability of Hall's account of the events of this year see J. P. Cooper, 'The Supplication against the Ordinaries Reconsidered', EHR, LXXII (1957), 617–20.

comprise all the peers of the kingdom.[1] Indeed, we cannot exclude the possibility that the raising of their demands was a deliberate scheme on the part of the King and his advisers to strengthen the chances of the successful passage through the Commons of legislation which would reduce the Crown's financial losses through uses. In the event of strong opposition they wanted room to manœuvre. If in the event the Crown's demands had to be reduced from a half to one-third to mollify the opposition, its gains would nevertheless be the same as those originally projected. This suggestion is supported by the fact that Hall was clearly under the impression that the King was ready to reduce his demands. And the rumour that this was so may have led Chapuys to believe that the King was demanding one-third in wardship.[2] Unfortunately, we possess no other information about the bill's reception in the Commons.[3]

The failure of the Crown's efforts in 1532 requires little explanation. It is clear that the bill had received the consent of the nobility before it was laid before the Commons, although our evidence does not permit us to be certain whether it was discussed formally in the Lords or whether the Crown had simply employed the procedure of an agreement with the nobility whereby they undertook to give the bill their support when it came before them in the Upper House. Neither the correspondence of Chapuys nor the chronicle of Hall mentions any bill to abolish entails for all save the nobility. It is quite possible that

[1] If we can accept Hall's statement that all the lords had consented thereto, it is possible that the agreement on which the bill actually presented in the Lords was based did not include an undertaking whereby the signatories agreed that, if they died before it became law, its provisions should nevertheless take effect between their heirs and the Crown. The Crown certainly made no attempt to invoke any such undertaking when Thomas Dacre, lord Fiennes, died in September 1533. On the other hand, it is possible that it deliberately waived its rights thereunder in order to exploit the legal opportunities which lord Dacre's dispositions presented.   [2] *L & P*, V. 380 (no. 805).

[3] It does appear to have achieved two readings (ibid., VI. 52 (no. 120)). The suggestion (*EHR*, LXXXII (1967), 683) that this refers to the second session of 1532 conflicts with Hall's account. For the purpose of the enrolment of statutes the two sessions of 1532 were treated as one.

its omission from these sources is accidental. On the other hand it is equally possible that this portion of the Crown's schemes had been dropped, or its introduction into parliament deferred, until the bill relating to uses had gone through, a possibility which is quite likely in view of the fact that its benefits were conferred mainly on the nobility. At any rate, our sources leave us in no doubt that nothing would have successfully commended the Crown's proposals to a majority of the Commons. Chapuys in his letter of 14 February 1532 told the Emperor that the King's 'demand has been the occasion of strange words against the King and Council',[1] an account which is supported by Hall's description of the bill's reception.[2] Most of the Commons would have held some land under feudal tenure and the bill before them, especially if the King was demanding a half in wardship, would severely damage the benefits they derived from uses. We must assume that the bill, like the previous agreement with the nobility, conferred on all mesne lords the same proportion of their tenants' lands in wardship as the Crown secured in respect of both its tenants-in-chief and its other tenants. If so, the peers would certainly have profited, some of them quite substantially, from the bill when it became law, a fact which must have helped them to decide to support it. But it is unlikely that those members of the Commons who were feudal lords would have gained in terms of wardship to the same extent as their social superiors. Such additional profits as they could expect would not be enough to compensate them adequately for the reduction in their powers to devise which the Crown's proposals would have achieved.

(ii) The Statute of Uses (1536)

One of the most remarkable features of the relations between King and Reformation Parliament is the fact that, having failed in 1532 to secure a reform which left a substantial part of his subjects' gains from uses intact, four years later in the Statute of Uses Henry VIII secured a reform which abolished such gains alto-

[1] ibid., V. 380 (no. 805).   [2] Hall, p. 204.

gether. Holdsworth was well aware of the need to explain the
contrast between the strong and successful opposition of the
Commons in 1532 and their weakness and complaisance in 1536.
His explanation placed its main emphasis on the skill of the King
and his advisers in handling the Commons in 1536:

> . . . It was clearly impossible to carry the original scheme through the
> House of Commons. The alliance between the king and his nobility
> had been found to be useless for this purpose. There must be a new
> scheme founded on a new alliance between the king and one of the
> interests in the House of Commons which had blocked the original
> scheme.
>
> There could be little doubt which of these interests it would be the
> most easy to win. It was not likely that the landowners would ever
> consent to any scheme which would deprive them of the power of
> making secure family settlements and secret conveyances. On the other
> hand, the lawyers, and probably other classes in the community, were
> prepared to admit that uses often furthered fraudulent dealing . . .
> Probably the perception of the common lawyers was quickened by
> their professional jealousy of the Chancery. Many of them no doubt
> would have liked to capture for their own courts jurisdiction over this
> new form of property, which was making the fortune of the court of
> Chancery . . . Clearly there was the possibility of drawing a measure
> which would both give the king what he wanted and command the
> approval of the lawyers.
>
> The way in which the king went to work was characteristic of his
> diplomatic methods. He frightened the landowners by the stringency
> of his enquiries into settlements which deprived him of his rights; and
> he frightened the lawyers by listening to a petition against abuses in the
> administration of the law.[1]

But it is difficult to accept this account of the reasons for the
success of the Crown's policies. Holdsworth cited only two instances of stringent enquiries into settlements.[2] His discussion of
the attitude of the lawyers is unsatisfactory because it both mis-
construes their motives and exaggerates their importance in the

---

[1] Holdsworth, IV. 453–4.
[2] ibid., IV. 454, n. 4. One of these involved the dispositions of lord Dacre,
discussed below.

deliberations of the Commons. Although the courts of common law were now distinct from that of the Chancery, there is no convincing evidence of a conflict of jurisdictions early in the sixteenth century and it is likely that many of those who practised in the courts of common law also did so in the Chancery. It may be unwise to dismiss altogether the notion that the lawyers in the Commons would have regarded any proposals for the reform of the law with distaste, since their professional pride and profits might be damaged. But it is difficult to believe that legal ingenuity would not within a short time have thwarted such reforms. Moreover, those lawyers who were landowners would have lost more through the removal of their personal benefits from uses than from reforms in their professional activities. On these grounds alone, therefore, it would seem most unlikely that the King's threats to reform the law would have seriously frightened the lawyers or his proposals to reform uses have appealed to the professional interests of the common law. But, even if they did, it is difficult to see in such effects a convincing explanation for the passing of the Statute of Uses. Although we do not know how many of the members of the Commons were lawyers,[1] they could not have been so numerous as to provide a majority that would have enabled the King to push through a bill which injured the interests of all landowners who were feudal lords. Above all, Holdworth's remarks contain nothing which explains why the Commons on this occasion accepted a measure which went much further than one that they had bitterly and successfully opposed four years before.

In fact, the King got his way by means of a series of extra-parliamentary manœuvres which ultimately gave him a victory over uses in the courts of law and thus presented the Commons

---

[1] In the parliament of 1422 between a fifth and a quarter of the Commons were men of law. But in the parliament of 1584 the practising lawyers returned to the Commons numbered 53 out of a total of 460—that is, roughly an eighth, although the total of those who had undergone some sort of legal education had in the meanwhile increased (J. S. Roskell, *The Commons in the Parliament of 1422*, Manchester, 1954, p. 65). In the light of these figures it is difficult to believe that the proportion of those in the Commons who were professionally involved in the practice of the law was greater than in 1422.

with a *fait accompli*. According to Hall,[1] the King warned the Commons that this was his intention on 18 March 1532: '. . . Therefore I assure you, if you will not take some reasonable end now when it is offered, I will search out the extremity of the law, and then will I not offer you so much again.' Hall went on to tell what then happened: '. . . For after this, the King called the Judges and the best learned men of his Realm, and they disputed the matter in Chancery, and agreed that land could not be willed by the order of the common law, whereupon an act was made, that no man might declare his will of no part of his land.'

Hall's remarks are the only contemporary description we possess of the manœuvres employed to secure the passing of the Statute of Uses. A study of the available records confirms his statement that uses were found to be illegal at common law and that there was a connexion between this and the passing of the statute. But there are three points on which Hall's knowledge is weak and superficial. In the first place, the precise nature of the assembly which 'disputed' in the Chancery is by no means clear. It is possible that his words refer to the actual case which ended in the Crown's favour. If so, his language is hardly appropriate to the description of a legal action. On the other hand, Hall may be referring to an assembly in which the Crown consulted its legal advisers about the best means of proceeding at common law. It is very likely that there was such a meeting, although we have no other mention of it. But, if Hall is referring to this, he omits to describe the actual case which followed. In the second place, the word 'whereupon', without further details, begs the vitally important question of how a decision at common law persuaded the Commons to alter their attitude. In the third place, Hall's description of the Statute of Uses, though an accurate summary of its consequences, is oversimplified. Nevertheless, he was the only contemporary who has left us any account of the means by which the Crown secured its victory.

The methods employed were both ingenious and ruthless. By means of its escheators, and the inquisitions held by them when landowners died, the Crown had an opportunity to investigate

[1] Hall, II. 203–4.

the settlements made by deceased tenants-in-chief. If the jurors in an inquisition *post mortem* entered a finding which was in the Crown's favour, then it had the right at common law to proceed accordingly. Such a finding could be challenged by an interested party—for instance, one who claimed the land belonged to him, not to the deceased—by means of the procedure on the 'common law' side of Chancery which was known as a 'traverse',[1] in which the Chancellor, having enquired into the facts at issue, gave his judgement. The King's advisers—perhaps Thomas Cromwell himself, though there is no positive evidence to suggest this[2]— hatched a scheme whereby this procedure was to be manipulated against uses. If uses which had been created by a deceased tenant-in-chief could be found to have been made in collusion to de-fraud the King of his rights, the Crown could seize the lands so conveyed. If the deceased's feoffees then sought to traverse the inquisition's findings, the Chancellor would uphold the finding of collusion. If the use so found to be collusive was of the kind which the Crown had so far been prepared to regard as having been made in good faith, a new point of law would thus have been established. The King's escheators would henceforward be able to insist that all such uses were collusive and any attempts by feoffees to traverse such findings would fail—indeed, it would not be worth while to make them. Such a scheme entailed an un-scrupulous manipulation of the processes of law in two respects. First, it ran counter to the precedents of the courts of common law and royal administrative practice since the late fourteenth century and, in particular, to the terms of the statute of 1490. Doctrines had developed which envisaged the existence of uses which were not in any way collusive at law.[3] Second, in the last resort the scheme depended upon the co-operation of the Chancellor and his finding that the use in question was collusive: in passing such a judgement he would be ignoring the precedents of

[1] See above, p. 209.

[2] See the discussion below of the events which led to the passing of the Statute of Wills. This lends support to the view that Thomas Cromwell was the author of the policies which led to the Statute of Uses.

[3] See above, pp. 186–7, 242–3 and 248.

a hundred and fifty years and making a legal decision which was based solely on extra-legal considerations.

To succeed this scheme required the death of a tenant-in-chief who had created uses of a hitherto non-collusive nature and was important enough for any action to be taken by the Crown to become easily known to all leading landowners and, in particular, to those sitting in the Lords and Commons. The King did not have long to wait after his threat to the Commons in March 1532.[1] On 9 September 1533 Thomas Fiennes, lord Dacre, died, leaving as his heir his grandson Thomas who was eighteen years of age. His estates comprised manors in thirteen counties, though just over two-fifths of his revenues came from those in Sussex alone.[2] The bulk of these lands appear to have been in the hands of feoffees. In his 'last will' he laid down that the revenues from a number of these manors were to be employed for the performance of his testament and the payment of various legacies for as long as was necessary for this purpose. Some manors were left in tail male, with various remainders to other members of his family, to his two younger sons. The most important of his dispositions directed his feoffees to convey the residue of the lands held by them to his heir when he attained the age of twenty-four years. In the meanwhile, his executors were to employ the revenues for the maintenance of the heir and pay to Anne Fiennes, his granddaughter and the heir's sister, a marriage portion of 500 marks: any surplus revenues were to be handed over to the heir when he reached the age of twenty-four.[3] Inquisitions *post mortem* which were held in Kent and Sussex in January 1534 found that the testament and 'last will' were

drawn up, made and declared by the abovesaid Thomas, late lord Dacre, by fraud and collusion . . . by and between the same Thomas in his

---

[1] This was the first death of a peer of the realm since the failure to secure legislation in 1532.

[2] This figure is based on the valuations contained in PRO, S.P. 1/58/ff. 85–9, calendared in *L & P*, IV (3), 2996 (no. 6647).

[3] Full transcripts of the testament and 'last will' are to be found in the record of the Chancery case which is cited below. For a summary of the financial provisions see *L & P*, VI. 649 (no. 1590). For the inquisitions *post mortem* held in Kent and Sussex, see PRO, Chan., inq. p.m., C. 142/80/24 and 25.

lifetime and the said Thomas Polstead and William Threle[1] and other counsellors and adherents of the said Thomas, late lord Dacre, in order to defraud . . . the lord King, his heirs and executors of the custody, ward and marriage of the body of the same Thomas, kin and heir of the said Thomas late lord Dacre, and of the custody, possession and ward . . . of all . . . the lands . . . which were of the said Thomas, late lord Dacre, and of the issues and profits of the same.

On 11 February 1535 the feoffees appeared in Chancery to traverse the findings in respect of the Kent[2] inquisition, denying that lord Dacre's testamentary dispositions were collusive. Since the facts given in the inquisition were not denied, no further inquisitions were ordered and the proceedings seem to have revolved solely around the points of law involved. The discussion appears to have been adjourned to the Exchequer Chamber during the following Easter term where the legal issues raised were discussed by the judges of both benches and the serjeants.[3] The record of the case tells us that the Chancellor Sir Thomas Audley decided that the inquisition's findings were good in law and that those lands late of lord Dacre comprised therein should remain in the King's hands.

There can be no doubt that the dispositions made by lord Dacre gave the Crown the opportunity it required to construct the test case which would enable it to win its victory over uses. If Thomas Cromwell was not himself responsible for the conception of this policy, he was clearly behind its successful execution. An entry in Cromwell's *Remembrances*, which belongs to the year 1533, indicates not merely that it was intended to use the Dacre settlements to achieve the Crown's ends but also that this intention had been formed before full details of lord Dacre's

[1] These were two of the executors.

[2] They probably brought their action in respect of this, and not the Sussex, inquisition because the manors in Kent were stated to be held of the King in chief, whereas the Sussex inquisition stated that it was not known of whom the manors it named were held. Success in respect of the former would *ipso facto* lead to the removal of the King's hands from the latter.

[3] PRO, Chancery, Common Law Pleadings, C. 43/2/32. Holdsworth did not consult the record of this case and wrongly concluded (Holdsworth, IV. 447–8) from the account in the Year Book that the feoffees were successful.

dispositions were available to the Crown: 'Finding offices of the collusion of my lord Dacres and to get a copy of the will.'[1] Another such document of the same year refers to 'The book containing the will of lord Dacres of the South.'[2] At some stage then Crown's intentions in respect of the projected inquisitions *post mortem* became known to the late lord's executors who appear to have offered some sort of bargain—presumably either money or a division of the inheritance between themselves and the Crown—which would persuade it to drop its plans.[3] The fact that the Crown's plans regarding the Dacre estates were associated in some way with parliamentary legislation is confirmed by a document entitled 'Things to be moved on the King's behalf unto his attorney, to be put afterwards in order and determination by the learned counsel against the next assembly of his Parliament', since these include, 'Lord Dacre's will of the South to be examined.'[4]

The points of law which the Crown successfully established by means of the Dacre's case deserve careful examination. A study both of the existing law and of lord Dacre's dispositions shows that the Crown in no way needed to claim and, in fact, could not claim, that lord Dacre's uses had deprived it of the wardship of the body and marriage of the heir. As we have seen,[5] royal lawyers and administrators had claimed such rights for the Crown by virtue of its prerogative even when the whole of the lands of a tenant-in-chief had been conveyed to uses and he had declared his will. But, in any case, lord Dacre had not enfeoffed his feoffees of all his estates. While none of those of which he died seised in fee appears definitely to have been held of the King in chief, he died seised of a number of manors in Yorkshire which included two held of the King as of honours—one of Richmond and one of Knaresborough.[6] Moreover, the relevant escheator's account states that the Lincolnshire manor of Wintringham was

---

[1] *L & P*, VI. 551 (no. 1382).   [2] ibid., VI. 648 (no. 1589).
[3] Three sets of *Remembrances* contain references to 'the executors of Lord Dacres of the South, and to show the King their offer', one assigned by the editor to 1533 and two to 1534 (ibid., VI. 545 (no. 1371); ibid., VII. 54 (no. 143 (ii)) and 110 (no. 263)).   [4] ibid., VI. 549 (no. 1381).   [5] See above, pp. 251-2.
[6] PRO, Esch. Accts., LTR, E. 357/142, 25–26 Hen. VIII.

T

also held by him in fee and that it was not known of whom it was held, a fact which would *ipso facto* enable the Crown to hold it in wardship.[1] These details serve only to emphasize the determination of the Crown to exploit the legal aspects of lord Dacre's dispositions as part of its efforts to bring uses under control, since it is obvious that the loss of wardship of the body and marriage which was claimed in the findings of collusion in Kent and Sussex had not in fact occurred.

Can we trace evidence of fraudulent intent in the details of lord Dacre's dispositions? This question must be answered in the light of the development of doctrines of collusion in the late fourteenth and fifteenth centuries[2] and the working of the statute of 1490. Directions that feoffees provide the executors with the revenues required for the performance of the testament or convey estates to younger sons were by this date invariably found in testamentary documents. A consideration of two particular dispositions of lord Dacre confirms the view that in terms of the law that was then accepted his arrangements were not collusive. First, he laid down that certain manors, worth roughly £195 a year, should provide such revenues as were required for the performance of his testament. The expenditure, however, involved in this must have totalled at least £900 over and above the cost of two important items—the payment of his debts and the costs of his burial. It is likely that the need to calculate the amount of the revenues available to the executors explains the presence in the Kent inquisition of the statement that the money, goods and chattels owned by lord Dacre at his death were worth £576 11s. 1d. But it is clear that the whole of this sum could not have been available to the executors, since lord Dacre had bequeathed all his household goods and equipment to his heir. Even if we assume that they were able to dispose of the deceased's money and valuables as well as use the revenues allotted to them, it is difficult to see how the performance of the testatment could have been completed before the heir came of age, in view of the fact that he was over eighteen years of age at the time of his grandfather's

---

[1] PRO, Esch. Accts., LTR, E. 357/82, 24–25 Hen. VIII.
[2] See above, Ch. IV (i).

death. But, even if this were the case, the Crown would have no grounds for claiming collusion since it was accepted legal doctrine that it could seize the lands once the will was performed:[1] the existence of a will meant, not that its rights were excluded, but that they were simply deferred.

The other disposition made by lord Dacre which deserves detailed attention is that which lays down that the executors should receive the issues of the residue of the estates until the twenty-fourth birthday of the heir. The direction that they should maintain him out of these might be regarded as an example of the tendency to intrude on the lord's rights of wardship which can be seen in some fifteenth-century wills.[2] On the other hand, this direction may well have been quite innocuous. There was nothing to indicate that lord Dacre wished his executors to exercise those rights of wardship which belonged to the Crown. Moreover, the heir's sister's marriage portion had to be raised from these same revenues. Since this process may well not have been completed before he came of age, it is quite likely that, in issuing his direction in these terms, lord Dacre was simply assuming that moneys would only be available for the heir's maintenance after he had come of age. If so, his apparent encroachment on royal rights might easily have been construed as the result of careless phrasing, not real intention. Nevertheless, even if the marriage portion had been raised some time before the heir came of age, the Crown did not need a finding of 'collusion' to have the right to the wardship of the lands forthwith.

There can be no doubt that all these arguments were well known to Thomas Cromwell and the Crown's lawyers. The *Letters and Papers* contain[3] both a valuation of all lord Dacre's estates and a summary of the financial provisions of his testament and 'last will'. Moreover, they were well aware of the ways in which the statute of 1490 was interpreted—indeed, the agreement with the nobility of a few years before had been framed in the light of these. Of course, although in strict law it was accepted

---

[1] See above, p. 253.   [2] See above, pp. 222–5 and 228–9.
[3] *L & P*, IV (3), 2996 (no. 6647) and ibid., VI. 649 (no. 1590). The originals have been consulted and provide all financial calculations made in the text.

that the Crown could exercise its rights once the will had been performed, the application of this doctrine would have been a highly complex administrative task. But Thomas Cromwell was hardly a minister who flinched from the thorough prosecution of royal rights. Again, the administrative developments which were soon to result in the Court of Wards had been in progress for some years: the Crown certainly possessed administrative resources for the exploitation of wardships that were superior to those of the previous reign, or even the early years of Henry VIII. It is, therefore, difficult to believe that the Crown, had it wished to do so, was not in a position to attempt the enforcement of its rights once a will had been performed.

All these arguments lead inexorably to one conclusion: the finding of collusion in respect of lord Dacre's dispositions was based on the ground that any devise of land by a tenant-in-chief who died leaving an heir under age was *ipso facto* fraudulent because it must employ revenues which were the Crown's by virtue of its prerogative. It is quite impossible to argue that the Crown based its claims on lord Dacre's directions that his heir should be granted the residue of the estates on his twenty-fourth birthday and that the executors should take the issues in the meanwhile. Indeed, certain manors were included in the jury's finding of collusion despite the fact that the deceased's directions regarding them in no way involved the heir—in Kent one manor left to his younger son John Fiennes and a number of manors in Sussex devised to provide revenues for the performance of his testament. For over a century and a half before the Dacre's case dispositions of this type had been regarded as perfectly proper. The Crown, in fact, acted as though any devise by will of lands held of it in chief was illegal. All the estates which lord Dacre had held as a *cestui que use* were seized by the escheators;[1] and letters[2] written to Cromwell after the heir had come of age show that it was only then that the executors were able to proceed with the performance of the will.

[1] PRO, Esch. Accts., LTR, E. 357/77 (Kent), 25–26 Hen. VIII and –/125 (Sussex), 25–26 Hen. VIII, where it is stated that the issues thereof were to be accounted for by the Receiver-general of the King's wardships.

[2] *L & P*, XIII (1), 49 (no. 143) and 67 (nos. 197–98).

In his judgement that the finding of collusion was good in law the Chancellor was stating a point of law of exceptional importance. Henceforward it would be possible for the Crown by means of such a finding to upset any devise of land by means of uses if made by a tenant-in-chief who left an heir under age. The judgement raised further points of law, since it referred to lands held in chief only. Would a similar finding be possible if only lands held of mesne lords were devised by a tenant-in-chief, thus ousting the King from his 'prerogative wardship'? Would it also be possible in the case of lands held solely of the Crown as of the Duchy of Lancaster or an escheated honour? The Crown's success in the Dacre's case, and the resources it enjoyed by virtue of its prerogative, suggest that it would have found no difficulty in securing success in these respects also.

The extent to which the Chancellor's judgement overrode existing legal doctrines needs little emphasis. What lord Dacre had done had hitherto been clearly permissible under the practices which were followed by all landowners and respected by the Crown and the courts of law.[1] But those doctrines of collusion that already existed were now at one blow widened to comprise any testamentary devises of his lands, for any purpose, by any tenant-in-chief who left an heir under age. In effect, the statute of 1490 which allowed such dispositions, if properly made, was completely by-passed. It is especially interesting to note that the Crown's lawyers appear to have taken care to plan their operations in such a way as to minimize the effectiveness of existing doctrines and past precedents if these were used against royal claims. The finding of collusion which they secured was made in respect of lord Dacre's testament and 'last will', not his conveyance of the lands concerned to his feoffees. By so doing they obtained for themselves more room to manœuvre in two respects in the legal arguments which ensued. In the first place, previous doctrines of collusion had been stated with reference to feoffments of the lands, not the testamentary dispositions of the deceased: while the terms of the latter might constitute evidence of

---

[1] The Statute of Uses (cl. 9) virtually admitted this by providing that all devises made by those who died before 1 May 1536 should stand.

fraudulent intent,[1] it was the original enfeoffment at which any finding of collusion was directed. The obvious counter-argument for the feoffees to employ in such a case was that their enfeoffment by the deceased was an unconditional one. But a finding of collusion in respect of the testamentary dispositions met this plea in advance by by-passing it and making it completely irrelevant to the point at issue. In the second place, there was the strong likelihood that lord Dacre's feoffees would point to the fact that he had complied with the terms of the statute of 1490 by declaring his will. The Crown sought to meet this point by attempting to make the contents of the will, as distinct from its mere existence, the central issue at law.[2] And the surviving accounts of the proceedings show that this tactic enabled the Crown to argue that, because lands held by feudal tenure were not devisable at common law, lord Dacre's will was *ipso facto* collusive. At any rate, such a view would help to explain why the Chancellor arrived at a judgement which ran counter to past precedents and the statute of 1490. Even so, in the light of these, his case was far from good in law. But the fact that the Crown deliberately launched its attack against the testamentary dispositions of lord Dacre, not his original enfeoffment of feoffees, illustrates the skill and ingenuity which were devoted to the planning of its manœuvres.

In the light of this discussion it is quite clear that if the Chancellor had based his judgement on existing precedents, legislation and practice, the Dacre's case would have reached a different conclusion. It is unfortunate that the extant Year Book account[3] of the discussion which occurred in the Exchequer Chamber is defective: only five counsel are recorded as taking part and none of these was a judge of either bench[4] or had reached the rank of king's serjeant. It is certainly difficult to believe that the judges of the

[1] See above, pp. 182 and 188–90.

[2] Of the five speakers who took part in the discussion reported in the Year Book, all devoted their arguments to the consideration of whether or not the will was collusive. Three discussed the relevance of the terms of the statute of 1490. [3] *YBVE*, 27 Hen. VIII, Pasch., pp. 7–10, pl. 22.

[4] Holdsworth (IV. 447) is wrong in describing Montague as Chief Justice at this time. He did not become a king's serjeant until 1537, and Chief Justice of the King's Bench until 1539.

court of Common Pleas could have been sympathetic to the Crown's claims, in view of the discussion that occurred in their own court in another case in 1536–7.[1] But notes[2] left by a King's Bench judge tell how they were all summoned to debate the issues with the Chancellor and Cromwell and were then called before the King himself who remonstrated with them, promising his 'good thanks' for their support. Only after this royal intervention did those judges who opposed the Crown's claims give in. Presumably they all then stated their acceptance of the royal case in the Exchequer Chamber. Strictly speaking, while the Chancellor was under an obligation to consult the judges on an important point of law, he was certainly not bound to accept their views.[3] But the Crown no doubt required the judges' unanimity to impress any parliamentary opposition.[4] It is, then, impossible to avoid the conclusion that the Chancellor's decision in the Dacre's case was motivated solely by the needs of royal policy and paid no regard to commonly accepted legal doctrines. The result which was thus achieved would have been quite feasible in the late fourteenth or early fifteenth centuries when the legal problems posed by the evasion of uses first emerged. But the years since then had witnessed the acceptance of uses by the Crown, culminating in the statute of 1490. In the Dacre's case the Chancellor overturned the legal *status quo* in the financial interests of the Crown.

In the absence of the relevant journals of the Lords and Commons, and of material in the *Letters and Papers*,[4] we are unable to

[1] Dyer, I. 7b–13a (no. 11).

[2] BM. MS. Hargreaves, 388, ff. 96–7. The relevant portion is translated by A. W. B. Simpson in *University of Toronto Law Journal*, XVI (1965), 8–9. The assembly described, although it took place in the Exchequer Chamber, was not a formal meeting of that court, since Cromwell was present.

[3] Coke, *Fourth Institute*, pp. 79 and 84.

[4] The evidence does not support the view that this was a 'judicial decision that uses were of no legal validity' (*EHR*, LXXXII (1967), 692). Any rule of law established could only have applied to cases of wardship (see below, pp. 284–5). And, if the Chancellor had simply ceased to protect the performance of wills of land, this would not have stopped them being made. It is essential to distinguish between the grounds for the decision and the decision itself. Hall (II. 204) is referring to the former when he states that they 'agreed that land could not be willed by order of the common law'.

reconstruct the details of the way in which the Crown manipulated the result of the Dacre's case to get its way in parliament. All we know is that the Statute of Uses[1] was passed in the parliamentary session which began on 4 February, and ended on 14 April 1536, the first session which occurred after the Dacre's case. What is, however, abundantly clear is that parliament was presented with a *fait accompli*: the Crown could now expel any feoffees in the event of the minority of an heir of a *cestui que use* who had been its tenant prior to their enfeoffment to his use. But it was undesirable to leave matters thus and legislation was necessary in the interests both of the Crown and of all other feudal lords.

On the one hand, from the standpoint of the Crown, there would be two weaknesses in any settlement which was based on the result of the Dacre's case alone. The first was administrative in nature. Whenever a wardship occurred, royal officials would have to ensure that, if necessary, a finding of collusion was made in the relevant inquisition *post mortem*. Not only would they always have to maintain constant vigilance but there was also the risk that any jury empanelled by an escheator would be obdurate and refuse to make the required finding. The second weakness in the Crown's position was that, although its rights of wardship and marriage were now recovered, the result of the Dacre's case did not protect those incidents which were due when the heir was of age—primer seisin, livery and relief. Although wardship and marriage constituted by far the most valuable of the incidents of tenure, some of the financial losses caused by uses still remained. On the other hand, from the standpoint of those landowners who held land of the Crown, the position was extremely unsatisfactory. Not only did they lose the right to devise their lands if they left an heir under age but at the same time they had no redress against their own tenants when these willed their lands. The result of the Dacre's case related solely to the Crown's rights of wardship and marriage: it stated no principle which would enable mesne lords to secure the wardship of heirs whose lands were held of them.

[1] *Statutes*, III. 539–42 (27 Hen. VIII, c. 10). The most important clauses are printed in Digby, pp. 347–54.

Nor can there have been any real hope that the courts of common law would assist mesne lords in this respect. It is doubtful whether they were under any obligation to accept the principle on which the Chancellor acted in the Dacre's case, especially since this appears to have been stated in opposition to common law doctrines.[1] Moreover, even if they had been prepared to do so in theory, in practice the cumbrous procedures and the technical snares which befell litigants in the common law courts would in the end have deprived mesne lords of any effective redress. Thus, although the Crown gained a great deal of what it wanted, mesne lords gained nothing, and, if they were tenants-in-chief, the Crown's gains were at their expense.

It may be argued that in this situation it was obviously in the interests of the Lords and Commons, many of whom must have been mesne lords, to protest. They may well have done so; but it is equally likely that fear of royal displeasure dissuaded them from this course of action. Indeed, it is probable that they were conscious of the fact that, now the break with Rome had been achieved, the King was even less likely than before to be deterred by their anger, while the hope of personal benefits from grants of the lands of the monasteries which were about to be dissolved made some of them more complaisant towards the King's will. Moreover, by February 1536 the Commons, about to embark on their eighth session since November 1529, must have felt somewhat weary of parliamentary business. Perhaps, indeed, it is unnecessary to engage in guesses about the influences that affected the attitudes of Lords and Commons, since these may easily be attributed to a recognition on their part that any protests made by them would be wasted effort. The Crown had achieved already the major part of its ends by extra-parliamentary means: even if a protest and a demand for the reversal of its policy were made in parliament, it was unlikely it would achieve anything. *Le Roy s'advisera* was the most that the Lords or Commons could hope

---

[1] It was not mentioned at all by the judges and counsel who took part in the reported discussion of a case relating to the wardship of an heir's body which was claimed by a mesne lord, though the principle involved was highly relevant (Dyer, I. 7b–13a (no. 11).

for. And, when this parliament was dissolved, royal administrators would continue their extra-parliamentary methods. In
short, it was to the advantage of the landowners who sat in parliament to accept the *fait accompli* and agree to a legislative reform
which, although it improved the Crown's position, would confer
benefits on them as well.

A study of the Statute of Uses shows that it gave both the
Crown and mesne lords what they wanted. Its most important
provision (cl. 1) laid down that

> where any person or persons stand, or be seised, or at any time here-
> after shall happen to be seised, of and in any honours, castles, manors,
> lands, tenements, rents, services, reversions, remainders or other heredi-
> taments, to the use, confidence or trust of any other person or persons,
> or of any body politic, by reason of any bargain, sale, feoffment, fine,
> recovery, covenant, contract, agreement, will, or otherwise, by any
> manner of means whatsoever it be; ... in every such case, all and every
> such person and persons, and bodies politic, that have or hereafter shall
> have any such use, confidence or trust, in fee simple, fee tail, for term
> of life, or for years, or otherwise, or any use, confidence or trust, in
> remainder or reverter, shall from henceforth stand and be seised,
> deemed, and adjudged in lawful seisin, estate and possession of and in
> the same ... hereditaments, with their appurtenances, to all intents,
> constructions and purposes in the law, of and in such like estates, as
> they had or shall have in use, trust, or confidence of or in the same;
> And ... the estate, right title, right and possession that was in such
> person or persons that were or shall be hereafter seised of any ...
> hereditaments, to the use, confidence or trust of any such person or
> persons, or of any body politic, be from henceforth clearly deemed and
> adjudged to be in him or them that have, or hereafter shall have, such
> use, confidence or trust, after such quality, manner, form and condition
> as they had before, in or to the use, confidence, or trust that was in
> them.

The next two clauses applied this principle to cases where a number of persons were seised to the use of one of them (cl. 2) and
where persons were seised of hereditaments to the use that some
other person or persons should have a rent out of them (cl. 3).
All devises of land by will made by those who died before 1 May
1536 were to remain valid (cl. 9). From the same date the King

was to be entitled to primer seisin, livery, ouster le main, fines for alienation, reliefs or heriots as a result of the statute and other lords entitled to fines, reliefs and heriots (cl. 10).

The effect of these and other provisions[1] of the statute was to convert the equitable estate of the *cestui que use* into a legal estate: whereas previously the estate enjoyed by the *cestui que use* was not recognized by the courts of common law but was only accepted as legally valid in the court of Chancery, now an act of parliament declared that the *cestui que use* was the real owner of the land. Henceforward, when a feudal tenant died, his lord, whether the Crown or a mesne, would be able to proceed on the basis of the fact that he had died seised of the land. Whether or not his heir was of age, therefore, it would be impossible for him to evade any of the relevant incidents of feudal tenure or devise by will the lands which were held to his use. When the lord had obtained whatever incidents were due to him, the heir would be able to enter on all the lands which his ancestor had held, whether in fee or as the beneficiary of a use. It is important to note that the statute did not attempt to abolish uses and there was, therefore,

[1] Cl. 4 laid down that any wife who held lands settled on her and her husband in any form of joint settlement or was the beneficiary of any use jointly with her husband should, after his death, be deprived of all right to sue dower from her husband's estates. Cl. 7 stated that, unless it had been created by act of parliament, she was to have the right to surrender any jointure made after marriage and instead sue her dower. It has always been argued that these provisions were made necessary by the main principle laid down by the statute, since as a result a husband would no longer be able to deprive his wife of dower after his death by enfeoffing his lands to uses (Holdsworth, III. 196). It is certainly true that the statute here assisted widows, since henceforth a *cestui que use* would be regarded as the legal owner of all his estates and his widow would have no difficulty in insisting on her rights to dower from the whole of them. But this view overlooks the fact that she might have secured her rights in the courts of common law. Furthermore, it misinterprets the effects of uses upon the position of widows, since they often secured thereby estates which were larger than what they would have obtained from dower alone. In the light of these considerations it is more likely that this aspect of the statute's provisions is better understood as an attempt to curtail as much as possible the proportion of an inheritance which lay outside the hands of a lord during the minority of an heir. Henceforth a widow would have to choose between her jointure and her right to dower.

nothing in law to prevent their continued existence. But what the Statute of Uses achieved was the abolition of the fiction that separated the effective possession of land from its legal ownership. Although uses might continue, they could no longer mask the identity of the individual who occupied the land and drew its profits.

The royal officials who drafted the statute[1] must have given careful attention to the problem of securing the best possible means whereby the rights of all feudal lords to the incidents of tenure might be safeguarded. What reasons, then, impelled them to draw up a reform along the lines we see in the Statute of Uses? It might be argued that their aims could be achieved by a piece of legislation which expressly saved the incidents of tenure for the benefit of the lords concerned and forbade their evasion by means of uses. Although we possess no contemporary account of the reasons why such a course of action was not followed, it is not difficult to explain its rejection. No doubt it was realized that legislation which expressly sought to save the incidents of tenure would be difficult to enforce, if uses were retained. True, the Crown was in a position to employ the *post mortem* inquisitions of its escheators; but to ensure that its rights were properly safe-guarded thereby would entail both constant vigilance on its part

---

[1] For some discussion of the drafts which have survived, with references to the *Letters and Papers*, see Holdsworth, IV. 456–7. It is impossible to accept Holdsworth's views on one of the drafts which he prints in full (IV. 580–1). He states that 'it would not have stopped the practice of devising land'. But cl. 4 of the draft reads 'Item, every person and persons, having the use in any lands, tenements or hereditaments, shall be admitted taken and reputed, in all conditions and to all intents and purposes, tenants to the chief lords of whom the lands, tenements or hereditaments, whereof they have such use, shall be holden, in like manner, form and condition in every behalf, as if they had had such estate in the possession, reversion or remainder of the lands tenements or hereditaments, whereof they have such use, as they have in the use.' These words reveal a clear desire to end the power to devise and save the lord's in-cidents, though the point is laid down in a manner that is clumsy in comparison with the actual statute passed. No doubt this explains why this draft was dis-carded. But it is, therefore, impossible to accept Holdsworth's view that it was 'a scheme put forward by the landowners' which was 'useless, or almost useless, to the king'.

and the ever-present risk that escheators would be inefficient and juries difficult to manage. At the same time, mesne lords, in order to protect their interests, would often be driven to seek the remedies of the courts of common law where technical hazards and cumbrous procedures would endanger any prospects of their success. They might, then, feel that a legislative reform of this type gave their rights insufficient protection: those of them who sat in parliament might, despite the result of the Dacre's case, be loath to give the proposed measure their support. A possible alternative was a statute which forbade the devising by will of all lands held by feudal tenure. But this would be equally unlikely to achieve much. Both for the Crown and mesne lords the problem of searching out all enfeoffments to uses made by deceased tenants would still have remained, while a simple prohibition of the practice would merely have encouraged a search for other evasive devices. The most radical of all the possibilities that were available was the outright prohibition of uses. But this would have presented enormous difficulties in view of the fact that uses had now become part and parcel of the country's legal institutions. By this time, for example, they were employed not merely in the devising of lands by will but also in the conveyance of lands from one person to another by means of bargain and sale. The employment of uses certainly led to a great deal of inconvenience, since it often concealed the real identity of those involved in conveyances of land.[1] But, although some of the King's subjects to whom, for example, debts were owed or who had claims to lands which had thus secretly been conveyed to others, might suffer from the employment of uses on the part of those against whom they had claims, the fact remained that they themselves might at some time find it to their advantage to employ uses for similar purposes. It

[1] For full details of the disadvantages of uses, from the standpoint both of the Crown and its subjects, see the document from the government's records printed by Holdsworth IV. 577–80. Its complaints should not be taken too seriously since from the standpoint of the King's subjects it is clear that any disadvantages in the administration of the law were much more than outweighed by the advantages. Holdsworth is probably right in suggesting that 'it may well have been the raw material upon which those who drew the preamble to the statute worked' (ibid., IV. 456).

was in the interests of good government that all transactions in land and the identities of those engaged therein should be easily traceable. But this need not entail the abolition of uses, since it could be achieved by a system of compulsory registration of conveyances. It is true that the preamble to the Statute of Uses complained that 'scantly any person can be certainly assured of any lands by them purchased, nor know surely against whom they shall use their actions or execution for their rights, titles and duties'. Nevertheless, these words are not reliable evidence of the motives which lay behind the Crown's policies, since the preamble was intended to recite as many criticisms of uses as could be collected so as to create the strongest possible justification for the reforms that were to follow in the body of the statute. In fact, it is quite clear that the government never considered the abolition of uses as a practical policy. Instead, it intended to deal with the inconveniences that might arise through uses in the administration of the law by means of a scheme whereby all conveyances of land were henceforth to be enrolled by officials in each shire who were to be appointed by the Crown.[1]

In these circumstances the Crown chose to adopt the approach which we see in the Statute of Uses whereby uses were permitted to continue but it was laid down that the *cestui que use* should be regarded as possessing a legal estate in the lands of which the feoffees were seised to his use. Certain precedents pointed towards its adoption. A statute of 1484 had transferred to the *cestuis que usent* of Richard III the legal estates which he had held in use before he became King.[2] The same year it was enacted that the *cestui que use* could make legal conveyances of the land which was held to his use.[3] Henry VII's statutes of 1490[4] and 1504[5] had both accepted the fact of the *cestui use*'s occupation of the land. Indeed, in practical terms the approach of the Statute of Uses really adopted an attitude towards uses which would have been possible on the part of the courts of common law when they first began to emerge[6]—

---

[1] This is discussed and printed by Holdsworth (Holdsworth, IV. 457–60 and 582–6).   [2] *Statutes*, II. 480 (1 Ric. III, c. 5).
[3] ibid., II. 477—8 (1 Ric. III, c. 1).   [4] ibid., II. 540–1 (4 Hen. VII, c. 17).
[5] ibid., II. 660 (19 Hen. VII, c. 15).   [6] See above, pp. 191–2.

the rule that the legal estate was to be vested in the *cestui que use* approached the problem of the ownership of the land so enfeoffed from the standpoint of an enquiry into its physical occupation.

But, although such precedents help to explain the appearance of the legal doctrine we see stated in the Statute of Uses, they do not account for the Crown's decision to adopt this particular method of combating uses. The motives of Henry VIII's government can only be understood in the light of the fact that it was concerned, not with the reform of the land law in the interests of good government, but with the protection of the incidents of feudal tenure in the interests both of the Crown and all other feudal lords. In the event, indeed, although the reasons for its change of plan are not known, it dropped its grandiose scheme for the compulsory registration of all conveyances of land, for the much less radical Statute of Enrolments[1] which provided only for the compulsory enrolment of bargains and sales. There were weighty objections against all the other available legislative remedies, whereas the Statute of Uses possessed the great advantages of practicality and simplicity. The principle which was laid down in its first clause and worked out in the rest of its provisions raised the straightforward issue of the identity of the person or persons to whose use the feoffees were seised, stating that he or they were to be regarded as having the legal estate in the land concerned. In the four centuries or so which have elapsed since the passing of this statute legal commentators have drawn attention to its omissions and ambiguities and to the complexities to which these gave rise in the courts of law. But in the context of the problems which faced the government of Henry VIII it is anachronistic to expect the King or his advisers to exercise any qualities of prescience in the field of legal developments or to assume that their efforts were devoted to the end of reforming all the legal problems that were posed by uses. Their aim was merely to lay down a rule of law which would enable all feudal lords to secure from their tenants those incidents of tenure which were their due.

[1] *Statutes*, III. 549 (27 Hen. VIII, c. 16), also printed in Digby, p. 368. The Statute of Uses had increased the risks of fraud through bargains and sales, since now the vendor did not need to execute the legal estate.

In this analysis the Statute of Uses appears as a double com-promise—between the respective interests of the feudal lords in-volved, the Crown and mesne lords, and between the various legal remedies that were available and the consequences that would follow from their adoption. The Crown was now able to regain all its incidents of feudal tenure. Mesne lords regained all that was due to them from their tenants; and, although the Crown's gains, if they were its tenants, were at their expense, they lost less than they would have lost through the result of the Dacre's case. Indeed, if the Crown was to be allowed to recover its feudal revenues completely, the Statute of Uses was the sort of reform that was best suited to the interests of mesne lords: it laid down provisions from which they as well as the Crown might benefit, while it permitted uses to continue. Nevertheless, although these arguments may explain the Crown's success in securing the passing of the Statute of Uses through parliament and the form the statute took, the fact remains that the Crown's gains were very much greater than those of any of its subjects. The landowners of England were compelled to accept a reform which gave the Crown benefits much greater than those the Commons had refused to grant four years earlier. Although we possess no contemporary complaint about the methods the Crown had employed to get its way, it is reasonable to infer that the skilful manipulation of the resources of its prerogative aroused much bitterness. Above all, whatever gains those landowners who were mesne lords received from the statute must have seemed slight in comparison with their losses. They had suddenly lost powers which many of their ancestors had been able to exercise over their lands for more than two hundred years past: they were deprived of all opportunity to employ their landed revenues after their deaths for the payment of debts or provision for their younger children. In effect, the Statute of Uses had destroyed part of the financial resources of the landowning familes of England, great and small.

(iii) THE STATUTE OF WILLS (1540)

The Crown's success in pushing through the Statute of Uses was short-lived. In the parliamentary session of April–July 1540 another statute—the Statute of Wills[1]—was passed which restored to all landowners, with effect from 20 July 1540, the power of devising by will the greater part of their lands. The most important clause of all laid down that every tenant-in-chief

shall have full power and authority by his last will, by writing or otherwise, by any act or acts lawfully executed in his life, to give, dispose, will or assign two parts of [his] manors, lands, tenements or hereditaments in three parts to be divided, or else as much . . . as shall extend or amount to the yearly value of two parts of the same in three parts to be divided in certainty and by special divisions as it may be known in severalty, to and for the advancement of his wife, preferment of his children, and payment of his debts or otherwise at his will and pleasure; any law, statute, custom or other thing to the contrary thereof notwithstanding.

The whole of any lands held in socage might be similarly devised. In the case of lands held in chief the King obtained the right to the wardship of a third thereof, if the heir was under age, and, if the deceased held by military service of other lords, of a third of all the lands so held. A similar right to devise was conferred on those who held solely of mesne lords who also obtained the right to a third in wardship. In its last clause the act ensured that all lords should enjoy the wardship of one-third of a deceased tenant's lands by laying down that a widow was to receive her dower or jointure from the two-thirds that were devised.

A number of clauses made real efforts to safeguard the King's rights to feudal incidents other than wardship. Every royal tenant was to sue for liveries and reliefs as before the act and fines for alienation were to continue in respect of all lands alienated by a tenant-in-chief (clauses 2, 3 and 7). In clause 9 it was stated that, if two or more persons held of the King by knight's service jointly to them and the heirs of one of them, in the event of the

---

[1] *Statutes*, III. 744–6 (32 Hen. VIII, c. 1). For excerpts, see Digby, pp. 387–9.

U

latter's death the King was to have the wardship and marriage of his heir if under age.

The basic provisions of the act clearly comprised an enactment of the proposals of the agreement made with the nobility in 1530–1. But, whereas the latter had assumed the continuous existence of uses, the Statute of Wills takes the form of a concession of the right to devise lands on the part of the Crown to its subjects. The act contains a number of provisions conferring benefits upon the Crown alone. But against these must be set the fact that all royal tenants were now able to devise lands held in socage, a concession which had not been made in 1530–1. The details of the Act of Wills show clearly that in consenting to its promulgation Henry VIII was surrendering a large part of the gains he had secured through the Statute of Uses.

There can be no doubt that the Statute of Wills constituted a *volte face* on the part of the Crown which can only be explained in terms of the hostility which the Statute of Uses had aroused among the country's landowners. But the precise nature of the ways in which their resentment over royal policies was manifested and brought to bear upon the Crown presents a complex problem. Anger at the loss of their power to devise by means of uses was a powerful motive—perhaps the most important—behind the participation of many of the northern gentry in the Pilgrimage of Grace some months after the passing of the Statute of Uses. Among the demands made by the rebels was one that the statute be repealed.[1] Not only had they come to regard uses as an accepted means of settling land that was available to every landowner but many of them must already have employed them to make arrangements for the needs of younger children and the payment of debts and were now involved, as a result of the statute, in financial problems which threatened real difficulties for their families in the future. Such feelings remained strong after the Pilgrimage of Grace had been suppressed and were a source of concern to the government whenever rebellion was in the air. A witness who was interrogated in 1538 in the course of investiga-

---

[1] *L & P*, XI. 272 (no. 705), 303 (no. 780), 507 (no. 1246); ibid., XII (1), 4 (no. 6), and 12 (no. 16). See also Hall, p. 272.

tions into the activities of the Poles stated that 'when the Act of Uses was passed Lord De La Warr showed him of it, saying it was a very sore act and that he grudged much at it'.[1]

It soon became apparent that the resentment felt by the land-owning classes over the loss of their power to devise land was leading them to search feverishly for means of evading the Statute of Uses. Robert Aske, when interrogated after the Pilgrimage of Grace, warned the government that such developments were inevitable.[2] He stated that

it would be profitable for worshipful men having lands that the said statute should be annulled or qualified so that they might declare their will of parcel of their lands for payment of their debts and marriage of their children; for . . . if a man study to defeat the King of the marriage of his son and heir and of the lands or both, there are more ways of doing it than before.

It is difficult to see how Aske could have shown how the Statute of Uses had increased the number of opportunities for evasive practices. When questioned further on this point, he disclaimed detailed knowledge on the ground that it was a long time since he had examined the authorities.[3] But he pointed out that, if a man held of the King as of the Crown or of the Duchy of Lancaster and with a licence[4] alienated to another on condition that he execute an estate to him for life, with remainder to his son and heir apparent in tail, with remainder in fee simple to a younger son or daughter or a stranger, neither the son and heir nor his lands

[1] *L & P*, XIII (2), 331 and 344 (nos. 822 and 831).

[2] ibid., XII (1), 406-8 (no. 901).

[3] Aske's knowledge on these points was obviously derived from the Year Book cases discussed above, Ch. IV (i). The particular instance of legal evasion he cites must be based on the doctrines stated in the case of 1455 which is discussed above (*YBVE*, Pasch., 33 Hen. VI, pp. 14-16, pl. 6).

[4] Aske makes no distinction between lands held in chief and those held of the Duchy of Lancaster and wrongly assumed that alienations of the latter required a licence to alienate. Strictly speaking, while the settlement he envisages was feasible in the case of a holding of the Duchy of Lancaster, it might be frustrated in the case of lands held in chief by the refusal of the necessary licence unless it provided for the reservation in the hands of the tenant of a portion of the lands, however minute.

would be in wardship since he obtained the latter as a 'purchaser'
—that is, by virtue of the settlement, not inheritance. At the same
time it would be impossible to claim that the conveyance was
collusive, since the heir acquired a life-interest only and the fee
simple lay in another. In February 1538 lord De La Warr had
declared that a settlement of lands he had made for the performance of his last will and testament 'was of such a nature that it
would abar the Statute of Uses'.[1] There can be no doubt that, as
soon as the statute was passed, lawyers were consulted, and the
Year Books and their abridgements searched, for means by which
it might be evaded.

The desire to seek such devices was so strong that it even involved royal officials. Hall tells how on 23 February 1540

were four readers sent for to the Star Chamber, of every house of the
four principal Inns of Court one, where sat the Lord Chancellor, the
lord Privy Seal and xiiii. of the chief of the King's council, and there
the lord Chancellor declared how Sir John Shelton, knight, had by the
advice of Sir Humphrey Brown, the King's Serjeant, Sir Nicholas
Hare, knight, the King's Councillor, and Speaker of the Parliament,
and William Coningsby, esquire, attorney of the Duchy of Lancaster,
all being his servants and of his fee, declared a fraudulent will of his
lands, contrary to the statute made, *anno* xxvii., and also to the evil
example of all other, that should defraud the lords of their seigniories.
Wherefore the said Sir Humphrey Brown and Sir Nicholas Hare were
that day by the whole Council of the King dismissed of their offices
and service to the King and sent to the Tower: and within three days
after was William Coningsby sent thither, where they remained ten
days and after were delivered: but they three lost all their offices that
they had of the King.[2]

According to a statute passed a few years later,[3] Sir John Shelton
had conveyed his lands in three separate parcels to a feoffee on
condition that he should execute certain estates within fifteen

---

[1] *L & P*, XIII (2), 334 (no. 828).

[2] Hall, II. 303. These events are referred to in a letter from the French
ambassador on 3 March 1540 (*L & P*, XV. 120 (no. 289). See also ibid., XV. 71
(no. 195), 120 (no. 291), 130 (no. 322) and 180 (no. 438).

[3] *Statutes*, III. 866–7 (33 Hen. VIII, c. 26).

days—one to Sir John himself and his assigns for term of ninety-nine years, one to Anne his wife for term of her life, with remainder to Sir John for life, with remainder to his son and heir for sixty years, and the third to his wife for ninety-nine years and, in the event of her death, to Sir John, his executors and assigns for the residue of the term—all eventually with remainder to Ralph, son and heir-apparent of Sir John's son and heir, in tail male. By these means it was intended that John Shelton the heir, who was of age, should enter without undergoing livery or primer seisin. The resemblance of these complicated and ingenious arrangements to that instanced as possible at law by Aske needs no emphasis. It is likely that the discovery of these settlements led Thomas Cromwell to make investigations into the extent to which similar conveyances had been, or were being, prepared by other landowners, since there has survived among his papers a petition addressed to him in which the writer declared that he had not 'devised any estates to bring a term of years to the owner of the inheritance of any lands with a remainder over to declare a will' and went on to detail the settlements with which he had been associated as counsel since the Statute of Uses.[1] From this document it is clear that Cromwell had heard of another means by which the statute might be evaded.[2]

In the light of this evidence it might be argued that in the Statute of Wills the government of Henry VIII recognized the inescapable fact that the Statute of Uses was bitterly disliked and landowners would never cease from searching for devices to evade its provisions. Seeing that the enforcement of the statute would fail to prevent the evasion of royal rights, it decided on a compromise whereby landowners had most of their power to devise lands restored to them, in the hope that evasive practices would cease, what was left of royal rights remain intact, and landowners

---

[1] *L & P*, XV. 510–11 (no. 1028).

[2] Cf. Holdsworth, IV. 465, n. 2, where it is wrongly assumed that settlements of the type made by Sir John Shelton came within the category dealt with in the petition addressed to Cromwell. But, while the former involved an estate for a term of years for the owner, it contained no remainder to declare a will.

in general become more friendly disposed towards royal policies.[1] Undoubtedly the discovery of the complicity of royal officials in evasive practices must have come as a severe shock and driven home the difficulties that would be involved in the successful enforcement of the Statute of Uses. There are, however, a number of reasons for regarding this explanation of the passing of the Statute of Wills as an unsatisfactory one. In the first place, if the fear of another Pilgrimage of Grace was a real one, it is odd that nothing was done in this respect in the first and second sessions of the parliament of 1539–40. In the second place, while Thomas Cromwell's *Remembrances*[2] refer to the legislation which was to set up the Court of Wards and which was passed in the same session as the Statute of Wills, they contain no reference to the latter. In the third place, it would have been quite possible for the government, whenever it discovered methods of evasion in operation, to have statutes passed which made them illegal. Indeed, it did so in 1542 and 1543.[3] Such a policy would have required constant watchfulness and a recourse to fresh legislation as soon as a new method of evasion was discovered. Nevertheless, it would have been in the traditions of royal policy over the last few years. If the Crown was free to pursue the policy of its choice, we would expect it to defend the gains it had recently made, rather than surrender a large part of them without any apparent struggle.

In the light of these considerations it is difficult to view the Statute of Wills as a compromise with his subjects entered into freely by Henry VIII. And this conclusion is supported by an examination of the Lords' Journals. The bill setting up the Court of Wards was read for the first time in the Lords on 3 June 1540 and again on 7 June. Its third reading and its despatch to the Commons occurred on 10 June, the day on which Thomas Cromwell was committed to the Tower for treason.[4] The bill 'that every man might freely dispose of two-thirds of his property' was read

---

[1] This appears to be the view advanced in Holdsworth, IV. 465.
[2] *L & P*, XV. 180 (no. 438). Cf. ibid., XV. 221 (no. 503).
[3] 33 Hen. VIII, c. 26; 34 & 35 Hen VIII, c. 5.
[4] *Journals of the House of Lords*, I. 141–3.

for the first time in the Lords on 9 July and for the third time on 14 July, when it was sent to the Commons: it returned thence two days later.[1] It is quite clear from these details that no effort was made by the government to deal with the legislation relating to the Court of Wards and wills of land together, although they dealt with two aspects of the same problem. If both were ready at the beginning of the session, it is odd that they were not introduced together or, at any rate, within a very short time of one another. Indeed, it might be argued that it was to the Crown's advantage to have them introduced together, since the benefits offered to landowners through the proposed Statute of Wills might assist the passage of the statute which was to set up the Court of Wards. Furthermore, the bill dealing with wills was not introduced until after Cromwell's arrest and passed through Parliament while he lay in the Tower awaiting his fate.

Two further facts suggest both that the Statute of Wills was pushed through in some haste and that it is unlikely that Thomas Cromwell was associated with its drafting. In 1542 a statute was passed which declared null and void the fraudulent conveyances effected some years before by Sir John Shelton.[2] And in 1543 another statute was made 'for the explanation of the Statute of Wills', dealing with a number of points on which it was ambiguous or defective.[3] In particular, it dealt with the problem of lands held by knight's service which had since 20 July 1540 been conveyed to 'any other person or persons for term of years, life or lives, with one remainder over in fee, or with divers remainders over for term of years, life, or in tail, with a remainder over in fee simple to any person or persons or to his or their right heirs'. If found by office to be covinous, they were to be treated as null and void: the King was to have his rights and other lords writs of right of ward. Those responsible for the drafting of this statute inserted this provision in order to deal with both the settlements effected by Sir John Shelton and the other evasive devices of which Thomas Cromwell had certainly been aware on the eve of

[1] ibid., I. 154 and 156–7.
[2] *Statutes*, III. 866–7 (33 Hen. VIII, c. 26).
[3] ibid., III. 901–4 (34 & 35 Hen. VIII, c. 5).

the parliamentary session which passed the Statute of Wills. Had Cromwell been responsible for the latter, it is difficult to understand how a draftsman of his skill and experience, with the knowledge that he had recently acquired of evasive practices, could have omitted clauses which would have prevented their continuance in the future. Indeed, we know that he had in mind legislation of this kind when the parliamentary session began in April 1540, since some of his *Remembrances* which refer to 'the establishing of a law for the Court of the Wards' also mention 'an Act to be devised for devices contrary to divers statutes made by learned men.'[1] The fact that the Statute of Wills did nothing in this direction suggests that it was planned by those who had no knowledge of Cromwell's intentions. Moreover, it seems likely that they worked in a hurry and thus gave insufficient attention to the legal difficulties their legislation entailed.

Although we must beware of reading too much significance into these details, there are obviously strong grounds for suggesting that the passing of the Statute of Wills was in some way connected with the events of Thomas Cromwell's fall from power. Certainly there is no evidence to show that, when the bill setting up the Court of Wards was introduced, the government had any intentions of giving up the gains it had won in 1536. It seems likely that the change of plan that then occurred was made after Thomas Cromwell's fall from power. His opponents were able to persuade the King to agree to the resurrection in statutory form of the provisions of the agreement that had been made with the nobility in 1530–1. It may be no coincidence that their leader, the duke of Norfolk, was one of those who had been involved in the negotiations of almost ten years before. We cannot say with any certainty why Henry VIII now agreed to the rejection of the policies he had previously followed. One possible explanation is that Norfolk and his allies persuaded the King that a compromise over the right to will lands was to his political advantage. It is is also possible that the policies now jettisoned had been mainly conceived by Thomas Cromwell and that, while the King had consented to them, he had not been directly involved in the

[1] *L & P*, XV. 180 (no. 438).

machinations which secured the passing of the Statute of Uses. If so, it would have been all the easier to persuade him to a drastic alteration of these policies. But, in any event, it is difficult to believe that the Statute of Wills was planned by Thomas Cromwell.

The Statute of Wills was a measure from which the King only lost and his subjects only gained. The Crown was deprived of the greater part of the gains it had made in 1536, since in the event of the death of its tenant leaving an heir under age, two-thirds of his lands were out of wardship, while the landowners of England won a specific right to devise this proportion of their lands. As a result the ultimate beneficiaries of the legislation of 1536 and 1540 were the King's subjects. Since Henry VII's reign the King had insisted on his right to the wardship of the body and the marriage of his tenant's heir when all the lands had been properly conveyed to uses and, in consequence, the only real benefit which the Crown derived from its efforts in the decade which preceded the Statute of Wills was the wardship of one-third of the lands. But by the Statute of Uses mesne lords had recovered their own rights of wardship of the body and marriage of which they had previously been completely deprived when all the lands held of them had been enfeoffed to uses; and now both they and their tenants won the right at common law to devise by will the greater part of their lands. Since the Crown did not lose its gains of 1536 completely, it is fair to regard the Statute of Wills as a compromise between its interests and those of its landowning subjects; but it was a compromise which masked a real and substantial defeat.

Conclusions

THE years between 1215 and 1540 witnessed two struggles over the future of feudal institutions in England. In both the basic issue was the same—whether feudal lords and, in particular, the greatest of them all, the Crown, should be able to prevent the decline which was occurring in their profits from the incidents of feudal tenure. In the first struggle, which finally ended in 1327, this issue arose because of the consequences of unchecked subinfeudation. From the standpoint of mesne tenants it largely ended with the abolition of subinfeudation in the Statute of *Quia Emptores* in 1290 and, from the standpoint of tenants-in-chief, with the formal recognition by the Crown in a statute of 1327 of their right to alienate. The second struggle arose because of the losses of feudal incidents through the employment of uses. It is clear that mesne lords played a far less active part in this struggle than in the first and very soon abandoned any efforts to recover their rights, since it was very much in their interests to employ uses themselves. It was left to the Crown to attempt to combat uses but it made no all-out efforts to bring its losses under control until the last two decades of the fifteenth century. And then, although Henry VII failed to recover royal rights completely, he nevertheless succeeded in stopping the Crown's loss of rights proceeding further, since the royal prerogative was used to retain wardship of the body and the marriage of the heir when all lands had been conveyed to uses. At the same time his ministers engaged in a ruthless and efficient exploitation of the rights that were saved. Although in the Statute of Uses in 1536 Henry VIII succeeded for a short time in recovering all royal losses completely, his success was short-lived and the Statute of Wills of 1540 permitted all feudal tenants, whether of the King or mesne lords, to devise two-thirds of their lands by will.

These developments justify the view that the thirteenth, four-teenth and fifteenth centuries saw a real decline in the value of feudal incidents in England. Although they survived in law for a further century and a half, feudal lords never recovered their losses completely. The policies directed towards this end by the first two Tudors secured only a partial success. The King and other lords kept the rights of wardship of the body and marriage but the right to two-thirds of the deceased's lands in wardship had gone for ever. There can be no doubt that it was the King's subjects who benefited from these changes and that their gains more than outweighed any success the Crown had achieved by 1540 in defending its own rights. Those who were mesne lords lost in that they remained powerless to prevent their tenants from alienating and the fruits of the victory they won in the Statute of *Quia Emptores* disappeared when their profits from feudal incidents were eroded away through the growth of uses. But every mesne lord was also a tenant and such losses as he incurred were more than compensated for by the gains he himself made through the employment of uses. In any case, the Statutes of Uses and Wills recovered for all mesne lords the rights of wardship of the body and marriage and wardship of one-third of their tenants' lands. From the standpoint of the Crown, the same period witnessed a lasting deterioration in its position as feudal overlord. The small financial gains and additions to its prerogative it made through the licensing of acquisitions in mortmain and alienations in chief did not compensate for the absence of any absolute power to prevent alienations in chief, especially when this exposed it to the erosion of its feudal revenues by uses. And such measure of recovery as it achieved by 1540 left its tenants with much of their gains. Since it was always lord and never tenant, the Crown was bound to be the residuary victim of any decline in the resources of feudal lords.

The present study has been concerned with the analysis of these developments and the motives and issues which underlay them. To investigate thoroughly the consequences which flowed from them would require a comprehensive study of all the available evidence relating to the landowners of England in the fourteenth, fifteenth and early sixteenth centuries. Nevertheless, it is possible to indicate in general terms the social and economic benefits which uses must have conferred upon the landowners of England. It is abundantly clear that they thereby secured a degree of control over their inheritances which their predecessors of the thirteenth century had not possessed. They were now able to devise their lands by will, either employing the revenues therefrom after their deaths or devising interests therein to younger children or other persons of their choice. The precise assessment of the value of these benefits is a difficult task which cannot be satisfactorily attempted until the records relating to many families have been thoroughly examined. It might be suggested that a father who employed the powers that uses gave him to devise some portion of the inheritance was damaging its future prospects in that his heir was being deprived of the lands devised. But it is likely that the heads of landed houses would have exercised great caution in acting thus; and if a family was adding to its territorial wealth by marriage or purchase, the gains from these sources might well replace any losses through devises to cadet branches. In any case, before uses emerged, it had always been the practice to provide for younger sons by means of entails and for daughters by *maritagia*.

Nor is it easy to see how an heir would lose in the long run to any serious extent if his ancestor had employed uses to provide for the payment of his debts. If he was under age at the time of his accession to his inheritance, the debts would largely, if not completely, be paid out of revenues which had previously belonged to his lord. If he was of age, although he would remain without the revenues concerned until repayment was completed, he in his turn would be in a position to provide for the repayment of his own debts in the same way. Moreover, the fact that uses were available must have made it easier to borrow money whether for the performance of family responsibilities, to pay for personal extravagance or make preparations for military service overseas.

Although any final conclusions must await the results of further research, it would seem certain that the benefits obtained through uses more than outweighed any disadvantages, since otherwise they would not have been so popular. No doubt the margin of advantage would have depended upon the circumstances of the individual family. And these would be influenced by a number of factors. Two were especially important because they were present in every landed inheritance in the fourteenth and fifteenth centuries. One was the volume of the profits made during service in the French wars: the other was the extent to which landed revenues were in decline. But historians who study these developments must remember that the generation which saw both the opening of the Hundred Years' War and the ravages of the Black Death also witnessed the beginnings of the adoption of uses by the English nobility and upper gentry. How far the profits of service in France compensated for the decline of landed revenues in England is a difficult problem in itself. It is further complicated by the growth in the popularity of uses in the same period, since the power to devise lands by will which English landowners now exercised led to an expansion in their capital resources. Uses enabled them to break free from the most irksome of the bonds of feudal tenure; and this freedom opened up sources of wealth denied to their ancestors.

Quia Emptores *and 'Bastard Feudalism'*

A STUDY of the consequences of feudal tenure in later medieval England cannot be complete without some examination of current views concerning the effects of the Statute of *Quia Emptores* on feudal institutions. Professor Plucknett has suggested that, 'When the relationship of lord and man again became a potent social force in the fifteenth century, *Quia Emptores* prevented that relationship being coupled with dependent land tenure, and so gave a peculiar character to what it is customary to call "bastard feudalism".'[1] In his discussion of fourteenth-century evidence on this subject, Dr. Holmes has declared that, 'It is not clear how far bastard feudalism had developed in the thirteenth century but, in any case, *Quia Emptores* made it inescapable.'[2]

In considering these suggestions we must define the term 'bastard feudalism' with care. Within the body of social relationships to which historians have affixed this label there were three elements. In one a lord granted to his man by charter an annual fee or annuity to be received from his landed revenues. It was granted in return for the man's past and future services, either during the lord's pleasure or for the life of the recipient. Another form of relationship was created when a landowner wished to recruit men to follow him to the King's wars. He gave the man a money fee to be received annually in return for his undertaking to follow his lord. During the lengthy foreign wars of the period it was in the interests of each great magnate to maintain a nucleus of personnel on whom he could call for service when required. Hence the practice arose of retaining a man for peace and war. This form of agreement between lord and man was made in indentures of retinue between them.[3] The third type of relationship was

---

[1] Plucknett, *Ed. I*, pp. 107–8. [2] Holmes, p. 83.
[3] The payments made to retainers were generally described as fees. But for one called an annuity, see Bean, p. 95, n. 3.

temporary, whereas the other two possessed some degree of permanence. When an urgent need to recruit a following arose—perhaps in time of civil war—a great lord could grant his livery to those who joined him. They bore his badge or crest as a mark of their allegiance to him: and in return for the assistance they gave him they received either pay or patronage.

The triple character of 'bastard feudalism' must be borne in mind when we estimate its debt to *Quia Emptores*. It is quite clear that the statute could not have led to the granting of liveries. This practice was as feasible before 1290 as after. In the case of the retainer system, it might be argued that before *Quia Emptores* lords would have rewarded their retainers with grants of land. However, even if this were true, it would only have been one influence on the situation. The retainer system could never have developed on any scale without lengthy wars which impelled great lords to create bodies of retainers on whose services they could call when necessary. In the case, however, of a simple grant of a fee or annuity from landed revenues, we see a practice to which a grant of lands was certainly an alternative.

Any influence exercised by *Quia Emptores* upon this situation would have resulted from its abolition of subinfeudation. Can we then say it was because of this that the practice developed of granting fees and annuities out of landed revenues instead of lands? And, for the same reason, did the relationship between lord and retainer become one of money, not tenure? In answering these questions we are hampered by the almost complete absence of records relating to great baronial estates in the thirteenth century. There are, however, three general grounds on which we may reject the suggestion that there were connexions between *Quia Emptores* and 'bastard feudalism'. First, it underrates the undoubted existence of money relationships in war for a considerable time before 1290. Mercenaries had been well known in England since the Norman Conquest, if not earlier. Second, it assumes that without *Quia Emptores* English magnates would have wanted to reward their men with lands. But all the available evidence indicates that subinfeudation in return for military service had virtually ceased before the close of the twelfth century. Above all, the views of

Professor Plucknett and others misconstrue the terms of the statute. Its provisions applied only to grants of land made in fee simple. There was thus no reason after 1290 why a landowner should not reward a follower with a grant of lands for life, or for a term of years.

Such details as we can discover in the available evidence support these arguments. In a number of passages Bracton reveals that he is well aware of the existence of fees paid out of landed revenues. In one he states that, 'There is likewise a certain kind of rent, which is paid by someone, to be derived from a certain thing, with distraint or not, which is not called a service, but is as it were a free tenement upon enfeoffment.'[1] It has been realized for many years that the financial contracts for military service between lord and man, out of which the retainer system grew, can be traced back as far as the Welsh campaign of 1277.[2] Messrs. Richardson and Sayles have recently printed a contract, dated 20 July 1270, in which Adam of Jesmond agreed to accompany the lord Edward on crusade to the Holy Land with four knights for a period of one year, in return for a sum of 600 marks and transport.[3] In view of this evidence, it is reasonable to conclude that financial contracts for military service were being drawn up in writing at least twenty years before *Quia Emptores*.

The most striking evidence on this point, however, is to be found in letters patent in which Henry III inspected and confirmed letters patent of his son Edmund, earl of Lancaster.[4] In these, dated 1 February 1271, he granted to his knight, Sir Robert Turberville, because he was about to cross the sea with him, the manor of Minsterworth for a term of three years. In this grant it was stated that Turberville had previously received £20 a year from the issues of the manor; and, when it reverted to Edmund at the end of the three years' term, it was to remain charged with this rent. It is quite clear from these details that the practice already

[1] Bracton, II. 113. See also ibid., III. 59 and IV. 342.
[2] J. E. Morris, *The Welsh Wars of Edward I* (Oxford, 1901), pp. 68–9.
[3] H. G. Richardson and G. O. Sayles, *The Governance of Medieval England from the Conquest to Magna Carta* (Edinburgh, 1963), pp. 463–5.
[4] *CPR*, 1266–72, p. 515.

existed of paying for a contract for military service out of landed revenues. It is, of course, true that the relationship between earl Edmund and this knight was not the same as that which later existed between lord and retainer: there is nothing to indicate that there was any indenture between them, or that he was retained. But it is obvious that Sir Robert Turberville's position was no different from that of a man who after 1290 held a fee or annuity from his lord.

These two documents, drawn up within a few months of one another in 1270–1, suggest that the relationships we meet in the fourteenth and fifteenth centuries were not yet fully developed. Where the lord Edward recruited by means of a financial contract, his brother chose to employ a grant of land for a term of years. But financial relationships between lords and men in England already existed in 1270–1. Moreover, Sir Robert Turberville's money fee confirms Bracton's acceptance of such grants as common practice. Meagre though this evidence is, it leaves no doubt that the origins of the basic features of 'bastard feudalism' can be traced back well before *Quia Emptores*.

x

APPENDIX II

Uses Recorded in Inquisitions Post Mortem, 1327–77[1]

— = no lands in this category.
S = seised in fee in this category.
AF = all lands in this category conveyed to feoffees to uses.
PF = some lands in this category conveyed to feoffees to uses; seised in fee of the remainder.

Name of deceased	Date of death	Heir: under or over age	Held of King in chief	Held of King ut de honore[2]	Held of mesne lords[3]
William Claydon[4]	1330	under	—	—	PF
William St. John[5]	1331	under	—	—	PF
Edward Peverel[6]	1332	under	—	—	PF
Edmund Benstead[7]	1334	under	AF	—	—
Alexander Cobeldike[8]	1334	under	—	S	PF

[1] Two cases have not been included: (1) Robert, lord Clifford who died in 1344 (*CIPMA*, VIII. 383 (no. 531); cf. *CPR, 1343–5*, pp. 188–9; *CCR, 1343–6*, pp. 633–4); (2) Sir Robert Bertram who died in 1363 (*CIPMA*, XI. 369–71 (no. 487)). In both feoffees had been enfeoffed for the specific purpose of making a settlement in tail on their feoffor, but he died before they could effect it. In view of these details, these cases cannot be considered as falling within the category of uses.

[2] This column includes lands held of the King (or Queen) in socage or burgage. Lands held of the honours of Peverel, Boulogne and Hagenet are treated as holdings in chief (see above, p. 10).

[3] This column includes lands held of mesne lords in socage. On the few occasions when the inquisitions omit to mention tenures, it has been assumed that the lands concerned were held of mesne lords.

[4] *CIPMA*, VII. 205–6 (no. 281).   [5] ibid., VII. 252–3 (no. 343).
[6] ibid., VII. 256–9 (no. 356).   [7] ibid., VII. 398 (no. 568).
[8] ibid., VII. 408 (no. 597).

Name of deceased	Date of death	Heir: under or over age	Held of King in chief	Held of King ut de honore	Held of mesne lords
David Strabolgi, earl of Athol[9]	1335	under	PF	PF	S
Robert Howel[10]	1336	under	—	—	AF
Walter Clerebek[11]	1338	under	AF	—	—
John Goldington[12]	1338	under	S	S	PF
Robert del Isle[13]	1342	over	—	—	PF
Edward Despenser[14]	1342	under	—	—	PF
John son of Ingram Berenger[15]	1343	under	PF	—	S
John Cliff[16]	1343	under	—	—	AF
John Shardelowe[17]	1344	over	—	—	PF
Cecily, late the wife of Brian Hickling[18]	1344	under	PF	—	PF
William Bulsham[19]	1345	over	—	—	AF
William de la Plaunk[20]	1347	under	S	—	AF
John Wake[21]	1348	under	S	—	PF
Laurence Hastings, earl of Pembroke[22]	1348	under	S	—	PF
John Tidilminton[23]	1348	heir unknown	AF	—	S
William Botreaux[24]	1349	under	S	—	AF
Sibyl Cornwall[25]	1349	under	—	—	PF
John son of John Mautravers[26]	1349	under	—	S	PF
Peter Faucomberge[27]	1349	over	AF	—	AF

[9] ibid., VII. 503–4 (no. 713).
[10] ibid., VIII. 503–4 (no. 676).
[11] ibid., VIII. 99 (no. 157).
[12] ibid., VIII. 110–12 (no. 179).
[13] ibid., VIII. 256–7 (no. 386). He did not die, but assumed the habit of religion.
[14] ibid., VIII. 265–6 (no. 395).
[15] ibid., VIII. 312–15 (nos. 467–8).
[16] ibid., VIII. 283 (no. 424).
[17] ibid., VIII. 365–6 (no. 519).
[18] ibid., VIII. 396 (no. 544).
[19] ibid., VIII. 421 (no. 586).
[20] ibid., IX. 14–15 (no. 31).
[21] ibid., IX. 109–13 (no. 117).
[22] ibid., IX. 127 (no. 118).
[23] ibid., IX. 83 (no. 89).
[24] ibid., IX. 156 (no. 164).
[25] ibid., IX. 161 (no. 175).
[26] ibid., IX. 173–4 (no. 190).
[27] ibid., IX. 176 (no. 197).

Name of deceased	Date of death	Heir: under or over age	Held of King in chief	Held of King ut de honore	Held of mesne lords
John Willoughby[28]	1349	under	S	—	PF
John Constable[29]	1349	under	—	PF	S
Simon Rugeley[30]	1349	under	—	—	AF
Richard Winchester[31]	1349	under	PF	—	—
William Well[32]	1349	under	S	—	PF
Richard Well[33]	1349	under	—	—	PF
Alan Twytham[34]	1349	under	—	—	AF
Walter Heslarton[35]	1349	under	—	—	AF
Adam Pykworth[36]	1349	heir unknown	—	—	AF
John Caltoft[37]	1351	under	—	AF	AF
Thomas Bekering, kt.[38]	1352	under	S	—	PF
Robert Wyard, kt.[39]	1354	under	S	—	PF
Nicholas, lord Cauntelo[40]	1355	over	—	—	AF
Richard Talbot the elder, kt.[41]	1356	over	PF	—	S
John Avenel, kt.[42]	1359	over	—	—	AF
John Shardelowe[43]	1359	over	—	—	AF
Richard Plays, kt.[44]	1360	under	S	—	PF
Thomas Bradeston, kt.[45]	1360	under	S	S	PF

[28] *CIPMA*, IX. 181 (no. 201).

[29] ibid., IX. 219–23 (no. 226). The formalities of transferring seisin to the feoffees had not been properly observed by the deceased.

[30] ibid., IX. 345 (no. 437).

[31] ibid., IX. 270 (no. 298). The alienation to the feoffees had, in fact, been made by his parents.

[32] ibid., IX. 323 (no. 423).

[33] ibid., IX. 416–17 (no. 597).

[34] ibid., IX. 427 (no. 628).

[35] ibid., IX. 431–2 (no. 639).

[36] ibid., XI. 191–2 (no. 225).

[37] ibid., X. 73 (no. 71).

[38] ibid., X. 17–18 (no. 39).

[39] ibid., X. 140–1 (no. 161).

[40] ibid., X. 195–7 (no. 217).

[41] ibid., X. 277–9 (no. 326).

[42] ibid., X. 393–4 (no. 498).

[43] ibid., X. 441–2 (no. 543).

[44] ibid., X. 464–6 (no. 598).

[45] ibid., X. 478–81 (no. 614).

Name of deceased	Date of death	Heir: under or over age	Held of King in chief	Held of King ut de honore	Held of mesne lords
Marmaduke Fag[46]	1360	under	—	—	AF
John Vere, earl of Oxford[47]	1360	over	PF	S	PF
William Bohun, earl of Northampton[48]	1360	under	PF	PF	PF
Roger Mortimer, earl of March[49]	1360	under	PF	PF	PF
John Colville, kt.[50]	1360	over	—	—	AF
John Aleyn[51]	?	under	—	—	AF
Thomas Berkeley of of Ule[52]	1361	under	S	—	PF
William Kerdiston, kt.[53]	1361	over	S	—	PF
William Lancaster[54]	1361	under	S	—	AF
Henry, duke of Lancaster[55]	1361	over	PF	—	S
John, lord Mowbray[56]	1361	over	PF	—	—
Thomas Trekenesford[57]	1361	under	—	PF	—
John Welles[58]	1361	under	S	—	PF
Thomas Drokenesford[59]	1361	heir unknown	—	—	AF
Richard Danvers[60]	1361	under	AF	—	—
William Aumale, kt.[61]	1361	under	S	—	AF
William Kirkland[62]	1361	under	—	—	AF

[46] ibid., X. 482 (no. 616).
[47] ibid., X. 513–23 (no. 638).
[48] ibid., X. 523–30 (no. 639).
[49] ibid., X. 530–40 (no. 640).
[50] ibid., X. 550–1 (no. 655).
[51] ibid., XI. 4 (no. 8).
[52] ibid., XI. 6–7 (no. 10).
[53] ibid., XI. 72–9 (no. 102).
[54] ibid., XI. 87–8 (no. 115).
[55] ibid., XI. 92–116 (no. 118).
[56] ibid., XI. 138–45 (no. 144).
[57] ibid., XI. 182–3 (no. 209).
[58] ibid., XI. 186–8 (no. 217).
[59] ibid., XI. 199 (no. 242).
[60] ibid., XI. 200–1 (no. 244).
[61] ibid., XI. 216 (no. 272).
[62] ibid., XI. 273–4 (no. 351).

Name of deceased	Date of death	Heir: under or over age	Held of King in chief	Held of King ut de honore	Held of mesne lords
Richard Turberville, kt.[63]	1361	under	—	—	PF
Giles Nekton[64]	1361	under	—	—	AF
Roger Brome[65]	1361	under	—	—	AF
John Lysours, kt[66]	1361	under	—	—	AF
John Berners, kt.[67]	1361	under	—	AF	S
William Bleseby[68]	1362	under	S	—	PF
John Coges[69]	1362	under	S	—	PF
Thomas Courtenay, kt.[70]	1362	under	S	—	PF
Agnes, late the wife of William Hunter[71]	?	heir unknown	—	—	PF
Susan, late the wife of John Canynges[72]	1362	under	—	PF	S
Cecily de la Lynde[73]	1362	under	—	—	AF
Thomas Berden[74]	1363	none	—	AF (in free burgage in London only)	—
William Ingoldesthorpe, kt.[75]	1363	under	S	—	AF
Geoffrey Cornwall, kt.[76]	1365	under	PF	—	PF
Margery, late the wife of John Norwich[77]	1366	under	S	—	PF

[63] CIPMA, XI. 340 (no. 444).
[64] ibid., XI. 397–8 (no. 522).
[65] ibid., XII. 4–7 (no. 7).
[66] ibid., XIII. 28 (no. 35).
[67] ibid., XIV. 255–7 (no. 246).
[68] ibid., XI. 18 (no. 27).
[69] ibid., XI. 241 (no. 306).
[70] ibid., XI. 242–4 (no. 309).
[71] ibid., XI. 434–5 (no. 572).
[72] ibid., XII. 27–8 (no. 28).
[73] ibid., XII. 40–1 (no. 50).
[74] ibid., XII. 85–6 (no. 108).
[75] ibid., XIII. 158–9 (no. 188).
[76] ibid., XII. 10–13 (no. 12).
[77] ibid., XII. 51–3 (no. 72).

Name of deceased	Date of death	Heir: under or over age	Held of King in chief	Held of King ut de honore	Held of mesne lords
William de la Pole the younger, kt.[78]	?	?	—	—	AF
Maud, late the wife of John Vere, earl of Oxford[79]	1366	over	S	PF	S
Ralph Bulmer[80]	1366	under	S	—	PF
John Bohun, kt.[81]	1367	under	PF	S	S
Adam Clifton, kt.[82]	1367	under	S	—	PF
Thomas Engaine, kt.[83]	1367	over	PF	—	PF
John Tiptoft, kt.[84]	1367	over	S	S	PF
John Wodehull, kt.[85]	1367	under	S	—	PF
Anthony, lord Lucy[86]	1368	under	S	—	PF
Roger Trumpington[87]	1368	over	AF	—	AF
Bartholomew Burwash, kt.[88]	1369	over	S	—	PF
Thomas Beauchamp, earl of Warwick[89]	1369	over	S	—	PF
Joan, late the wife of Reynold, lord Cobham[90]	1369	over	S	S	PF
John Delves, kt.[91]	1369	over	S	—	AF
John Leyham[92]	1369	under	AF	—	—
Michael, lord Poynings[93]	1369	under	S	—	PF
Richard Salteby[94]	1369	under	—	S	PF
Leonard Carew[95]	1369	under	—	S	AF

[78] ibid., XII. 56 (no. 76).
[80] ibid., XII. 97–100 (no. 125).
[82] ibid., XII. 105–6 (no. 128).
[84] ibid., XII. 150–2 (no. 171).
[86] ibid., XII. 207–13 (no. 233).
[88] ibid., XII. 297–9 (no. 322).
[90] ibid., XII. 326–9 (no. 335).
[92] ibid., XII. 354 (no. 371).
[94] ibid., XII. 402–3 (no. 415).

[79] ibid., XII. 60–4 (no. 81).
[81] ibid., XII. 100–5, (no. 127).
[83] ibid., XII. 113–16 (no. 139).
[85] ibid., XII. 154–5 (no. 173).
[87] ibid., XII. 405–6 (no. 420).
[89] ibid., XII. 303–12 (no. 326).
[91] ibid., XII. 332–3 (no. 342).
[93] ibid., XII. 389–93 (no. 404).
[95] ibid., XII. 417–18 (no. 436).

Name of deceased	Date of death	Heir: under or over age	Held of King in chief	Held of King ut de honore	Held of mesne lords
William Vavasour[96]	1369	under	—	—	AF
Warin Bassing-bourne, kt.[97]	1369	over	AF	—	AF
Andrew Sackville[98]	1369	?	—	AF	—
Margaret, daughter of Richard Baslingthorpe, kt.[99]	1369	over	S	—	PF
Robert Caston[100]	1369	under	—	—	AF
John Clerk[101]	1369	under	—	—	AF
John Corbet[102]	1370	under	S	—	PF
Richard Merton[103]	1370	under	PF	—	S
Sir John Lisle[104]	1370	under	S	S	PF
Ralph Hempnall, kt.[105]	1370	under	AF	—	—
William, lord Ferrers of Groby[106]	1371	under	S	—	PF
John Blebury[107]	?	over	AF	—	—
Joan Stubbs[108]	1371–2	?	—	—	AF
Thomas Camoys, kt.[109]	1372	heir unknown	—	—	PF
Robert Tiptoft, kt.[110]	1372	under	S	S	PF
Roger Widdrington[111]	1372	under	AF	—	AF
Alice, late the wife of of John Howard, kt.[112]	1372	over	—	—	AF
John Man[113]	1372	under	AF	—	AF

[96] *CIPMA*, XIII. 5 (no. 6).
[97] ibid., XIII. 11–12 (no. 13).
[98] ibid., XIII. 44 (no. 58).
[99] ibid., XIV. 5–7 (no. 9).
[100] ibid., XIV. 17–18 (no. 17).
[101] ibid., XIII. 228–9 (no. 252).
[102] ibid., XIII. 17–18 (no. 20).
[103] ibid., XIII. 32–3 (no. 42).
[104] ibid., XIII. 60–2 (no. 80).
[105] ibid., XIII. 64–5 (no. 85).
[106] ibid., XIII. 65–71 (no. 87).
[107] ibid., XIII. 127–8 (no. 162).
[108] ibid., XIV. 268 (no. 262).
[109] ibid., XIII. 150–1 (no. 173).
[110] ibid., XIII. 190–5 (no. 212).
[111] ibid., XIII. 198–200 (no. 215).
[112] ibid., XIII. 267 (no. 301).
[113] ibid., XIV. 270 (no. 267).

Name of deceased	Date of death	Heir: under or over age	Held of King in chief	Held of King ut de honore	Held of mesne lords
William Haclut[114]	1373	over	S	AF	PF
Humphrey Bohun, earl of Hereford and Essex[115]	1373	under	S	S	PF
Nicholas Longford, kt.[116]	1373	over	S	S	PF
William Luffwick[117]	1373	under	—	—	AF
John Loudham[118]	1374	under	S	—	AF
John Norwich, kt.[119]	1374	over	S	—	AF
Richard Rous[120]	1374	under	S	—	PF
Thomas Belhouse, kt.[121]	1374	under	—	—	AF
John son of Walter Baskerville, kt.[122]	1374	under	S	—	AF
Henry Coggeshall, kt.[123]	1375	under	S	AF	AF
Sir William Cauntelo[124]	1375	over	S	—	PF
Simon Draycote[125]	1375	over	—	—	AF
Ralph, lord Dacre[126]	1375	over	PF	—	S
John Hastings, earl of Pembroke[127]	1375	under	PF	AF	AF
Edward Kendal, kt.[128]	1375	over	PF	—	PF
Nicholas Lovaine, kt.[129]	1375	under	PF	—	—
Thomas, lord Poynings[130]	1375	under	S	S	PF

[114] ibid., XIII. 236–7 (no. 262).
[115] ibid., XIII. 130–46 (no. 167).
[116] ibid., XIII. 240–2 (no. 265).
[117] ibid., XIV. 183–4 (no. 170).
[118] ibid., XIV. 38–9 (no. 39).
[119] ibid., XIV. 43–5 (no. 46).
[120] ibid., XIV. 83–4 (no. 83).
[121] ibid., XIV. 89–90 (no. 88).
[122] ibid., XIV. 94 (no. 98).
[123] ibid., XIV. 99–101 (no. 104).
[124] ibid., XIV. 105–7 (no. 108).
[125] ibid., XIV. 114–15 (no. 115).
[126] ibid., XIV. 117–19 (no. 119).
[127] ibid., XIV. 143–64 (no. 148).
[128] ibid., XIV. 167–8 (no. 152).
[129] ibid., XIV. 184–5 (no. 172).
[130] ibid., XIV., 197–201 (no. 190).

Name of deceased	Date of death	Heir: under or over age	Held of King in chief	Held of King ut de honore	Held of mense lords
Arnold Savage, kt.[131]	1375	under	S	PF	AF
Edward, lord Despenser[132]	1375	under	PF	S	PF
William Baude, kt.[133]	1375	under	—	AF	AF
John, lord Mohun[134]	1375	no heir	AF	—	—
Roger Gyney, kt.[135]	1376	under	AF	—	—
William Huntingfield, kt.[136]	1376	over	S	—	PF
Richard Meynell, kt.[137]	1376	under	S	—	PF
John Kiriel, kt.[138]	1377	under	AF	—	—

[131] *CIPMA*, XIV. 209–10 (no. 202).
[132] ibid., XIV. 214–27 (no. 209).
[133] ibid., XIV. 240–4 (no. 227).
[134] ibid., XIV. 304 (no. 322).
[135] ibid., XIV. 263 (no. 255).
[136] ibid., XIV. 265–8 (no. 261).
[137] ibid., XIV. 272–3 (no. 271).
[138] ibid., XIV. 299 (no. 313).

LIST OF CASES

Full details of the sources will be found in the List of Abbreviations or the relevant footnote.

			Pages
Rolls of the Justices in Eyre			
	no. 257	(1221)	107n
	no. 1013	(1221)	107
Bracton's Note Book	pl. 754	(1233)	108, 157
	pl. 999	(1224)	107, 157
	pl. 1248	(1238–9)	43–4n
	pl. 1683	(1225)	107–8, 157
	pl. 1838	(1227)	191
	pl. 1851	(1226–7)	108n, 157
S.C. King's Bench, I. 47–9		(1279)	70n
Placitorum Abbreviatio			
	p. 272, col. 1		
	(Suff., Hil., 9 Ed. I)	(1281)	29n
YBRS, 21 & 22 Ed. I, p. 70		(1293)	30
	pp. 272–7	(1293)	88
	pp. 640–1	(1294)	80
Year Books of Edward II			
	2 & 3 Ed. II pp. 84–6	(1309)	9n
	3 Ed. II pp. 185–6	(1310)	111n
S.C. Council, pp. 33–4		(1350)	163–4
Fitzherbert, *Collusion*, no. 29		(1357)	183n
Garde, no. 33		(1358)	183, 187, 193
YBVE, 45 Ed. III, pl. 25		(1371)	183, 187, 193
Fitzherbert, *Garde*, no. 102		(1373)	183, 187, 193, 194nn
Bellewe, *Les Ans du Roy Richard le second*, pp. 99–100		(1384)	184, 187, 193, 194nn
Year Books of Richard II:			
11 Richard II, pp. 118–19		(1387)	159n
S.C. Chan., no. 40		(1398–1403)	169n
	no. 45	(1396–1403)	172n
	no. 71	(1396–1403)	172n
	no. 72	(1396–1403)	172n

LIST OF STATUTES[1]

[1] This does not include *Prerogativa Regis*.

321

INDEX

Y

DATE DUE